Kaplan Publishing are constantly fi
ways to make a difference to your s
exciting online resources really do
different to students looking for exam success.

This book comes with free MyKaplan online resources so that you can study anytime, anywhere. This free online resource is not sold separately and is included in the price of the book.

Having purchased this book, you have access to the following online study materials:

CONTENT	ACCA (including FFA,FAB,FMA)		FIA (excluding FFA,FAB,FMA)	
	Text	Kit	Text	Kit
Electronic version of the book	✓	✓	✓	✓
Check Your Understanding Test with instant answers	✓			
Material updates	✓	✓	✓	✓
Latest official ACCA exam questions*		✓		
Extra question assistance using the signpost icon**		✓		
Timed questions with an online tutor debrief using clock icon***		✓		
Interim assessment including questions and answers	✓		✓	
Technical answers	✓	✓	✓	✓

* Excludes F1, F2, F3, F4, FAB, FMA and FFA; for all other papers includes a selection of questions, as released by ACCA

** For ACCA P1-P7 only

*** Excludes F1, F2, F3, F4, FAB, FMA and FFA

How to access your online resources

Kaplan Financial students will already have a MyKaplan account and these extra resources will be available to you online. You do not need to register again, as this process was completed when you enrolled. If you are having problems accessing online materials, please ask your course administrator.

If you are not studying with Kaplan and did not purchase your book via a Kaplan website, to unlock your extra online resources please go to www.mykaplan.co.uk/addabook (even if you have set up an account and registered books previously). You will then need to enter the ISBN number (on the title page and back cover) and the unique pass key number contained in the scratch panel below to gain access.

You will also be required to enter additional information during this process to set up or confirm your account details.

If you purchased through Kaplan Flexible Learning or via the Kaplan Publishing website you will automatically receive an e-mail invitation to MyKaplan. Please register your details using this email to gain access to your content. If you do not receive the e-mail or book content, please contact Kaplan Publishing.

Your Code and Information

This code can only be used once for the registration of one book online. This registration and your online content will expire when the final sittings for the examinations covered by this book have taken place. Please allow one hour from the time you submit your book details for us to process your request.

Please scratch the film to access your MyKaplan code.

Please be aware that this code is case-sensitive and you will need to include the dashes within the passcode, but not when entering the ISBN. For further technical support, please visit www.MyKaplan.co.uk

KAPLAN PUBLISHING

ACCA

Applied Skills

Financial Reporting (FR)

Study Text

British Library Cataloguing-in-Publication Data

A catalogue record for this book is available from the British Library.

Published by:
Kaplan Publishing UK
Unit 2 The Business Centre
Molly Millar's Lane
Wokingham
Berkshire
RG41 2QZ

ISBN: 978-1-78740-392-5

Printed and bound in Great Britain.

Acknowledgements

These materials are reviewed by the ACCA examining team. The objective of the review is to ensure that the material properly covers the syllabus and study guide outcomes, used by the examining team in setting the exams, in the appropriate breadth and depth. The review does not ensure that every eventuality, combination or application of examinable topics is addressed by the ACCA Approved Content. Nor does the review comprise a detailed technical check of the content as the Approved Content Provider has its own quality assurance processes in place in this respect.

Contents

Introduction

This document references IFRS® Standards and IAS® Standards, which are authored by the International Accounting Standards Board (the Board), and published in the 2018 IFRS Standards Red Book.

How to use the Materials

These Kaplan Publishing learning materials have been carefully designed to make your learning experience as easy as possible and to give you the best chances of success in your examinations.

The product range contains a number of features to help you in the study process. They include:

1 Detailed study guide and syllabus objectives

2 Description of the examination

3 Study skills and revision guidance

4 Study text

5 Question practice

The sections on the study guide, the syllabus objectives, the examination and study skills should all be read before you commence your studies. They are designed to familiarise you with the nature and content of the examination and give you tips on how best to approach your learning.

The **Study Text** comprises the main learning materials and gives guidance as to the importance of topics and where other related resources can be found. Each chapter includes:

- The **learning objectives** contained in each chapter, which have been carefully mapped to the examining body's own syllabus learning objectives or outcomes. You should use these to check you have a clear understanding of all the topics on which you might be assessed in the examination.
- The **chapter diagram** provides a visual reference for the content in the chapter, giving an overview of the topics and how they link together.
- The **content** for each topic area commences with a brief explanation or definition to put the topic into context before covering the topic in detail. You should follow your studying of the content with a review of the illustration/s. There are worked examples which will help you to better understand how to apply the content to the topic.
- **Test your understanding** sections provide an opportunity to assess your understanding of the key topics by applying what you have learned to short questions. Answers can be found at the back of each chapter.
- **Summary diagrams** complete each chapter to show the important links between topics and the overall content of the paper. These diagrams should be used to check that you have covered and understood the core topics before moving on.

Quality and accuracy are of the utmost importance to us so if you spot an error in any of our products, please send an email to mykaplanreporting@kaplan.com with full details, or follow the link to the feedback form in MyKaplan.

Our Quality Coordinator will work with our technical team to verify the error and take action to ensure it is corrected in future editions.

Icon Explanations

Definition – Key definitions that you will need to learn from the core content.

Key point – Identifies topics that are key to success and are often examined.

Test your understanding – Exercises for you to complete to ensure that you have understood the topics just learned.

Illustration – Worked examples help you understand the core content better.

Supplementary reading – These sections will help to provide a deeper understanding of core areas. The supplementary reading is **NOT** optional reading. It is vital to provide you with the breadth of knowledge you will need to address the wide range of topics within your syllabus that could feature in an exam question. **Reference to this text is vital when self-studying.**

Tutorial note – Included to explain some of the technical points in more detail.

Footsteps – Helpful tutor tips.

On-line subscribers

Our on-line resources are designed to increase the flexibility of your learning materials and provide you with immediate feedback on how your studies are progressing.

If you are subscribed to our on-line resources you will find:

1 On-line reference-ware: reproduces your Study Text on-line, giving you anytime/anywhere access.

2 On-line testing: provides you with additional on-line objective testing so you can practise what you have learned further.

3 On-line performance management: immediate access to your on-line testing results. Review your performance by key topics and chart your achievement through the course relative to your peer group.

Syllabus

Core areas of the syllabus

- A conceptual framework for financial reporting.
- A regulatory framework for financial reporting.
- Financial statements.
- Business combinations.
- Analysing and interpreting financial statements.

ACCA Performance Objectives

In order to become a member of the ACCA, as a trainee accountant you will need to demonstrate that you have achieved nine performance objectives. Performance objectives are indicators of effective performance and set the minimum standard of work that trainees are expected to achieve and demonstrate in the workplace. They are divided into key areas of knowledge which are closely linked to the exam syllabus.

There are five Essential performance objectives and a choice of fifteen Technical performance objectives which are divided into five areas.

The performance objectives which link to this exam are:

1 Ethics and professionalism (Essential)

2 Stakeholder relationship management (Essential)

6 Record and process transactions and events (Technical)

7 Prepare external financial reports (Technical)

8 Analyse and interpret financial reports (Technical)

The following link provides an in-depth insight into all of the performance objectives:

https://www.accaglobal.com/content/dam/ACCA_Global/Students/per/PER-Performance-objectives-achieve.pdf

Progression

There are two elements of progression that we can measure: first how quickly students move through individual topics within a subject; and second how quickly they move from one course to the next. We know that there is an optimum for both, but it can vary from subject to subject and from student to student. However, using data and our experience of student performance over many years, we can make some generalisations.

A fixed period of study set out at the start of a course with key milestones is important. This can be within a subject, for example 'I will finish this topic by 30 June', or for overall achievement, such as 'I want to be qualified by the end of next year'.

Your qualification is cumulative, as earlier papers provide a foundation for your subsequent studies, so do not allow there to be too big a gap between one subject and another. We know that exams encourage techniques that lead to some degree of short term retention, the result being that you will simply forget much of what you have already learned unless it is refreshed (look up Ebbinghaus Forgetting Curve for more details on this). This makes it more difficult as you move from one subject to another: not only will you have to learn the new subject, you will also have to relearn all the underpinning knowledge as well. This is very inefficient and slows down your overall progression which makes it more likely you may not succeed at all.

In addition, delaying your studies slows your path to qualification which can have negative impacts on your career, postponing the opportunity to apply for higher level positions and therefore higher pay.

You can use the following diagram showing the whole structure of your qualification to help you keep track of your progress.

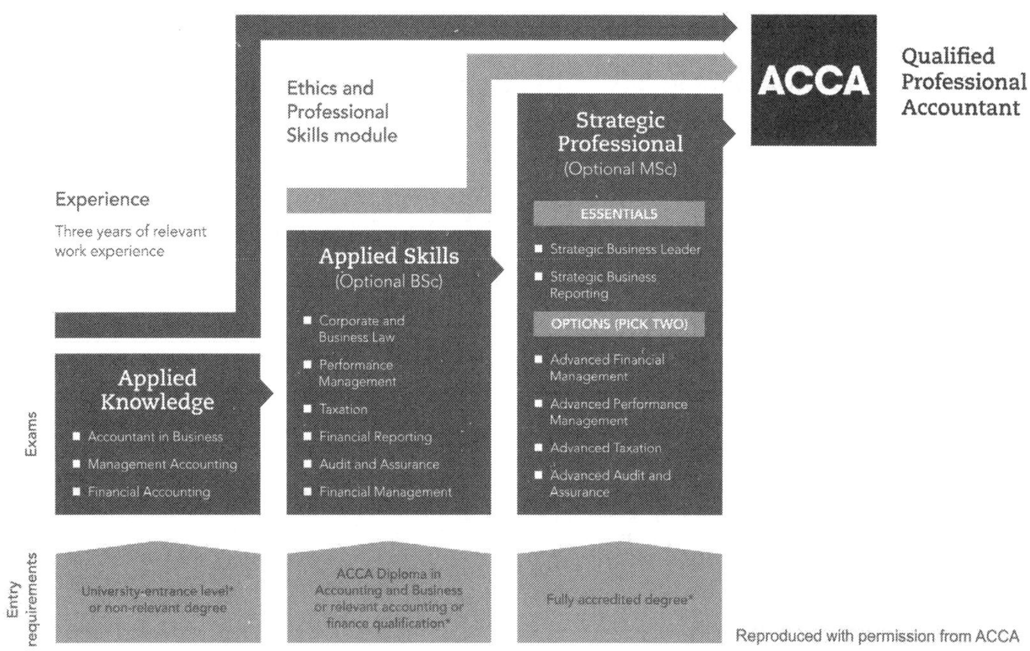

Reproduced with permission from ACCA

Syllabus objectives and chapter references

We have reproduced the ACCA's syllabus from September 2019 to June 2020, showing where the objectives are explored within this book. Within each chapter we have broken down the extensive information found in the syllabus into easily digestible and relevant sections, called Content Objectives. These correspond to the objectives at the beginning of each chapter.

Syllabus learning objective			Chapter reference
A	**THE CONCEPTUAL AND REGULATORY FRAMEWORK FOR FINANCIAL REPORTING**		
1	**The need for a conceptual framework and the characteristics of useful information**		
	(a)	Describe what is meant by a conceptual framework for financial reporting.[2]	6
	(b)	Discuss whether a conceptual framework is necessary and what an alternative system might be.[2]	6
	(c)	Discuss what is meant by relevance and faithful representation and describe the qualities that enhance these characteristics.[2]	6
	(d)	Discuss whether faithful representation constitutes more than compliance with accounting standards.[1]	6
	(e)	Discuss what is meant by understandability and verifiability in relation to the provision of financial information.[2]	6
	(f)	Discuss the importance of comparability and timeliness to users of financial statements.[2]	6
	(g)	Discuss the principle of comparability in accounting for changes in accounting policies.[2]	8
2	**Recognition and measurement**		
	(a)	Define what is meant by 'recognition' in financial statements and discuss the recognition criteria.[2]	6
	(b)	Apply the recognition criteria to:[2] (i) assets and liabilities. (ii) income and expenses.	6

Syllabus learning objective			Chapter reference
	(c)	Explain and compute amounts using the following measures:[2] (i) historical cost (ii) current cost (iii) value in use (iv) fair value	7
	(d)	Discuss the advantages and disadvantages of historical cost accounting.	7
	(e)	Discuss whether the use of current value accounting overcomes the problems of historical cost accounting.[2]	7
	(f)	Describe the concept of financial and physical capital maintenance and how this affects the determination of profits.[1]	7
3	**Regulatory framework**		
	(a)	Explain why a regulatory framework is needed, including the advantages and disadvantages of IFRS over a national regulatory framework.[2]	6
	(b)	Explain why accounting standards on their own are not a complete regulatory framework.[2]	6
	(c)	Distinguish between a principles based and a rules based framework and discuss whether they can be complementary.[1]	6
	(d)	Describe the IASB's standard setting process including revisions to and interpretations of standards.[2]	6
	(e)	Explain the relationship of national standard setters to the IASB in respect of the standard setting process.[2]	6
4	**The concepts and principles of groups and consolidated financial statements**		
	(a)	Describe the concept of a group as a single economic unit.[2]	17
	(b)	Explain and apply the definition of a subsidiary within relevant accounting standards.[2]	17
	(c)	Using accounting standards and other regulation, identify and outline the circumstances in which a group is required to prepare consolidated financial statements.[2]	17

Syllabus learning objective			Chapter reference
	(d)	Describe the circumstances when a group may claim exemption from the preparation of consolidated financial statements.[2]	17
	(e)	Explain why directors may not wish to consolidate a subsidiary and when this is permitted by accounting standards and other applicable regulation.[2]	17
	(f)	Explain the need for using coterminous year ends and uniform accounting policies when preparing consolidated financial statements.[2]	17
	(g)	Explain why it is necessary to eliminate intra group transactions.[2]	17
	(h)	Explain the objective of consolidated financial statements.[2]	17
	(i)	Explain why it is necessary to use fair values for the consideration for an investment in a subsidiary together with the fair values of a subsidiary's identifiable assets and liabilities when preparing consolidated financial statements.[2]	18
	(j)	Define an associate and explain the principles and reasoning for the use of equity accounting.[2]	20
B	**ACCOUNTING FOR TRANSACTIONS IN FINANCIAL STATEMENTS**		
1	**Tangible non-current assets**		
	(a)	Define and compute the initial measurement of a non-current asset (including borrowing costs and an asset that has been self-constructed).[2]	2
	(b)	Identify subsequent expenditure that may be capitalised, distinguishing between capital and revenue items.[2]	2
	(c)	Discuss the requirements of relevant accounting standards in relation to the revaluation of non-current assets.[2]	2
	(d)	Account for revaluation and disposal gains and losses for non-current assets.[2]	2
	(e)	Compute depreciation based on the cost and revaluation models and on assets that have two or more significant parts (complex assets).[2]	2

Syllabus learning objective			Chapter reference
	(f)	Discuss why the treatment of investment properties should differ from other properties.[2]	2
	(g)	Apply the requirements of relevant accounting standards to an investment property.[2]	2
2	**Intangible non-current assets**		
	(a)	Discuss the nature and accounting treatment of internally generated and purchased intangibles.[2]	3
	(b)	Distinguish between goodwill and other intangible assets.[2]	3
	(c)	Describe the criteria for the initial recognition and measurement of intangible assets.[2]	3
	(d)	Describe the subsequent accounting treatment, including the principle of impairment tests in relation to goodwill.[2]	3, 18
	(e)	Indicate why the value of purchase consideration for an investment may be less than the value of the acquired identifiable net assets and how the difference should be accounted for.[2]	18
	(f)	Describe and apply the requirements of relevant accounting standards to research and development expenditure.[2]	3
3	**Impairment of assets**		
	(a)	Define, calculate and account for an impairment loss.[2]	4
	(b)	Account for the reversal of an impairment loss on an individual asset.	4
	(c)	Identify the circumstances that may indicate impairments to assets.[2]	4
	(d)	Describe what is meant by a cash generating unit.[2]	4
	(e)	State the basis on which impairment losses should be allocated, and allocate an impairment loss to the assets of a cash generating unit.[2]	4
4	**Inventory and biological assets**		
	(a)	Describe and apply the principles of inventory valuation.[2]	8
	(b)	Apply the requirements of relevant accounting standards for biological assets.[2]	8

Syllabus learning objective			Chapter reference
5	**Financial instruments**		
	(a)	Explain the need for an accounting standard on financial instruments.[1]	9
	(b)	Define financial instruments in terms of financial assets and financial liabilities.[1]	9
	(c)	Explain and account for the factoring of receivables.	9
	(d)	Indicate for the following categories of financial instruments how they should be measured and how any gains and losses from subsequent measurement should be treated in the financial statements:[1] (i) amortised cost (ii) fair value through other comprehensive income (including where an irrevocable election has been made for equity investments that are not held for trading). (iii) fair value through profit or loss.[2]	9
	(e)	Distinguish between debt and equity capital.[2]	9
	(f)	Apply the requirements of relevant accounting standards to the issue and finance costs of:[2] (i) equity (ii) redeemable preference shares and debt instruments with no conversion rights (principle of amortised cost). (iii) convertible debt	9
6	**Leasing**		
	(a)	Account for right of use assets and lease liabilities in the records of the lessee.[2]	12
	(b)	Explain the exemption from the recognition criteria for leases in the records of the lessee.[2]	12
	(c)	Account for sale and leaseback agreements.[2]	12
7	**Provisions and events after the reporting period**		
	(a)	Explain why an accounting standard on provisions is necessary.[2]	15
	(b)	Distinguish between legal and constructive obligations.[2]	15
	(c)	State when provisions may and may not be made and demonstrate how they should be accounted for.[2]	15

Syllabus learning objective				Chapter reference
	(d)	Explain how provisions should be measured.[1]		15
	(e)	Define contingent assets and liabilities and describe their accounting treatment and required disclosures.[2]		15
	(f)	Identify and account for: [2]		15
		(i)	warranties/guarantees	
		(ii)	onerous contracts	
		(iii)	environmental and similar provisions	
		(iv)	provisions for future repairs or refurbishments	
	(g)	Events after the reporting period		
		(i)	distinguish between and account for adjusting and non-adjusting events after the reporting period.[2]	15
		(ii)	identify items requiring separate disclosure, including their accounting treatment and required disclosures.[2]	15
8	**Taxation**			
	(a)	Account for current taxation in accordance with relevant accounting standards.[2]		13
	(b)	Explain the effect of taxable temporary differences on accounting and taxable profits.[2]		13
	(c)	Compute and record deferred tax amounts in the financial statements.[2]		13
9	**Reporting financial performance**			
	(a)	Discuss the importance of identifying and reporting the results of discontinued operations.[2]		5
	(b)	Define and account for non-current assets held for sale and discontinued operations.[2]		5
	(c)	Indicate the circumstances where separate disclosure of material items of income and expense is required.[2]		1, 5
	(d)	Account for changes in accounting estimates, changes in accounting policy and correction of prior period errors.		8

Syllabus learning objective			Chapter reference
	(e)	Earnings per share (eps)	
		(i) calculate the eps in accordance with relevant accounting standards (dealing with bonus issues, full market value issues and rights issues).[2]	14
		(ii) explain the relevance of the diluted eps and calculate the diluted eps involving convertible debt and share options (warrants).[2]	14
10	**Revenue**		
	(a)	Explain and apply the principles of recognition of revenue:	
		(i) identification of contracts	11
		(ii) identification of performance obligations	11
		(iii) determination of transaction price	11
		(iv) allocation of the price to performance obligations	11
		(v) recognition of revenue when/as performance obligations are satisfied	11
	(b)	Explain and apply the criteria for recognising revenue generated from contracts where performance obligations are satisfied over time or at a point in time.[2]	11
	(c)	Describe the acceptable methods for measuring progress towards complete satisfaction of a performance obligation.[2]	11
	(d)	Explain and apply the criteria for the recognition of contract costs.[2]	11
	(e)	Apply the principles of recognition of revenue, and specifically account for the following types of transaction:[2]	11
		(i) principal versus agent	
		(ii) repurchase agreements	
		(iii) bill and hold arrangements	
		(iv) consignments	
	(f)	Prepare financial statement extracts for contracts where performance obligations are satisfied over time.[2]	11

Syllabus learning objective			Chapter reference
11	**Government grants**		
	(a)	Apply the provisions of relevant accounting standards in relation to accounting for government grants.[2]	2
12	**Foreign currency transactions**		
	(a)	Explain the difference between functional and presentation currency and explain why adjustments for foreign currency transactions are necessary.	10
	(b)	Account for the translation of foreign currency transactions and monetary/non-monetary foreign currency items at the reporting date.	10
C	**ANALYSING AND INTERPRETING THE FINANCIAL STATEMENTS OF SINGLE ENTITIES AND GROUPS**		
1	**Limitations of financial statements**		
	(a)	Indicate the problems of using historic information to predict future performance and trends.[2]	22
	(b)	Discuss how financial statements may be manipulated to produce a desired effect (creative accounting, window dressing).[2]	22
	(c)	Explain why figures in a statement of financial position may not be representative of average values throughout the period for example, due to:[2]	
		(i) seasonal trading	
		(ii) major asset acquisitions near the end of the accounting period.	22
	(d)	Explain how the use of consolidated financial statements might limit interpretation techniques.	22, 18, 19
2	**Calculation and interpretation of accounting ratios and trends to address users' and stakeholders' needs**		
	(a)	Define and compute relevant financial ratios.[2]	22
	(b)	Explain what aspects of performance specific ratios are intended to assess.[2]	22
	(c)	Analyse and interpret ratios to give an assessment of an entity's/group's performance and financial position in comparison with:[2]	22
		(i) previous period's financial statements	
		(ii) another similar entity/group for the same reporting period	
		(iii) industry average ratios.	

Syllabus learning objective			Chapter reference
	(d)	Interpret an entity's financial statements to give advice from the perspectives of different stakeholders.[2]	22
	(e)	Discuss how the interpretation of current value based financial statements would differ from those using historical cost based accounts.[1]	22
3	**Limitations of interpretation techniques**		
	(a)	Discuss the limitations in the use of ratio analysis for assessing corporate performance.[2]	22
	(b)	Discuss the effect that changes in accounting policies or the use of different accounting policies between entities can have on the ability to interpret performance.[2]	22
	(c)	Indicate other information, including non-financial information, that may be of relevance to the assessment of an entity's performance.[1]	22
	(d)	Compare the usefulness of cash flow information with that of a statement of profit or loss or a statement of profit or loss and other comprehensive income.[2]	16
	(e)	Interpret a statement of cash flows (together with other financial information) to assess the performance and financial position of an entity.[2]	16
		(i) explain why the trend of eps may be a more accurate indicator of performance than a company's profit trend and the importance of eps as a stock market indicator.[2]	14
		(ii) discuss the limitations of using eps as a performance measure.[3]	14
4	**Specialised, not-for-profit and public sector entities**		
	(a)	Explain how the interpretation of the financial statement of a specialised, not-for-profit or public sector organisation might differ from that of a profit making entity by reference to the different aims, objectives and reporting requirements.[1]	6, 22

Syllabus learning objective			Chapter reference
D	**PREPARATION OF FINANCIAL STATEMENTS**		
1	**Preparation of single entity financial statements**		
	(a)	Prepare an entity's statement of financial position and statement of profit or loss and other comprehensive income in accordance with the structure and content prescribed within IFRS and with accounting treatments as identified within syllabus areas A, B and C.[2]	1
	(b)	Prepare and explain the contents and purpose of the statement of changes in equity.[2]	1
	(c)	Prepare a statement of cash flows for a single entity (not a group) in accordance with relevant accounting standards using the indirect method.[2]	16
2	**Preparation of consolidated financial statements including an associate**		
	(a)	Prepare a consolidated statement of financial position for a simple group (parent and one subsidiary and associate) dealing with pre- and post-acquisition profits, non-controlling interests and consolidated goodwill.[2]	18, 20
	(b)	Prepare a consolidated statement of profit or loss and consolidated statement of profit or loss and other comprehensive income for a simple group dealing with an acquisition in the period and non-controlling interest. [2]	19, 20
	(c)	Explain and account for other reserves (e.g. share premium and revaluation surplus).[1]	18
	(d)	Account for the effects in the financial statements of intra-group trading.[2]	18, 19
	(e)	Account for the effects of fair value adjustments (including their effect on consolidated goodwill) to:[2] (i) depreciating and non-depreciating non-current assets (ii) inventory (iii) monetary liabilities (iv) assets and liabilities not included in the subsidiary's own statement of financial position, including contingent assets and liabilities	18, 19
(f)	Account for goodwill impairment.[2]		18, 19
(g)	Describe and apply the required accounting treatment of consolidated goodwill.[2]		18, 19

Syllabus learning objective	Chapter reference
(h) Explain and illustrate the effect of a disposal of a parent's investment in a subsidiary in the parent's individual financial statements and/or those of the group (restricted to disposals of the parent's entire investment in the subsidiary).	21

The numbers in square brackets indicate the intellectual depth at which the subject area could be assessed within the examination. Level 1 (knowledge and comprehension) broadly equates with the Knowledge module, Level 2 (application and analysis) with the Skills module and Level 3 (synthesis and evaluation) to the Professional level. However, lower level skills can continue to be assessed as you progress through each module and level.

The Examination

Examination format

All questions are compulsory. The examination will contain both computational and discursive elements.

Some questions will adopt a scenario/case study approach.

Section A of the examination comprises 15 objective test (OT) questions of 2 marks each.

Section B of the examination comprises three objective case questions (OT cases) worth 10 marks each. Each case has five objective test questions of 2 marks each.

Section C of the examination comprises two constructed response (CR) questions, worth 20 marks each.

The 20 mark questions will examine the interpretation and preparation of financial statements for either a single entity or a group. The section A and section B questions can cover any areas of the syllabus.

An individual question may often involve elements that relate to different subject areas of the syllabus. For example, the preparation of an entity's financial statements could include matters relating to several accounting standards.

Questions may ask candidates to comment on the appropriateness or acceptability of management's opinion or chosen accounting treatment. An understanding of accounting principles and concepts and how these are applied to practical examples will be tested.

Questions on topic areas that are also included in Financial Accounting (FA) will be examined at an appropriately greater depth in this examination.

Candidates will be expected to have an appreciation of the need for specific accounting standards and why they have been issued. For detailed or complex standards, candidates need to be aware of their principles and key elements.

	Number of marks
Section A – Fifteen 2-mark objective test questions	30
Section B – Three 10-mark objective case questions, comprising of five 2-mark questions each	30
Section C – Two 20-mark constructed response questions	40
	100

Examination tips

Individual students will have different approaches to tackling the FR exam.

The time allowed for the examination is 3 hours for computer-based and 3 hours 15 minutes for the paper-based.

For the computer-based examination (CBE) students should allocate 1.8 minutes per mark, meaning that a 20 mark section C question should be completed in approximately 36 minutes, with a 10 mark section B question taking approximately 18 minutes.

For the paper-based examination students may wish to use the additional 15 minutes as reading time, then allocate 1.8 minutes per mark as for the CBE. An alternative suggestion is to allocate 1.95 minutes to each mark available, so a 20 mark section C question should be completed in approximately 39 minutes, with a 10 mark section B question taking approximately 19 minutes.

Unless you know exactly how to answer the question, spend some time planning your answer. Stick to the question and tailor your answer to what you are asked. Pay particular attention to the verbs in the question.

If you **get completely stuck** with a question, take a guess, move on and return to it later.

If you do not understand what a question is asking, state your assumptions.

Even if you do not answer in precisely the way the examiner hoped, you should be given some credit, if your assumptions are reasonable.

You should do everything you can to make things easy for the marker. The marker will find it easier to identify the points you have made if your answers are well laid out.

Short narrative response: Your answer should be concise but specific, explaining terms where required. Short narrative responses will often require comment on the correct accounting treatment of items, so an ability to discuss this is essential, rather than simply providing calculations.

Computations: It is **absolutely essential** to include all your workings in your answers.

Many computational questions require the use of a standard format. Be sure you know these formats thoroughly before the exam and use the layouts that you see in the answers given in this book and in model answers.

Interpretation style response: Longer form responses are likely to contain some form of interpreting information. A good interpretation answer takes account of the information contained within the question and is structured well, with good use of headings and sections.

ACCA Support

For additional support with your studies please also refer to the ACCA Global website.

Study skills and revision guidance

This section aims to give guidance on how to study for your ACCA exams and to give ideas on how to improve your existing study techniques.

Preparing to study

Set your objectives

Before starting to study decide what you want to achieve – the type of pass you wish to obtain. This will decide the level of commitment and time you need to dedicate to your studies.

Devise a study plan

Determine which times of the week you will study.

Split these times into sessions of at least one hour for study of new material. Any shorter periods could be used for revision or practice.

Put the times you plan to study onto a study plan for the weeks from now until the exam and set yourself targets for each period of study – in your sessions make sure you cover the course, course assignments and revision.

If you are studying for more than one examination at a time, try to vary your subjects as this can help you to keep interested and see subjects as part of wider knowledge.

When working through your course, compare your progress with your plan and, if necessary, re-plan your work (perhaps including extra sessions) or, if you are ahead, do some extra revision/practice questions.

Effective studying

Active reading

You are not expected to learn the text by rote, rather, you must understand what you are reading and be able to use it to pass the exam and develop good practice. A good technique to use is SQ3Rs – Survey, Question, Read, Recall, Review:

1 **Survey the chapter** – look at the headings and read the introduction, summary and objectives, so as to get an overview of what the chapter deals with.

2 **Question** – whilst undertaking the survey, ask yourself the questions that you hope the chapter will answer for you.

3 **Read** through the chapter thoroughly, answering the questions and making sure you can meet the objectives. Attempt the exercises and activities in the text, and work through all the examples.

4 **Recall** – at the end of each section and at the end of the chapter, try to recall the main ideas of the section/chapter without referring to the text. This is best done after a short break of a couple of minutes after the reading stage.

5 **Review** – check that your recall notes are correct.

You may also find it helpful to re-read the chapter to try to see the topic(s) it deals with as a whole.

Note-taking

Taking notes is a useful way of learning, but do not simply copy out the text. The notes must:

- be in your own words
- be concise
- cover the key points
- be well-organised
- be modified as you study further chapters in this text or in related ones.

Trying to summarise a chapter without referring to the text can be a useful way of determining which areas you know and which you don't.

Three ways of taking notes:

1 **Summarise the key points of a chapter.**

2 **Make linear notes** – a list of headings, divided up with subheadings listing the key points. If you use linear notes, you can use different colours to highlight key points and keep topic areas together. Use plenty of space to make your notes easy to use.

3 **Try a diagrammatic form** – the most common of which is a mind-map. To make a mind-map, put the main heading in the centre of the paper and put a circle around it. Then draw short lines radiating from this to the main sub-headings, which again have circles around them. Then continue the process from the sub-headings to sub-subheadings, advantages, disadvantages, etc.

Highlighting and underlining

You may find it useful to underline or highlight key points in your study text – but do be selective. You may also wish to make notes in the margins.

Revision

The best approach to revision is to revise the course as you work through it.

Also try to leave four to six weeks before the exam for final revision. Make sure you cover the whole syllabus and pay special attention to those areas where your knowledge is weak. Here are some recommendations:

Read through the text and your notes again and condense your notes into key phrases. It may help to put key revision points onto index cards to look at when you have a few minutes to spare.

Review any assignments you have completed and look at where you lost marks – put more work into those areas where you were weak.

Practise exam standard questions under timed conditions. If you are short of time, list the points that you would cover in your answer and then read the model answer, but do try to complete at least a few questions under exam conditions.

Also practise producing answer plans and comparing them to the model answer.

If you are stuck on a topic find somebody (a tutor) to explain it to you.

Read good newspapers and professional journals, especially ACCA's Student Accountant – this can give you an advantage in the exam.

Ensure you know the structure of the exam – how many questions and of what type you will be expected to answer.

During your revision attempt all the different styles of questions you may be asked.

Further reading

'A student's guide to International Financial Reporting Standards' by Clare Finch.

'A student's guide to Preparing Financial Statements' by Sally Baker.

'A student's guide to Group Accounts' by Tom Clendon.

You can find further reading and technical articles under the student section of ACCA's website.

Examinable Documents

This text has been updated to reflect Examinable Documents September 2019 to June 2020 issued by ACCA.

Chapter

1

Introduction to published accounts

Chapter learning objectives

Upon completion of this chapter you will be able to:

- prepare an entity's financial statements in accordance with prescribed structure and content
- prepare and explain the contents and purpose of the statement of changes in equity.

PER

One of the PER performance objectives (PO7) is to prepare external financial reports. You take part in preparing and reviewing financial statements – and all accompanying information – and you do it in accordance with legal and regulatory requirements. Working though this chapter should help you understand how to demonstrate that objective.

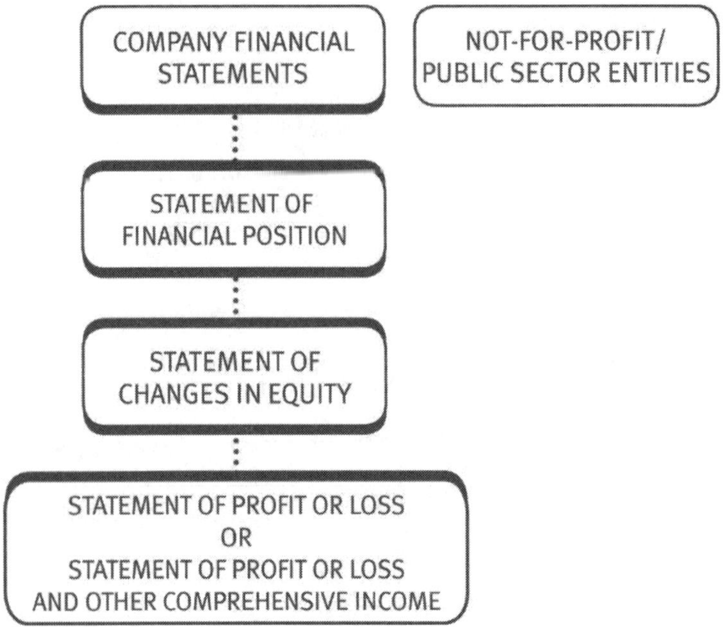

Preparation of single entity financial statements could be examined as one of the constructed response questions in section C of the FR examination. This chapter will look at the techniques and principles behind the construction of this. It is important to note that Chapters 2 to 15 contain information on specific accounting standards, any of which could be included within the construction of single entity financial statements. Once you have worked through these chapters, Chapter 23 provides practice of single entity financial statements with those standards incorporated into them.

1 Preparation of financial statements for companies

IAS 1 Presentation of Financial Statements

IAS 1 *Presentation of Financial Statements* states that a complete set of financial statements comprises:

- a statement of financial position
- either
  - a statement of profit or loss and other comprehensive income, or
  - a statement of profit or loss plus a statement showing other comprehensive income
- a statement of changes in equity
- a statement of cash flows
- accounting policies and explanatory notes.

IAS 1 (revised) does not require the above titles to be used by companies. It is likely in practice that many companies will continue to use the previous terms of balance sheet rather than statement of financial position, income statement instead of statement of profit or loss, and cash flow statement rather than statement of cash flows.

Exceptional items

Exceptional items is the name often given to material items of income and expense of such size, nature or incidence that disclosure is necessary in order to explain the performance of the entity.

The accounting treatment is to:

- include the item in the standard statement of profit or loss line
- disclose the nature and amount in the notes.

In some cases it may be more appropriate to show the item separately on the face of the statement of profit or loss.

Examples include:

- write down of inventories to net realisable value (NRV)
- impairment of property, plant and equipment
- restructuring costs
- gains/losses on disposal of non-current assets
- discontinued operations
- litigation settlements
- reversals of provisions

Statement of financial position

A recommended format is as follows:

XYZ: Statement of financial position as at 31 December 20X8

Assets	$	$
Non-current assets:		
Property, plant and equipment		X
Investments		X
Intangibles		X
		——
		X
Current assets:		
Inventories	X	
Trade receivables	X	
Cash and cash equivalents	X	
Asset held for sale	X	
	——	X
		——
Total assets		X
		——
Equity and liabilities		
Capital and reserves:		
Share capital	X	
Retained earnings	X	
Other components of equity	X	
	——	X
		——
Total equity		X
Non-current liabilities:		
Long-term borrowings	X	
Deferred tax	X	
	——	X
Current liabilities:		
Trade and other payables	X	
Short-term borrowings	X	
Current tax payable	X	
Short-term provisions	X	
	——	X
		——
Total equity and liabilities		X
		——

Note that IAS 1 requires an asset or liability to be classified as current if:

- it will be settled within 12 months of the reporting date, or
- it is part of the entity's normal operating cycle.

Within the equity section of the statement of financial position, other components of equity include:

- revaluation surplus
- share premium
- investment reserve (see financial instruments, Chapter 9).

Statement of changes in equity (SOCIE)

The statement of changes in equity provides a summary of all changes in equity arising from transactions with owners in their capacity as owners.

This includes the effect of share issues and dividends.

Other non-owner changes in equity, such as comprehensive income, are disclosed in aggregate only.

XYZ Group

Statement of changes in equity for the year ended 31 December 20X8

	Share capital	Share premium	Revaluation surplus	Retained earnings	Total equity
	$	$	$	$	$
Balance at 31 December 20X7	X	X	X	X	X
Prior year adjustment (IAS 8) (See Chapter 8)				(X)	(X)
Restated balance	X	X	X	X	X
Dividends				(X)	(X)
Issue of share capital	X	X			X
Total comprehensive income			X	X	X
Transfer to retained earnings (See Chapter 2)			(X)	X	–
Balance at 31 December 20X8	X	X	X	X	X

Statement of profit or loss and other comprehensive income

Total comprehensive income is the realised profit or loss for the period, plus other comprehensive income.

Other comprehensive income (OCI) is income and expenses that are not recognised in profit or loss (i.e. they are recorded in reserves rather than as an element of the realised profit for the period). For the purposes of FR, other comprehensive income includes any change in the revaluation of non-current assets (IAS 16, covered in Chapter 2) and fair value through other comprehensive income financial assets (IFRS 9, covered in Chapter 9).

Presentation of other comprehensive income

The amendments to IAS 1 (revised) change how items of OCI are presented in the financial statements – they do not change which items should be presented in OCI. In principle, items of OCI must be classified as follows:

- Items that **might be reclassified** (or recycled) to profit or loss in subsequent accounting periods
  - Foreign exchange gains and losses arising on translation of a foreign operation (IAS 21) (not on FR syllabus)
  - Effective parts of cash flow hedging arrangements (IAS 39) (not on FR syllabus)
  - Remeasurement of **debt** instruments designated to be classified as fair value through OCI (IFRS 9, Chapter 9)
- Items that **will not be reclassified** (or recycled) to profit or loss in subsequent accounting periods
  - Changes in revaluation surplus (IAS 16, Chapter 2 & IAS 38, Chapter 3)
  - Remeasurement of **equity** instruments designated to be classified as fair value through OCI (IFRS 9, Chapter 9)

IAS 1 *Presentation of Financial Statements* requires that you prepare either:

1. A statement of profit or loss and other comprehensive income showing total comprehensive income, or
2. A statement of profit or loss showing the realised profit or loss for the period PLUS a statement showing other comprehensive income.

Statement of profit or loss and other comprehensive income

A recommended format is as follows:

XYZ: Statement of profit or loss and other comprehensive income for the year ended 31 December 20X8

	$
Revenue	X
Cost of sales	(X)
	——
Gross profit	X
Distribution costs	(X)
Administrative expenses	(X)
	——
Profit from operations	X
Finance costs	(X)
Investment income	X
	——
Profit before tax	X
Income tax expense	(X)
	——
Profit for the year	X
Other comprehensive income	
Gain/loss on revaluation (IAS 16)	X
Gain/loss on fair value through other comprehensive income financial assets (IFRS 9)	X
	——
Total comprehensive income for the year	**X**
	——

Alternative presentation

Statement of profit or loss plus statement of comprehensive income

A recommended format for the statement of profit or loss is as follows:

XYZ
Statement of profit or loss for the year ended 31 December 20X8

	$
Revenue	X
Cost of sales	(X)
Gross profit	X
Distribution costs	(X)
Administrative expenses	(X)
Profit from operations	X
Finance costs	(X)
Investment income	X
Profit before tax	X
Income tax expense	(X)
Profit for the year	X

A recommended format for the presentation of other comprehensive income is:

XYZ
Statement of other comprehensive income for the year ended 31 December 20X8

	$
Profit for the year	X
Other comprehensive income	
Gain/loss on property revaluation	X
Gain/loss on fair value through other comprehensive income financial assets	X
Total comprehensive income for the year	X

2 Introduction to published accounts

The following questions enable preparation of published accounts utilising knowledge gained at Financial Accounting (FA). In order to be able to complete an FR published accounts question these basic preparation techniques must be followed and the accounting standards in Chapters 2–15 must first be learned.

Example 1 – Published accounts

The following information has been extracted from the books of Picklette for the year to 31 March 20X9.

	$000	$000
Administrative expenses	170	
Interest paid	5	
Called up share capital (ordinary shares of $1 each)		200
Dividend	6	
Cash at bank and in hand	9	
Income tax (remaining balance from previous year)	10	
Warranty provision		90
Distribution costs	240	
Land and buildings:		
at cost (Land $110,000, Buildings $100,000)	210	
accumulated depreciation (at 1 April 20X8)		48
Plant and machinery:		
at cost	125	
accumulated depreciation (at 1 April 20X8)		75
Retained earnings (at 1 April 20X8)		270
10% Loan note (issued in 20X7)		80
Purchases	470	
Sales		1,300
Inventory (at 1 April 20X8)	150	
Trade payables		60
Trade receivables	728	
	2,123	2,123

Additional information

1 Inventory at 31 March 20X9 was valued at $250,000.

2 Buildings and plant and machinery are depreciated on a straight-line basis (assuming no residual value) at the following rates:

On cost:	Buildings	5%
	Plant and machinery	20%

3 There were no purchases or sales of non-current assets during the year to 31 March 20X9.

4 The depreciation charges for the year to 31 March 20X9 are to be apportioned as follows:

Cost of sales	60%
Distribution costs	20%
Administrative expenses	20%

5 Income taxes for the year to 31 March 20X9 are estimated to be $135,000.

6 The 10% loan note was issued on 1 April 20X7 and is repayable five years from that date.

7 The year-end provision for warranty claims has been estimated at $75,000. Warranty costs are charged to administrative expenses.

Required:

Prepare Picklette's statement of profit or loss for the year to 31 March 20X9 and a statement of financial position as at that date.

Solution

Picklette: Statement of profit or loss

	$000
Revenue	1,300
Cost of sales (470 + 150 (Op Inv) – 250 (Cl Inv) + (60% × 30 (W1)))	(388)
Gross profit	912
Distribution (240 + (20% × 30 (W1)))	(246)
Administration (170 + (20% × 30 (W1)) + – 15 (Warranty)	(161)
Profit from operations	505
Finance costs (80 × 10%)	(8)
Profit before tax	497
Income Tax (135 + 10)	(145)
Profit for the year	352

Statement of financial position

	$000	$000
Non-current assets		
Property, plant and equipment **(W1)**		182
Current assets		
Inventory	250	
Receivables	728	
Bank	9	
		987
		1,169
Share capital	200	
Retained earnings **(W2)**	616	
		816
Non-current liabilities		
Loan	80	
Provision for warranties (90 (TB) – 15)	75	
		155
Payables		
(60 + 3 (accrued interest))	63	
Tax liability	135	
		198
		1,169

Working 1:

	Land	Buildings	Plant and machinery	Total
	$000	$000	$000	$000
Cost b/f	110	100	125	335
Depreciation b/f	–	(48)	(75)	(123)
Charge (5%/20% of cost)		(5)	(25)	(30)
Carrying amount c/f	110	47	25	182

Working 2:

	$000
Retained earnings b/f	270
Profit for the year	352
Dividends	(6)
Retained earnings c/f	616

Test your understanding 1

The following trial balance has been extracted from the books of Arran as at 31 March 20X7:

	$000	$000
Administration expenses	250	
Distribution costs	295	
Share capital $1		270
Share premium		80
Revaluation surplus		20
Dividend paid	27	
Cash at bank and in hand	3	
Receivables	233	
Interest paid	25	
Dividends received		15
Interest received		1
Land and buildings at cost (land 380, buildings 100)	480	
Land and buildings: accumulated depreciation		30
Plant and machinery at cost	400	
Plant and machinery: accumulated depreciation		170
Retained earnings account (at 1 April 20X6)		235
Purchases	1,260	
Sales		2,165
Inventory at 1 April 20X6	140	
Trade payables		27
Bank loan		100
	3,113	3,113

Additional information

1 Inventory at 31 March 20X7 was valued at a cost of $95,000. Included in this balance were goods that had cost $15,000. These goods had become damaged during the year and it is considered that the goods could be sold for $5,000, after paying commission of $500.

2 Depreciation for the year to 31 March 20X7 is to be charged against cost of sales as follows:

Buildings	5% on cost (straight line)
Plant and machinery	30% on carrying amount (reducing balance)

3 Land is to be revalued upwards by $100,000.

4 Income tax of $165,000 is to be provided for the year to 31 March 20X7.

5 The bank loan is repayable in five years' time.

Prepare the statement of profit or loss and other comprehensive income, statement of changes in equity and statement of financial position for year ended 31 March 20X7.

Note: Show all workings, notes are not required.

3 Not-for-profit and public sector entities

Not-for-profit and public sector entities

Comparison of aims

The main aims of not-for-profit and public sector entities are very different to those of profit-orientated entities:

Profit-orientated sector	Not-for-profit/public sector
Financial aim is to make profit and increase shareholder wealth.	Financial aim is to achieve value for money/provide service.
Directors are accountable to shareholders.	Managers are accountable to trustees/government/public.
External finance freely available in the form of loans and share capital.	Finance generally limited to donations/ government subsidies.

Accounting standards and not-for-profit and public sector entities

Accounting standards are designed to:

- measure financial performance accurately and consistently
- report the financial position accurately and consistently
- account for the directors' stewardship of resources and assets.

Not-for-profit and public sector organisations:

- do not aim to achieve a profit but have to account for their income and costs
- have to account for their effectiveness, economy and efficiency
- do not have to produce financial statements for the public (but in many cases may do so).

Some measurement accounting standards will be relevant such as those relating to inventory, non-current assets, leasing, etc. Others relating purely to reporting such as earnings per share (eps) will not be so relevant.

4 Chapter summary

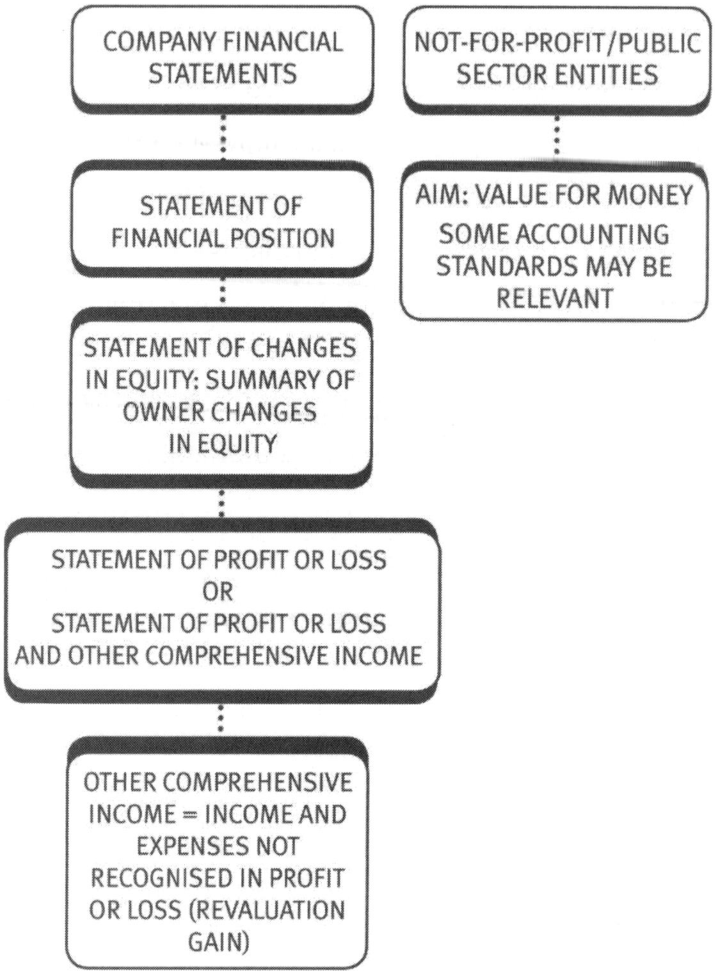

Test your understanding 2

The following trial balance relates to P at 31 March 20X1:

	$000	$000
Revenue		5,300
Cost of sales	1,350	
Dividends received		210
Administration expenses	490	
Distribution costs	370	
Interest paid	190	
Prepayments	25	
Dividends paid	390	
Property, plant and equipment	4,250	
Short-term investments	2,700	
Inventory at 31 March 20X1	114	
Trade receivables	418	
Cash and cash equivalents	12	
Trade payables		136
Long-term loans (repayable 20X9)		1,200
Share capital		1,500
Share premium		800
Retained earnings at 31 March 20X0		1,163
	10,309	10,309

The following information should also be taken into account:

1 The tax charge for the year has been estimated at $470,000.

2 The directors declared a final dividend of $270,000 on 3 April 20X1.

Required:

Prepare, in a form suitable for publication, the statement of profit or loss and other comprehensive income, statement of financial position and statement of changes in equity for the year ended 31 March 20X1.

Test your understanding answers

Test your understanding 1

Arran Statement of profit or loss and other comprehensive income for the year ended 31 March 20X7

	$000
Revenue	2,165
Cost of sales **(W1)**	(1,389)
Gross profit	776
Administration	(250)
Distribution	(295)
Operating profit	231
Finance cost	(25)
Interest receivable	1
Investment income	15
Profit before tax	222
Income tax expense	(165)
Profit for the year	57
Other comprehensive income	
Gain on land revaluation	100
Total comprehensive income for the year	157

Arran Statement of changes in equity

	Share capital	Share premium	Revaluation surplus	Retained earnings	Total equity
	$000	$000	$000	$000	$000
B/f	270	80	20	235	605
Total comprehensive income			100	57	157
Dividends				(27)	(27)
C/f	270	80	120	265	735

Arran Statement of financial position as at 31 March 20X7

	$000	$000
Non-current assets:		
Property, plant and equipment **(W2)**		706
Current assets:		
Inventory	85	
Receivables	233	
Bank	3	
		321
		1,027
Share capital (from SOCIE)		270
Share premium (from SOCIE)		80
Revaluation surplus (from SOCIE)		120
Retained earnings (from SOCIE)		265
		735
Non-current liabilities		100
Current liabilities		
Trade payables	27	
Tax liability	165	
		192
		1,027

Workings:

(W1) Cost of sales

	$
Opening inventory	140
Purchases	1,260
Closing inventory (95 – 10)	(85)
Depreciation: plant & machinery (W2)	69
Depreciation: building (W2)	5
Total	1,389

(W2) Property, plant and equipment

	Land	**Buildings**	**Plant & machinery**	**Total**
	$000	$000	$000	$000
Cost	380	100	400	
Accumulated depreciation		(30)	(170)	
			230	
Revaluation	100			
Depreciation charge				
100 × 5%		(5)		
230 × 30%			(69)	
Carrying amount c/f	480	65	161	706

Note that the only use of the total column is to calculate the total carrying amount to enter onto the statement of financial position, any other totals are unnecessary. Similarly the only subtotal needed is for plant and machinery, where the subtotal is used to calculate depreciation.

Test your understanding 2

P Statement of profit or loss and other comprehensive income for the year ended 31 March 20X1

	$000
Revenue	5,300
Cost of sales	(1,350)
Gross profit	3,950
Distribution costs	(370)
Administration expenses	(490)
Profit from operations	3,090
Income from investments	210
Finance cost	(190)
Profit before tax	3,110
Income tax expense	(470)
Profit for period	2,640
Other comprehensive income	–
Total comprehensive income for the period	2,640

P Statement of changes in equity for the year ended 31 March 20X1

	Share capital	Share premium	Retained earnings	Total
	$	$	$	$
Balance at 1 April 20X0	1,500	800	1,163	3,463
Total comprehensive income			2,640	2,640
Dividends			(390)	(390)
Balance at 31 March 20X1	1,500	800	3,413	5,713

Note: Dividends declared after the year end will not be adjusted for.

P Statement of financial position as at 31 March 20X1

Non-current assets	$000	$000
Property, plant and equipment		4,250
Current assets		
Inventories	114	
Trade receivables	418	
Prepayments	25	
Investments	2,700	
Cash and cash equivalents	12	
		3,269
Total assets		7,519
Equity and liabilities		
Capital and reserves		
Issued ordinary share capital		1,500
Share premium		800
Retained earnings		3,413
		5,713
Non-current liabilities		
Long-term loans		1,200
Current liabilities		
Trade payables	136	
Income tax	470	
		606
Total equity and liabilities		7,519

Chapter

2

Tangible non-current assets

Chapter learning objectives

Upon completion of this chapter you will be able to:

- define the cost of a non-current asset
- calculate the initial cost measurement of a non-current asset
- calculate the initial cost measurement of a self-constructed non- current asset
- distinguish between capital and revenue expenditure
- identify the subsequent expenditure that may be capitalised
- explain the treatment of borrowing costs per IAS 23
- explain the requirements of IAS 16 in relation to the revaluation of non-current assets
- account for revaluation of non-current assets
- account for gains and losses on disposal of non-current assets
- calculate depreciation based on the cost model
- calculate depreciation based on the revaluation model
- calculate depreciation on assets that have two or more significant parts (complex assets)
- apply the provisions of IAS 20 in relation to accounting for government grants
- define investment properties
- discuss why the treatment of investment properties should differ from other properties
- apply the requirements of IAS 40 for investment properties.

PER

One of the PER performance objectives (PO6) is to record and process transactions and events. You use the right accounting treatments for transactions and events. These should be both historical and prospective – and include non-routine transactions. Working though this chapter should help you understand how to demonstrate that objective.

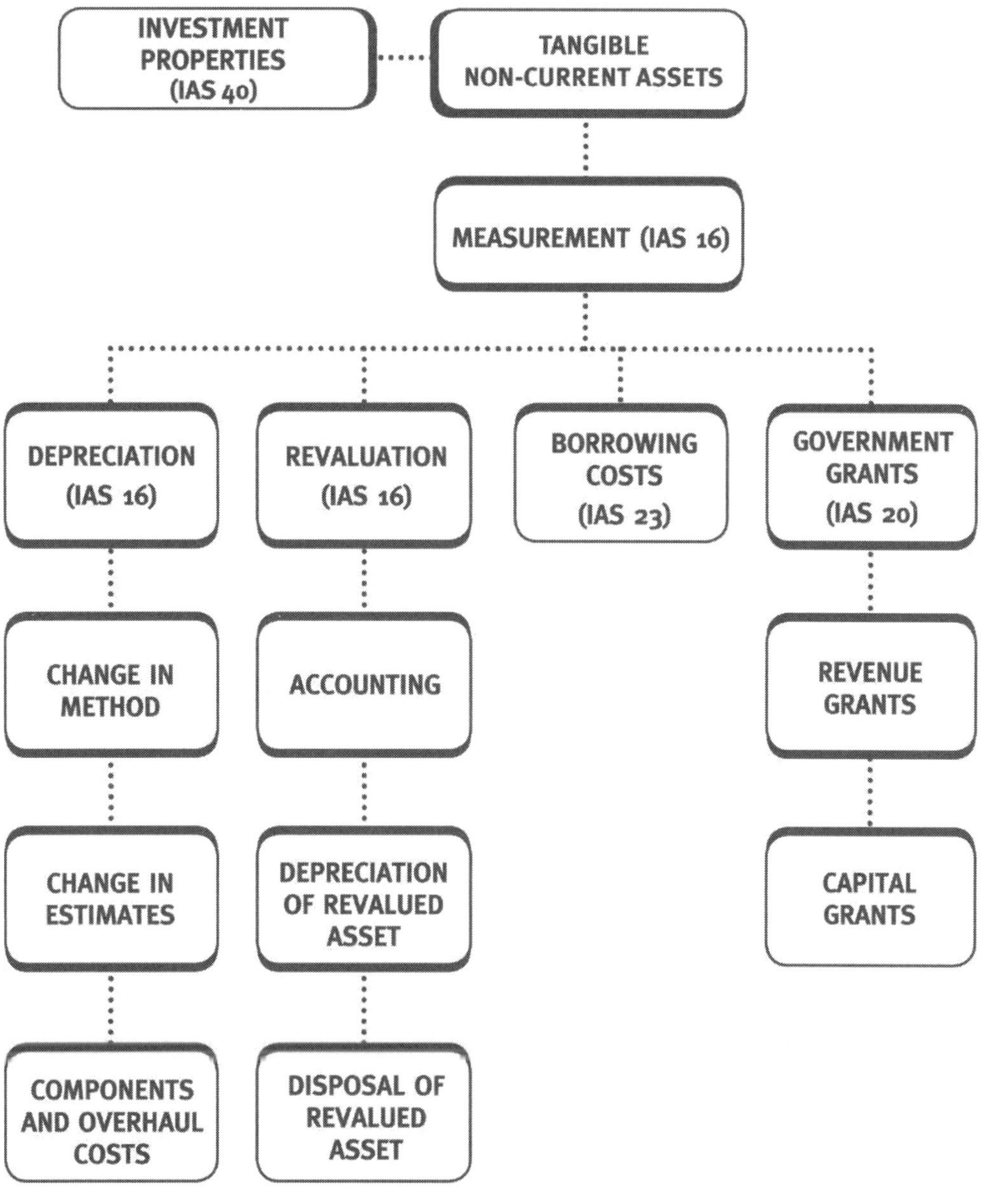

1 IAS 16 Property, Plant and Equipment

Property, plant and equipment

Property, plant and equipment are tangible assets held by an entity for more than one accounting period for use in the production or supply of goods or services, for rental to others, or for administrative purposes.

Recognition

An item of property, plant and equipment should be recognised as an asset when:

- **'it is probable that future economic benefits associated with the asset will flow to the entity; and**
- **the cost of the asset can be measured reliably**' (IAS 16, para 7).

Initial measurement

An item of property, plant and equipment should initially be measured at its cost:

- include all costs involved in bringing the asset into working condition
- include in this initial cost capital costs such as the cost of site preparation, delivery costs, installation costs, borrowing costs (in accordance with IAS 23 – see later in this chapter).
- revenue costs should be written off as incurred.
- dismantling costs – the present value of these costs should be capitalised, with an equivalent liability set up. The discount on this liability would then be unwound over the period until the dismantling costs are paid. This means that the liability increases by the interest rate each year, with the increase taken to finance costs in the statement of profit or loss.
  - You may need to use the interest rate given and apply the discount fraction where r is the interest rate and n the number of years to settlement.

$$\frac{1}{(1 + r)^n}$$

e.g

Illustration 1

If an oil rig was built in the sea, the cost to be capitalised is likely to include the cost of constructing the asset and the present value of the cost of dismantling it. If the asset cost $10 million to construct, and would cost $4 million to remove in 20 years, then the present value of this dismantling cost must be calculated. If interest rates were 5%, the present value of the dismantling costs are calculated as follows:

$4 million × $1/1.05^{20}$ = $1,507,558

The total to be capitalised would be $10 million + $1,507,558 = $11,507,558.

This would be depreciated over 20 years, so 11,507,558 × 1/20 = $575,378 per year.

Each year, the liability would be increased by the interest rate of 5%.

In year 1 this would mean the liability increases by $75,378 (making the year end liability $1,582,936).

This increase is taken to the finance costs in the statement of profit or loss.

Test your understanding 1

An entity started construction on a building for its own use on 1 April 20X7 and incurred the following costs:

	$000
Purchase price of land	250,000
Stamp duty	5,000
Legal fees	10,000
Site preparation and clearance	18,000
Materials	100,000
Labour (period 1 April 20X7 to 1 July 20X8)	150,000
Architect's fees	20,000
General overheads	30,000
	583,000

The following information is also relevant:

- Material costs were greater than anticipated. On investigation, it was found that materials costing $10 million had been spoiled and therefore wasted and a further $15 million was incurred on materials as a result of faulty design work.
- As a result of these problems, work on the building ceased for a fortnight during October 20X7 and it is estimated that approximately $9 million of the labour costs relate to this period.
- The building was completed on 1 July 20X8 and occupied on 1 September 20X8.

You are required to calculate the cost of the building that will be included in tangible non-current asset additions.

Subsequent expenditure

Subsequent expenditure on property, plant and equipment should only be capitalised if:

- it enhances the economic benefits provided by the asset (this could be extending the asset's life, an expansion or increasing the productivity of the asset)
- it relates to an overhaul or required major inspection of the asset – the costs associated with this should be capitalised and depreciated over the time until the next overhaul or safety inspection
- it is replacing a component of a complex asset. The replaced component will be derecognised. A complex asset is an asset made up of a number of components, which each depreciate at different rates, e.g. an aircraft would comprise body, engines and interior.

All other subsequent expenditure should be recognised in the statement of profit or loss, because it merely maintains the economic benefits originally expected e.g. the cost of general repairs should be written off immediately (revenue expenditure).

e.g

Illustration 2 – Subsequent expenditure

A piece of machinery has an annual service costing $10,000. During the most recent service it was decided to replace part of the engineering meaning that it will work faster and produce more units of product per hour. The cost of the replacement part is $20,000.

Would this expenditure be treated as capital or revenue expenditure?

Solution

- $10,000 servicing cost is revenue expenditure, written off to the statement of profit or loss.
- $20,000 replacement part enhances future economic benefits and so is capital expenditure and increases the cost of non-current assets in the statement of financial position.

2 Depreciation

Definitions

'Depreciation is the systematic allocation of the depreciable amount of an asset over its useful life' (IAS 16, para 6).

'Depreciable amount is the cost of an asset, or other amount substituted for cost, less its residual value' (IAS 16, para 6)

Depreciation must be charged from the date the asset is available for use, i.e. it is capable of operating in the manner intended by management.

This may be earlier than the date it is actually brought into use, for example if staff need to be trained to use it. Depreciation is continued even if the asset is idle.

The depreciation method used should reflect as fairly as possible the pattern in which the asset's economic benefits are consumed by the entity. Possible methods include:

- straight line
- reducing balance
- machine hours.

A change from one method of providing depreciation to another:

- is permissible only on the grounds that the new method will give a fairer presentation of the results and of the financial position
- does not constitute a change of accounting policy
- is a change in accounting estimate.

The carrying amount should be written off over the remaining useful life, commencing with the period in which the change is made.

If an asset is classed as a complex asset, it may be thought of as having separate components within a single asset, e.g. an engine within an aircraft will need replacing before the body of the aircraft needs replacing. Each separate part of the asset should be depreciated over its useful life.

Illustration 3 – Depreciable amount

An asset costs $100,000 and has an expected useful life of ten years. The purchaser intends to use the asset for six years at which point the expected residual value will be $40,000 (at current prices).

What is the depreciable amount?

Solution

The depreciable amount is $(100,000 – 40,000) = $60,000 spread over six years.

Review of useful lives and residual values

Useful life and residual value should be reviewed at the end of each reporting period and revised if expectations are significantly different from previous estimates.

The carrying amount of the asset at the date of revision less any residual value should be depreciated over the revised remaining useful life.

Illustration 4 – Revision of useful life

An entity purchased an asset for $20,000 on 1 January 20X3. Straight-line depreciation of $5,000 per annum has been charged, assuming a four-year useful life with no residual value. On 1 January 20X5 the annual review of asset lives was undertaken and the remaining useful life for this asset was estimated at four years.

The financial statements for the year ended 31 December 20X5 are being prepared.

What is the depreciation charge for the year ended 31 December 20X5?

Major inspection or overhaul costs

Inspection and overhaul costs are generally expensed as they are incurred.

They are, however, capitalised as a non-current asset to the extent that they satisfy the IAS 16 rules for separate components.

Where this is the case they are then depreciated over their useful lives, i.e. until the next inspection or overhaul is due

e.g

Illustration 5 – Overhaul costs

An entity purchases an aircraft that has an expected useful life of 20 years with no residual value. The aircraft requires substantial overhaul at the end of years 5, 10 and 15. The aircraft cost $25 million and $5 million of this figure is estimated to be attributable to the economic benefits that are restored by the overhauls. In year 6, the cost of the overhaul is estimated to be $6 million.

Calculate the annual depreciation charge for the years 1–5 and years 6–10.

Solution

The aircraft is treated as two separate components for depreciation purposes:

Years 1–5	$m
Initial overhaul value $5m depreciated over 5 years	1
Balance of $20m depreciated over 20 years	1
Depreciation charge per annum	2

When the first overhaul is completed at the end of year 5 **at a cost of, say, $6 million**, then this cost is capitalised and depreciated to the date of the next overhaul:

Years 6–10	$m
Overhaul $6m depreciated over 5 years	1.2
Aircraft depreciation	1.0
Depreciation charge per annum	2.2

3 Revaluation of non-current assets

IAS 16 treatments

IAS 16 allows a choice of accounting treatment for property, plant and equipment:

- the cost model
- the revaluation model.

The cost model

Property, plant and equipment should be valued at cost less accumulated depreciation.

The revaluation model

Property, plant and equipment may be carried at a revalued amount less any subsequent accumulated depreciation.

If the revaluation alternative is adopted, two conditions must be complied with:

- Revaluations must subsequently be made with sufficient regularity to ensure that the carrying amount does not differ materially from the fair value at each reporting date.
- When an item of property, plant and equipment is revalued, the entire class of assets to which the item belongs must be revalued.

Accounting for a revaluation

Steps:

(1) Restate asset's cost to the new valuation.

(2) Eliminate any existing accumulated depreciation for the asset.

(3) Show the total increase in Other Comprehensive Income, at the foot of the statement of profit or loss. This would then be taken to the revaluation surplus (much like the profit for the year gets taken to retained earnings).

Journal (assuming revalued amount is greater than original cost):

		$	$
Dr	Non-current assets cost/valuation (revalued amount – cost)	X	
Dr	Accumulated depreciation (eliminate accumulated balance)	X	
Cr	Other Comprehensive Income (revaluation surplus)		X

Recognising revaluation gains and losses

Revaluation gains are recorded as a component of other comprehensive income either within the statement of profit or loss and other comprehensive income or in a separate statement. This gain is then carried in a revaluation surplus within equity. This revaluation surplus is a capital reserve and is therefore not permitted to be distributed to the shareholders.

Revaluation losses, which represent an impairment of the asset value, are recognised in the statement of profit or loss. When a revaluation loss arises on a previously revalued asset it should be deducted first against the previous revaluation gain and can therefore be taken to other comprehensive income in the year. Any excess impairment will then be recorded as an impairment expense in the statement of profit or loss.

Note that offset of gains and losses between different properties is **not permitted**.

e.g

Illustration 6 – Revaluation of non-current assets

Recognition of revaluation gain

An entity revalues its buildings and decides to incorporate the revaluation into its financial statements.

Extract from the statement of financial position at 31 December 20X7:	$000
Buildings:	
Cost	1,200
Depreciation	(144)
	1,056

The building is revalued at 1 January 20X8 at $1,400,000. Its useful life is 40 years at that date.

Show the relevant extracts from the financial statements at 31 December 20X8.

Solution

The relevant extracts from the financial statements at 31 December 20X8 are as follows:

Statement of profit or loss and other comprehensive income (extract)

	$000
Depreciation (W1)	(35)
Other comprehensive income:	
Gain on revaluation (W1)	344

Statement of financial position (extract)

	$000
Non-current assets	
Land and buildings **(W1)**	1,365
Equity	
Revaluation surplus (SOCIE)	344

Statement of changes in equity (extract)

	Revaluation surplus $000
1 January 20X8 b/f	–
Revaluation gain **(W1)**	344
31 December 20X8 c/f	344

(W1) PPE Note

Land and buildings	$000
1 January 20X8	1,056
Revaluation (β)	344
Valuation	1,400
Depreciation (1,400/40 years)	(35)
31 December 20X8	1,365

Depreciation of revalued assets

Once an asset has been revalued the following treatment is required.

- Depreciation must be charged, based on valuation less residual value, over the remaining useful life of the asset
- The whole charge must go to the statement of profit or loss for the year.
- An annual reserves transfer **may** be made, from revaluation surplus to retained earnings, for the **additional** depreciation charged on the revalued amount compared to cost.This permitted treatment under IAS 16 is to address the imbalance between a non-distributable gain held in revaluation surplus and the reduction in retained earnings due to the increased depreciation charge.
- This transfer would be shown on the SOCIE.

Journals

Dr	Statement of profit or loss – depreciation charge	X
Cr	Accumulated depreciation	X

And:

Dr	Revaluation surplus (depreciation on valuation – depreciation on original cost)	X
Cr	Retained earnings	X

Note: This transfer is not part of other comprehensive income, it is shown on the **SOCIE only.**

Test your understanding 2

On 1 April 20X8 the fair value of Xu's property was $100,000 with a remaining life of 20 years. Xu's policy is to revalue its property at each year end. At 31 March 20X9 the property was valued at $86,000. The balance on the revaluation surplus at 1 April 20X8 was $20,000 which relates entirely to the property.

Xu does not make a transfer to realised profit in respect of excess depreciation.

Required:

1 **Prepare extracts of Xu's financial statements for the year ended 31 March 20X9 reflecting the above information.**

2 **State how the accounting would be different if the opening revaluation surplus did not exist.**

Test your understanding 3

An entity revalued its land and buildings at the start of the year to $60 million ($15 million for the land). The property cost $30 million ($6 million for the land) ten years prior to the revaluation. The total expected useful life of 40 years remained unchanged. The entity's policy is to make an annual transfer of realised amounts to retained earnings.

Show the effects of the above on the financial statements for the year.

Disposal of revalued non-current assets

The profit or loss on disposal of a revalued non-current asset should be calculated as the difference between the net sale proceeds and the carrying amount.

There are two steps to disposing of a revalued asset:

(1) It should be accounted for in the statement of profit or loss of the period in which the disposal occurs.

(2) Any balance on the revaluation surplus relating to this asset should now be transferred to retained earnings.

Note: This does not affect other comprehensive income, which is only altered when the asset is actually revalued upwards or downwards.

Test your understanding 4

Derek purchased a property costing $750,000 on 1 January 20X4 with a useful life of 10 years. It has no residual value. At 31 December 20X4 the property was valued at $810,000 resulting in a gain on revaluation being recorded in other comprehensive income of $135,000. There was no change to its useful life. Derek does not make a transfer to realised profits in respect of excess depreciation on revalued assets.

On 31 December 20X6 the property was sold for $900,000.

Required:

How should the disposal on the previously revalued asset be treated in the financial statements for the year ended 31 December 20X6?

4 IAS 20 Accounting for Government Grants and Disclosure of Government Assistance

Introduction

Governments often provide money or incentives to companies to export their goods or to promote local employment.

Government grants could be:

- revenue grants, e.g. contribution towards payroll costs
- capital grants, e.g. contribution towards purchase of non-current assets.

General principles

IAS 20 follows two general principles when determining the treatment of grants:

Prudence: grants should not be recognised until the conditions for receipt have been complied with and there is reasonable assurance the grant will be received.

Accruals: grants should be matched with the expenditure towards which they were intended to contribute.

Definitions (IAS 20, para 3)

'Government refers to government, government agencies and similar bodies whether local, national or international.'

'Government assistance is action by government designed to provide an economic benefit specific to an entity or range of entities qualifying under certain criteria' e.g. the grant of a local operating licence.

'Government grants are assistance by government in the form of transfers of resources to an entity in return for past or future compliance with certain conditions relating to the operating activities of the entity.'

'Grants related to assets are government grants whose primary condition is that an entity qualifying for them should purchase, construct or otherwise acquire long-term assets.'

'Grants related to income are government grants other than those related to assets – known as revenue grants.'

Revenue grants

The recognition of the grant will depend upon the circumstances.

- If the grant is paid when evidence is produced that certain expenditure has been incurred, the grant should be matched with that expenditure.
- If the grant is paid on a different basis, e.g. achievement of a non-financial objective, such as the creation of a specified number of new jobs, the grant should be matched with the identifiable costs of achieving that objective.

Presentation of revenue grants

IAS 20 allows such grants to either be:

- presented as a credit in the statement of profit or loss, or
- deducted from the related expense.

Revenue grant presentation

Presentation as credit in the statement of profit or loss

Supporters of this method **'claim that it is inappropriate to net income and expense items, and that separation of the grant from the expense facilitates comparison with other expenses not affected by a grant'** (IAS 20, para 30).

Deduction from related expense

It is argued that with this method, **'the expenses might well not have been incurred by the entity if the grant had not been available, and presentation of the expense without offsetting the grant may therefore be misleading'** (IAS 20, para 30).

Illustration 7

An entity is given $300,000 on 1 January 20X1 to keep staff employed within a deprived area. The entity must not make redundancies for the next three years, or the grant will need to be repaid.

By 31 December, 20X1, no redundancies have taken place and none are planned.

The grant should be released over three years, meaning that $100,000 is taken to the statement of profit or loss each year.

This can be shown as a separate line in the statement of profit or loss or deducted from administrative expenses (or wherever the staff costs are charged).

As $100,000 has been released to the statement of profit or loss, the remaining $200,000 will be held in deferred income, to be recognised over the next two years.

Of this, $100,000 will be released within the next year, so will be held within current liabilities. The remaining $100,000 will be held as a non-current liability.

Capital grants

IAS 20 permits two treatments:

- Write off the grant against the cost of the non-current asset and depreciate the reduced cost.
- Treat the grant as a deferred credit and transfer a portion to revenue each year, so offsetting the higher depreciation charge on the original cost.

Treatment of capital grants

Grants for purchases of non-current assets should be recognised over the expected useful lives of the related assets.

IAS 20 permits two treatments. Both treatments are equally acceptable and capable of giving a fair presentation.

Method 1

On initial recognition, deduct the grant from the cost of the non-current asset and depreciate the reduced cost.

Method 2

Recognise the grant initially as deferred income and transfer a portion to revenue each year, so offsetting the higher depreciation charge based on the original cost.

Method 1 is obviously far simpler to operate. Method 2, however, has the advantage of ensuring that assets acquired at different times and in different locations are recorded on a uniform basis, regardless of changes in government policy.

In some countries, legislation requires that non-current assets should be stated by companies at purchase price and this is defined as actual price paid plus any additional expenses. Legal opinion on this matter is that enterprises subject to such legislation should not deduct grants from cost. In such countries Method 1 may only be adopted by unincorporated bodies.

Test your understanding 5

Capital grants

An entity opens a new factory and receives a government grant of $15,000 in respect of capital equipment costing $100,000. It depreciates all plant and machinery at 20% pa straight-line.

Show the statement of profit or loss and statement of financial position extracts in respect of the grant in the first year under both methods.

Other types of government assistance may include the provision of interest- free loans or guarantees. These should be disclosed in the notes to the accounts.

Repayment of grants

In some cases grants may need to be repaid if the conditions of the grant are breached.

If there is an obligation to repay the grant and the repayment is probable, then it should be provided for in accordance with the requirements of IAS 37 (see Chapter 15).

If the deferred income method for capital grants has been used, then the remaining grant would be repaid to the government. Any amounts released to profit or loss may also need to be reversed, depending on the level of repayment required.

If the netting-off method for capital grants has been used, then the cost of the asset must be increased to recognise the full cost of the asset without the grant. A liability will be set up for the grant repayment.

5 IAS 23 Borrowing Costs

IAS 23 treatment

IAS 23 *Borrowing Costs* regulates the extent to which entities are allowed to capitalise borrowing costs incurred on money borrowed to finance the acquisition of certain assets.

- Borrowing costs **must** be capitalised as part of the cost of an asset if that asset is a **qualifying** asset (one which **'necessarily takes a substantial period of time to get ready for its intended use or sale'** (IAS 23, para 5)).

Commencement of capitalisation

IAS 23 states that capitalisation of borrowing costs should commence when **all** of the following conditions are met:

- expenditure for the asset is being incurred
- borrowing costs are being incurred
- activities that are necessary to prepare the asset for its intended use or sale are in progress.

The rate of interest to be taken

Where funds are borrowed specifically to acquire a qualifying asset, borrowing costs which may be capitalised are those actually incurred, less any investment income on the temporary investment of the borrowings during the capitalisation period.

Test your understanding 6

Wilson received an $18 million 5% loan on 1 January 20X8 to finance construction of a new factory. As the funds were not all required immediately Wilson invested $6 million in 2% bonds until 31 May 20X8.

Construction of the factory began on 1 March 20X8 and was completed on 31 December 20X8.

Calculate the amount of interest to be capitalised in respect of the factory as at 31 December 20X8.

Where funds for the project are taken from general borrowings the weighted average cost of general borrowings is taken.

Illustration 8

If an entity had a $10 million 6% loan and a $2 million 8% loan, the weighted average cost of borrowing would be:

$$\frac{(\$10m \times 6\%) + (\$2m \times 8\%)}{\$12m}$$

$$= \$760k/\$12m = 6.33\%$$

The amount to be capitalised would be the amount spent on the asset multiplied by 6.33% per annum.

Cessation of capitalisation

Capitalisation of borrowing costs should cease when **either**:

- 'substantially all the activities necessary to prepare the qualifying asset for its intended use or sale are complete' (IAS 23, para 21), or
- construction is suspended, e.g. due to industrial disputes.

Test your understanding 7

On 1 January 20X5, Sainsco began to construct a supermarket which had an estimated useful life of 40 years. It purchased the site for $25 million. The construction of the building cost $9 million and the fixtures and fittings cost $6 million. The construction of the supermarket was completed on 30 September 20X5 and it was brought into use on 1 January 20X6.

Sainsco borrowed $40 million on 1 January 20X5 in order to finance this project. The loan carried interest at 10% pa. It was repaid on 30 June 20X6.

Required:

Calculate the total amount to be included at cost in property, plant and equipment in respect of the development at 31 December 20X5.

6 IAS 40 Investment Property

IAS 40 Definition

Investment property is land or a building **'held to earn rentals or for capital appreciation or both'** (IAS 40, para 5), rather than for use by the entity or for sale in the ordinary course of business.

Owner-occupied property is excluded from the definition of investment property, so these are properties not used by the entity in general operations.

These could be spare properties rented out to third parties, or specifically bought in order to profit from a gain in value.

There could be a situation where a building can be accounted for in two different ways. If an entity occupies a premises but rents out certain floors to other companies, then the part occupied will be classed as property, plant and equipment per IAS 16, with the floors rented out classed as investment property per IAS 40.

Consolidated accounts

If a building is rented by a subsidiary of the entity, then the building will be classed as an investment property in the individual accounts, but will be classed as property, plant and equipment per IAS 16 in the consolidated financial statements.

This is because the asset will be used by the group, so must be accounted for in accordance with IAS 16.

Accounting treatment

Investment properties should initially be measured at cost.

IAS 40 then gives a choice for subsequent measurement between the following:

- cost model
- fair value model.

Once the model is chosen it must be used for all investment properties.

Cost model

Under the cost model the asset should be accounted for in line with the cost model laid out in IAS 16.

Fair value model

Under the fair value model:

- the asset is revalued to fair value at the end of each year
- the gain or loss is shown directly in the **statement of profit or loss** (not other comprehensive income)
- no depreciation is charged on the asset.

Fair value is normally established by reference to current prices on an active market for properties in the same location and condition.

Test your understanding 8

Celine, a manufacturing entity, purchases a property for $1 million on 1 January 20X1 for its investment potential. The land element of the cost is believed to be $400,000, and the buildings element is expected to have a useful life of 50 years. At 31 December 20X1, local property indices suggest that the fair value of the property has risen to $1.1 million.

Required:

Show how the property would be presented in the financial statements as at 31 December 20X1 if Celine adopts:

(a) **the cost model**

(b) **the fair value model.**

If an asset is transferred from property, plant and equipment to investment property and the fair value model for investment property is used:

- The asset **must first be revalued per IAS 16** (creating a revaluation surplus in equity) and then transferred into investment property at fair value.

If the cost model is used for investment properties:

- The asset is transferred into investment properties at the current carrying amount and continues to be depreciated.

If an asset is transferred from investment property to property, plant and equipment and the fair value model for investment property is used:

- **Revalue the property first per IAS 40** (taking the gain or loss to the statement of profit or loss) and then transfer to property, plant and equipment at fair value.

If the cost model is used for investment properties:

- The asset is transferred into property, plant and equipment at the current carrying amount and continues to be depreciated.

Test your understanding 9

Kyle Co purchased an investment property some year ago and carries it under the fair value model. At 1 January 20X1, the property had a fair value in Kyle Co's financial statements of $12 million. On 1 July 20X1 Kyle Co decided to move into the property and use it for its own business. At this date the asset had a fair value of $14 million and a remaining useful life of 14 years.

What amount should be recorded in Kyle Co's statement of profit or loss for the year ended 31 December 20X1?

7 Chapter summary

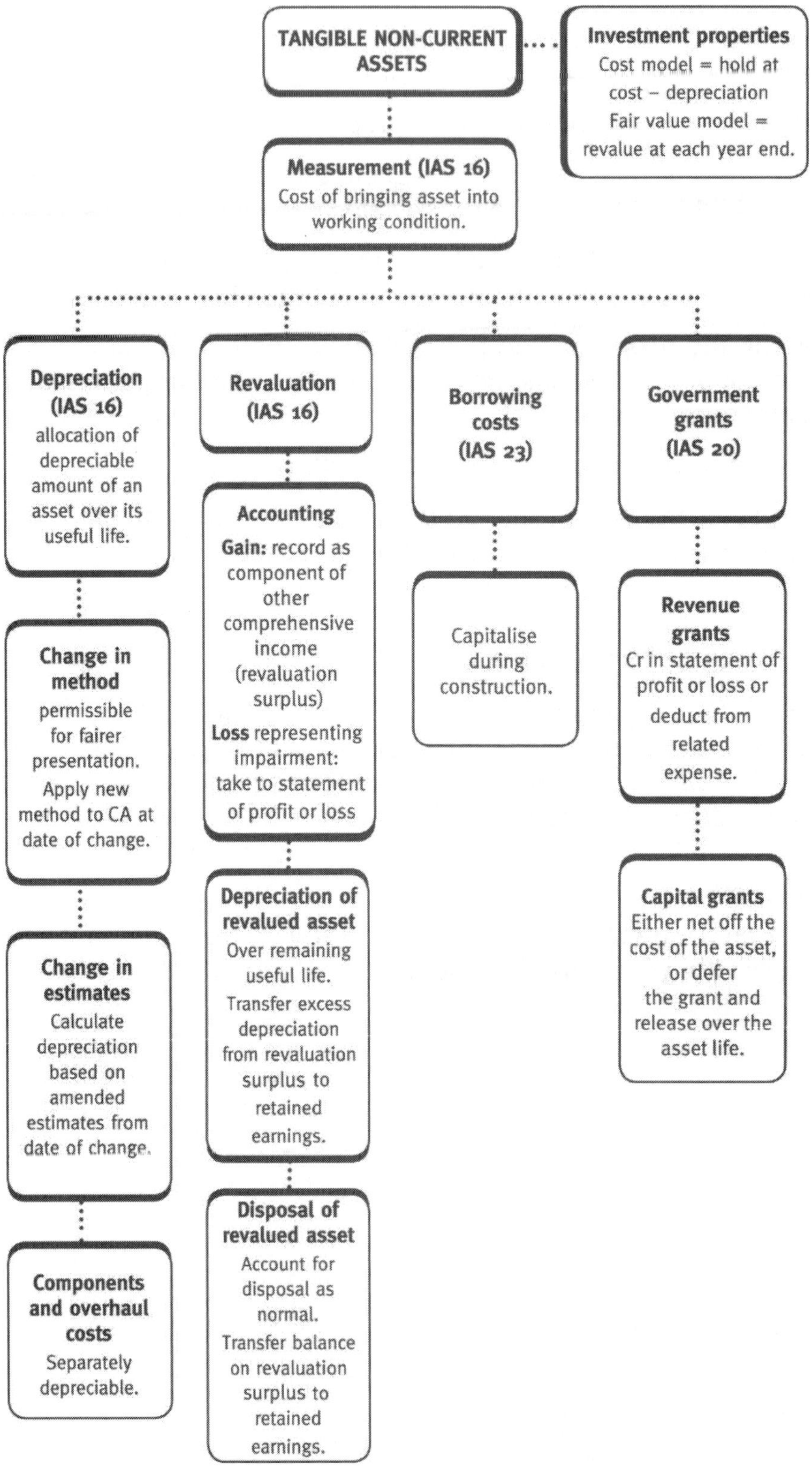

Test your understanding 10

During the year to 30 September 20X3 Hudson built a new mining facility to take advantage of new laws regarding on-shore gas extraction. The construction of the facility cost $10 million, and to fund this Hudson took out a $10 million 6% loan on 1 October 20X2, which will not be repaid until 20X6. The 6% interest was paid on 30 September 20X3. Construction work began on 1 October 20X2, and the work was completed on 31 August 20X3. As not all the funds were required immediately, Hudson invested $3 million of the loan in 4% bonds from 1 October 20X2 until 31 January 20X3. Mining commenced on 1 September 20X3 and is expected to continue for 10 years.

As a condition of being allowed to construct the facility, Hudson is required by law to dismantle it on 1 October 20Y3. Hudson estimated that this would cost a further $3 million.

As the equipment is extremely specialised, Hudson invested significant resources in recruiting and training employees. Hudson spent $600,000 on this process in the year to 30 September 20X3, believing it to be worthwhile as it anticipates that most employees will remain on the project for the entire 10 year duration.

Hudson has a cost of capital of 6%.

Required:

Show, using extracts, the correct financial reporting treatment for the above items in the financial statements for Hudson for the year ended 30 September 20X3.

Test your understanding 11

(1) An entity purchased a property 15 years ago at a cost of $100,000 and have been depreciating it at a rate of 2% per annum, on the straight line basis. The entity have had the property professionally revalued at $500,000.

What is the revaluation surplus that will be recorded in the financial statements in respect of this property?

A $400,000

B $500,000

C $530,000

D $430,000

(2) An entity owns two buildings, A and B, which are currently recorded in the books at carrying amounts of $170,000 and $330,000 respectively. Both buildings have recently been valued as follows:

Building A $400,000

Building B $250,000

The entity currently has a balance on the revaluation surplus of $50,000 which arose when building A was revalued several years ago. Building B has not previously been revalued.

What double entry will need to be made to record the revaluations of buildings A and B?

A	Dr	Non-current assets	$150,000
	Dr	Statement of profit or loss	$80,000
	Cr	Other comprehensive income (revaluation surplus)	$230,000
B	Dr	Non-current assets	$150,000
	Dr	Statement of profit or loss	$30,000
	Cr	Other comprehensive income (revaluation surplus)	$180,000
C	Dr	Non-current assets	$150,000
	Cr	Other comprehensive income (revaluation surplus)	$150,000
D	Dr	Non-current assets	$150,000
	Dr	Statement of profit or loss	$50,000
	Cr	Other comprehensive income (revaluation surplus)	$200,000

(3) On 1 April 20X0 Slow and Steady Co held non-current assets that cost $312,000 and had accumulated depreciation of $66,000 at this date. During the year ended 31 March 20X1, Slow and Steady Co disposed of non-current assets which had originally cost $28,000 and had a carrying amount of $11,200.

Slow and Steady Co's policy is to charge depreciation of 40% on the reducing balance basis, with no depreciation charged in the year of disposal.

What is the depreciation charge to the statement of profit or loss for the year ended 31 March 20X1?

$ ________

(4) A building contractor decides to construct an office building to be occupied by his own staff. Tangible non-current assets are initially measured at cost.

Which TWO of the following expenses incurred by the building contractor cannot be included as a part of the cost of the office building?

A Interest incurred on a specific loan taken out to pay for the construction of the new offices

B Direct building labour costs

C A proportion of the contractor's general administration costs

D Hire of plant and machinery for use on the office building site

E Additional design work caused by initial design errors

F Delivery costs in getting the raw materials onto site

(5) **The purpose of depreciation is to:**

A Allocate the cost less residual value on a systematic basis over the asset's useful life

B Write the asset down to its realisable value each period

C Accumulate a fund for asset replacement

D Recognise that assets lose value over time

(6) An entity uses funds from its general borrowings to build a new production facility. Details of the entity's borrowings are shown below:

– $10 million 6% loan

– $6 million 8% loan

The entity used $12 million of these funds to construct the facility, which was under construction for the entire year.

How much interest should be capitalised as part of the cost of the asset?

$ _________

(7) A manufacturing entity is entitled to a grant of $3 million for creating 50 jobs and maintaining them for three years. $1.5m is received when the jobs are created and the remaining $1.5m is receivable after three years, provided that the 50 jobs are still in existence. The entity creates 50 jobs at the beginning of year one and there is reasonable assurance that this level of employment will be maintained.

What is the deferred income balance at the end of the first year?

$ _________

(8) On 1 January 20X1, Sly received $2m from the local government on the condition that they employ at least 100 staff each year for the next 4 years. On this date, it was virtually certain that Sly would meet these requirements. However, on 1 January 20X2, due to an economic downturn and reduced consumer demand, Sly no longer needed to employ 100 staff. The conditions of the grant required full repayment.

What should be recorded in the financial statements?

A Reduce deferred income balance by $1,500,000

B Reduce deferred income by $1,500,000 and recognise a loss in the financial statements of $500,000

C Reduce deferred income by $2,000,000

D Reduce deferred income by $2,000,000 and recognise a gain in the financial statements of $500,000

(9) An entity purchased an investment property on 1 January 20X3 for a cost of $3.5m. The property had an estimated useful life of 50 years, with no residual value, and at 31 December 20X5 had a fair value of $4.2m. On 1 January 20X6 the property was sold for net proceeds of $4m.

Calculate the profit or (loss) on disposal under both the cost and fair value (FV) model.

A Cost: $0.71m FV: ($0.2m)

B Cost: $0.2m FV: $0.2m

C Cost $0.5m FV: ($0.2m)

D Cost $0.71m FV: $0.5m

(10) An investment property with a useful life of 10 years was purchased by Akorn on 1 January 20X9 for $200,000. By 31 December 20X9 the fair value of the property had risen to $300,000. Akorn measures its investment properties under the fair value model.

What values would go through the statement of profit or loss in the year?

A Gain: $100,000 and Depreciation $30,000

B Gain: $0 and Depreciation of $30,000

C Gain: $100,000 and Depreciation of 0

D Gain: $120,000 and Depreciation of $20,000

(11) **With regards to borrowing costs relating to specific borrowings used for the construction of a qualifying asset, match the description to the correct accounting treatment in the table below.**

	Include in calculation of non-current asset	**Investment income**	**Finance cost**
Interest earned on the investment of surplus borrowings before the construction period begins			
Interest incurred after the construction period has ended			
Interest incurred during the construction period			
Interest earned on the investment of surplus borrowings during the construction period			

Test your understanding answers

Test your understanding 1

- Only those costs which are directly attributable to bringing the asset Into working condition for its intended use should be included
- administration and other general overhead costs cannot be included
- costs included should only be normal, not abnormal, costs.

The amount included in property, plant and equipment is computed as follows:

	Total	**Exclude**	**Include**
	$000	$000	$000
Purchase price of land	250,000		250,000
Stamp duty	5,000		5,000
Legal fees	10,000		10,000
Site preparation and clearance	18,000		18,000
Materials **(Note 1)**	100,000	25,000	75,000
Labour **(Note 2)**	150,000	9,000	141,000
Architect's fees	20,000		20,000
General overheads	30,000	30,000	
	583,000	64,000	519,000

Notes:

(1) The costs of spoiled material and faulty design are abnormal costs.

(2) The $9 million labour cost incurred during the period of the stoppage is an abnormal cost and is excluded.

Test your understanding 2

(1) **Extracts of the financial statements for Xu at 31 March 20X9**

Statement of profit or loss and other comprehensive income (extract)

	$
Depreciation **(W1)**	(5,000)
Other comprehensive income:	
Revaluation loss **(W2)**	(9,000)

Statement of financial position (extract)

Non-current assets	
Property (at valuation)	86,000
Equity	
Revaluation surplus (20,000 – 9,000)	11,000

Statement of changes in equity (extract)

	Revaluation surplus
Balance at 1 April 20X8	20,000
Revaluation of leasehold **(W2)**	(9,000)
Balance at 31 March 20X9	11,000

Workings:

(W1) Depreciation

$100,000/20 years = $5,000

(W2) Revaluation

Carrying amount of leasehold at 31 March 20X9 (100,000 – 5,000 **(W1)**)	95,000
Leasehold valuation at 31 March 20X9	86,000
Loss on revaluation	(9,000)

(2) If the opening revaluation surplus did not exist, then the revaluation loss of $9,000 would need to be taken through the statement of profit or loss as an impairment expense.

Test your understanding 3

Statement of profit or loss and other comprehensive income (extract)

	$000
Depreciation **(W1)**	(1,500)
Other comprehensive income:	
Revaluation gain **(W1)**	36,000

Statement of financial position (extract)

Non-current assets	$000
Land and buildings **(W1)**	58,500
Equity	
Revaluation surplus (SOCIE)	35,100

Statement of changes in equity (extract)	Revalualtion Surplus $000
Balance b/f	–
Revaluation gain **(W1)**	36,000
Transfer to retained earnings **(W2)**	(900)
Balance c/f	35,100

(W1)	**Land**	**Buildings**	**Total**
Cost	6,000	24,000	30,000
Depreciation ($^{10}/_{40}$)		(6,000)	(6,000)
Carrying amount	6,000	18,000	24,000
Revaluation gain (bal)	9,000	27,000	36,000
Revaluation	15,000	45,000	60,000
Depreciation ($^{1}/_{30}$)		(1,500)	(1,500)
	15,000	43,500	58,500

(W2) Annual transfer		
New depreciation (W1)		1,500
Old depreciation	($24m/40 years)	(600)
Annual transfer		900

Test your understanding 4

Profit on disposal

	$000	$000
Sale proceeds		900
Valuation at 31 December 20X4	810	
Less: Depreciation ((810 ÷ 9 yrs) × 2 yrs)	(180)	
Carrying amount at 31 Dec 20X6		(630)
Profit on disposal		270

Transfer remaining balance on revaluation surplus

	$000
Dr Revaluation surplus	135
Cr Retained earnings	135

Test your understanding 5

Method 1: Deduct from asset

Statement of profit or loss (extract)

	$
Depreciation (85,000 × 20%)	(17,000)

Statement of financial position (extract)

	$
Non-current assets:	
Plant & machinery (100,000 – 15,000)	85,000
Accumulated depreciation	(17,000)
	68,000

Method 2: Treat grant as deferred income

Statement of profit or loss (extract)

	$
Depreciation (100,000 × 20%)	(20,000)
Government grant credit **(W1)**	3,000

Statement of financial position (extract)

	$
Non-current assets:	
Plant & machinery	100,000
Accumulated depreciation	(20,000)
	80,000
Non-current liabilities	
Government grant (12,000 **(W1)** – 3,000 (current liability))	9,000
Current liabilities	
Government grant (15,000 × 20%)	3,000

(W1) Government grant deferred income

	$		$
Transfer to profit or loss (15,000 × 20%)	3,000	Grant cash received	15,000
Balance c/f	12,000		
	15,000		15,000

Test your understanding 6

Answer

Interest will only be capitalised during the period of construction from 1 March 20X8 to 31 December 20X8, i.e. 10 months. Any interest earned during the period of construction will be deducted from the capitalised cost. Interest incurred or earned before construction commences will be recognised within the statement of profit or loss (SPL).

		\$000
Interest payable: \$18m × 5%		900
Pre-construction: charged to SPL ($\$18m \times 5\% \times {}^{2}/_{12}$)		(150)
		———
Capitalised interest cost		750
Interest earned: \$6m × 2% × 5/12	50	
Pre-construction: credited to SPL ($\$6m \times 2\% \times {}^{2}/_{12}$)	(20)	
	———	(30)
		———
Net interest capitalised		720
		———

Test your understanding 7

Total amount to be included in property, plant and equipment at 31 December 20X5:

	\$m
Site	25,000
Building	9,000
Fittings	6,000
Interest capitalised (40,000 × 10% × 9/12)	3,000
	———
	43,000
	———

Only nine months' interest can be capitalised, because IAS 23 states that capitalisation of borrowing costs must cease when substantially all the activities necessary to prepare the asset for its intended use or sale are complete.

Test your understanding 8

(a) **Cost model**

Depreciation in the year is = $12,000 (Building $600,000 × $^{1}/_{50}$)

Therefore:

– in the statement of profit or loss, there will be a depreciation charge of $12,000

– in the statement of financial position, the property will be shown at a carrying amount of $1,000,000 – $12,000 = $988,000.

(b) **Fair value model**

– In the statement of financial position, the property will be shown at its fair value of $1.1 million.

– In the statement of profit or loss, there will be a gain of $0.1 million representing the fair value adjustment.

– No depreciation is charged.

Test your understanding 9

On the date that Kyle Co moves into the property, it should be classed as property, plant and equipment. As Kyle Co uses the fair value model for investment properties, this should be revalued to fair value at the date of reclassification, resulting in a fair value gain of $2 million being recorded in the statement of profit or loss.

Following this, the asset should then be depreciated over its remaining useful life of 14 years. Therefore Kyle Co will also have a depreciation expense of $500,000, being $14m/14 years, for the last six months of the year.

Test your understanding 10

Statement of profit or loss for the year ended 30 September 20X3

Depreciation **(W3)**	$100,753
Staff recruitment and training	$600,000
Finance costs ($50,000 **(W1)** + $94,822 **(W2)**	$144,822

Statement of financial position as at 30 September 20X3

Non-current assets:	
Property, plant and equipment **(W3)**	$11,989,610
Non-current liabilities:	
Provision ($1,580,363 + $94,822 **(W2)**)	$1,675,185
Loan	$10,000,000

(W1) Borrowing costs

The interest should be capitalised from 1 October to 1 September, net of the income earned from the temporary investment of the $3 million for the 4 months.

Interest payable: $10 million × 6% = $600,000 × 11/12 = $550,000

Interest income earned: $3 million × 4% = $120,000 × 4/12 = $40,000.

Amount to be capitalised = $550,000 – $40,000 = **$510,000**.

Also, as the asset was completed on 1 September, the interest for September needs to be charged to the statement of profit or loss as an expense ($600,000 × 1/12 = **$50,000**).

(W2) Provision for dismantling

The $3 million should be initially discounted to present value using Hudson's cost of capital of 6% and capitalised. $3 million payable in 11 years' time (from October 20X2 to October 20Y3):

$3,000,000 × $1/1.06^{11}$ = **$1,580,363**

The discount on the provision must also be unwound over the year.

$1,580,363 × 6% = **$94,822** to be added to finance costs and to the closing provision.

(W3) Property, plant and equipment

	$
Construction cost	10,000,000
Borrowing costs capitalised **(W1)**	510,000
Present value of dismantling costs **(W2)**	1,580,363
Total to be capitalised	**12,090,363**

This should be depreciated over the useful life of 10 years. As mining begins on 1 September, depreciation should begin from this date.

Depreciation = $12,090,363/10 × 1/12 = **$100,753**

Carrying amount = $12,090,363 – $100,753 = **$11,989,610**

Test your understanding 11

(1) **D**

Current value	500,000
Carrying amount at date of revaluation (100,000 – (100,000 × 2% × 15 yrs))	(70,000)
Revaluation gain	430,000

(2) **A**

	Building A	**Building B**
Current value	400,000	250,000
Carrying amount	(170,000)	(330,000)
Revaluation gain/(loss)	230,000	(80,000)

The gain on Building A will be credited to other comprehensive income and the revaluation surplus.

The loss on Building B will be debited to the statement of profit or loss expenses because we do not have a balance on the revaluation surplus in respect of building B to offset the loss.

We make an overall debit to non-current assets of $230,000 – $80,000 = $150,000

(3) The answer is **$93,920**

Carrying amount at 1 April 20X0 ($312,000 cost – $66,000 depreciation)	$246,000
Carrying amount of disposal	($11,200)
Carrying amount at 31 March 20X1	$234,800
Depreciation at 40%	$93,920

(4) **C and E** – Direct costs relating to the acquisition of the asset can be included such as labour costs, interest on loans to acquire the asset and hire costs. The administration cost is not a direct cost. Also costs relating to errors or wastage cannot be capitalised.

(5) **A**

(6) As general borrowings are being used, the weighted average cost of borrowing should be used. This is calculated by working out the interest on both loans, and then dividing by the total borrowings. Therefore the weighted average cost of borrowings = (($10m × 6%) + ($6m × 8%))/$16m = 6.75%.

As $12m has been used, the interest to be capitalised = $12m × 6.75% = **$810,000**

(7) **$500,000**. The total grant income is $3m, to be recognised over a three-year period. Annual income is therefore $1m. At the end of the first year the entity has received $1.5m of which $1m has been recognised in the statement of profit or loss, leaving $500,000 deferred into future periods.

(8) **B** – The $2,000,000 received will be credited to the statement of profit or loss over the 4 year grant period at a rate of $500,000 pa. Therefore after one year $500,000 will have been released to the SPL and a balance of $1,500,000 will remain in deferred income. Full repayment of the grant is required, so the income recognised in the first year will now be reversed, and the balance remaining on deferred income will be derecognised.

(9) **A** – Under the cost model the property will be depreciated over 50 years for 3 years up to the date of disposal. Therefore, at the disposal date the carrying value would have been $3.5m – ($3.5m/50 × 3 years) = $3.29m and the profit on disposal $0.71m ($4m – $3.29). Under the fair value model the property will not be depreciated hence the loss on disposal would be $0.2m ($4m – $4.2m).

(10) **C** – Under the fair value model the property will not be depreciated hence the gain on valuation would be $100,000 ($300,000 – $200,000).

(11)

	Include in calculation of non-current asset	**Investment income**	**Finance cost**
Interest earned on the investment of surplus borrowings before the construction period begins		✓	
Interest incurred after the construction period has ended			✓
Interest incurred during the construction period	✓		
Interest earned on the investment of surplus borrowings during the construction period	✓		

Chapter

3

Intangible assets

Chapter learning objectives

Upon completion of this chapter you will be able to:

- explain the nature of internally-generated and purchased intangible assets
- explain the accounting treatment of internally-generated and purchased intangible assets
- distinguish between goodwill and other intangible assets
- describe the criteria for the initial recognition of intangible assets
- describe the criteria for the initial measurement of intangible assets
- explain the subsequent accounting treatment of goodwill
- explain the principle of impairment tests in relation to goodwill
- explain why the value of the purchase consideration for an investment may be less than the value of the acquired net assets
- explain how this difference should be accounted for
- define research expenditure and development expenditure according to IAS 38
- explain the accounting requirements of IAS 38 for research expenditure and development expenditure
- account for research expenditure and development expenditure.

PER

One of the PER performance objectives (PO6) is to record and process transactions and events. You use the right accounting treatments for transactions and events. These should be both historical and prospective – and include non-routine transactions. Working though this chapter should help you understand how to demonstrate that objective.

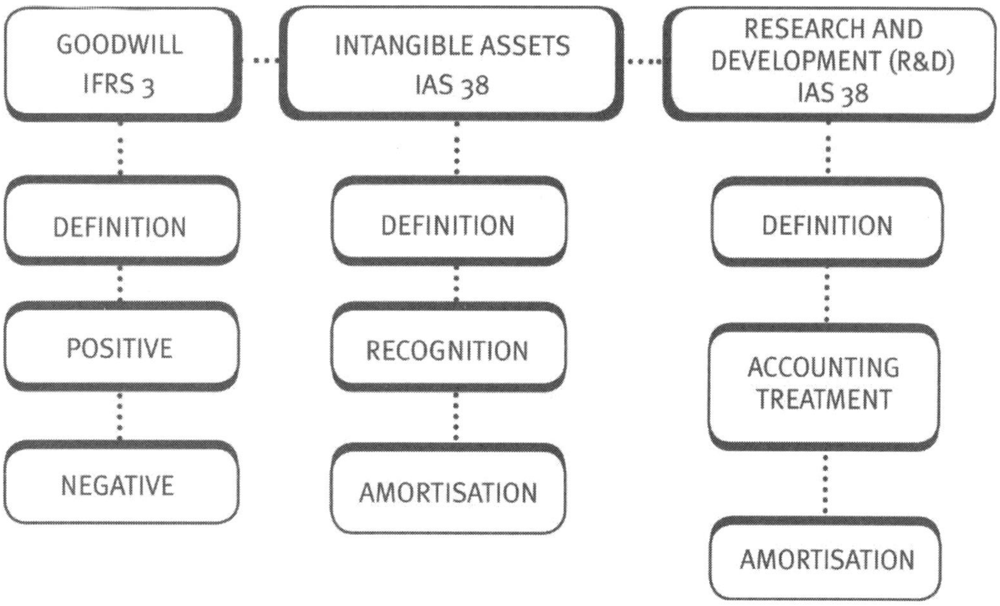

Definition

'An intangible asset is an identifiable non-monetary asset without physical substance' (IAS 38, para 8)

Intangible assets include items such as:

- licences and quotas
- intellectual property, e.g. patents and copyrights
- brand names
- trademarks

For an asset to be identifiable IAS 38 *Intangible Assets* states that it must fall into one of two categories:

1 It is separable – the asset can be bought or sold separately from the rest of the business

2 It arises from legal/contractual rights – this will arise as part of purchasing an entire company. This will be looked at further in the consolidated financial statements chapters.

It must also meet the normal definition of an asset:

- controlled by the entity as a result of past events (normally by enforceable legal rights)
- a resource from which future economic benefits are expected to flow (either from revenue or cost saving).

Recognition

To be recognised in the financial statements, an intangible asset must meet

- **'the definition of an intangible asset, and**
- **meet the recognition criteria'** of the framework (IAS 38, para 18)
  - it is probable that future economic benefits attributable to the asset will flow to the entity
  - the cost of the asset can be measured reliably.

If these criteria are met, the asset should be initially recognised at cost.

Purchased intangible assets

If an intangible asset is purchased separately (such as a licence, patent, brand name), it should be recognised initially at cost.

Measurement after initial recognition

There is a choice between:

- the cost model
- the revaluation model.

The cost model

- The intangible asset should be carried at cost less amortisation and any impairment losses.
- This model is more commonly used in practice.

Amortisation works the same as depreciation. The intangible asset is amortised over the useful life, with the annual expense being shown in the statement of profit or loss each year.

An intangible asset with a **finite useful life** must be amortised over that life, normally using the straight-line method with a zero residual value.

An intangible asset with an **indefinite useful life:**

- should not be amortised
- should be tested for impairment annually, and more often if there is an actual indication of possible impairment.

The revaluation model

- The intangible asset may be revalued to a carrying amount of fair value less subsequent amortisation and impairment losses.
- Fair value should be determined by reference to an active market.

An active market is a market in which transactions for the asset take place with sufficient frequency and volume to provide pricing information on an ongoing basis.

IAS 38 states that active markets for intangible assets are rare, and specifically prohibits the revaluation of patents, brand names, trademarks and publishing rights.

As a guide, indicators of an active market would include:

- the items traded within the market are homogeneous (identical)
- prices are available to the public.

Most intangible assets have value because of their uniqueness, and are therefore unlikely to be homogeneous. Certain licences may fit this model and could possibly be revalued, but most other intangible assets will not.

Internally-generated intangible assets

Generally, internally-generated intangible assets cannot be capitalised, as the costs associated with these cannot be identified separately from the costs associated with running the business.

The following internally-generated items may never be recognised:

- goodwill ('inherent goodwill')
- brands
- mastheads
- publishing titles
- customer lists

Brands

- The accounting treatment of brands has been a matter of controversy for some years. IAS 38 *Intangible Assets* has now ended the controversy by stating that internally-generated brands and similar assets may never be recognised.
- Expenditure on internally-generated brands cannot be distinguished from the cost of developing the business as a whole, so should be written off as incurred.
- Where a brand name is separately acquired and can be measured reliably, then it should be separately recognised as an intangible non-current asset, and accounted for in accordance with the general rules of IAS 38.

Illustration 1 – Intangible classification

How should the following intangible assets be treated in the financial statements?

- A publishing title acquired as part of a subsidiary company.
- A licence purchased in order to market a new product.

Solution

- **Publishing title** – The answer depends on whether the asset can be valued reliably. If this is possible, the title will be recognised at its fair value, otherwise it will be treated as part of goodwill on acquisition of the subsidiary.
- **Licence** – As the licence has been purchased separately from a business, it should be initially capitalised at cost.

Goodwill

The nature of goodwill

Goodwill is the difference between the value of a business as a whole and the aggregate of the fair values of its separable net assets.

Separable net assets are those assets and liabilities which can be identified and sold off separately without necessarily disposing of the business as a whole. They include identifiable intangible assets such as patents, licences and trademarks.

Fair value is defined in IFRS 13 as '**the price that would be received to sell an asset or paid to transfer a liability in an orderly transaction between market participants at the measurement date**' (IFRS 13 Appendix A) (i.e. an exit price).

Goodwill may exist because of any combination of a number of possible factors:

- reputation for quality or service
- technical expertise
- possession of favourable contracts
- good management and staff.

Purchased and non-purchased goodwill

Purchased goodwill:

- arises when one business acquires another as a going concern
- includes goodwill arising on the consolidation of a subsidiary
- will be recognised in the financial statements as its value at a particular point in time is certain.

Non-purchased goodwill:

- is also known as inherent goodwill
- has no identifiable value
- is not recognised in the financial statements.

IFRS 3 Business Combinations

IFRS 3 governs accounting for all business combinations and deals with the accounting treatment of goodwill (see Chapter 18).

Goodwill is defined as **'an asset representing the future economic benefits arising from assets acquired in a business combination that are not individually identified and separately recognised'** (IFRS 3, Appendix A). Negative goodwill (gain on a bargain purchase) is treated as income, as the purchaser has paid less than the fair value of the identifiable net assets. This will be covered further in Chapter 18.

Accounting for non-purchased goodwill

Non-purchased goodwill should not be recognised in the financial statements. It certainly exists, but fails to satisfy the recognition criteria in the Framework, since it is not capable of being measured reliably.

Research and development

Definitions

'Research is original and planned investigation undertaken with the prospect of gaining new scientific knowledge and understanding' (IAS 38, para 8).

'Development is the application of research findings or other knowledge to a plan or design for the production of new or substantially improved materials, devices, products, processes, systems or services before the start of commercial production or use' (IAS 38, para 8).

Accounting treatment

Research expenditure: write off as incurred to the statement of profit or loss.

Development expenditure: recognise as an intangible asset if, and only if, an entity can demonstrate all of the following:

- **P**robable flow of economic benefit from the asset, whether through sale or internal cost savings.
- **I**ntention to complete the intangible asset and use or sell it
- **R**eliable measure of development cost
- **A**dequate resources to complete the project
- **T**echnical feasibility of completing the intangible asset so that it will be available for use or sale
- **E**xpected to be profitable, i.e. the costs of the project will be exceeded by the benefits generated.

It is only expenditure incurred after the recognition criteria have been met which should be recognised as an asset. Development expenditure recognised as an expense in profit or loss cannot subsequently be reinstated as an asset.

If an item of plant is used in the development process, the depreciation on the plant is added to the development costs in intangible assets during the period that the project meets the development criteria. That is because the economic benefit gained from the plant in this period is only realised when the development project is complete and production is underway. It will be taken to the statement of profit or loss as amortisation within the amortisation of the development costs.

Amortisation

Development expenditure should be amortised over its useful life as soon as commercial production begins.

Test your understanding 1

An entity has incurred the following expenditure during the current year:

(a) $100,000 spent on the initial design work of a new product – it is anticipated that this design will be taken forward over the next two year period to be developed and tested with a view to production in three years' time.

(b) $500,000 spent on the testing of a new production system which has been designed internally and which will be in operation during the following accounting year. This new system should reduce the costs of production by 20%.

How should each of these costs be treated in the financial statements of the entity?

Test your understanding 2

An entity has incurred the following expenditure during the current year:

(i) A brand name relating to a specific range of chocolate bars, purchased for $200,000. By the year end, a brand specialist had valued this at $250,000.

(ii) $500,000 spent on developing a new line of confectionery, including $150,000 spent on researching the product before management gave approval to fully fund the project.

(iii) Training costs for staff to use a new manufacturing process. The total training costs amounted to $100,000 and staff are expected to remain for an average of 5 years.

Explain the accounting treatment for the above issues.

Illustration 2 – Amortisation of development expenditure

Improve has deferred development expenditure of $600,000 relating to the development of New Miracle Brand X. It is expected that the demand for the product will stay at a high level for the next three years. Annual sales of 400,000, 300,000 and 200,000 units respectively are expected over this period. Brand X sells for $10.

How should the development expenditure be amortised?

Solution

There are two possibilities for writing off the development expenditure:

- Write off in equal instalments over the three-year period, i.e. $200,000 pa.
- Write off in relation to total sales expected (900,000 units).
  Year 1 (400,000/900,000) × $600,000 = 266,667
  Year 2 (300,000/900,000) × $600,000 = 200,000
  Year 3 (200,000/900,000) × $600,000 = 133,333

Chapter summary

GOODWILL IFRS 3

Definition

Difference between the value of a business as a whole and the aggregate of the fair values of its separable net assets.

May be:

- purchased
- inherent.

Positive purchased goodwill

- Capitalise
- Do not amortise
- Test for impairment.

Negative purchased goodwill

- Check calculation
- Credit to Statement of profit or loss

INTANGIBLE ASSETS IAS 38

Definition

Identifiable non-monetary asset without physical substance.

Recognition

To be recognised must:

- meet the definition of an intangible asset, and
- meet the recognition criteria of the framework.

Value using cost model or revaluation model.

Amortisation

- If finite useful life, amortise to zero residual value.
- If indefinite useful life, do not amortise but test for impairment.

R&D

Definitions

Research: investigation undertaken to gain new scientific knowledge and understanding.

Development: application of research findings before the start of commercial production or use.

Accounting treatment

Research costs: write off to statement of profit or loss

Development costs: capitalise if criteria met.

Amortisation

Amortise capitalised development costs over useful life.

Test your understanding 3

1 Cowper plc has spent $20,000 researching new cleaning chemicals in the year ended 31 December 20X0. They have also spent $40,000 developing a new cleaning product which will not go into commercial production until next year. The development project meets the criteria laid down in IAS 38 *Intangible Assets*.

How should these costs be treated in the financial statements of Cowper plc for the year ended 31 December 20X0?

A $60,000 should be capitalised as an intangible asset on the statement of financial position.

B $40,000 should be capitalised as an intangible asset and should be amortised; $20,000 should be written off to the statement of profit or loss.

C $40,000 should be capitalised as an intangible asset and should not be amortised; $20,000 should be written off to the statement of profit or loss.

D $60,000 should be written off to the statement of profit or loss

2 **Which TWO of the following items below could potentially be classified as intangible assets?**

A purchased brand name

B training of staff

C internally generated brand

D licences and quotas

3 Sam Co has provided the following information as at 31 December 20X6:

(i) Project A – $50,000 has been spent on the research phase of this project during the year.

(ii) Project B – $80,000 had been spent on this project in the previous year and $20,000 this year. The project was capitalised in the previous year however, it has been decided to abandon this project at the end of the year.

(iii) Project C – $100,000 was spent on this project this year. The project meets the criteria of IAS 38 and is to be capitalised.

Which of the following adjustments will be made in the financial statements as at 31 December 20X6?

A Reduce profit by $70,000 and increase non-current assets by $100,000

B Reduce profit by $150,000 and increase non-current assets by $100,000

C Reduce profit by $130,000 and increase non-current assets by $180,000

D Reduce profit by $130,000 and increase non-current assets by $100,000

4 **Which of the following statements concerning the accounting treatment of research and development expenditure are true, according to IAS 38 *Intangible Assets?***

(i) Research is original and planned investigation undertaken with the prospect of gaining new knowledge and understanding.

(ii) Development is the application of research findings.

(iii) Depreciation of plant used specifically on developing a new product can be capitalised as part of development costs.

(iv) Expenditure once treated as an expense cannot be reinstated as an asset.

A (i), (ii) and (iii)

B (i), (ii) and (iv)

C (ii), (iii) and (iv)

D All of the above

5 **Which of the following should be included in a company's statement of financial position as an intangible asset under IAS 38 *Intangible Assets*?**

A Internally developed brands

B Internally generated goodwill

C Expenditure on completed research

D Payments made on the successful registration of a patent.

6 During the year to 31 December 20X8 X Co incurred $200,000 of development costs for a new product. In addition, X Co spent $60,000 on 1 January 20X8 on machinery specifically used to help develop the new product and $40,000 on building the brand identity. Commercial production is expected to start during 20X9.

The machinery is expected to last 4 years with no residual value.

What value should be included within Intangible Assets in respect of the above in X Co's Statement of Financial Position as at 31 December 20X8?

$ __________

7 **Which TWO of the following criteria must be met before development expenditure is capitalised according to IAS 38 *Intangible Assets*?**

A the technical feasibility of completing the intangible asset

B future revenue is expected

C the intention to complete and use or sell the intangible asset

D there is no need for reliable measurement of expenditure

8 **For each issue, identify the correct accounting treatment in Madeira's financial statements:**

	Capitalise as intangible	**Expense**
$400,000 developing a new process which will bring in no revenue but is expected to bring significant cost savings		
$400,000 developing a new product. During development a competitor launched a rival product and now Madeira is hesitant to commit further funds to the process		
$400,000 spent on marketing a new product which has led to increased sales of $800,000		
$400,000 spent on designing a new corporate logo for the business		

Test your understanding answers

Test your understanding 1

(a) These are research costs as they are only in the early design stage and therefore should be written off to the statement of profit or loss in the period.

(b) These would appear to be development stage costs as the new production system is due to be in place fairly soon and will produce economic benefits in the shape of reduced costs. Therefore these should be capitalised as development costs.

Test your understanding 2

(i) The brand name is a purchased intangible asset, so can be capitalised at the cost of $200,000.

Intangible assets can only be revalued if an active market exists. This is unlikely here, as the brand name will not be a homogeneous item. Therefore the item should be held under the cost model.

The brand should be written off over its expected useful life. If this has an indefinite useful life then no amortisation is charged. However, an annual impairment review would be required.

(ii) The $500,000 relates to research and development. Of the total, $150,000 should be expensed to the statement of profit or loss, as management had not displayed either the intention to complete, or the release of the resources to complete.

Therefore $350,000 can be capitalised as an intangible asset as development costs.

(iii) The training costs must be expensed in the statement of profit or loss. The movement of staff cannot be controlled, and therefore there is no way of restricting the economic benefits. If the staff leave, the company receives no benefit.

Test your understanding 3

1 **C** – $20,000 is research and should be written off as incurred. $40,000 should be capitalised as a development asset, but is not amortised until commercial production begins.

2 **A and D** – Training cannot be capitalised as a firm cannot control the future economic benefits by limiting the access of others to the staff. Internally generated brands cannot be capitalised.

3 **B** – The expenditure in relation to projects A and B should be written off. Project C should be capitalised and will therefore increase the value of non-current assets.

4 **D** – All of the statements are true.

5 **D** – Internally generated intangible assets cannot be recognised, and research costs are written off as incurred.

6 **$215,000** – The development costs of $200,000 can be capitalised, as can the depreciation on the asset while the project is being developed. The asset is used for a year on the project, so the depreciation for the first year ($60,000/4 years = $15,000) can be added to intangible assets. The $40,000 is an internally generated brand and cannot be capitalised.

7 **A and C** – There is no need for revenue, there needs to be probable economic benefits which may come in the form of cost savings as well as revenue.

8

	Capitalise as intangible	**Expense**
$400,000 developing a new process which will bring in no revenue but is expected to bring significant cost savings	✓	
$400,000 developing a new product. During development a competitor launched a rival product and now Madeira is hesitant to commit further funds to the process		✓
$400,000 spent on marketing a new product which has led to increased sales of $800,000		✓
$400,000 spent on designing a new corporate logo for the business		✓

Chapter

4

Impairment of assets

Chapter learning objectives

Upon completion of this chapter you will be able to:

- define an impairment loss
- list the circumstances which may indicate impairment to assets
- describe a cash generating unit (CGU)
- explain the basis on which impairment losses should be allocated
- allocate an impairment loss to the assets of a CGU.

PER

One of the PER performance objectives (PO6) is to record and process transactions and events. You use the right accounting treatments for transactions and events. These should be both historical and prospective – and include non-routine transactions. Working though this chapter should help you understand how to demonstrate that objective.

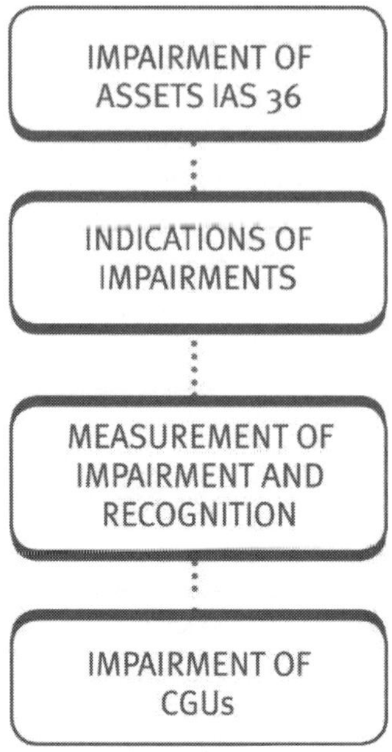

1 Impairment of individual assets

Objective of IAS 36 Impairment of Assets

The objective is to set rules to ensure that the assets of an entity **'are carried at no more than their recoverable amount'** (IAS 36, para 1).

Excluded assets

IAS 36 applies to all assets other than:

- inventories (IAS 2)
- construction contracts (IAS 11)
- deferred tax assets (IAS 12)
- assets arising from employee benefits (IAS 19 is excluded from FR)
- financial assets included in the scope of IFRS 9
- investment property measured at fair value (IAS 40)
- non-current assets classified as held for sale (IFRS 5).

Impairment

An asset is impaired if its recoverable amount is below the value currently shown on the statement of financial position – the asset's current carrying amount.

Recoverable amount is taken as the higher of:

- fair value less costs to sell (net realisable value), and
- value in use.

An impairment exists if:

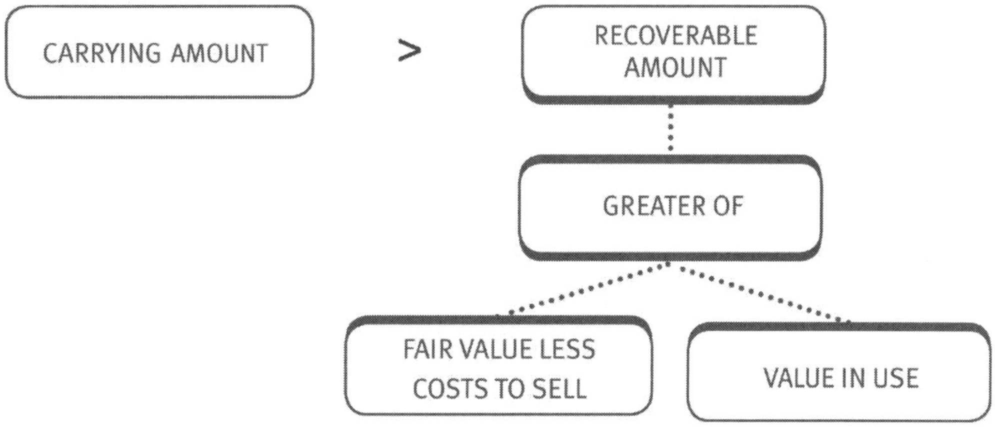

Measurement of recoverable amount

Measurement of fair value less costs to sell

Measurement may be by way of:

- a binding sale agreement
- the current market price less costs of disposal (where an active market exists).

Measurement of value in use

Value in use is determined by estimating future cash inflows and outflows to be derived from the use of the asset and its ultimate disposal, and applying a suitable discount rate to these cash flows.

Cash flows relating to financing activities or income taxes should not be included.

Illustration 1 – Recoverable amount

The following information relates to three assets:

	A	B	C
	$000	$000	$000
Carrying amount	100	150	120
Net realisable value	110	125	100
Value in use	120	130	90

What is the recoverable amount of each asset?

Calculate the impairment loss for each of the three assets.

Solution

The recoverable amounts for each asset are as follows:

A $120,000

B $130,000

C $100,000

The impairment loss for each asset is as follows:

A Nil

B $20,000

C $20,000

Indicators of impairment

IAS 36 requires that at each reporting date, an entity must assess whether there are indications of impairment.

Indications may be derived from within the entity itself (internal sources) or the external market (external sources).

External sources of information

- The asset's market value has declined more than expected.
- Changes in the technological, market, economic or legal environment have had an adverse effect on the entity.
- Interest rates have increased, thus increasing the discount rate used in calculating the asset's value in use.

Internal sources of information

- There is evidence of obsolescence of, or damage to, the asset.
- Changes in the way the asset is used have occurred or are imminent.
- Evidence is available from internal reporting indicating that the economic performance of an asset is, or will be, worse than expected.

If an indicator of impairment exists then an impairment review must be performed.

Annual impairment reviews

Where there is no indication of impairment then no further action need be taken.

An exception to this rule is:

- goodwill acquired in a business combination
- an intangible asset with an indefinite useful life
- an intangible asset not yet available for use.

IAS 36 requires annual impairment reviews for these assets irrespective of whether there is any indication of impairment.

Recognition and measurement of an impairment

Where there is an indication of impairment, an impairment review should be carried out:

- the recoverable amount should be calculated
- the asset should be written down to recoverable amount and
- the impairment loss should be immediately recognised in the statement of profit or loss.

The only exception to this is if the impairment reverses a previous gain taken to the revaluation surplus.

In this case, the impairment will be taken first to the revaluation surplus (and so disclosed as other comprehensive income) until the revaluation gain is fully exhausted, then any excess is taken to the statement of profit or loss.

Test your understanding 1

Recoverable amount

An entity owns a car that was involved in an accident at the year end. It is barely useable, so the value in use is estimated at $1,000. However, the car is a classic and there is a demand for the parts. This results in a fair value less costs to sell of $3,000. The opening carrying amount was $8,000 and the car was estimated to have a life of eight years from the start of the year.

Identify the recoverable amount of the car and any impairment required.

Test your understanding 2

An entity owns a property which was revalued to $500,000 on 31 March 20X3 with a revaluation gain of $200,000 being recognised as other comprehensive income and recorded in the revaluation surplus. At 31 March 20X5 the property had a carrying amount of $460,000 but the recoverable amount of the property was estimated at only $200,000.

What is the amount of impairment and how should this be treated in the financial statements?

2 Reversal of an impairment loss

The calculation of impairment losses is based on predictions of what may happen in the future. Sometimes, actual events turn out to be better than predicted. If this happens, the recoverable amount is re-calculated and the previous write-down is reversed.

- Impaired assets should be reviewed at each reporting date to see whether there are indications that the impairment has reversed.
- A reversal of an impairment loss is recognised immediately as income in profit or loss. If the original impairment was charged against the revaluation surplus, it is recognised as other comprehensive income and credited to the revaluation surplus.
- The reversal must not take the value of the asset above its depreciated historical cost, i.e. the amount it would have been if the original impairment had never been recorded. The depreciation that would have been charged in the meantime must be taken into account.
- The depreciation charge for future periods should be revised to reflect the changed carrying amount.

An impairment loss recognised for goodwill cannot be reversed in a subsequent period. The reason for this is that once purchased goodwill has become impaired, any subsequent increase in its recoverable amount is likely to be an increase in internally generated goodwill, rather than a reversal of the impairment loss recognised for the original purchased goodwill. Internally generated goodwill cannot be recognised.

Indicators of impairment reversal

External indicators of an impairment reversal are:

- Increases in the asset's market value
- Favourable changes in the technological, market, economic or legal environment
- Decreases in interest rates.

Internal indicators of an impairment reversal are:

- Favourable changes in the use of the asset
- Improvements in the asset's economic performance.

Illustration 2 – Reversal of impairment

Boxer purchased a non-current asset on 1 January 20X1 at a cost of $30,000. At that date, the asset had an estimated useful life of ten years. Boxer does not revalue this type of asset, but accounts for it on the basis of depreciated historical cost. At 31 December 20X2, the asset was subject to an impairment review and had a recoverable amount of $16,000.

At 31 December 20X5, the circumstances which caused the original impairment to be recognised have reversed and are no longer applicable, with the result that the recoverable amount is now $40,000.

Required:

Explain, with supporting computations, the impact on the financial statements of the two impairment reviews.

Solution

Year ended 31 December 20X2	$
Asset cost at 1 January 20X1	30,000
Depreciation to 31 December 20X2 (30,000 × $^2/_{10}$)	(6,000)
Carrying amount at 31 December 20X2	24,000
Recoverable amount	(16,000)
Impairment loss	8,000

The asset is written down to $16,000 and the impairment loss of $8,000 is charged to profit or loss. The depreciation charge per annum in future periods will be $2,000 ($16,000 × $^1/_8$).

Year ended 31 December 20X5	$
Carrying amount at 31 December 20X2 as above	16,000
Depreciation to 31 December 20X5 ($^3/_8$)	(6,000)
Carrying amount at 31 December 20X5	10,000
Recoverable amount	40,000
Impairment loss	Nil

There has been no impairment loss. In fact, there has been a complete reversal of the first impairment loss. The asset can be reinstated to its depreciated historical cost i.e. to the carrying amount at 31 December 20X5 if there never had been an earlier impairment loss.

	$
Asset historical cost at 1 January 20X1	30,000
Historical cost depreciation to 31 December 20X5 ($^5/_{10}$)	(15,000)
Historical carrying amount at 31 December 20X5	15,000
Impaired carrying amount as above	10,000
Reversal of impairment loss	5,000

The reversal of the loss is recognised by increasing the asset by $5,000 ($15,000 – $10,000) and recognising a gain of $5,000 in profit or loss.

It should be noted that the whole $8,000 original impairment cannot be reversed. The impairment can only be reversed to a maximum amount of depreciated historical cost, based upon the original cost and estimated useful life of the asset.

3 Cash generating units (CGUs)

What is a CGU?

When assessing the impairment of assets it will not always be possible to base the impairment review on individual assets.

- The value in use calculation may be impossible on a single asset because the individual asset does not generate distinguishable cash flows.
- In this case, the impairment calculation should be based on a CGU.

Definition of a CGU

A CGU is defined as **'the smallest identifiable group of assets that generates cash inflows that are largely independent of the cash inflows from other assets'** (IAS 36, para 6).

Illustration 3 – CGUs

In a restaurant chain, the smallest group of assets might be the assets within a single restaurant, but with a mining company, all the assets of the company might make up a single cash generating unit.

The impairment calculation

The impairment calculation is done by:

- assuming the cash generating unit is one asset
- comparing the carrying amount of the CGU to the recoverable amount of the CGU.

CARRYING AMOUNT OF CGU = carrying amounts of all assets in CGU added together.	>	RECOVERABLE AMOUNT CGU = recoverable amount of all assets in CGU added together.

As previously, an impairment exists where the carrying amount exceeds the recoverable amount.

Impairment of a CGU

Deal with any specifically impaired assets first, then impair the CGU. IAS 36 requires that an impairment loss attributable to a CGU should be allocated to write down the assets in the following order:

1. Purchased goodwill
2. The other assets (including other intangible assets) in the CGU on a pro-rata basis based on the carrying amount of each asset in the CGU.

Note: No individual asset should be written down below its recoverable amount. This means that, unless specifically impaired, current assets are unlikely to be impaired as part of a CGU, as they are already likely to be carried at their recoverable amounts. Inventory, as noted above, is outside the scope of IAS 36.

Test your understanding 3

Sebb Co runs a unit that suffers a massive drop in income due to the failure of its technology on 1 January 20X8. The following carrying amounts were recorded in the books immediately prior to the impairment:

	$m
Goodwill	20
Technology	5
Brands	10
Land	50
Buildings	30
Other net assets	40

The recoverable value of the unit is estimated at $85 million. The technology is worthless, following its complete failure.

The other net assets include inventory and receivables. It is considered that the carrying amount of other net assets is a reasonable representation of their net realisable value.

Show the impact of the impairment on 1 January 20X8.

4 Chapter summary

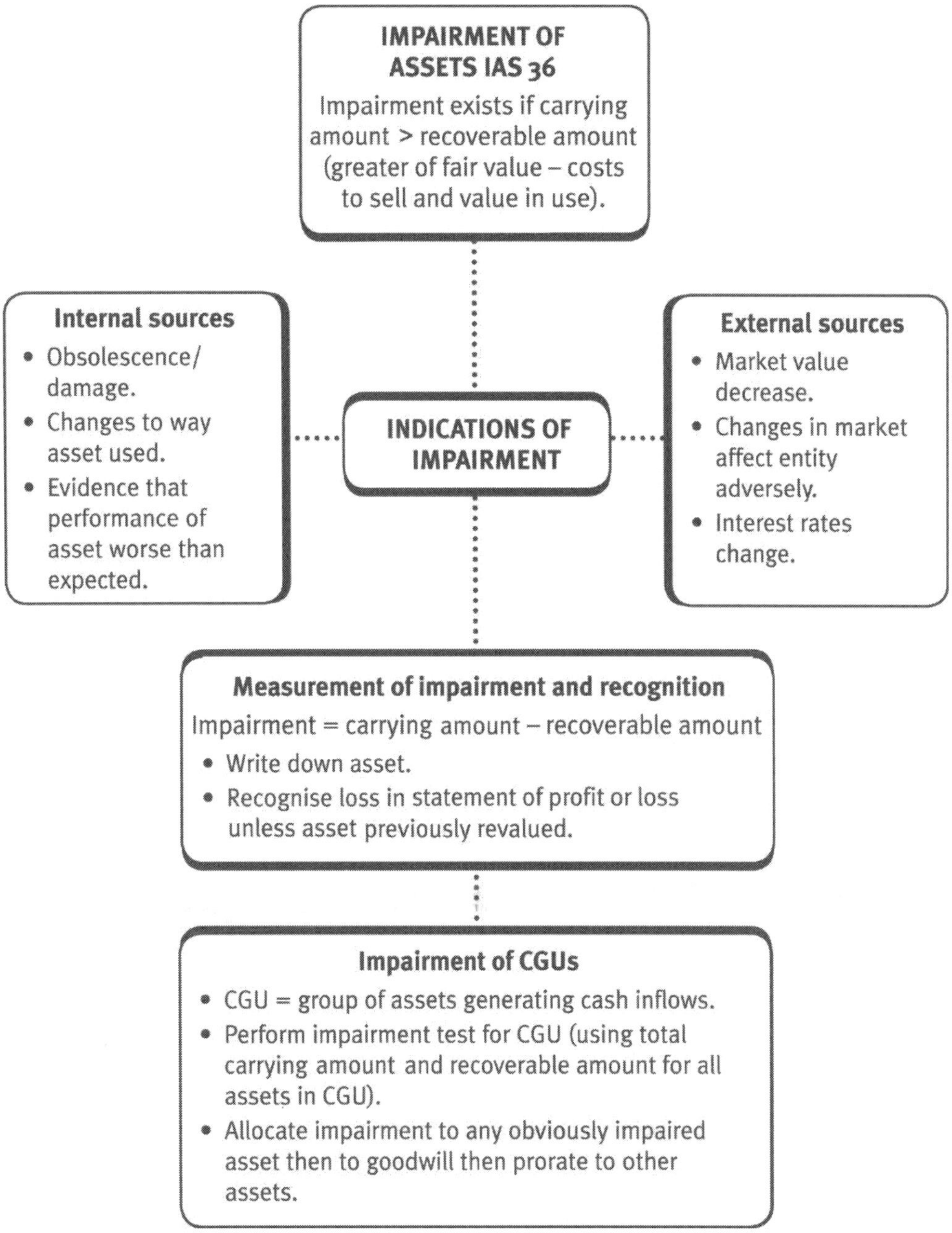

Test your understanding 4

Impairment of assets

The following trial balance relates to Hume at 30 June 20X7:

	$	$
Revenue		390,000
Cost of sales	210,600	
Distribution costs	6,800	
Administration expenses	12,700	
Loan interest paid	3,600	
Property – cost	150,000	
Property – depreciation at 1 July 20X6		38,400
Plant and equipment – cost	176,200	
Plant and equipment – depreciation at 1 July 20X6		48,600
Trade receivables	31,600	
Inventory – 30 June 20X7	18,100	
Bank	1,950	
Trade payables		25,400
Ordinary shares $1		50,000
Share premium		9,000
12 % Loan note (issued 1 July 20X6)		40,000
Taxation	1,300	
Retained earnings at 1 July 20X6		11,450
	612,850	612,850

The following notes are relevant:

1 Property includes land at a cost of $30,000. The building is being depreciated on a straight-line basis over its estimated useful life of 25 years.

2 Plant and equipment is being depreciated on the reducing balance basis at a rate of 20% per annum.

3 The balance on plant and equipment included a piece of specialist machinery that cost $70,000 on 1 July 20X5. On 30 June 20X7 a fork-lift truck reversed into the machinery causing severe damage. Hume has identified two possible options:

(i) **Sell the machine**

A potential buyer has been located, who has indicated that she would pay 80% of the carrying amount at 30 June 20X7. However, she has insisted that the machine is repaired before she buys it. The repair work will be done by Hume's employees and will take about 120 hours of skilled labour, the associated cost with this labour is $2,160.

In addition Hume will have to deliver the machine to the buyer at a cost of $2,100 and there will be a single premium insurance cost of $580 for the journey.

(ii) **Repair the machine and continue to use it**

The financial controller has estimated that the present value of cash flows generated from future use (including the repair cost) amount to $31,800.

4 All depreciation is charged to cost of sales.

5 The directors have estimated the provision for income tax for the year to 30 June 20X7 at $6,500.

Required:

Prepare the statement of profit or loss for Hume for the year to 30 June 20X7 and a statement of financial position at that date.

Test your understanding 5

1 The following information relates to three assets held by a company:

	Asset A	Asset B	Asset C
	$	$	$
Carrying amount	100	50	40
Value in use	80	60	35
Fair value less cost to sell	90	65	30

What is the total impairment loss?

$ _________

2 The following information relates to four assets held by the company:

	A	B	C	D
	$m	$m	$m	$m
Carrying amount	120	30	40	70
Value in use	80	70	80	20
Fair value less costs to sell	90	40	70	30

What is the total impairment loss?

$ _________ m

3 **In accordance with IAS 36 *Impairment of Assets* which of the following statements are true?**

1 An impairment review must be carried out annually on all intangible assets.

2 If the fair value less costs to sell of an asset exceed the carrying amount there is no need to calculate a value in use.

3 Impairment is charged to the statement of profit or loss unless it reverses a gain that has been recognised in equity in which case it is offset against the revaluation surplus.

A All three.

B 1 and 2 only.

C 1 and 3 only.

D 2 & 3 only.

4 **Which TWO of the following could be an indication that an asset may be impaired according to IAS 36 *Impairment of Assets?***

A Decrease in market interest rates

B Increase in market values for the asset

C Damage caused to the asset

D Management intention to reorganise the business

5 Finsbury Co has a cash generating unit (CGU) that suffers a large drop in income due to reduced demand for its products. An impairment review was carried out and the recoverable amount of the cash generating unit was determined at $100m. The assets of the CGU had the following carrying amounts immediately prior to the impairment:

	$m
Goodwill	25
Intangibles	60
Property, plant and equipment	30
Inventory	15
Trade receivables	10
	140

The inventory and receivables are considered to be included at their recoverable amounts.

What is the carrying amount of the intangibles once the impairment loss has been allocated?

A $45m

B $50m

C $55m

D $60m

Test your understanding answers

Test your understanding 1

Recovorable amount is higher of:

- fair value less costs to sell $3,000
- value in use $1,000

Therefore $3,000.

This indicates an impairment as follows:

Motor vehicle:	$000
Carrying amount b/f	8
Depreciation (8 × $^1/_8$)	(1)
Impairment (balancing figure)	(4)
Recoverable amount c/f	3

Test your understanding 2

Impairment = $460,000 – 200,000 = $260,000

Of this $200,000 is debited to the revaluation surplus to reverse the previous upward revaluation (and recorded as other comprehensive income) and the remaining $60,000 is charged to the statement of profit or loss.

Test your understanding 3

- Carrying amount is $155 million.
- Recoverable amount is $85 million.
- Therefore an impairment of $70 million is required.

Technology is considered to be completely worthless and therefore must first be written down to nil.

Dr Impairment expense $5m
Cr Technology $5m

Following the write down of technology – the impairment loss to allocate against the remaining CGU assets is $65m.

Dr Impairment expense $65m
Cr CGU **(W1)** $65m

(W1)

	Carrying amount		Impairment	Impaired value
Goodwill	20		(20)	0
Brands	10	**(W2)**	(5)	5
Land	50	**(W2)**	(25)	25
Buildings	30	**(W2)**	(15)	15
Other net assets	40		–	40
CGU	**150**		**(65)**	**85**

(W2) Pro-rate remaining loss

		$m
Total impairment remaining		65
Allocate first to goodwill		(20)
Remaining		45
Pro-rate based on carrying amount:		
Brands	45 × 10/(10 + 50 + 30) =	5
Land	45 × 50/(10 + 50 + 30) =	25
Buildings	45 × 30/(10 + 50 + 30) =	15

As the other net assets are held at a reasonable representation of the realisable value, no impairment should be allocated to these. No assets should be written down to below their recoverable amount. On this basis, the other net assets are left at their current carrying amount.

Test your understanding 4

Statement of profit or loss for the year ended 30 June 20X7

	$
Revenue	390,000
Cost of sales **(W1)**	(253,920)
Gross profit	136,080
Distribution costs	(6,800)
Administrative expenses	(12,700)
Profit from operations	116,580
Finance costs (3,600 + 1,200 accrual)	(4,800)
Profit before tax	111,780
Tax (1,300 + 6,500)	(7,800)
Profit for the year	103,980

Statement of financial position as at 30 June 20X7

	$	$
Non-current Assets		
Property **(W2)**		106,800
Plant and Equipment **(W2)**		89,080
		195,880
Current Assets		
Inventory	18,100	
Receivables	31,600	
Bank	1,950	
		51,650
		247,530
Equity		
Share capital		50,000
Share premium		9,000
Retained earnings (11,450 + 103,980)		115,430
		174,430

Non-current liabilities		
12% Loan notes		40,000
Current liabilities		
Payables	25,400	
Accrued loan note interest ((12% × 40,000) – 3,600)	1,200	
Income tax	6,500	
		33,100
		247,530

Workings:

(W1) Cost of Sales

Per TB	210,600
Plant & equipment depreciation **(W2)**	25,520
Building depreciation **(W2)**	4,800
Impairment **(W3)**	13,000
	253,920

(W2) Non-current assets

	Property	**Plant & equip't**
Cost per TB	150,000	176,200
Acc dep'n per TB	(38,400)	(48,600)
Charge for year (150,000 – 30,000)/25 years	(4,800)	
20% × (176,200 – 48,600)		(25,520)
Impairment **(W3)**		(13,000)
	106,800	89,080

The impaired asset is not damaged until the year-end and therefore is subject to depreciation as normal during the year.

(W3) Impairment

Carrying amount at 30 June 20X7	44,800
Recoverable amount (higher of fair value less costs to sell and VIU)	31,800
Impairment loss	13,000
Carrying amount at 30 June 20X7	
Cost at 1 July 20X5	70,000
Depreciation 20X6 (20% × 70,000)	(14,000)
	56,000
Depreciation 20X7 (20% × 56,000)	(11,200)
	44,800
Fair value less costs to sell at 30 June 20X7	
Selling price (80% × 44,800)	35,840
Repair costs	(2,160)
Delivery costs	(2,100)
Insurance	(580)
	31,000

Value in use (VIU) – $31,800 per question

Test your understanding 5

1

	Asset A	Asset B	Asset C
	$	$	$
Carrying amount	100	50	40
Value in use	80	60	35
Fair value less cost to sell	90	65	30
Valued at higher of value in use/fair value less costs to sell	90	65	35
Impairment	10	Nil	5

Total Impairment = **$15**

2 The total impairment is **$70m**.

Asset A is impaired by $30m ($120m – $90m recoverable amount) and asset D is impaired by $40m ($70m – $30m recoverable amount). Assets B and C are not impaired, as their recoverable amounts exceed the carrying amount.

3 **D** – Item 1 is untrue. An annual impairment review is only required for intangible assets with an indefinite life.

4 **C and D** – A decrease in interest rates would reduce the discount applied to future cash flows in calculating the value in use, therefore increasing the value in use. An increase in market values will lead to the asset value increasing rather than being impaired.

5 **B – $50m:** The impairment would be allocated to goodwill first, then pro-rata across other assets based on their carrying amounts. No asset should be reduced to below its recoverable amount, so inventory and receivables will remain unimpaired. After the goodwill of $25m has been impaired, the remaining $15m should be allocated to intangibles and PPE on the following basis:

Intangibles = ($60m/$90m) × $15m = $10m.

PPE = ($30m/$90m) × $15m = $5m

	$m	**Imp** ($m)	**Carrying amount** ($m)
Goodwill	25	(25)	–
Intangibles	60	(10)	50
Property, plant and equipment	30	(5)	25
Inventory	15	–	15
Trade receivables	10	–	10
	140	(40)	100

Chapter

5

Non-current assets held for sale and discontinued operations

Chapter learning objectives

Upon completion of this chapter you will be able to:

- explain the importance of identifying and reporting the results of continuing and discontinued operations
- define non-current assets held for sale
- account for non-current assets held for sale
- define discontinued operations
- account for discontinued operations
- identify circumstances where separate disclosure of material items of income and expense is required.

PER

One of the PER performance objectives (PO6) is to record and process transactions and events. You use the right accounting treatments for transactions and events. These should be both historical and prospective – and include non-routine transactions. Working though this chapter should help you understand how to demonstrate that objective.

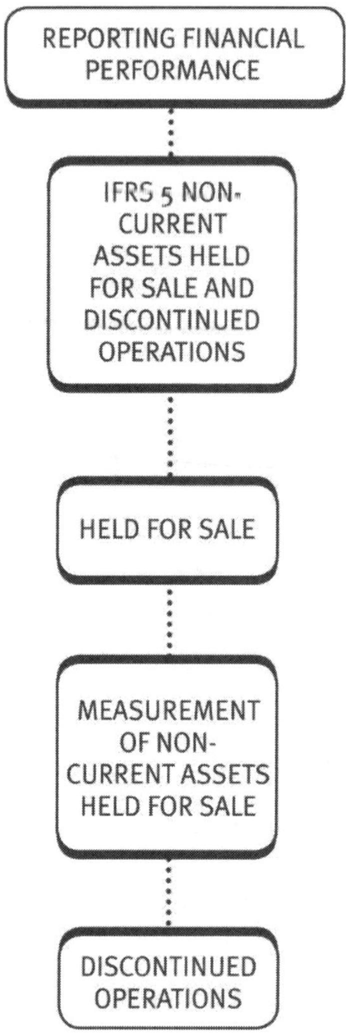

1 IFRS 5 Non-current Assets Held for Sale and Discontinued Operations

Objective

The objectives of IFRS 5 are to set out:

- requirements for the classification, measurement and presentation of non-current assets held for sale, in particular requiring that such assets should be presented separately on the face of the statement of financial position
- updated rules for the presentation of discontinued operations, in particular requiring that the results of discontinued operations should be presented separately in the statement of profit or loss.

Classification as held for sale

'An entity shall classify a non-current asset as held for sale if its carrying amount will be recovered principally through a sale transaction rather than through continuing use' (IFRS 5, para 6).

For this to be the case, the following conditions must apply:

- the asset **'must be available for immediate sale in its present condition'** (IFRS 5, para 7)
- the sale must be highly probable, meaning that:
  - management are **'committed to a plan to sell the asset'**
  - there is an **'active programme to locate a buyer',** and
  - the asset is being **'actively marketed at a price that is reasonable'** (IFRS 5, para 8)
- the sale is expected to be completed **'within one year from the date of classification'** as held for sale (IFRS 5, para 8)
- **'it is unlikely that significant changes to the plan will be made or that the plan will be withdrawn'** (IFRS 5, para 8).

Measurement of non-current assets held for sale

Non-current assets that qualify as held for sale should be measured at the lower of:

- their carrying amount and
- fair value less costs to sell.

Held for sale non-current assets should be:

- presented separately on the face of the statement of financial position under current assets
- not depreciated.

Where assets held under the revaluation model are reclassified as held for sale, these assets should be revalued using the method in IAS 16 *Property, Plant and Equipment* or IAS 40 *Investment Property* as appropriate prior to reclassification.

Test your understanding 1

On 1 January 20X1, Michelle Co bought a stamping machine for $20,000. It has an expected useful life of 10 years and a nil residual value. On 30 September 20X3, Michelle Co decides to sell the machine and starts actions to locate a buyer. The machines are in short supply, so Michelle Co is confident that the machine will be sold fairly quickly. Its market value at 30 September 20X3 is $13,500 and it will cost $500 to dismantle the machine and make it available to the purchaser. The machine has not been sold at the year end.

At what value should the machine be stated in Michelle Co's statement of financial position at 31 December 20X3?

Discontinued operations

A **discontinued operation** is a **'component of an entity that has either been disposed of, or is classified as held for sale,** and:

- **represents a separate major line of business or geographical area of operations**
- **is part of a single co-ordinated plan to dispose of a separate major line of business or geographical area of operations,** or
- **is a subsidiary acquired exclusively with a view to resale'** (IFRS 5, para 32)

By showing the performance of discontinued operations separately, users can see the performance of the remaining operations, enabling them to predict future performance more accurately.

An entity must disclose a single amount on the face of the statement of profit or loss, **'comprising the total of:**

- **the post-tax profit or loss of discontinued operations,** and
- **the post-tax gain or loss recognised on the measurement to fair value less costs to sell or on the disposal of the assets constituting the discontinued operation'** (IFRS 5, para 33(a))

An analysis of this single amount must be presented, either in the notes or on the face of the statement of profit or loss.

The analysis must disclose:

- **'the revenue, expenses and pre-tax profit or loss of discontinued operations**
- **the related income tax expense**
- **the gain or loss recognised on the measurement to fair value less costs to sell or on the disposal of the assets constituting the discontinued operation'** (IFRS 5, para 33(b)).

Statement of profit or loss presentation (with a discontinued operation)

	20X9
	$
Continuing operations:	
Revenue	X
Cost of sales	(X)
	—
Gross profit	X
Distribution costs	(X)
Administration expenses	(X)
	—
Profit from operations	X
Finance costs	(X)
	—
Profit before tax	X
Income tax expense	(X)
	—
Profit for the period from continuing operations	X
Discontinued operations:	
Profit for the period from discontinued operations*	X
	—
Total profit for the period	X
	—

*The analysis of this single amount, as described above, would be given in the notes.

Alternatively the analysis could be given on the face of the statement of profit or loss, with separate columns for continuing operations, discontinued operations, and total amounts.

Test your understanding 2

St. Valentine produced cards and sold roses. However, half way through the year ended 31 March 20X6, the rose business was closed and the assets sold off, incurring losses on the disposal of non-current assets of $76,000 and redundancy costs of $37,000. The directors reorganised the continuing business at a cost of $98,000.

Trading results may be summarised as follows:

	Cards	**Roses**
	$000	$000
Revenue	650	320
Cost of sales	320	150
Distribution	60	90
Administration	120	110

Other trading information (to be allocated to continuing operations) is as follows:

	$000
Finance costs	17
Tax	31

Required:

(a) Draft the statement of profit or loss for the year ended 31 March 20X6.

(b) Explain how an IFRS 5 *Discontinued Operations* presentation can make information more useful to the users of financial statements.

2 Chapter summary

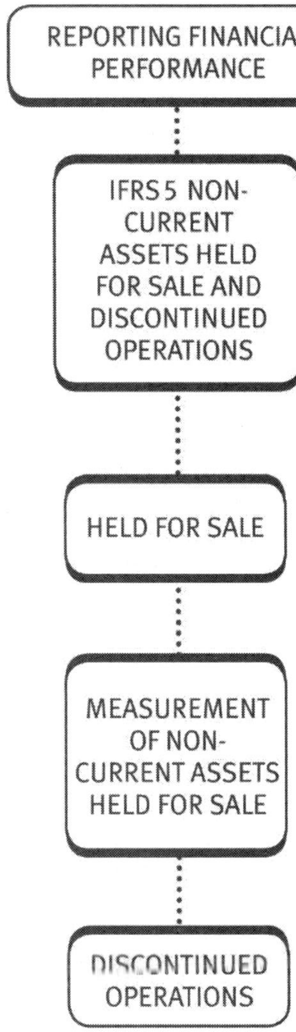

Test your understanding 3

Partway is in the process of preparing its financial statements for the year ended 31 October 20X6. The company's principal activity is in the travel industry, mainly selling package holidays (flights and accommodation) to the general public through the Internet and retail travel agencies. During the current year the number of holidays sold by travel agencies declined dramatically and the directors decided at a board meeting on 15 October 20X6 to cease marketing holidays through its chain of travel agents and sell off the related high-street premises. Immediately after the meeting the travel agencies' staff and suppliers were notified of the situation and an announcement was made in the press. The directors wish to show the travel agencies' results as a discontinued operation in the financial statements to 31 October 20X6. Due to the declining business of the travel agents, on 1 August 20X6 Partway expanded its Internet operations to offer car hire facilities to purchasers of its Internet holidays.

The following are extracts from Partway's statement of profit or loss results – years ended:

		31 October 20X6			**31 October 20X5**
	Internet	**Travel agencies**	**Car hire**	**Total**	**Total**
	$000	$000	$000	$000	$000
Revenue	23,000	14,000	2,000	39,000	40,000
Cost of sales	(18,000)	(16,500)	(1,500)	(36,000)	(32,000)
Gross profit/(loss)	5,000	(2,500)	500	3,000	8,000
Operating costs	(1,000)	(1,500)	(100)	(2,600)	(2,000)
Profit/(loss) before tax	4,000	(4,000)	400	400	6,000

The results for the travel agencies for the year ended 31 October 20X5 were: revenue $18 million, cost of sales $15 million and operating expenses of $1.5 million.

Required:

(a) State the definition of both non-current assets held for sale and discontinued operations and explain the usefulness of information for discontinued operations.

(b) Discuss whether the directors' wish to show the travel agencies' results as a discontinued operation is justifiable.

(c) Assuming the closure of the travel agencies is a discontinued operation, prepare the extracts from the statement of profit or loss of Partway for the year ended 31 October 20X6 together with comparatives. Show the required analysis of the discontinued operations.

Test your understanding 4

1 **According to IFRS 5 *Non-current Assets Held for Sale and Discontinued Operations* which TWO of the following relate to the criteria for an asset held for sale?**

A The item must be a major line of operations or geographical area

B The asset must be available for immediate sale

C The sale is expected to be completed within the next three months

D A reasonable price has been set

2 **According to IFRS 5 *Non-current Assets Held for Sale and Discontinued Operations* which of the following amounts in respect of a discontinued operation must be shown on the face of the statement of profit or loss?**

(i) Revenue

(ii) Gross profit

(iii) Profit after tax

(iv) Operating profit

A All of the above

B (iii) only

C (iii) and (iv)

D (iv) only

3 **According to IFRS 5 *Non-current Assets Held for Sale and Discontinued Operations* how should non-current assets held for sale be valued?**

A Lower of the carrying amount or the fair value

B Lower of the carrying amount or the fair value less costs of disposal

C Higher of the carrying amount or the fair value

D Higher of the carrying amount or the fair value less costs of disposal

4 Halfway through the year an asset is identified as an asset held for sale after meeting the criteria according to IFRS 5 *Non-current Assets Held for Sale and Discontinued Operations*. At the start of the year the carrying amount of the asset was $150,000 (original cost $200,000 two years ago). The asset is being depreciated on a straight-line basis.

What should the depreciation expense for the year be?

$ 12,500

5 At the reporting date an asset is identified as an asset held for sale after meeting the criteria according to *IFRS 5 Non-current Assets Held for Sale and Discontinued Operations.*

Where should the asset appear on the statement of financial position?

A Part of the property, plant and equipment under non-current assets

B It is not shown on the statement of financial position

C Separately below non-current assets

D Separately below current assets

6 Kat has a year-end of 31 December.

On the 1st January 20X9, it classified one of its freehold properties as held for sale. At that date the property had a carrying amount of $667,000 and had been accounted for according to the revaluation model. Its fair value was estimated at $825,000 and the costs to sell at $3,000.

In accordance with IFRS 5 *Non-current Assets Held for Sale and Discontinued Operations*, what amounts should be recognised in the financial statements for the year to 31 December 20X9?

A Statement of profit or loss gain $155,000
Statement of profit or loss impairment loss $3,000
Revaluation gain nil

B Statement of profit or loss gain $158,000
Statement of profit or loss impairment loss nil
Revaluation gain nil

C Statement of profit or loss gain nil
Statement of profit or loss impairment loss nil
Revaluation gain $155,000

D Statement of profit or loss gain nil
Statement of profit or loss impairment loss $3,000
Revaluation gain $158,000

7 **For each issue, identify the correct accounting treatment in Madeira's financial statements:**

	Asset held for sale	Discontinued operation	Neither
A loss-making division, which Madeira have agreed to close next year			
The factory of Madeira, which is being marketed at a reasonable price at year-end			
Madeira's specialised plant, which will be advertised for sale once it has been dismantled			

Test your understanding answers

Test your understanding 1

Carrying amount at 30 September 20X3:

	$
Cost	20,000
Depreciation year 1 (20,000/10 years)	(2,000)
Depreciation year 2	(2,000)
Depreciation year 3 (20,000/10 years × $^{9}/_{12}$)	(1,500)
	14,500

Fair value less costs to sell = $13,500 – $500 = $13,000

The machine qualifies as 'held for sale' on 30 September 20X3, so should be stated at the lower of $14,500 and $13,000, namely at $13,000.

The impairment loss of $1,500 incurred in writing down the machine to fair value less costs to sell will be charged to the statement of profit or loss.

The machine will no longer be depreciated once reclassified.

Test your understanding 2

(a) **Statement of profit or loss for St Valentine for the year ended 31 March 20X6**

	$000
Continuing operations:	
Revenue	650
Cost of sales	(320)
Gross profit	330
Administration costs	(120)
Distribution costs	(60)
Operating profit	150
Reorganisation costs	(98)
	52
Finance costs	(17)
Profit before tax	35
Income tax expense	(31)
Profit for the year from continuing operations	4
Discontinued operations:	
Loss for the year from discontinued operations	(143)
Total loss for the year	(139)

In the notes to the accounts disclose analysis of the discontinued operations figure:

	$000
Revenue	320
Cost of sales	(150)
Gross profit	170
Administration costs	(110)
Distribution costs	(90)
Operating loss	(30)
Loss on disposal	(76)
Redundancy costs	(37)
Overall loss	(143)

(b) **IFRS 5 presentation**

When a business segment or geographical area has been classified as a discontinued operation, IFRS 5 requires a separate presentation be made on the face of the statement of profit or loss. This separate presentation enables users to immediately identify that the performance relating to the discontinued segment or area will not continue in the future, hence making the information more relevant to users' decision-making. The user can choose to include the information when evaluating the past performance of the company or ignore it when forecasting future outcomes.

Test your understanding 3

(a) IFRS 5 *Non-current Assets Held for Sale and Discontinued Operations* defines non-current assets held for sale as those assets (or group of assets) whose carrying amounts will be recovered principally through a sale transaction rather than through continuing use. For this to be the case the assets must be available for immediate sale, the sale must be highly probable and. it must be expected to be completed within 12 months of the classification as held for sale.

A discontinued operation is a component of an entity that has either been disposed of, or is classified as 'held for sale' and:

- represents a separate major line of business or geographical area of operations
- is part of a single co-ordinated plan to dispose of such, or
- is a subsidiary acquired exclusively for sale.

IFRS 5 says that the discontinued component of an entity must have operations and cash flows that can be clearly distinguished from the rest of the entity and will in all probability have been a cash-generating unit (or group of such units) whilst held for use. This definition also means that a discontinued operation will also fall to be treated as a 'disposal group' as defined in IFRS 5. A disposal group is a group of assets (possibly with associated liabilities) that it is intended will be disposed of in a single transaction by sale or otherwise (closure or abandonment). Assets held for disposal (but not those being abandoned) must be presented separately from other assets, within current assets, rather than as non-current assets, at the lower of carrying amount or fair value less costs to sell. Any associated liabilities must be separately presented under liabilities. The results of a discontinued operation should, as a minimum, be disclosed separately as a single figure within the profit for the year in the statement of profit or loss, with more detailed figures disclosed either in the statement of profit or loss or in the notes.

The intention of this requirement is to improve the usefulness of the financial statements by improving the predictive value of the statement of profit or loss. Clearly the results from discontinued operations should have little impact on future operating results. Thus users can focus on the continuing activities in any assessment of future income and profit potential.

(b) The timing of the board meeting and consequent actions and notifications is within the accounting period ended 31 October 20X6. The notification of staff, suppliers and the press seems to indicate that the sale is highly probable, and the directors are committed to a plan to sell the assets and are actively seeking a buyer. From the financial and other information given in the question it appears that the travel agencies' operations and cash flows can be clearly distinguished from its other operations. The assets of the travel agencies appear to meet the definition of non-current assets held for sale. However the main difficulty is whether their sale and closure also represent a discontinued operation. The main issue is with the wording of 'a separate major line of business' in part (a) of the above definition of a discontinued operation. The company is still operating in the holiday business, but only through Internet selling. The selling of holidays through the Internet compared with through high street travel agencies requires very different assets, staff knowledge and training, and has a different cost structure. It could therefore be argued that although the company is still selling holidays the travel agencies do represent a separate line of business. If this is the case, it seems the announced closure of the travel agencies appears to meet the definition of a discontinued operation.

(c) **Partway statement of profit or loss and other comprehensive income year ended:**

	31 October 20X6	**31 October 20X5**
	$000	$000
Continuing operations		
Revenue	25,000	22,000
Cost of sales	(19,500)	(17,000)
Gross profit	5,500	5,000
Operating expenses	(1,100)	(500)
Profit/(loss) from continuing operations	4,400	4,500
Discontinued operations		
Profit/(loss) from discontinued operations	(4,000)	1,500
Total profit for the period	400	6,000

Analysis of discontinued operations

Revenue	14,000	18,000
Cost of sales	(16,500)	(15,000)
Gross profit/(loss)	(2,500)	3,000
Operating expenses	(1,500)	(1,500)
Profit/(loss) from discontinued operations	(4,000)	1,500

Note: Other presentations may be acceptable.

Test your understanding 4

1 **B and D** – The sale must be expected to complete within a year, not within three months. The asset does not need to represent a major line of operations or geographical area, as this is the criteria for a discontinued operation.

2 **B** – One line is shown in relation to a discontinued operation, with a full analysis of the figure being shown in the notes to the accounts.

3 **B** – This ensures that any loss will be recorded immediately, with any profit on disposal only recognised when the asset is actually sold.

4 **$12,500.** Depreciation should be charged for the first six months of the year, and then cease when the asset is classified as held for sale. As the carrying amount has decreased by $50,000 in two years, the depreciation must be $25,000 a year. Therefore six months' depreciation is $12,500.

5 **D** – This will be shown within current assets as it is expected to be sold within a year

6 **D** – The asset held for sale will be revalued to the fair value of $825,000 creating a gain of $158,000 to the revaluation surplus. The asset held for sale will then be reduced to the fair value less costs to sell value of $825,000 – $3,000, creating an impairment cost of $3,000. There will not be a gain recognised in profit or loss until the asset is sold and the gain is realised.

7

	Asset held for sale	Discontinued operation	Neither
A loss-making division, which Madeira have agreed to close next year			✓
The factory of Madeira, which is marketed at a reasonable price at year end	✓		
Madeira's specialised plant, which will be advertised for sale once it has been dismantled			✓

The loss-making division cannot be classed as a discontinued operation, even though it may be a major line of business as it has not been closed during the year and is not classed as held for sale. Items which are to be abandoned do not meet the criteria for being a discontinued operation.

The specialised plant cannot be classed as an asset held for sale as it is not available for sale in its present condition.

Chapter

6

A conceptual and regulatory framework

Chapter learning objectives

Upon completion of this chapter you will be able to:

- explain why a regulatory framework is needed
- explain why accounting standards on their own are not a complete regulatory framework
- distinguish between a principles-based and a rules-based framework
- describe the International Accounting Standards Board's standard-setting process including revisions to and interpretations of standards
- explain the relationship between national standard setters and the International Accounting Standards Board in respect of the standard-setting process
- describe a conceptual framework
- discuss what an alternative system to a conceptual framework might be
- define and discuss fundamental and enhancing qualitative characteristics
- define and explain the recognition in financial statements
- apply the recognition criteria to assets, liabilities, equity, income and expenses
- discuss what is meant by the financial position approach to recognition
- indicate when income and expense recognition should occur under the financial position approach.

PER

One of the PER performance objectives (PO6) is to record and process transactions and events. You use the right accounting treatments for transactions and events. These should be both historical and prospective – and include non-routine transactions. Working though this chapter should help you understand how to demonstrate that objective.

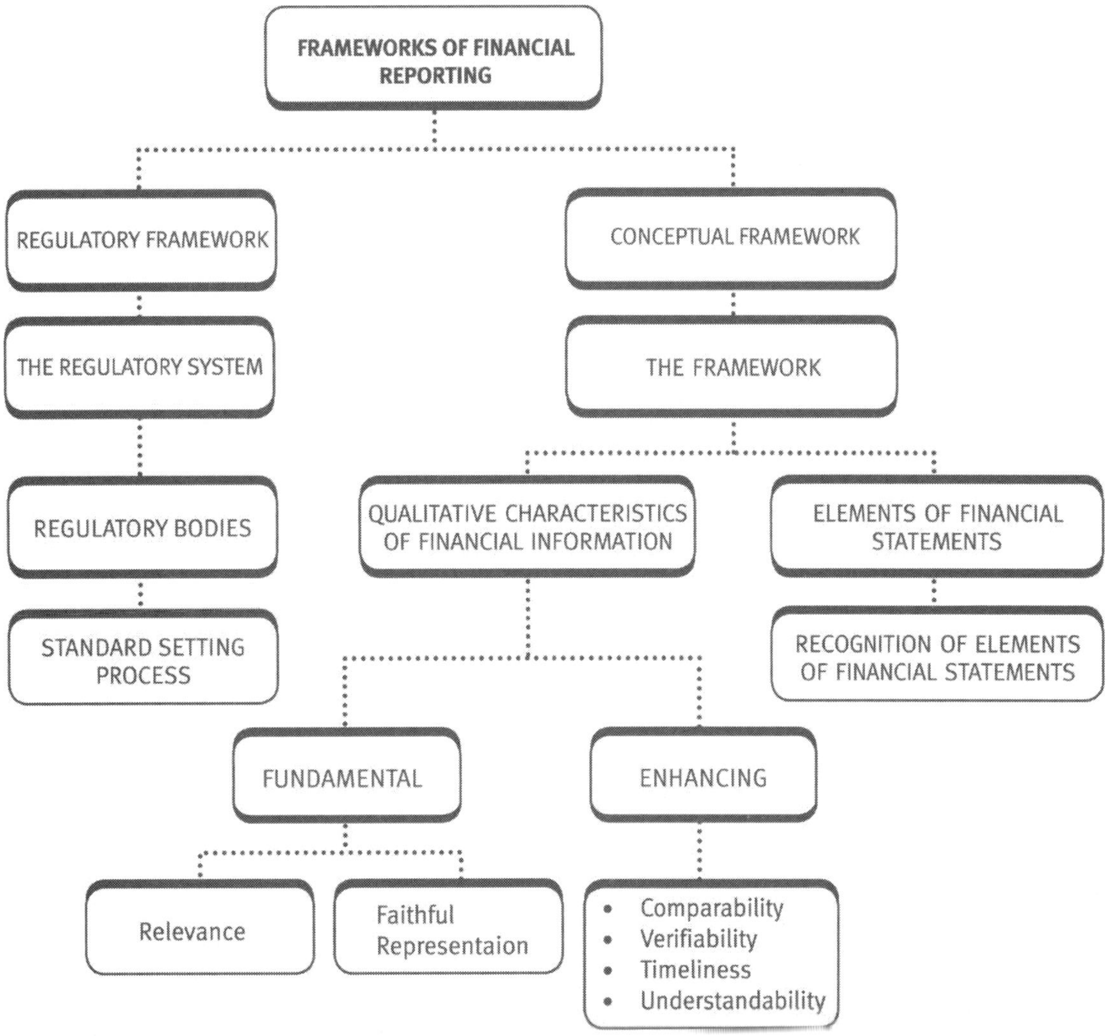

1 The need for a regulatory framework

The regulatory framework

The regulatory framework of accounting in each country which uses IFRS® Standards is affected by a number of legislative and quasi-legislative influences as well as IFRS Standards:

- national company law
- EU directives
- security exchange rules.

Why a regulatory framework is necessary

Regulation of accounting information is aimed at ensuring that users of financial statements receive a minimum amount of information that will enable them to make meaningful decisions regarding their interest in a reporting entity. A regulatory framework is required to ensure that relevant and reliable financial reporting is achieved to meet the needs of shareholders and other users.

Accounting standards on their own would not be a complete regulatory framework. In order to fully regulate the preparation of financial statements and the obligations of companies and directors, legal and market regulations are also required.

Principles-based and rules-based framework

Principles-based framework:

- based upon a conceptual framework such as the International Accounting Standards Board's (the Board's) Framework
- accounting standards are created using the conceptual framework as a basis.

Rules-based framework:

- 'Cookbook' approach
- accounting standards are a set of rules which companies must follow.

In the UK there is a principles-based framework in terms of the Statement of Principles and Accounting Standards and a rules-based framework in terms of the Companies Acts, EU directives and stock exchange rulings.

Advantages and disadvantages of harmonisation

There are a number of reasons why the harmonisation of accounting standards would be beneficial. Businesses operate on a global scale and investors make investment decisions on a worldwide basis. There is thus a need for financial information to be presented on a consistent basis.

The advantages of harmonisation:

I Multinational entities

(i) Access to international finance is easier as financial information is more understandable if it is prepared on a consistent basis

(ii) In a business that operates in several countries, the preparation of financial information is easier as it would all be prepared on the same basis

(iii) There is greater efficiency in accounting departments

(iv) Consolidation of financial statements is easier.

II Investors – If investors wish to make decisions based on the worldwide availability of investments, then better comparisons between entities are required. Harmonisation assists this process, as financial information would be consistent between different entities from different regions.

III Tax authorities – Tax liabilities of investors should be easier to calculate.

IV Large international accounting firms – Accounting firms would benefit as accounting and auditing is easier if similar accounting practices exist on a global basis.

The disadvantages of harmonisation:

(i) Difficult to introduce, apply and maintain or enforce in different countries, each of which has a range of social, political, economic and business factors to consider.

(ii) Different legal systems may prevent the application of certain accounting practices and restrict the options available.

(iii) Different purposes of financial reporting between countries. In some countries, the principal purpose of financial reporting is to serve as a basis for establishing tax liabilities. Equally, whether a particular entity applies a harmonised set of financial reporting standards may be of little practical relevance if it is essentially owner-managed.

(iv) Countries may be unwilling to accept another country's standards.

(v) Costly to develop a fully detailed set of accounting standards.

The role of national standard setters

- The harmonisation process has gathered pace in the last few years. From 2005 all European listed entities were required to adopt IFRS Standards in their group financial statements. Many other countries including Australia, Canada and New Zealand decided to follow a similar process. National standard setters are committed to a framework of accounting standards based on IFRS Standards.
- The overall impact of the above is that the trend towards closer international harmonisation of accounting practices is now set. It will become increasingly difficult for domestic standard setters to justify domestic standards at odds with IFRS Standards.

The standard setting process

The IFRS Foundation

International Financial Reporting Standards (IFRS) Foundation

- is the supervisory body for the Board
- is responsible for governance issues and ensuring each body is properly funded.

The objectives of the IFRS Foundation include:

- developing a set of global accounting standards of high quality which are understandable and enforceable
- promoting the use and application of these standards
- bringing about the convergence of national and international accounting standards.

International Accounting Standards Board (The Board)

The Board:

- is solely responsible for issuing International Financial Reporting Standards (IFRS Standards)

The Board and national standard setters

The intentions of the Board are to develop a single set of understandable and enforceable high quality worldwide accounting standards. However the Board cannot enforce compliance with IFRS standards, therefore it needs the co-operation of national standard setters.

In order to achieve this the Board works in partnership with the major national standard-setting bodies:

- All the most important national standard setters are represented on the Board and their views are taken into account so that a consensus can be reached.
- All national standard setters can issue Board discussion papers and exposure drafts for comment in their own countries, so that the views of all preparers and users of financial statements can be represented.

As far as possible, future international standards will be more rigorous than previously and will no longer allow alternative treatments. The former Chairman of the Board, Sir David Tweedie has already stated that there will not be 'convergence for the sake of convergence by the issue of a set of 'lowest common denominator' accounting standards'.

Because the Board on its own cannot enforce compliance with its standards, it needs the co-operation of national standard setters. Without their support, rigorous new international standards are unlikely to be adopted by everybody. Therefore, the Board works in partnership with the major national standard setting bodies, including the UK Financial Reporting Council (FRC) and the US Financial Accounting Standards Board (FASB).

Each major national standard setter 'leads' certain international standard-setting projects, e.g. the UK ASB carried out much of the work to develop an updated international standard on leasing.

All the major national standard-setters are now committed to international convergence.

IFRIC

International Financial Reporting Interpretations Committee (IFRIC®)

- issues rapid guidance on accounting matters where divergent interpretations of IFRS Standards have arisen
- these must be approved by the Board

The IFRIC addresses issues of reasonably widespread importance, rather than issues that are of concern to only a small minority of entities. The interpretations cover both:

- newly identified financial reporting issues not specifically dealt with in IFRS Standards, or
- issues where unsatisfactory or conflicting interpretations have developed, or seem likely to develop in the absence of authoritative guidance, with a view to reaching a consensus on the appropriate treatment.

IFRSAC

The IFRS Advisory Council (IFRSAC)

The IFRS Advisory Council provides a forum for the Board to consult a wide range of interested parties affected by the Board's work, with the objectives of:

- advising the Board on agenda decisions and priorities in the Board's work,
- informing the Board of the views of the organisations and individuals on the Council on major standard-setting projects, and
- giving other advice to the Board or to the Trustees.

Development of an IFRS Standard

The procedure for the development of an IFRS Standard is as follows:

- The Board identifies a subject and appoints an advisory committee to advise on the issues.
- The Board may issue a discussion paper to encourage comment.
- The Board publishes an exposure draft, being a draft version of the intended standard.
- Following the consideration of comments received on the draft, the Board publishes the final text of the IFRS Standard.
- The publication of an IFRS Standard, exposure draft or IFRIC Interpretation requires the votes of at least eight of the 15 Board members.

Status of IFRS Standards

Neither the IFRS Foundation, the Board nor the accountancy profession has the power to enforce compliance with IFRS Standards. Nevertheless, some countries adopt IFRS Standards as their local standards, and others ensure that there is minimum difference between their standards and IFRS Standards. In recent years, the status of the Board and its standards has increased, so IFRS Standards carry considerable persuasive force worldwide.

2 A conceptual framework

The meaning of a conceptual framework

Introduction

There are two main approaches to accounting:

- A principles-based or conceptual framework approach such as that used by the Board.
- A rules-based approach such as that used in the US.

What is a conceptual framework?

A conceptual framework is:

- a coherent system of interrelated objectives and fundamental principles
- a framework which prescribes the nature, function and limits of financial accounting and financial statements.

Why have a conceptual framework?

There are a variety of arguments for having a conceptual framework.

- It enables accounting standards and generally accepted accounting practice (GAAP) to be developed in accordance with agreed principles.
- It avoids 'fire-fighting', whereby accounting standards are developed in a piecemeal way in response to specific problems or abuses. Fire-fighting can lead to inconsistencies between different accounting standards, and between accounting standards and legislation.
- Lack of a conceptual framework may mean that certain critical issues are not addressed, e.g. until recently there was no definition of basic terms such as 'asset' or 'liability' in any accounting standard.
- As transactions become more complex and businesses become more sophisticated it helps preparers and auditors of financial statements to deal with transactions which are not the subject of an accounting standard.
- Accounting standards based on principles are thought to be harder to circumvent.
- A conceptual framework strengthens the credibility of financial reporting and the accounting profession.
- It makes it less likely that the standard-setting process can be influenced by 'vested interests' (e.g. large companies/business sectors).

This is the approach used in the UK and by the Board in its revised conceptual Framework issued in March 2018.

Alternative rules-based system

A possible alternative to a conceptual framework is a prescriptive 'cookbook' approach based on rules rather than principles. This is the approach in the US.

Principles are harder to circumvent and therefore preferable to a rules-based approach.

The purpose of the framework

The conceptual framework published by the Board is called the Conceptual Framework for Financial Reporting. It includes guidance with regard to

- the objective of financial reporting
- the qualitative characteristics of financial information
- the definition, recognition and measurement of the elements of financial statements
- concepts of capital and capital maintenance.

The purpose of the Framework is to:

- assist the International Accounting Standards Board to develop IFRS Standards that are based on consistent concepts
- assist preparers to develop consistent accounting policies when no Standard applies to a particular transaction or other event, or when a Standard allows a choice of accounting policy
- assist all parties to understand and interpret the Standards.

The Framework is not in itself an IFRS Standard and does not override any specific IFRS Standard. In any rare instances where there may be a conflict between the Framework and an IFRS Standard, the requirements of the IFRS Standard prevail over the Framework.

3 Objective of financial reporting

The objective of financial reporting is to provide financial information about the reporting entity that is useful to existing and potential investors, lenders and other creditors in making decisions about providing resources to the entity.

4 Qualitative characteristics

Introduction

Qualitative characteristics are the attributes that make information provided in financial statements useful to others.

The Framework splits qualitative characteristics into two categories:

(i) Fundamental qualitative characteristics

- Relevance
- Faithful representation

(ii) Enhancing qualitative characteristics

- Comparability
- Verifiability
- Timeliness
- Understandability

Underlying assumption

The Framework identifies that the underlying assumption governing financial statements is the **going concern concept** (Framework, para 3.9). The going concern basis assumes that the entity has neither the need nor the intention to liquidate or materially curtail the scale of its operations. If this is not the case then the financial statements would be prepared on a different basis, which must be disclosed.

Fundamental qualitative characteristics

Relevance

Information is relevant if:

- it has the ability to influence the economic decisions of users, and
- is provided in time to influence those decisions.

Materiality has a direct impact on the relevance of information.

Qualities of relevance

Information provided by financial statements needs to be relevant. Information that is relevant has predictive and/or confirmatory value.

- Predictive value enables users to evaluate or assess past, present or future events.
- Confirmatory value helps users to confirm or correct past evaluations and assessments.

Where choices have to be made between mutually-exclusive options, the option selected should be the one that results in the maximum relevance of information – in other words, the one that would be of most use in taking economic decisions.

Materiality

Materiality is an entity-specific aspect of relevance and depends on the size of the item or error judged in the particular circumstances of its omission or misstatement. Materiality is a threshold quality.

A threshold quality is:

- one that needs to be studied before considering the other qualities of that information
- a cut-off point – i.e. if any information does not pass the test of materiality, it does not need to be considered further.

Information is material if its omission or misstatement could influence the economic decisions of users taken on the basis of the financial statements.

Faithful representation

If information is to represent faithfully the transactions and other events that it purports to represent, they must be accounted for and presented in accordance with their substance and economic reality and not merely their legal form.

To be a perfectly faithful representation, financial information would possess the following characteristics:

- **Completeness** – To be understandable information must contain all the necessary descriptions and explanations.
- **Neutrality** – Information must be neutral, i.e. free from bias. Financial statements are not neutral if, by the selection or presentation of information, they deliberately influence the making of a decision or judgement in order to achieve a predetermined result or outcome.
- **Free from error** – Information must be free from error within the bounds of materiality. A material error or omission can cause the financial statements to be false or misleading, and thus unreliable and deficient in terms of their relevance.

Free from error does not mean perfectly accurate in all respects. For example, where an estimate has been used the amount must be described clearly and accurately as being an estimate.

e.g

Illustration 1 – Relevance

A business is a going concern with no intentions to reduce or curtail its operations.

Which would be the most relevant valuation for its machinery – the net realisable value of the machinery or its depreciated cost?

Solution

As the business is to continue into the future and therefore it can be assumed that the machinery is not going to be sold, the depreciated cost of the machinery would be a more relevant value than the net realisable value.

If circumstances changed and the business were not a going concern, the net realisable value would be more relevant to the users of the financial statements.

Enhancing qualitative characteristics

'Comparability, verifiability, timeliness and understandability are qualitative characteristics that enhance the usefulness of information that both is relevant and provides a faithful representation' (Framework, para 2.23).

Comparability

Users must be able to:

- compare the financial statements of an entity over time to identify trends in its financial position and performance
- compare the financial statements of different entities to evaluate their relative financial performance and financial position.

For this to be the case there must be:

- consistency and
- disclosure.

An important implication of comparability is that users are informed of the accounting policies employed in preparation of the financial statements, any changes in those policies and the effects of such changes. Compliance with accounting standards, including the disclosure of the accounting policies used by the entity, helps to achieve comparability.

Because users wish to compare the financial position and the performance and changes in the financial position of an entity over time, it is important that the financial statements show corresponding information for the preceding periods.

Verifiability

'Verification can be direct or indirect. Direct verification means verifying an amount or other representation through direct observation, for example, by counting cash. Indirect verification means checking the inputs to a model, formula or other technique and recalculating the outputs using the same methodology' e.g. recalculating inventory amounts using the same cost flow assumption such as first-in, first-out method (Framework, para 2.31).

Timeliness

'Timeliness means having information available to decision makers in time to be capable of influencing their decisions. Generally, the older the information is the less useful it is'
(Framework, para 2.33).

Understandability

Understandability depends on:

- the way in which information is presented
- the capabilities of users.

It is assumed that users:

- **'have a reasonable knowledge of business and economic activities'**
- **'review and analyse the information diligently'**

(Framework, Para 2.36)

For information to be understandable users need to be able to perceive its significance.

5 Elements of the financial statements

Assets

'An asset is

- **a present economic resource controlled by the entity**
- **as a result of past events'**

(Framework, para 4.3)

'An economic resource is a right that has the potential to produce economic benefit.' (Framework, para 4.4)

Liabilities

'A liability is

- **a present obligation of the entity**
- **to transfer an economic resource as a result of past events'**

(Framework, para 4.26).

Equity interest

'Equity is the residual interest in the assets of the entity after deducting all its liabilities' (Framework, para 4.63)

Income

'Income is

- **increases in assets or decreases in liabilities, that result in increases in equity, other than those relating to contributions from holders of equity claims'** (Framework, para 4.68)

This definition follows a statement of financial position approach rather than the more traditional profit or loss approach to recognising income.

Expenses

'Expenses are

- **decreases in assets or increases in liabilities, that result in decreases in equity, other than those relating to distributions to holders of equity claims.'** (Framework, para 4.69).

Assets, liabilities and equity interest

Assets

'An asset is a present economic resource controlled by the entity as a result of past events' (Framework, para 4.3)

To explain further the parts of the definition of an asset:

- **Controlled by the entity** – control is the ability to obtain the economic benefits and to restrict the access of others (e.g. by an entity being the sole user of its plant and machinery, or by selling surplus plant and machinery).
- **Past events** – the event must be 'past' before an asset can arise. For example, equipment will only become an asset when there is the right to demand delivery or access to the asset's potential. Dependent on the terms of the contract, this may be on acceptance of the order or on delivery.

Liabilities

'A liability is a present obligation of the entity to transfer an economic resource as a result of past events.' (Framework, Para 4.26)

To explain further the parts of the definition of a liability:

- **Obligation** – this may be legal or constructive. A constructive obligation is an obligation which is the result of expected practice rather than required by law or a legal contract. An example of a constructive obligation may be an environmental provision created by an entity which has a published policy of clearing up damage done to the environment, regardless of whether any legislation exists enforcing this.
- **Past events** – similar points are made here to those under assets.

Complementary nature of assets and liabilities – as should be evident from the above, assets and liabilities are seen as mirror images of each other. Sometimes they are offset, e.g. a credit note issued to a customer will be set against the debt rather than being recorded as a separate liability.

Equity

'Equity is the residual interest in the assets of the entity after deducting all its liabilities' (Framework, para 4.6)

The definition describes the residual nature of equity interest. Owners' wealth can be increased whether or not a distribution is made. The sharing may be in different proportions. Equity interest is usually analysed in financial statements to distinguish interest arising from owners' contributions from that resulting from other events. The latter is split into different reserves which may have different applications or legal status.

Recognition of the elements

Recognition

Items are only recognised in the financial statements if they meet the definition of one of the elements. However, not all items meeting these definitions are recognised.

Elements are recognised if recognition provides users with useful financial information. In other words recognition must provide:

- relevant information
- a faithful representation of the asset or liability, and resulting income, expenses or equity movements.

Recognition might not provide relevant information if there is uncertainty over the existence of the element or if there is a low probability of an inflow or outflow of economic resources.

Recognition – an example

IAS 37 *Provisions, Contingent Liabilities and Contingent Assets* prohibits recognition of contingent liabilities and assets because it is not probable that resources will flow to or from the entity.

Recognition of an element might not provide a faithful representation if there is a very high degree of measurement uncertainty.

Judgement is required in deciding if recognition of an element is appropriate. This is why specific recognition criteria vary from one IFRS Standard to another.

If an asset or liability is not recognised, disclosures may be required to ensure users fully understand the reporting entity's economic transactions and the implications that these may have on future earnings and future cash flows.

Financial position approach to recognition

It can be seen therefore that:

- income is an increase in an asset or decrease in a liability
- expenses are an increase in a liability or decrease in an asset.

As income and expenses are therefore recognised on the basis of changes in assets and liabilities this is known as a financial position (or balance sheet) approach to recognition.

Derecognition

Derecognition is the removal of some or all of an asset or liability from the statement of financial position. This normally occurs when the entity:

- loses control of the asset, or
- has no present obligation for the liability.

Accounting for derecognition should faithfully represent the changes in an entity's net assets, as well as any assets or liabilities retained.

This is achieved by:

- derecognising any transferred, expired or consumed component, and
- recognising a gain or loss on the above, and
- recognising any retained component.

Sometimes an entity might appear to have transferred an asset or liability. However, derecognition would not be appropriate if exposure to variations in the element's economic benefits is retained.

e.g **Derecognition – an example**

An entity sells a building for $2 million and retains the right to buy it back for $3 million in five years' time. At the date of sale, the building had a fair value of $7 million. Property prices are expected to rise.

The entity does not derecognise the building from its statement of financial position. The entity has not lost control over the building because its ability to buy the building back for substantially less than fair value enables it to benefit from future price rises.

The cash received would be recognised as a loan liability.

6 Chapter summary

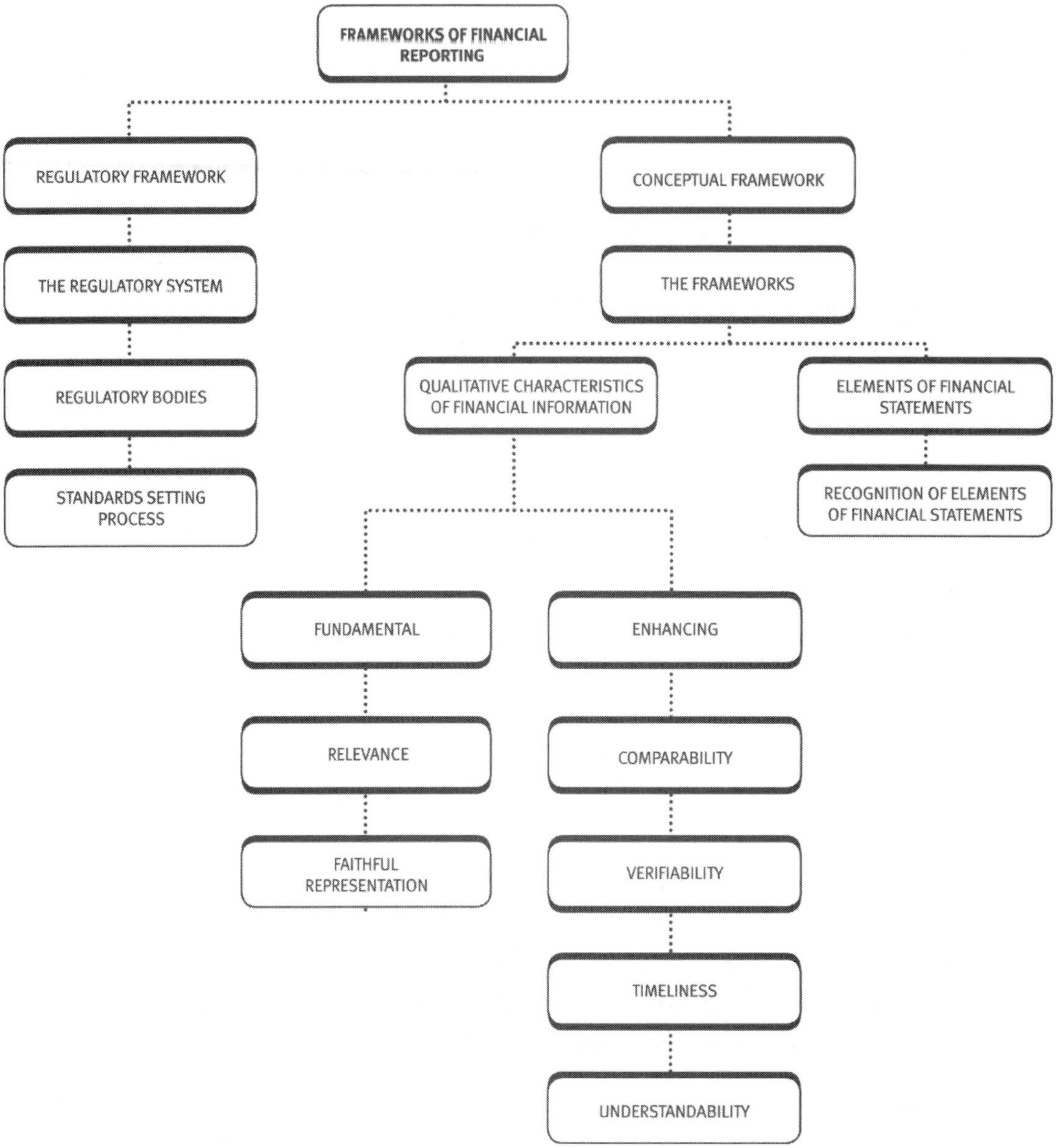

Test your understanding 1

1 **Under the current structure of regulatory bodies, which of the bodies listed below acts as the overall supervisory body?**

A IFRS Interpretations Committee

B International Accounting Standards Board

C IFRS Advisory Council

D IFRS Foundation

2 **Which of the bodies listed below is responsible for issuing International Financial Reporting Standards and guidance on their application?**

A IFRS Interpretations Committee

B International Accounting Standards Board

C IFRS Advisory Council

D IFRS Foundation

3 **Which of the bodies listed below is responsible for the approval of Draft Interpretations?**

A IFRS Interpretations Committee

B International Accounting Standards Board

C IFRS Advisory Council

D IFRS Foundation

4 **Which of the following best describes the role of the IFRS Advisory Council?**

A To prepare interpretations of IFRS Standards

B To provide the Board with the views of its members on standard setting projects

C To promote the use of IFRS Standards amongst its members

D To select the members of the Board

Test your understanding 2

The International Accounting Standards Board's (The Board's) Conceptual Framework for Financial Reporting identifies two fundamental and four enhancing qualitative characteristics of financial information.

Required:

Identify and explain EACH of the TWO fundamental qualitative characteristics of financial information listed in the Board's Framework.

Test your understanding 3

The Conceptual Framework for Financial Reporting has a number of purposes, including:

- assisting the Board in the development of future IFRS Standards and in its review of existing IFRS Standards
- assisting the Board in promoting harmonisation of regulations, accounting standards and procedures relating to the presentation of financial statements by providing a basis for reducing the number of alternative treatments permitted by IFRS Standards
- assisting preparers of financial statements in applying IFRS Standards and in dealing with topics that are yet to be covered in an IFRS Standard.

Required:

Discuss how The Conceptual Framework could help the Board achieve these objectives.

Test your understanding 4

The Conceptual Framework for Financial Reporting was first published in 1989 then updated in 2010 and 2018.

Required:

Explain the purposes of the Framework.

Test your understanding 5

1 **Under the Conceptual Framework for Financial Reporting, which of the following is the 'threshold quality' of useful information?**

A Relevance

B Reliability

C Materiality

D Understandability

2 **According to The Conceptual Framework for Financial Reporting, which of the following is the underlying assumption of a set of financial statements?**

A Going Concern

B Prudence

C Accruals

D Comparability

3 **Link the terms below to whether they relate to the principle of relevance or faithful representation.**

	Relevance	Faithful representation
Free from bias		✓
Materiality	✓	
Confirmatory value	✓	
Complete		✓

4 The Board's Framework identifies qualitative characteristics.

(i) Relevance

(ii) Comparability

(iii) Verifiability

(iv) Understandability

(v) Faithful representation.

Which of the above are not listed as enhancing characteristics?

A (i), (iv) and (v)

B (ii), (iii) and (iv)

C (ii) and (iii)

D (i) and (v)

5 The Conceptual Framework for Financial Reporting provides definitions of the elements of financial statements. One of the elements defined by the framework is 'expenses'.

In no more than 35 words, give the Framework's definition of expenses.

6 The International Accounting Standards Board's Conceptual Framework for Financial Reporting sets out two fundamental qualitative characteristics of financial information, relevance and faithful representation.

Which characteristics would you expect information to possess if it is to provide faithful representation?

7 **According to the International Accounting Standards Board's Framework for Financial Reporting, what is the objective of financial reporting?**

Test your understanding answers

Test your understanding 1

1 **D**

2 **B**

3 **A**

4 **B**

Test your understanding 2

The two principal qualitative characteristics are:

Relevance – Information is relevant when it influences the economic decisions of users by helping them evaluate past, present or future events or confirming or correcting their past evaluations.

The relevance of information can be affected by its nature and materiality. Some items may be relevant to users simply because of their nature whereas some items may only become relevant once they are material. Hence, materiality is a threshold quality of information rather than a primary characteristic.

According to the Framework, information is material if its omission or misstatement could influence the decisions of users.

Faithful representation – If information is to represent faithfully the transactions and other events that it purports to represent, they must be accounted for and presented in accordance with their substance and economic reality and not merely their legal form.

To be a faithful representation of financial performance and position, the following characteristics should be evident:

Completeness

To be understandable information must contain all the necessary descriptions and explanations.

Neutrality

Information must be neutral, i.e. free from bias. Financial statements are not neutral if, by the selection or presentation of information, they deliberately influence the making of a decision or judgement in order to achieve a predetermined result or outcome.

Free from error

Information must be free from error within the bounds of materiality. A material error or an omission can cause the financial statements to be false or misleading and thus unreliable and deficient in terms of their relevance.

Free from error does not mean perfectly accurate in all respects. For example, where an estimate has been used the amount must be described clearly and accurately as being an estimate.

Test your understanding 3

A conceptual Framework provides guidance on the broad principles of financial reporting. It highlights how items should be recorded, measured and presented. The setting of broad principles could assist in the development of accounting standards, ensuring that the principles are followed consistently as standards and rules are developed.

A conceptual Framework can provide guidance on how similar items are treated. By providing definitions and criteria that can be used in deciding the recognition and measurement of items, conceptual Frameworks can act as a point of reference for those setting standards, those preparing and those using financial information.

The existence of a conceptual Framework can remove the need to address the underlying issues over and over again. Where underlying principles have been established and the accounting standards are based on these principles, there is no need to deal with them fully in each of the standards. This will save the standard-setters time in developing standards and will again ensure consistent treatment of items.

Where a technical issue is raised but is not specifically addressed in an accounting standard, a conceptual Framework can help provide guidance on how such items should be treated. Where a short-term technical solution is provided by the standard-setters, the existence of a conceptual Framework will ensure that the treatment is consistent with the broad set of agreed principles.

Test your understanding 4

According to the Framework, its purpose is to:

- assist the International Accounting Standards Board to develop IFRS Standards that are based on consistent concepts
- assist preparers to develop consistent accounting policies when no Standard applies to a particular transaction or other event, or when a Standard allows a choice of accounting policy
- assist all parties to understand and interpret the Standards.

The Framework is not in itself an IFRS Standard and does not override any specific IFRS Standard. In any rare instances where there may be a conflict between the Framework and an IFRS Standard, the requirements of the IFRS Standard prevail over the Framework.

Test your understanding 5

1 **C**

2 **A**

3

	Relevance	**Faithful representation**
Free from bias		✓
Materiality	✓	
Confirmatory value	✓	
Complete		✓

4 **D**

5 Expenses are decreases in assets or increases in liabilities that result in decreases in equity, other than those relating to distributions to holders of equity claims. (Framework, para 4.69).

6 Completeness, neutrality and free from error.

7 The objective of financial reporting is to provide financial information about the reporting entity that is useful to existing and potential investors, lenders and other creditors in making decisions about providing resources to the entity.

Chapter

7

Conceptual framework: Measurement

Chapter learning objectives

Upon completion of this chapter you will be able to:

- define historical cost and compute an asset value using historical cost
- define and compute fair value/current value
- define and compute net realisable value (NRV)
- define and compute the present value (PV) of future cash flows
- describe the advantages and disadvantages of historical cost accounting
- discuss whether the use of current value accounting overcomes the problems of historical cost accounting
- describe the concepts of financial and physical capital maintenance.

PER

One of the PER performance objectives (PO6) is to record and process transactions and events. You use the right accounting treatments for transactions and events. These should be both historical and prospective – and include non-routine transactions. Working though this chapter should help you understand how to demonstrate that objective.

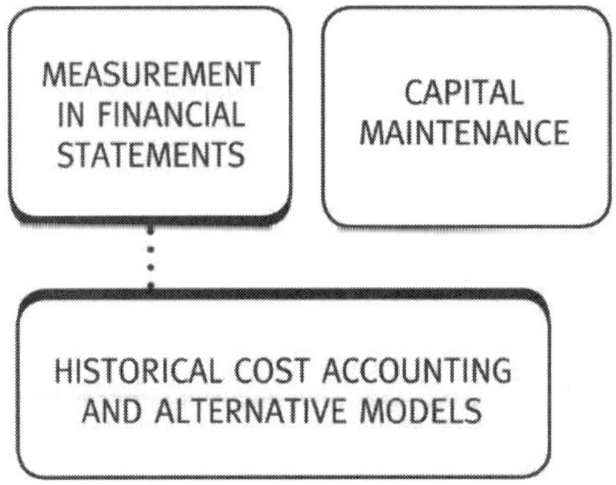

Measurement bases

There are a number of measurement bases mentioned in the International Accounting Standards Board's Conceptual Framework for Financial Reporting. These are:

- Historical cost (Framework, para 6.4 – 6.9) – The actual amount of cash paid or consideration given for the item
- Current cost (Framework, para 6.21 – 6.22) – The cash that would be paid to replace the asset at current values, reflecting the asset's age and condition
- Fair value (Framework, para 6.12 – 6.16) – The amount the item would realise in an orderly arm's length disposal
- Value in use (Framework, para 6.17 - 6.20) – The discounted value of future cash flows

Most items are held at historical cost.

Current cost is normally only used as an alternative to historical cost accounting, taking into account inflation. This will be investigated further within this chapter.

Some items, such as revalued assets or investments, may be revalued to fair value, being the realisable value.

Present value may be used in respect of items with cash flows receivable/payable in a future period.

Historical cost

Traditionally, accounts have been presented using the historical cost convention:

- assets are stated in the statement of financial position at their cost,
- less any amounts written off, e.g. depreciation of tangible non-current assets.

The objective of financial statements is to provide information about the reporting entity's financial performance and position that is useful to certain types of user for assessing the stewardship of directors and for making economic decisions.

Whilst being both easy to ascertain and objective, the historical cost basis of measurement fails to relate directly to any of the three decisions that might reasonably be made about an asset:

- Another, similar asset might be purchased. Management need to know the current replacement cost, which might have changed substantially since the present asset was purchased at its historical cost.
- The asset might be sold. Management need to know the amount which would be realised from sale, less any costs involved in disposal, i.e. the net realisable value. Again, this may bear no relationship to historical cost.
- The asset might be used in the business. Management need to estimate the future cash flows arising from the asset and discount these to their present value, i.e. their 'economic value'. Clearly, there is no direct link with historical cost in this case.

Historical cost accounting

The traditional approach to accounting has the following features:

- Accounting transactions are recorded at their original historical monetary cost.
- Items or events for which no monetary transaction has occurred are usually ignored altogether.
- Income for each period is normally taken into account only when revenue is realised in the form of cash or in some form which will soon be converted into cash.
- Profit for the period is found by matching income against the cost of items consumed in generating the revenue for the period (such items include non-current assets which depreciate through use, obsolescence or the passage of time).

These features of accounting have served users well over many years in assessing the stewardship of the directors.

Advantages of historical cost accounting

- Easy to understand
- Straightforward to produce
- Historical cost accounts are objective and free from bias
- Historical cost values are reliable and original values can be confirmed based on original invoices/accompanying documents
- Historical cost financial statements do not record gains until they are realised

Disadvantages of historical cost financial statements

In periods in which prices change significantly, historical cost financial statements have grave deficiencies:

- Carrying amount of non-current assets is often substantially below current value
- Inventory in the statement of financial position reflects prices at the date of purchase or manufacture rather than those current at the year end
- Statement of profit or loss expenses do not reflect the current value of assets consumed, so profit in real terms is exaggerated
- If profit were distributed in full, the level of operations would have to be curtailed
- No account is taken of the effect of increasing prices on monetary items (items designated or settled in cash) and
- The overstatement of profits and the understatement of assets prevent a meaningful calculation of return on capital employed (ROCE).

As a result of the above, users of financial statements find it extremely difficult to assess a company's progress from year to year or to compare the results of different operations.

e.g

Illustration 1 – Deficiencies of historical cost accounting

Company A acquires a new machine in 20X4. This machine costs $50,000 and has an estimated useful life of ten years.

Company B acquires an identical one-year old machine in 20X5. The cost of the machine is $48,000 and it has an estimated useful life of nine years.

Depreciation charges (straight-line basis, nil residual value) in 20X5 are as follows.

Company A	$50,000/10	= $5,000
Company B	$48,000/9	= $5,333

Carrying amounts at the end of 20X5 are:

Company A $50,000 – (2 × $5,000)	= $40,000
Company B $48,000 – $5,333	= $42,667

Both companies are using identical machines during 20X5, but the statements of profit or loss will show quite different profit figures because of adherence to historical cost.

Other asset values

Replacement cost is the cost to the entity of replacing the asset. However, in a non-current asset situation you will need to determine the asset's net replacement cost. Net replacement cost is the replacement cost of an asset less an appropriate amount of depreciation.

For example, an asset with a historical cost of $500,000 and a life of 5 years would have a carrying amount at the end of year 2 of $300,000 ($500,000 less 2 years' depreciation at $100,000 a year). If the current purchase price of an equivalent new asset at the end of year 2 was $600,000, then the value using replacement cost would be $360,000 ($600,000 less 2 years' depreciation at $120,000 a year).

Net realisable value (also known as fair value less costs to sell) is the estimated sales proceeds less any costs involved in selling the asset.

Economic value (value in use) is the present value of the future cash flows from an asset.

e.g

Illustration 2 – Other asset values

A company owns a machine which it purchased four years ago for $100,000. The accumulated depreciation on the machine to date is $40,000. The machine could be sold to another manufacturer for $50,000 but there would be dismantling costs of $5,000. To replace the machine with a new version would cost $110,000. The cash flows from the existing machine are estimated to be $25,000 for the next two years followed by $20,000 per year for the remaining four years of the machine's life.

The relevant discount rate for this company is 10% and the discount factors are:

Year 1	0.909
Year 2	0.826
Years 3 – 6 inclusive	2.619 (annuity rate)

Calculate the following values for the machine:

(a) Historical cost

(b) Net realisable value

(c) Replacement cost

(d) Economic value

Solution

(a) **Historical cost**

	$
Cost	100,000
Less: Depreciation	(40,000)
	60,000

(b) **Net realisable value**

	$
Selling price	50,000
Less: Costs to sell	(5,000)
	45,000

(c) **Replacement cost**

	$
Replacement cost for new asset	110,000
Less: 4 years' depreciation (4 × $^{1}/_{10}$ × $110,000)	(44,000)
	66,000

(d) **Economic value**

$25,000 × 0.909	22,725
$25,000 × 0.826	20,650
$20,000 × 2.619	52,380
	95,755

Alternatives to historical cost accounting

As historical cost accounting has been criticised for providing information that is out of date and potentially understates asset values, current value accounting has arisen as an alternative. This largely takes two forms:

- constant purchasing power (CPP), or
- current cost accounting (CCA).

Constant purchasing power (CPP)

Key features

- Financial statements are adjusted to show all figures in terms of money with the same purchasing power.
- A general price index is used for this, applying a general level of inflation.
- Figures in the statement of profit or loss and statement of financial position are adjusted by the CPP factor.
- CPP factor = (Index at the reporting date/Index at date of initial recognition)

In converting the figures in the basic historical cost financial statements into those in the CPP statement, a distinction is drawn between:

- monetary items
- non-monetary items.

Monetary items are those whose amounts are fixed by contract or otherwise in terms of numbers of units of currency, regardless of changes in general price levels. Examples of monetary items are cash, receivables, payables and loan capital.

Holders of monetary assets lose general purchasing power during a period of inflation to the extent that any income from the assets does not adequately compensate for the loss in purchasing power. The converse applies to those having monetary liabilities.

Non-monetary items include such assets as inventory and non-current assets. Retaining the historical cost concept requires that holders of non-monetary assets are assumed neither to gain nor to lose purchasing power by reason only of changes in the purchasing power of the unit of currency.

The owners of a company's equity capital have the residual claim on its net monetary and non-monetary assets. The equity interest is therefore neither a monetary nor a non-monetary item.

Advantages and disadvantages of CPP accounts

Advantages

- CPP accounting is both simple and objective. It relies on a standard index.
- It adjusts for changes in the unit of measurement and therefore is a true system of inflation accounting.
- It measures the impact on the entity in terms of shareholders' purchasing power.

Disadvantages

- It fails to capture economic substance when specific and general price movements diverge
- The unfamiliarity of information stated in terms of current purchasing power units.
- CPP does not show the current values to the business of assets and liabilities
- The general price index used is not necessarily appropriate for all assets in all businesses
- The physical capital of the business is not maintained.

Current cost accounting (CCA)

The key features of CCA are as follows:

- It is based on deprival values or value to the business. Deprival value is equal to the loss suffered if deprived of the asset and is usually represented by the replacement cost.
- Inventory and non-current assets are valued at deprival value.
- Monetary assets (cash, receivables, payables, loans) are not adjusted.
- An additional charge to the statement of profit or loss reflects the deprival value of inventory within cost of sales.
- An additional charge in the statement of profit or loss reflects deprival value of non-current assets (depreciation).

Current cost (or replacement cost) accounting is not a single system of accounting – there are several variants. We will concentrate on general principles, in particular those relating to inventory and non-current assets.

- The current cost statement of profit or loss is charged with the value to the business of assets consumed during the period. In particular, the charges for consuming inventory (cost of sales) and non-current assets (depreciation) are based on current rather than historical values.
- The current cost statement of financial position reflects the current value of inventory and non-current assets.

Advantages and disadvantages of CCA

Advantages

- The most important advantage of CCA is its relevance to users.
- Users will be able to assess the current state or recent performance of the business.
- Physical capital is maintained.
- Assets are stated at their value to the business.

Disadvantages

- Possibly greater subjectivity and lower reliability than historical cost.
- Lack of familiarity.
- Complexity.
- CCA only adjusts values for non-monetary assets not all assets/liabilities.

- Practical problems:
  - it is not always easy to obtain an index which is perfectly suitable for measuring the movement in the current cost of a particular type of asset
  - it is often difficult to obtain a suitable market value for specialist items, but indices may be constructed as an alternative
  - there may be no modern equivalent asset due to the advance of technology.

e.g

Illustration 3 – Current cost accounting

Describe the types of business that would be most heavily affected by the replacement of historical cost accounting with a system based on current values.

Solution

Businesses with the following characteristics will be most heavily affected by the change to current value accounting.

- Large quantities of inventory held for long periods of time – the resulting adjustments will impact heavily on the statement of profit or loss.
- High levels of non-current assets acquired a long time ago – the resulting depreciation adjustment will adversely affect profit.
- High levels of monetary assets – a charge is made to the statement of profit or loss to reflect their fall in value when prices are rising.
- High levels of borrowings – a credit is made in the statement of profit or loss to reflect the beneficial effect of borrowing in inflationary times.

Capital maintenance

Capital maintenance is a theoretical concept which tries to ensure that excessive dividends are not paid in times of changing prices.

Capital maintenance concepts can be classified as follows:

- Physical capital maintenance (PCM), alternatively known as operating capital maintenance (OCM). PCM is associated with CCA.
- Financial capital maintenance (FCM).

Physical capital maintenance (PCM) (Framework, para 8.3 (b))

PCM sets aside profits in order to allow the business to continue to operate at current levels of activity. In practice, this tends to mean adjusting opening capital by **SPECIFIC** price changes

Example

Business starts on 1 Jan 20X1 with contribution of $1,000 from owners. This is used to purchase 100 units at $10 each, which are sold for $1,100 cash. Opening capital is $1,000 and closing is $1,100 so profit is usually measured as $100.

However, over the year, the price of the units has increased to $10.75 (a specific price change hitting the business, rather than general). This is a price increase of 7.5%.

Therefore increase opening capital by 7.5% × 1000 = $1,075

Profit is therefore $1,100 – 1,075 = $25

Even if the profit is paid out, the business is left with cash of $1,075. This is enough to buy 1000 more units at $10.75 each. In other words, the productive capacity of the business, or physical capital, has been maintained.

Example

If price rises were 15% ($11.50), then the adjusted opening capital = 115% × $1000 = $1,150. So the profit of the business is $1,100 – $1,150 = $50 loss

Business has cash of $1,100 as there are no profits to pay out – can only purchase 95 units at $11.50 i.e. productive capacity has deteriorated.

Financial capital maintenance (FCM) (Framework, para 8.3 (a))

FCM sets aside profits in order to preserve the value of shareholders' funds in either monetary terms (money financial capital) or constant purchasing power (real financial capital).

We can measure the increase in

- Monetary terms
  - Business starts on 1 Jan X1 with contribution of $1,000 from owners. This is used to purchase 100 units at $10 each, which are sold for $1,100 cash.
  - Opening capital is $1,000 and closing is $1,100 so profit is measured as $100.
- Constant purchasing power

  Inflation over time makes comparisons difficult so constant purchasing power adjusts for general indices of inflation – e.g. retail prices index (RPI).
  - If increase in RPI is 5%
  - Increase opening capital by 5% × 1000 = $1,050
  - So profit is only $1,100 – $1,050 = $50.

Chapter summary

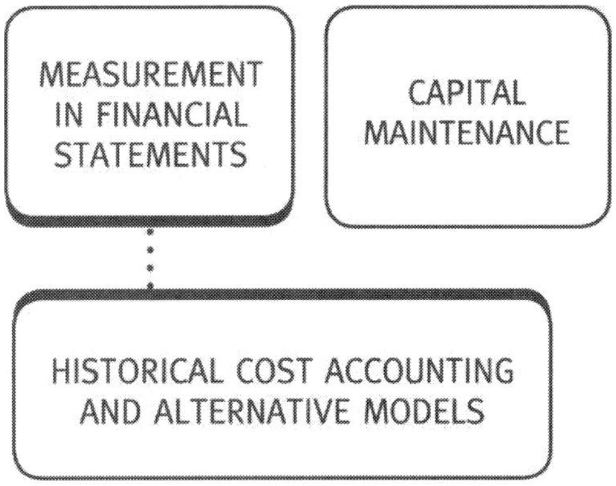

Test your understanding 1

1 **Which of the following measurement bases are referred to in the Board's Conceptual Framework?**

A Current Cost, Residual Value, Fair Value, Present Value

B Current Cost, Historical Cost, Fair Value, Present Value

C Current Cost, Fair Value, Present Value, Future Value

D Fair Value, Present Value, Future value, Residual Value

2 Ross Co made a profit of $350,000 for 20X9 based on historical cost accounting principles. Ross Co had opening capital of $1,000,000. Specific price indices increase during the year by 20% and general price indices by 5%.

How much profit should Ross Co record for 20X9 under three different capital maintenance concepts?

A $350,000 under real financial capital maintenance, $300,000 under money financial capital maintenance, and $150,000 under physical capital maintenance

B $350,000 under money financial capital maintenance, $150,000 under real financial capital maintenance, and $300,000 under physical capital maintenance

C $350,000 under money financial capital maintenance, $300,000 under real financial capital maintenance, and $150,000 under physical capital maintenance

D $150,000 under money financial capital maintenance, $350,000 under real financial capital maintenance, and $300,000 under physical capital maintenance

3 **Which of the following concepts measures profit in terms of an increase in the productive capacity of an entity?**

A Physical capital maintenance

B Historical cost accounting

C Financial capital maintenance

D Going concern concept

4 **Which of the following statements is true about historical cost accounts in times of rising prices?**

A Profits will be overstated and assets will be understated

B Asset values will be overstated

C Unrecognised gains will be recorded incorrectly

D Depreciation will be overstated

Test your understanding answers

Test your understanding 1

1 **B**

2 **C** – Money financial capital maintenance looks at the actual physical cash. Physical capital maintenance considers specific price rises while real financial capital maintenance considers general inflation.

3 **A** – Physical capital maintenance looks at profit in terms of the physical productive capacity of the business, taking into account specific price changes relevant to the entity.

4 **A** – In times of rising prices, asset values will be understated, as historical cost will not be a true representation of the asset values. Additionally, the real purchase cost of replacement items will not be incorporated, meaning that profits are overstated.

Chapter

8

Other standards

Chapter learning objectives

Upon completion of this chapter you will be able to:

- distinguish between an accounting policy and an accounting estimate
- describe how IAS 8 applies the principle of comparability where an entity changes its accounting policies
- account for a change in accounting policy and change in estimate
- recognise and account for a prior period adjustment
- describe and discuss fair value in accordance with IFRS 13
- explain the principles of IAS 2 with regard to the valuation of inventory
- define key terms in relation to agriculture per IAS 41
- apply the principles of IAS 41 with regard to the valuation of agriculture items.

PER

One of the PER performance objectives (PO6) is to record and process transactions and events. You use the right accounting treatments for transactions and events. These should be both historical and prospective – and include non-routine transactions. Working though this chapter should help you understand how to demonstrate that objective.

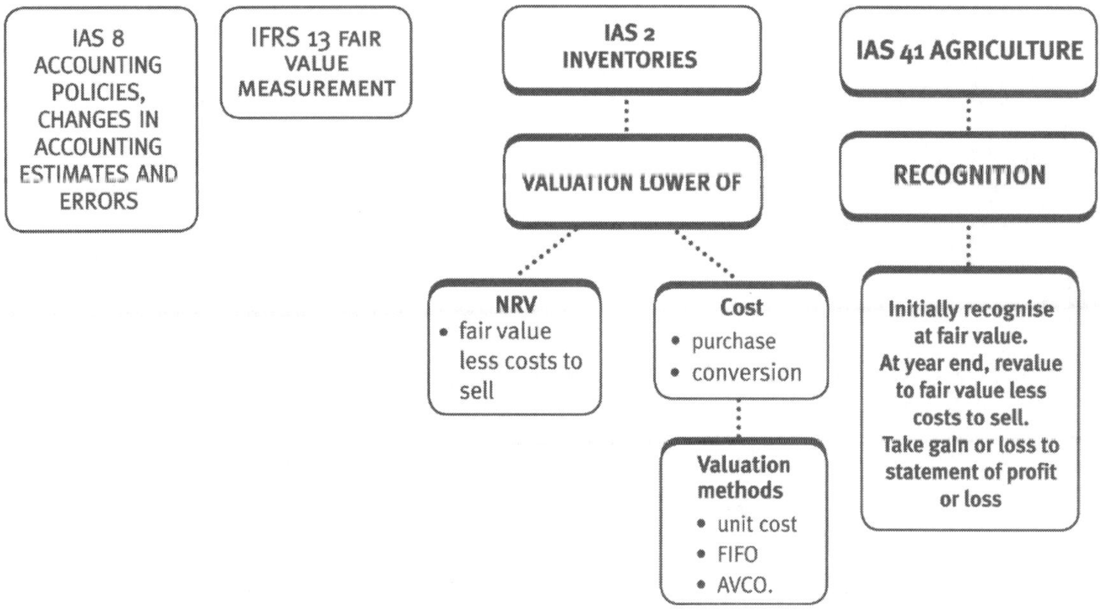

1 IAS 8 Accounting Policies, Changes in Accounting Estimates and Errors

IAS 8 Accounting Policies, Estimates and Errors

Introduction

IAS 8 governs the following topics:

- selection of accounting policies
- changes in accounting policies
- changes in accounting estimates
- correction of prior period errors.

Accounting policies

'Accounting policies are the specific principles, bases, conventions, rules and practices applied by an entity in preparing and presenting financial statements' (IAS 8, para 5).

IAS 8 requires an entity to select and apply appropriate accounting policies complying with International Financial Reporting Standards (IFRS Standards) and Interpretations to ensure that the financial statements provide **'information that is:**

- **relevant to the economic decision-making needs of users**
- **reliable in that the financial statements**
  - **represent faithfully the financial position, financial performance and cash flows of the entity**
  - **reflect the economic substance of transactions, other events and conditions and not merely the legal form**
  - **are neutral, i.e. free from bias**
  - **are prudent, and**
  - **are complete in all material respects'** (IAS 8, para 10)

Changing accounting policies

The general rule is that accounting policies are normally unchanged from period to period to ensure comparability of financial statements over time.

IAS 8 requires accounting policies to be changed **'only if the change:**

- **is required by an IFRS Standard** or
- **results in the financial statements providing reliable and more relevant information'** (IAS 8, para 14).

A change in accounting policy occurs if there has been a change in:

- recognition, e.g. an expense is now recognised rather than an asset
- presentation, e.g. depreciation is now included in cost of sales rather than administrative expenses, or
- measurement basis, e.g. stating assets at replacement cost rather than historical cost.

Accounting for a change in accounting policy

The required accounting treatment is that:

- the change should be applied retrospectively, with an adjustment to the opening balance of retained earnings in the statement of changes in equity
- comparative information should be restated unless it is impracticable to do so
- if the adjustment to opening retained earnings cannot be reasonably determined, the change should be adjusted prospectively, i.e. included in the current period's statement of profit or loss.

Accounting estimates

An **accounting estimate** is a method adopted by an entity to arrive at estimated amounts for the financial statements.

Most figures in the financial statements require some estimation:

- the exercise of judgement based on the latest information available at the time
- at a later date, estimates may have to be revised as a result of the availability of new information, more experience or subsequent developments.

Changes in accounting estimates

The requirements of IAS 8 are:

- The effects of a change in accounting estimate should be included in the statement of profit or loss in the period of the change and, if subsequent periods are affected, in those subsequent periods.
- The effects of the change should be included in the same income or expense classification as was used for the original estimate.
- If the effect of the change is material, its nature and amount must be disclosed.

Examples of changes in accounting estimates are changes in:

- the useful lives of non-current assets
- the residual values of non-current assets
- the method of depreciating non-current assets
- warranty provisions, based upon more up-to-date information about claims frequency and value.

e.g

Illustration 1 – Accounting estimates

If a non-current asset has a depreciable amount of $5,000 to be written off over five years, different depreciation methods such as straight line, reducing balance etc. all represent different estimation techniques.

The choice of method of depreciation would be the estimation technique whereas the policy of writing off the depreciable amount of non-current assets over their useful lives would be the accounting policy.

Estimation techniques therefore implement the measurement aspects of accounting policies.

e.g

Illustration 2 – Accounting policies v Accounting estimates

Which of the following is a change in accounting policy as opposed to a change in estimation technique?

1. An entity has previously charged interest incurred in connection with the construction of tangible non-current assets to the statement of profit or loss. Following the revision of IAS 23 *Borrowing Costs*, and in accordance with the revised requirements of that standard, it now capitalises this interest.
2. An entity has previously depreciated vehicles using the reducing balance method at 40% pa. It now uses the straight-line method over a period of five years.
3. An entity has previously shown certain overheads within cost of sales. It now shows those overheads within administrative expenses.
4. An entity has previously measured inventory at weighted average cost. It now measures inventory using the first in first out (FIFO) method.

Solution

For each of the items, ask whether this involves a change to:

- recognition
- presentation
- measurement basis.

If the answer to any of these is yes, the change is a change in accounting policy.

1 This is a change in recognition and presentation. Therefore this is a change in accounting policy.

2 The answer to all three questions is no. This is only a change in estimation technique.

3 This is a change in presentation and therefore a change in accounting policy.

4 This is a change in measurement basis and therefore a change in accounting policy.

Prior period errors

Prior period errors are omissions from, and misstatements in, the financial statements for one or more prior periods arising from a failure to use information that:

- was available when the financial statements for those periods were authorised for issue and
- could reasonably be expected to have been taken into account in preparing those financial statements.

Such errors include mathematical mistakes, mistakes in applying accounting policies, oversights and fraud.

Current period errors that are discovered in that period should be corrected before the financial statements are authorised for issue.

Correction of prior period errors

Prior period errors are dealt with by:

- restating the opening balance of assets, liabilities and equity as if the error had never occurred, and presenting the necessary adjustment to the opening balance of retained earnings in the statement of changes in equity
- restating the comparative figures presented, as if the error had never occurred
- disclosing within the accounts a statement of financial position at the beginning of the earliest comparative period. In effect this means that three statements of financial position will be presented within a set of financial statements:
  - at the end of the current year
  - at the end of the previous year
  - at the beginning of the previous year.

e.g

Illustration 3 – Prior period errors

During 20X1 a company discovered that certain items had been included in inventory at 31 December 20X0 at a value of $2.5 million but they had in fact been sold before the year end.

The original figures reported for the year ending 31 December 20X0 and the figures for the current year 20X1 are given below:

	20X1	**20X0**
	$000	$000
Sales	52,100	48,300
Cost of sales	(33,500)	(30,200)
Gross profit	18,600	18,100
Tax	(4,600)	(4,300)
Net profit	14,000	13,800

The retained earnings at 1 January 20X0 were $11.2 million. The cost of goods sold in 20X1 includes the $2.5 million error in opening inventory.

Show the 20X1 statement of profit or loss with comparative figures and the retained earnings for each year. Disclosure of other comprehensive income is not required. Assume that the adjustment will have no effect on the tax charge.

Solution

Statement of profit or loss

	20X1	**20X0**
	$000	$000
Sales	52,100	48,300
Cost of sales:		
20X1 (33,500 – 2,500)	(31,000)	
20X0 (30,200 + 2,500)		(32,700)
Gross profit	21,100	15,600
Tax	(4,600)	(4,300)
Net profit	16,500	11,300

Retained earnings

	20X1	20X0
Opening retained earnings	$000	$000
As previously reported		
$(11,200 + 13,800)	25,000	11,200
Prior period adjustment	(2,500)	–
As restated	22,500	11,200
Net profit for the year	16,500	11,300
Closing retained earnings	39,000	22,500

2 IFRS 13 Fair Value Measurement

The objective of IFRS 13 is to provide a single source of guidance for fair value measurement, where it is required by a reporting standard rather than being spread throughout several reporting standards. IFRS 13 will improve comparability between the many standards that require fair value measurement or fair value disclosures.

Definition

Fair value is the price that would be received to sell an asset or paid to transfer a liability in an orderly transaction between market participants at the measurement date (i.e. an exit price).

Fair value may be required to be measured on a recurring basis or a non-recurring basis see below).

IFRS 13 establishes a hierarchy that categorises the inputs to valuation techniques used to measure fair value as follows:

- Level 1 inputs comprise quoted prices ('observable') in active markets for identical assets and liabilities at the measurement date. This is regarded as providing the most reliable evidence of fair value and is likely to be used without adjustment.
- Level 2 inputs are observable inputs, other than those included within Level 1 above, which are observable directly or indirectly. This may include quoted prices for similar (not identical) assets or liabilities in active markets, or prices for identical or similar assets and liabilities in inactive markets. Typically, they are likely to require some degree of adjustment to arrive at a fair value measurement.
- Level 3 inputs are unobservable inputs for an asset or liability, based upon the best information available, including information that may be reasonably available relating to market participants.

Recurring and non-recurring basis

Recurring basis

Fair value on a recurring basis arises when a reporting standard requires fair value to be measured on an ongoing basis. An example of this is IAS 40 *Investment Property* (Chapter 2).

Non-recurring basis

Fair value on a non-recurring basis arises when a reporting standard requires fair value to be measured at fair value only in certain specified circumstances. This would apply, for example, with the application of IFRS 3 (Revised) *Business Combinations* (Chapter 18) where items are measured at fair value at the date of acquisition.

Measurement

When measuring fair value an entity shall take into account the characteristics of the asset or liability. Such characteristics include, for example, the following:

- the condition and location of the asset; and
- restrictions, if any, on the sale or use of the asset

An entity shall measure the fair value of an asset or a liability using the assumptions that market participants would use when pricing the asset or liability, assuming that market participants act in their economic best interest.

The fair value of an asset or liability shall not be adjusted for transaction costs (transaction costs will be accounted for in accordance with other IFRS Standards).

Exclusions from IFRS 13

IFRS 13 does not apply to IFRS 16 *Leases* (Chapter 12) or to situations where different measurements are required, such as net realisable value (IAS 2 *Inventories* – Chapter 8) or value in use (IAS 36 *Impairment of Assets* – Chapter 4) which may be required by some reporting standards.

Disclosure

An entity shall disclose information that helps users of its financial statements assess both of the following:

- for assets and liabilities that are measured at fair value on a recurring or non-recurring basis in the statement of financial position after initial recognition, the valuation techniques and inputs used to develop those measurements.
- for recurring fair value measurements using significant unobservable inputs, the effect of the measurements on profit or loss or other comprehensive income for the period.

3 Accounting for inventory

IAS 2 Inventories

Inventories are valued at the lower of cost and net realisable value (NRV).

Definition of cost

Cost is the cost of bringing items of inventory to their present location and condition (including cost of purchase and costs of conversion).

Definition of cost

Cost of purchase comprises:

- purchase price including import duties, transport and handling costs
- any other directly attributable costs, less trade discounts, rebates and subsidies.

Cost of conversion comprises:

- costs which are specifically attributable to units of production, e.g. direct labour, direct expenses and subcontracted work
- production overheads, which must be based on the normal level of activity
- other overheads, if any, attributable in the particular circumstances of the business to bringing the product or service to its present location and condition.

The following costs should be excluded and charged as expenses of the period in which they are incurred:

- abnormal waste
- storage costs
- administrative overheads which do not contribute to bringing inventories to their present location and condition
- selling costs.

Definition of Net Realisable Value (NRV)

NRV is the estimated selling price, in the ordinary course of business, less the estimated costs of completion and the estimated costs necessary to make the sale.

Inventory valuation methods

IAS 2 deals with three methods of arriving at cost:

- actual unit cost
- first in, first out (FIFO)
- weighted average cost (AVCO).

Where items of inventory are not ordinarily interchangeable (e.g. used cars), IAS 2 requires the actual unit cost valuation method to be used. Such items should be shown at their actual individual costs.

Where items are ordinarily interchangeable (e.g. tins of beans), the entity must choose between two cost formulae: the FIFO method and the AVCO method.

The same method of arriving at cost should be used for all inventories having similar nature and use to the entity. For inventories with a different nature or use, different cost methods may be justified.

Disclosure requirements

The main disclosure requirements of IAS 2 are:

- accounting policy adopted, including the cost formula used
- total carrying amount, classified appropriately
- amount of inventories carried at NRV
- amount of inventories recognised as an expense during the period
- details of any circumstances that have led to the write-down of inventories to their NRV.

Illustration 4 – Inventory valuation

Value the following items of inventory.

(a) Materials costing $12,000 bought for processing and assembly for a profitable special order. Since buying these items, the cost price has fallen to $10,000.

(b) Equipment constructed for a customer for an agreed price of $18,000. This has recently been completed at a cost of $16,800. It has now been discovered that, in order to meet certain regulations, conversion with an extra cost of $4,200 will be required. The customer has accepted partial responsibility and agreed to meet half the extra cost.

Solution

(a) Value at $12,000. $10,000 is irrelevant. The rule is lower of cost or NRV, not lower of cost or replacement cost. Since the special order is known to be profitable, the NRV will be above cost.

(b) Value at NRV, i.e. $15,900, as this is below cost of $16,800.

(NRV = contract price, $18,000 – our share of modification cost, $2,100).

4 IAS 41 Agriculture

Scope of IAS 41

IAS 41 *Agriculture* relates to Biological assets, government grants and agricultural produce **at the point of harvest**. Products which are the result of processing after harvest will be dealt with under IAS 2 *Inventories*, or other applicable standards.

The table below gives examples of each.

Biological assets (included in IAS 41, except bearer plants)	**Agricultural produce** (included in IAS 41 at the point of harvest, treated as inventory after that point)	**Products resulting from processing after harvest** (outside the scope of IAS 41)
Sheep	Wool	Yarn, carpet
Trees in a timber plantation	Felled trees	Logs, lumber
Dairy cattle	Milk	Cheese
Pigs	Carcass	Sausages, cured hams
Cotton plants	Harvested cotton	Thread, clothing
Sugarcane	Harvested cane	Sugar
Tobacco plants	Picked leaves	Cured tobacco
Tea bushes	Picked leaves	Tea
Grape vines	Picked grapes	Wine
Fruit trees	Picked fruit	Processed fruit
Oil palms	Picked fruit	Palm oil
Rubber trees	Harvested latex	Rubber products

Biological assets

A biological asset is a living animal or plant. A biological asset should be recognised if:

- It is probable that economic benefits will flow to the entity
- The cost or fair value of the asset can be reliably measured, and
- The entity controls the asset.

Recognition and measurement

Initial measurement is at:

- Fair value less any estimated 'point of sale' costs
- If there is no fair value, then the cost model should be used.

Subsequent measurement:

- Revalue to fair value less point of sale costs at year-end, taking any gain or loss to the statement of profit or loss.

Bearer plants

Bearer plants are accounted for under IAS 16 *Property, Plant and Equipment*, rather than IAS 41 *Agriculture*. A bearer plant is a living plant that:

- is used in the production or supply of agricultural produce;
- is expected to bear fruit for more than one period; and
- has a remote likelihood of being sold as agricultural produce, except for incidental scrap sales

Therefore items such as vines, tea bushes and fruit trees may be classed as bearer plants and treated as property, plant and equipment rather than being accounted for under the provisions of IAS 41 *Agriculture*.

Agricultural produce

At the date of harvest the produce should be recognised and measured at fair value less estimated costs to sell.

- Gains and losses on initial recognition are included in profit or loss (profit from operations) for the period.
- After produce has been harvested, IAS 41 ceases to apply. Agricultural produce becomes an item of inventory. Fair value less costs to sell at the point of harvest is taken as cost for the purpose of IAS 2 *Inventories*, which is applied from then onwards.

Fair value

Agriculture is fundamentally different from other types of business. Most non-current assets wear out or are consumed over time and therefore they are depreciated. Many agricultural assets grow, rather than wear out. Arguably, depreciation is irrelevant in this situation. Therefore biological assets are measured at fair value and changes in fair value are reported as part of profit for the period. This means that a farmer's profit for the year reflects the increase in the value of his productive assets as a whole, as well as the profit on any sales made during the year.

Many commentators have been wary of this departure from traditional realisation concepts, claiming that it is wrong to recognise profit before a sale has been made. Indeed, under IAS 41 profits could be recognised years before the products are even ready for sale. However, supporters of IAS 41 claim that the opposite is true. By requiring all changes in the value of a farm to be reported openly, farm managers will be unable to boost profits by selling off an unsustainable amount of produce.

For instance, under traditional accounting rules a forestry company could make huge short-term profits by felling all of its trees without replacing them. Profit would reflect the sales but ignore the fall in value of the forest.

IAS 41 contains a rebuttable presumption that the fair value of a biological asset can be measured reliably. Many biological assets are traded on an active market, so it is normally easy to determine the fair value of an asset by ascertaining the quoted price in that market.

If there is no active market for the asset then it may be possible to estimate fair value by using:

- the most recent market price
- the market price for a similar asset
- the discounted cash flows from the asset
- net realisable value.

If there is no active market and the alternative methods of estimating fair value are clearly unreliable, then a biological asset is measured at cost less depreciation on initial recognition until a reliable fair value can be established. For example, seedlings being grown on a plantation will not have any market value until they are a few years old.

Gains and losses can arise when a biological asset is first recognised. For example, a loss can arise because estimated selling costs are deducted from fair value. A gain can arise when a new biological asset (such as a lamb or a calf) is born.

Government grants and biological assets

Government grants

IAS 41 applies to government grants related to a biological asset.

- Unconditional government grants received in respect of biological assets measured at fair value are reported as income when the grant becomes receivable.
- If such a grant is conditional (including where the grant requires an entity not to engage in certain agricultural activity), the entity recognises it as income only when the conditions have been met.

Assets outside the scope of IAS 41

IAS 41 does not apply to intangible assets (e.g. production quotas) or to land related to agricultural activity.

- Intangible assets are measured the cost or fair value model in accordance with IAS 38 *Intangible Assets* in Chapter 3.
- Land is not a biological asset. It is treated as a tangible non-current asset and IAS 16 *Property, Plant and Equipment* applies. This means that (for example) when a forest is valued, the trees must be valued separately from the land that they grow on.

Test your understanding 1

A herd of five 4 year-old pigs was held on 1 January 20X3. On 1 July 20X3 a 4.5 year-old pig was purchased for $212.

The fair values less estimated point of sale costs were:

- 4 year-old pig at 1 January 20X3 $200
- 4.5 year-old pig at 1 July 20X3 $212
- 5 year-old pig at 31 December 20X3 $230

Required:

Calculate the amount that will be taken to the statement of profit or loss for the year ended 31 December 20X3.

Test your understanding 2

McDonald operates a dairy farm. At 1 January 20X1, he owns 100 cows worth $1,000 each on the local market. At 31 December 20X1, he owns 105 cows worth $1,100 each. During 20X1 he sold 40,000 gallons of milk at an average price of $5 a gallon. When cows are sold at the local market, the auctioneer charges a commission of 4%.

Show extracts from the financial statements for 20X1 for these activities, assuming that no cows were purchased or sold during the year.

5 Chapter summary

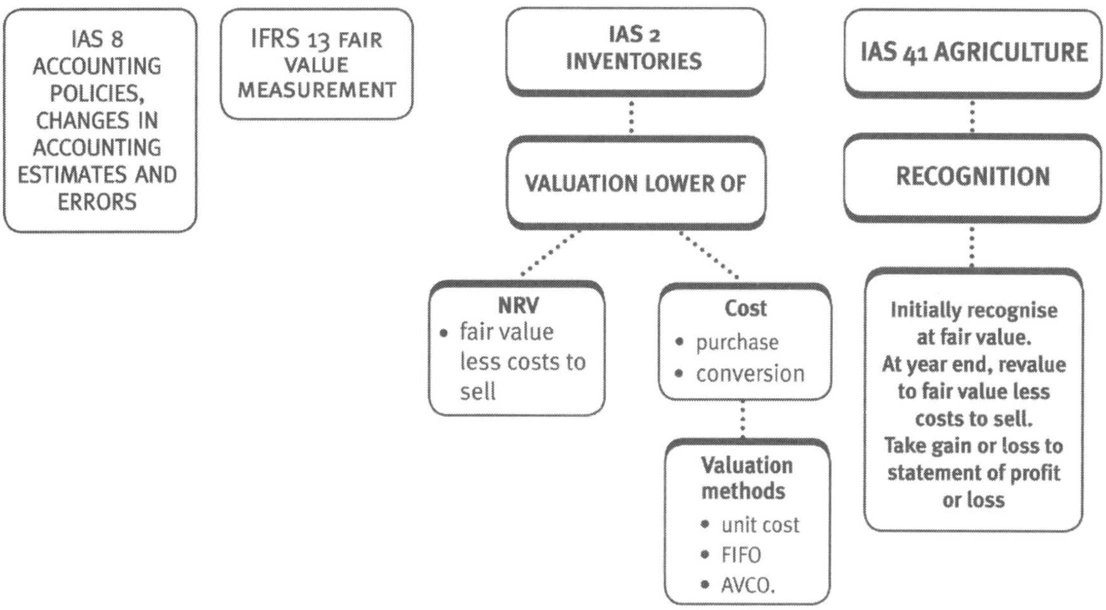

Test your understanding 3

1 **Which TWO of the following situations would not require a prior year adjustment per IAS 8 *Accounting Policies, Changes in Accounting Estimates and Errors*?**

A In last year's financial statements, inventories were understated by a material amount due to system error

B A company has changed its allowance for irrecoverable receivables from 10% of outstanding debt to everything over 120 days old

C A new accounting standard has been issued that requires a company to change its accounting policy but gives no guidance on the specific application of the change itself

D A company has chosen to value inventory using FIFO rather than AVCO as in previous periods

E A company has decided to move from charging depreciation on the straight line basis to the reducing balance basis

2 **In accordance with IAS 8 *Accounting Policies, Changes in Accounting Estimates and Errors* how is a change in accounting estimate accounted for?**

A By changing the current year figures but not the previous years' figures

B By changing the current year figures and the previous years' figures

C No alteration of any figures but disclosure in the notes

D Neither alteration of any figures nor disclosure in the notes

3 **Which ONE of the following statements regarding IFRS 13 *Fair Value Measurement* is NOT true?**

A Level 1 inputs are likely to be used without adjustment

B Level 1 inputs comprise quoted prices in active markets for identical assets and liabilities at the reporting date

C Level 2 inputs may include quoted prices for similar (but not identical) assets and liabilities in active markets

D Level 3 inputs are based on the best information available to market participants and are therefore regarded as providing the most reliable evidence of fair value

4 IAS 2 *Inventories* requires inventory to be valued at the lower of cost and net realisable value. Cost includes all expenditure incurred in bringing the items to their present location and condition.

Which of the following would NOT normally be included as part of the cost of inventory in a manufacturing business?

(i) Costs of transporting finished goods to customers' premises

(ii) Storage costs for raw materials, stored at the premises of a third party

(iii) Discounts allowed for prompt payment by customers

(iv) Discounts received for bulk purchases

A (ii) and (iv) only

B (iii) only

C (i) and (iii) only

D (i) and (iv) only

5 The following costs relate to a unit of goods:

Cost of raw materials $1, Direct labour $0.50

During the year $60,000 of production overheads were incurred. 8,000 units were produced during the year which is lower than the normal level of 10,000 units. This was as a result of a fault with some machinery which resulted in 2,000 units having to be scrapped. At the year-end, 700 units are in closing inventory.

What is the value of closing inventory?

$ _________

6 Posh plc has the following units in inventory at the end of 20X9.

	Units	**Cost per unit ($)**
Raw materials	5,000	25
Work in progress	2,000	30
Finished goods	1,000	35

Finished items usually sell for $50 per unit. However, water damage caused by improper storage of inventory will mean that 300 units of finished goods will be sold at 60% of the normal selling price less costs to sell of $5 per item. A further $5.50 per unit is still to be incurred to finish off the items of work in progress.

In accordance with IAS 2 *Inventories*, at what amount should inventories be stated in the statement of financial position of Posh plc as at the end of 20X9?

$ _________

7 Jacs owned a one year-old herd of cattle on 1 January 20X6, recognised in the financial statements at $140,000. At 31 December 20X6, the fair value of a two year-old herd of cattle is $170,000. Costs to sell are estimated to be $5,000.

What is the correct accounting treatment for the cattle at 31 December 20X6 according to IAS 41 *Agriculture*?

A Revalue to $165,000, taking gain of $25,000 to other comprehensive income

B Revalue to $165,000, taking gain of $25,000 to the statement of profit or loss

C Revalue to $170,000, taking gain of $30,000 to other comprehensive income

D Revalue to $170,000, taking gain of $30,000 to the statement of profit or loss

8 **Identify which of the following items would be accounted for under the provisions of IAS 41 *Agriculture*.**

Item	**Accounted for under IAS 41 *Agriculture***	**Not accounted for under IAS 41 *Agriculture***
Sheep		
Wine		
Wool		

Test your understanding answers

Test your understanding 1

The movement in the fair value less estimated costs to sell of the herd can be reconciled as follows.

	$
1 January 20X6 Pigs b/f 5 × $200	1,000
Purchased during year	212
	1,212
Gain to profit or loss (balancing figure)	168
31 December 20X6 Pigs c/f 6 × $230	1,380

Test your understanding 2

Statement of profit or loss:

Revenue from the sales of milk (40,000 × $5)	$200,000
Gain from increase in value of herd **(W1)**	$14,880

Statement of financial position:

Non-current assets

Herd of dairy cows **(W1)**	$110,880

(W1)

Valuation at 31 Dec X1: (105 × $1,100 × (100 – 4)%)	110,880
Valuation at 31 Dec X0: (100 × $1,000 × (100 – 4)%)	96,000
Increase in value	14,880

Test your understanding 3

1 **B and E** – A change in the calculation of the allowance for irrecoverable receivables, and a change in the depreciation method, are changes in accounting estimate so therefore require prospective adjustment only.

2 **A**

3 **D** – Level 3 inputs do include the best information available, but this is not regarded as the most reliable evidence of fair value, as level 1 inputs are likely to be the most reliable evidence.

4 **C**

5 **$5,250**

	$
Raw material	1.00
Direct labour	0.50
Production overheads ($60,000/10,000)	6.00
	7.50

$7.50 × 700 = **$5,250**

The allocation of fixed production overheads is based on the normal capacity of the production facilities. The amount of fixed overhead allocated to each unit of production is not increased as a consequence of low production or idle plant.

6 **$217,000.**

Inventory should be at the lower of cost and NRV. The costs are as follows:

	Units	Cost per unit ($)	Total cost ($)
Raw materials	5,000	25	125,000
Work in progress (WIP)	2,000	30	60,000
Finished goods	700	35	24,500

The NRV of the WIP is equal to the sale price less selling costs and costs to complete, $39.50 ($50 – $5 – $5.50). As this is above cost, the WIP is valued at cost.

The other 300 finished goods have a NRV below cost due to the damage. These could be sold for 60% of the normal selling price, which is $30, less the $5 selling costs = $25. The NRV of the finished goods is therefore 300 × $25 = $7,500

The total value of year-end inventory =
$125,000 + $60,000 + $24,500 + $7,500 = **$217,000**

7 **B** – Agriculture should be revalued to fair value less costs to sell, with the gain or loss being shown in the statement of profit or loss.

8

Item	**Accounted for under IAS 41 *Agriculture***	**Not accounted for under IAS 41 *Agriculture***
Sheep	X	
Wine		X
Wool	X	

Chapter

9

Financial assets and financial liabilities

Chapter learning objectives

Upon completion of this chapter you will be able to:

- explain the need for an accounting standard on financial instruments
- define financial instruments in terms of financial assets and financial liabilities
- distinguish between the categories of financial instruments
- indicate for the categories of financial instruments how they should be measured and how any gains and losses from subsequent measurement should be treated in the financial statements
- explain how fair value through profit or loss financial instruments should be measured and how any gains/losses from subsequent measurement should be treated in the financial statements
- distinguish between debt and equity capital
- account for the issue of redeemable preference shares and payment of preference share dividends
- account for the issue of debt instruments with no conversion rights and the payment of interest
- account for compound instruments
- account for the derecognition of financial instruments, including issues surrounding factoring.

PER

One of the PER performance objectives (PO6) is to record and process transactions and events. You use the right accounting treatments for transactions and events. These should be both historical and prospective – and include non-routine transactions. Working though this chapter should help you understand how to demonstrate that objective.

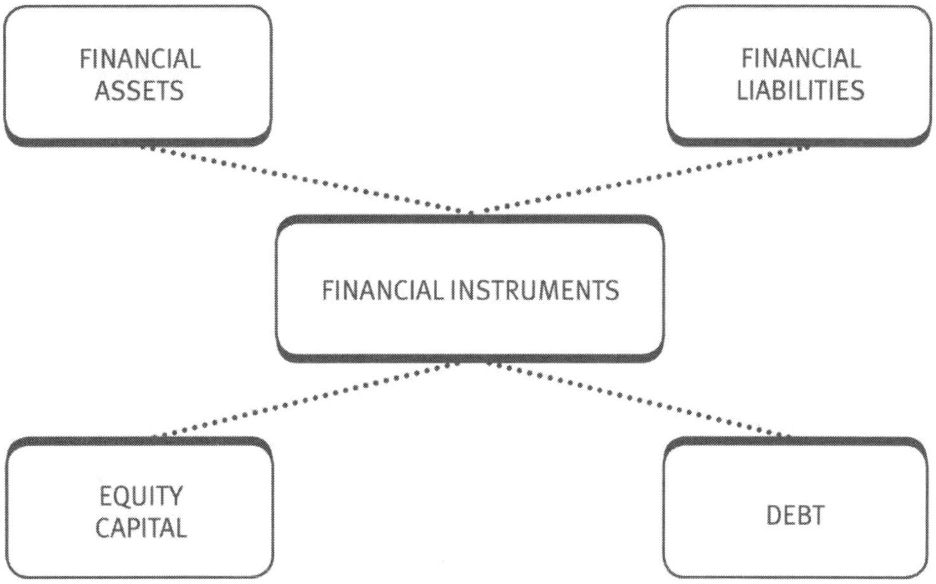

1 Financial instruments

Introduction

A **financial instrument** is any contract that gives rise to a financial asset of one entity and a financial liability or equity instrument of another entity.

Need for accounting standard

In recent years there has been a huge growth worldwide in the variety and complexity of financial instruments in international financial markets.

There were numerous concerns about the accounting practices used for financial instruments which led to demands for an accounting standard. The concerns included the following:

- there had been significant growth in the number and complexity of financial instruments
- accounting standards had not developed in line with the growth in instruments
- there had been a particular problem with derivatives (e.g. forwards, futures, swaps, etc.)
- unrealised gains/losses on many financial instruments were not recognised
- entities could choose when to recognise profits on instruments in order to smooth profits.

Accounting standards

There are three reporting standards that deal with financial instruments:

- IAS 32 ***Financial Instruments: Presentation***
- IFRS 7 ***Financial Instruments: Disclosures***
- IFRS 9 ***Financial Instruments***

IAS 32 deals with the classification of financial instruments and their presentation in financial statements.

IFRS 9 deals with how financial instruments are measured and when they should be recognised in financial statements.

IFRS 7 deals with the disclosure of financial instruments in financial statements.

Financial assets

A **financial asset** is any asset that is:

- **'cash'**
- **'a contractual right to receive cash or another financial asset from another entity'**
- **'a contractual right to exchange financial assets or liabilities with another entity under conditions that are potentially favourable'**
- **'an equity instrument of another entity'**

(IAS 32, para 11)

Examples of financial assets include:

- trade receivables
- options
- investments in equity shares.

Financial liabilities

A **financial liability** is any liability that is a contractual obligation:

- **'to deliver cash or another financial asset to another entity', or**
- **'to exchange financial assets or liabilities with another entity under conditions that are potentially unfavourable', or**
- **'that will or may be settled in the entity's own equity instruments.'**

(IAS 32, para 11)

Examples of financial liabilities include:

- trade payables
- debenture loans
- redeemable preference shares.

Illustration 1 – Financial instruments

Identify which of the following are financial instruments:

(a) inventories

(b) investment in ordinary shares

(c) prepayments for goods or services

(d) liability for income taxes

(e) a share option (an entity's obligation to issue its own shares).

Solution

(a) Inventory (or any other physical asset such as non-current assets) is not a financial instrument since there is no present contractual right to receive cash or other financial instruments.

(b) An investment in ordinary shares is a financial asset since it is an equity instrument of another entity.

(c) Prepayments for goods or services are not financial instruments since the future economic benefit will be the receipt of goods or services rather than a financial asset.

(d) A liability for income taxes is not a financial instrument since the obligation is statutory rather than contractual.

(e) A share option is a financial instrument since a contractual obligation exists to deliver an equity instrument.

2 Financial liabilities

Initial recognition of financial liabilities

A financial liability is initially recognised at its fair value. This is usually the **net proceeds of** the cash received less any costs of issuing the liability.

Subsequent measurement of financial liabilities

Financial liabilities will be carried at amortised cost, other than liabilities held for trading and derivatives that are liabilities, both of which are unlikely to be seen within FR.

Amortised cost is calculated as:

Initial value + effective interest – interest paid

The effective interest will be different to the interest paid if there are additional costs of borrowing, such as redemption premiums, issue costs or discounts on issue. An example of this type of liability is a deep-discount bond.

Deep discount bonds

One common form of financial instrument is a deep discount bond.

A deep-discount bond has the following features.

- This instrument is issued at a significant discount to its nominal value.
- Typically it has a coupon rate of interest much lower than the market rate.
- The full cost of borrowing is likely to include:
  - issue costs
  - discount on issue
  - annual interest payments
  - premium on redemption.

The initial carrying amount of the bond will be the net proceeds of issue.

The full finance cost will be charged over the life of the instrument so as to give a constant periodic rate of interest.

The constant periodic rate of interest (sometimes called the effective rate) can be calculated in the same way that an internal rate of return is calculated. In FR exam questions the effective rate of interest will be given.

These bonds, like most financial liabilities, will be measured at amortised cost:

Initial value + effective interest – interest paid

Illustration 2 – Measurement of financial liabilities

loan note is issued for $1,000. The loan note is redeemable at $1,250. The term of the loan is five years and interest is paid at 5.9% pa. The effective rate of interest is 10%.

Show how the value of the loan note changes over its life.

Solution

This financial liability should be valued at amortised cost.

The debt would initially be recognised at $1,000. The total finance cost of the debt is the difference between the payments required by the debt which total $1,545 ((5 × $59 interest) + $1,250 redemption) and the proceeds of $1,000, that is $545.

- The movements on the carrying amount of the debt over its term would be as follows:

Year	Balance at beginning of year	Finance cost for year (10%)	Cost paid during year	Balance at end of year
	$	$	$	$
1	1,000	100	(59)	1,041
2	1,041	104	(59)	1,086
3	1,086	109	(59)	1,136
4	1,136	113	(59)	1,190
5	1,190	119	(1,250 + 59)	–
		545		

- The amounts carried forward at each year end represent the amortised cost valuation to be shown in the statement of financial position.
- The carrying amount of the debt (amortised cost) is the net proceeds, plus finance charges recognised in the accounts, less payments made.

Test your understanding 1

1 A company issues 5% loan notes at their nominal value of $20,000 with an effective rate of 5%. The loan notes are repayable at par after 4 years.

What amount will be recorded as a financial liability when the loan notes are issued?

What amounts will be shown in the statement of profit or loss and statement of financial position for years 1–4?

2 A company issues 0% loan notes at their nominal value of $40,000. The loan notes are repayable at a premium of $11,800 after 3 years. The effective rate of interest is 9%.

What amount will be recorded as a financial liability when the loan notes are issued?

What amounts will be shown in the statement of profit or loss and statement of financial position for years 1–3?

3 A company issues 4% loan notes with a nominal value of $20,000.

The loan notes are issued at a discount of 2.5% and $534 of issue costs are incurred.

The loan notes will be repayable at a premium of 10% after 5 years. The effective rate of interest is 7%.

What amount will be recorded as a financial liability when the loan notes are issued?

What amounts will be shown in the statement of profit or loss and statement of financial position for year 1?

Preference shares

If irredeemable preference shares contain no obligation to make any payment, either of capital or dividend, they are classified as equity.

If preference shares are redeemable, or have a fixed cumulative dividend they are classified as a financial liability.

The key element is that where there is an obligation, the instrument represents a liability.

Preference shares

Some preference shares are irredeemable, in which case they are classified as equity. When a preference share provides for mandatory redemption by the issuer for a fixed or determinable amount at a fixed or determinable future date, or gives the holder the right to require the issuer to redeem the share at or after a particular date for a fixed or determinable amount, the instrument meets the definition of a financial liability and is classified as such.

Interest and dividends

The accounting treatment of interest and dividends depends upon the accounting treatment of the underlying instrument itself:

- equity dividends declared are reported directly in equity
- dividends on instruments classified as a liability are treated as a finance cost in the statement of profit or loss.

Test your understanding 2

On 1 April 20X7, a company issued 40,000 $1 redeemable preference shares with a coupon rate of 8% at par. They are redeemable at a large premium which gives them an effective finance cost of 12% per annum.

How would these redeemable preference shares appear in the financial statements for the years ending 31 March 20X8 and 20X9?

Classification as liability or equity

The substance of a financial instrument may differ from its legal form. Some financial instruments take the legal form of equity but in substance are liabilities. Others may combine features associated with both equity and liabilities.

The critical feature in differentiating a financial liability from an equity instrument is the existence of a contractual obligation on one party to the financial instrument (the issuer) either to deliver cash or another financial asset to the other party (the holder) or to exchange another financial asset/liability with the holder under conditions that are potentially unfavourable to the issuer. When such a contractual obligation exists, that instrument meets the definition of a financial liability regardless of the manner in which the contractual obligation will be settled.

A restriction on the ability of the issuer to satisfy an obligation, such as lack of access to foreign currency or the need to obtain approval for payment from a regulatory authority, does not negate the issuer's obligation or the holder's right under the instrument.

When a financial instrument does not give rise to such a contractual obligation, it is an equity instrument. Although the holder of an equity instrument may be entitled to receive a pro rata share of any dividends or other distributions declared by the issuer, the holder cannot under law force the issuer to declare dividends, so the issuer does not have a contractual obligation to make such distributions.

Compound instruments

A **compound instrument** is a financial instrument that has characteristics of both equity and liabilities, such as a convertible loan.

A convertible loan has the following characteristics:

- It is repayable, at the lender's option, in shares of the issuing company instead of cash
- The number of shares to be issued is fixed at the inception of the loan
- The lender will accept a rate of interest below the market rate for non-convertible instruments

As the lender is allowing the company a discounted rate in return for the potential issue of equity, these convertible instruments are accounted for using **split accounting**, recognising both their equity and liability components.

- There is a liability or debt element, as the issuer has the potential obligation to deliver cash
- There is also an equity element, as the investors may choose to convert the loan into shares instead.

The accounting for a convertible loan falls into two stages, initial and subsequent measurement.

Initial recognition

The liability is measured at its fair value. The fair value is the present value of the future cash flows (interest and capital) discounted using the market rate of interest for non-convertible debt instruments.

The equity element is equal to the loan proceeds less the calculated liability element.

Subsequent measurement

The liability is measured at amortised cost:

Initial value + market-rate interest – interest paid

The equity is not re-measured and remains at the same value on the statement of financial position until the debt is redeemed.

Convertible bonds

An entity issues a bond (debt) that can be converted into shares.

- The bondholder has the prospect of acquiring cheap shares in an entity, because the terms of conversion are normally quite generous. Even if the bondholder wants cash rather than shares, the deal may still be good. On maturity the cash-hungry bondholder will accept the conversion, and then sell the shares on the market for a profit.
- In exchange for this potential profit though, the bondholders normally have to accept a rate of interest below the market rate, and will have to wait some time before they receive the shares that form a large part of their return. There is also the risk that the entity's shares will underperform, making the eventual conversion unattractive.
- A compound financial instrument must be split into its component parts:
  - a financial liability (the debt)
  - an equity instrument (the option to convert into shares).
- These must be shown separately in the financial statements.

Illustration 3 – Compound instruments

Convert Co issues a convertible loan that pays interest of 2% per annum in arrears. The market rate is 8%, being the interest rate for an equivalent debt without the conversion option. The loan of $5 million is repayable in full after three years or convertible to equity. Discount factors are as follows:

Year	Discount factor at 8%
1	0.926
2	0.857
3	0.794

Required:

Split the loan between debt and equity at inception and calculate the finance charge for each year until conversion/redemption.

Solution

At inception

Year	Cash flow	Discount factor	Present value
	$000		$000
1	100	0.926	93
2	100	0.857	86
3	5,100	0.794	4,049

Debt	4,228
Equity (balancing figure)	772
Cash received	5,000

Year	Opening balance	Interest charged at 8%	Interest paid at 2%	Closing balance
1	4,228	338	(100)	4,466
2	4,466	357	(100)	4,723
3	4,723	377	(100)	5,000

Note: The carrying amount of the liability at the end of the 3 years will equal the amount to be repaid.

Test your understanding 3

1 An entity issues 2% convertible bonds at their nominal value of $36,000. Interest is payable annually in arrears.

The bonds are convertible at any time up to maturity into 40 ordinary shares for each $100 of bond. Alternatively the bonds will be redeemed at par after 3 years.

Similar non-convertible bonds would carry an interest rate of 9.1%. The present value of $1 payable at the end of year, based on rates of 2% and 9.1% are as follows:

End of year	2%	9.1%
1	0.98	0.92
2	0.96	0.84
3	0.94	0.77

What amounts will be shown as a financial liability and as equity when the convertible bonds are issued?

What amounts will be shown in the statement of profit or loss and statement of financial position for years 1–3?

Work to the nearest $000.

2 A company issues 4% convertible bonds at their nominal value of $5 million. Interest is payable annually in arrears.

Each $1,000 bond is convertible at any time up to maturity into 400 ordinary shares. Alternatively the bonds will be redeemed at par after 3 years.

The market rate applicable to non-convertible bonds is 6%.

The present value of $1 payable at the end of year, based on rates of 4% and 6% are as follows:

End of year	4%	6%
1	0.96	0.94
2	0.92	0.89
3	0.89	0.84

What amounts will be shown as a financial liability and as equity when the convertible bonds are issued?

What amounts will be shown in the statement of profit or loss and statement of financial position for years 1–3?

3 Financial assets

Initial recognition of financial assets

IFRS 9 deals with recognition and measurement of financial assets. **'An entity shall recognise a financial asset on its statement of financial position when, and only when, the entity becomes party to the contractual provisions of the instrument'** (IFRS 9, para 3.1.1)

Initial measurement of financial assets

At initial recognition, all financial assets are measured at fair value. This is likely to be the purchase consideration paid to acquire the financial asset. Transaction costs are included unless the asset is fair value through profit or loss.

4 Equity instruments

Equity instruments (purchases of shares in other entities) are measured at either:

- fair value through profit or loss, or
- fair value through other comprehensive income

Fair value through profit or loss

This is the default category for equity investments.

Any transaction costs associated with the purchase of these investments are expensed to profit or loss, and are not included within the initial value of the asset.

The investments are then revalued to fair value at each year-end, with any gain or loss being shown in the statement of profit or loss.

Fair value through other comprehensive income

Instead of classifying equity investments as fair value through profit or loss (FVPL), an entity may designate the investment as 'fair value through other comprehensive income' (FVOCI). This designation must be made on acquisition and can only be done if the investment is intended as a long- term investment. Once designated this category cannot later be changed to FVPL.

Under FVOCI:

- Transaction costs are capitalised
- The investments are revalued to fair value each year-end, with any gain or loss being shown in other comprehensive income and taken to an investment reserve in equity.

This is similar to a revaluation of property, plant and equipment under IAS 16. The main difference is that the investment reserve **can** be negative.

If a FVOCI investment is sold, the investment reserve can be transferred into retained earnings or left in equity.

Equity instruments – Further detail

The normal expectation is that equity instruments will have the designation of fair value through profit or loss, with the price paid to acquire the financial asset initially regarded as fair value. This could include unquoted equity investments, which may present problems in arriving at a reliable fair value at each reporting date. However, IFRS 9 does not include a general exception for unquoted equity investments to be measured at cost. Instead it provides guidance on when cost may, or may not, be regarded as a reliable indicator of fair value.

It is possible to designate an equity instrument as fair value through other comprehensive income, provided specified conditions have been complied with as follows:

- the equity instrument cannot be held for trading, and
- there must be an irrevocable choice for this designation upon initial recognition.

In this situation, initial recognition will also include directly attributable transaction costs. This may apply, for example, to strategic investments to be held on a continuing basis which are not held to take advantage of changes in fair value. The election to designate these investments at FVOCI would prevent any volatility in the share price being reflected within the entity's profits,

5 Debt instruments

Debt instruments (such as bonds or redeemable preference shares) are categorised in one of three ways:

- Fair value through profit or loss
- Amortised cost
- Fair value through other comprehensive income

The default category is again **fair value through profit or loss (FVPL)**. The other two categories depend on the instrument passing two tests:

- **Business model test.** This considers the entity's purpose in holding the investment.
- **Contractual cash flow characteristics test.** This looks at the cash that will be received as a result of holding the investment, and considers what it comprises.

Amortised cost

For an instrument to be carried at amortised cost, the two tests to be passed are:

- **Business model test.** The entity must intend to hold the investment to maturity.
- **Contractual cash flow characteristics test.** The contractual terms of the financial asset must give rise to cash flows that are solely of principal and interest.

If a debt instrument is held at amortised cost, the interest income (calculated using the effective interest as for liabilities) will be taken to the statement of profit or loss, and the year-end asset value is similarly calculated using an amortised cost table:

Balance b/f	Interest income	Payment received	Balance c/f
X	X	(X)	X

Fair value though other comprehensive income (FVOCI)

For an instrument to be carried at FVOCI, the two tests to be passed are:

- **Business model test.** The entity must intend to hold the investment to maturity but may sell the asset if the possibility of buying another asset with a higher return arises.
- **Contractual cash flow characteristics test.** The contractual terms of the financial asset must give rise to cash flows that are solely of principal and interest, as for amortised cost.

If a debt instrument is held at FVOCI

- The asset is initially recognised at fair value plus transaction costs
- Interest income is calculated using the effective rate of interest, in the same way as the amounts that would have been recognised in profit or loss if using amortised cost.
- At the reporting date, the asset will be revalued to fair value with the gain or loss recognised in other comprehensive income. This will be reclassified to profit or loss on disposal of the asset.

The contractual cash flow characteristics test

The contractual cash flow characteristics test determines whether the contractual terms of the financial asset give rise to cash flows on specified dates that are solely of principal and interest based upon the principal amount outstanding. If this is not the case, the test is failed and the financial asset must be measured at FVPL. For example, convertible bonds contain rights in addition to the repayment of interest and principal (the right to convert the bond to equity) and therefore would fail the test and must be accounted for at FVPL.

Debt instruments – Further detail

Even if a financial instrument passes both tests, it is still possible to designate a debt instrument as FVPL if doing so eliminates or significantly reduces a measurement or recognition inconsistency (i.e. accounting mismatch) that would otherwise arise from measuring assets or liabilities or from recognising the gains or losses on them on different bases.

Test your understanding 4

1 A company invests $5,000 in 10% loan notes. The loan notes are repayable at a premium after 3 years. The effective rate of interest is 12%. The company intends to collect the contractual cash flows which consist solely of repayments of interest and capital and have therefore chosen to record the financial asset at amortised cost.

What amounts will be shown in the statement of profit or loss and statement of financial position for the financial asset for years 1–3?

2 A company invested in 10,000 shares of a listed company in November 20X7 at a cost of $4.20 per share. At 31 December 20X7 the shares have a market value of $4.90.

Prepare extracts from the statement of profit or loss for the year ended 31 December 20X7 and a statement of financial position as at that date.

3 A company invested in 20,000 shares of a listed company in October 20X7 at a cost of $3.80 per share. At 31 December 20X7 the shares have a market value of $3.40. The company is not planning on selling these shares in the short term and elects to hold them as fair value through other comprehensive income.

Prepare extracts from the statement of profit or loss and other comprehensive income for the year ended 31 December 20X7 and a statement of financial position as at that date.

Test your understanding 5 – Bland

On 1 January 20X5 Bland bought a $10,000 6% bond for $9,000, incurring acquisition costs of $144. Interest is received annually in arrears, and the bond will be redeemed at a premium of $500 over its nominal value on 31 December 20X7. The effective rate of interest is 11%. The fair value of the bond was as follows:

31 December 20X5 $11,000

31 December 20X6 $10,400

Required:

Show how the bond will be accounted for over the three-year period if:

(a) **Bland planned to hold the bond until the redemption date.**

(b) **Bland may sell the bond if the possibility of an investment with a higher return arises.**

Offsetting financial assets/financial liabilities

In common with all IFRS Standards rules on offsetting, a financial asset and a financial liability may only be offset in very limited circumstances. The net amount may only be presented in the statement of financial position when the entity:

- has a legally enforceable right to set off the amounts, and
- intends either to settle on a net basis or to realise the asset and settle the liability simultaneously.

6 Derecognition

Derecognition of financial instruments

Financial instruments should be derecognised as follows:

- financial asset – **'when, and only when, the contractual rights to the cash flows from the financial asset expire'** (IFRS 9, para 3.2.3), e.g. when an option held by the entity has expired and become worthless or when the financial asset has been sold and the transfer qualifies for derecognition because substantially all the risks and rewards of ownership have been transferred from the seller to the buyer.
- financial liability – **'when, and only when, the obligation specified in the contract is discharged or cancelled or expires'** (IFRS 9, para 3.3.1).

On derecognition the difference between the carrying amount of the asset or liability, and the amount received or paid for it, should be included in the profit or loss for the period.

Factoring of receivables

Introduction

Factoring of receivables is where a company transfers its receivables balances to another organisation (a factor) for management and collection, and receives an advance on the value of those receivables in return.

Accounting for the factoring of receivables

Key question:

Is the seller in substance receiving a loan on the security of the receivables, or are the receipts an actual sale of those receivable balances?

Factors to consider:

- Who bears the risk (of slow payment and irrecoverable debts)?

A sale of receivables **with recourse** means that the factor can return any unpaid debts to the business, meaning the business retains the risk of irrecoverable debts. In this situation the transaction is treated as a secure loan against the receivables, rather than a sale.

A sale of receivables **without recourse** means the factor bears the risk of irrecoverable debts. In this case, this is usually treated as a sale and the receivables are removed from the entity's financial statements.

Factoring of receivables – Further detail

In most forms of factoring, receivables balances are sold to the factor, but the latter's degree of control over, and responsibility for, those debts will vary from one arrangement to another.

A significant accounting question is only likely to arise where the factoring arrangement leads to the receipt of cash earlier than would have been the case had the receivables been unfactored. If this is so, the question to be answered is whether the seller has in substance received either a loan on the security of the receivables, or has actually sold the receivable.

If the seller is in essence a borrower, and the factor a lender, then the arrangements will be such as to provide that the seller pays the equivalent of an interest charge to the factor on the amounts received from the factor until those amounts are collected by the factor from the receivable. Such payment would be in addition to any other charges.

The key factor in the analysis will be who **bears the risk** (of slow payment) and the benefit (of early payment) by the receivable. If the finance cost reflects events subsequent to transfer, then the transfer is likely to be equivalent to obtaining finance because the seller is bearing the risks and rewards of the receivable. If the cost is determined when the transfer is made, with no other variable costs, then it is likely to be a straightforward sale.

Test your understanding 6

An entity has an outstanding receivables balance with a major customer amounting to $12 million, and this was factored to Finance Co on 1 September 20X7. The terms of the factoring were:

Finance Co will pay 80% of the gross receivable outstanding account to the entity immediately.

- The balance will be paid (less the charges below) when the debt is collected in full. Any amount of the debt outstanding after four months will be transferred back to the entity at its full book value.
- Finance Co will charge 1% per month of the net amount owing from the entity at the beginning of each month. Finance Co had not collected any of the factored receivable amount by the year-end.
- the entity debited the cash from Finance Co to its bank account and removed the receivable from its accounts. It has prudently charged the difference as an administration cost.

How should this arrangement be accounted for in the financial statements for the year ended 30 September 20X7?

Disclosure of financial instruments

IFRS 7 provides the disclosure requirements for financial instruments. The major elements of disclosures required are:

- The carrying amount of each class of financial instrument should be recorded either on the face of the statement of financial position or within the notes.
- An entity must also disclose items of income, expense, gains and losses for each class of financial instrument either in the statement of profit or loss and other comprehensive income or within the notes.
- An entity must also make disclosures regarding the nature and extent of risks faced by the entity. This must cover the entity's exposure to risk, management's objectives and policies for managing those risks and any changes in the year.

7 Chapter summary

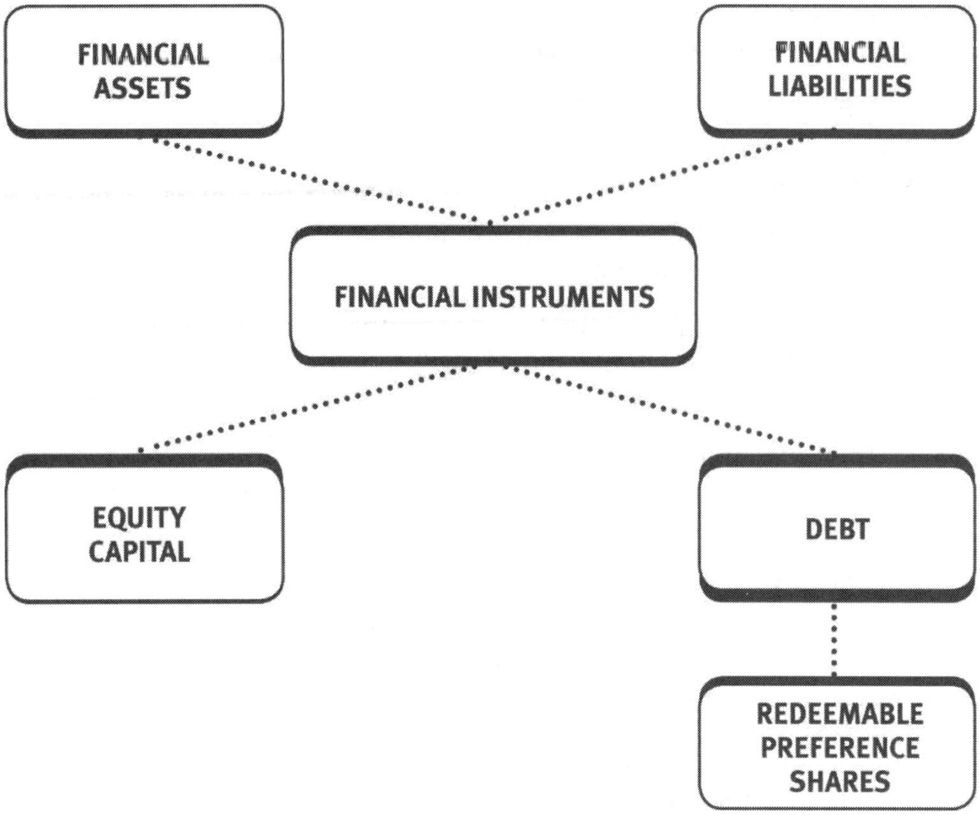

Test your understanding 7

Financial assets and liabilities

The following trial balance relates to JK at 30 September 20X7:

	$000	$000
Ordinary share capital $1 shares		100,000
Share premium		30,000
Revaluation surplus		145,000
Retained earnings reserve 1 October 20X6		285,611
6% Loan notes (note 3)		74,389
5% Convertible loan notes (note 4)		100,000
Revenue		565,000
Cost of sales	339,000	
Distribution costs	53,730	
Administrative expenses	44,810	
6% Loan note interest paid (note 3)	4,200	
5% Convertible loan note interest paid (note 4)	5,000	
Income tax (note 6)		2,150
Inventory at 30 September 20X7 (note 1)	64,320	
Bank	29,885	
Trade receivables	48,670	
Trade payables		69,650
Land and buildings – valuation (note 2)	450,000	
Plant and equipment – cost	265,585	
Plant and equipment – accumulated depreciation at 1 October 20X6 (note 2)		63,400
Financial assets (note 5)	130,000	
	1,435,200	1,435,200

Notes:

1 Included in inventory are some items at their cost of $25 million. Following damage that had taken place during the year, it is now thought that these items can be sold for $30 million but only after they have been repaired and repackaged at a cost of $8 million.

2 Land and buildings were revalued to $450 million (including land $100 million) from their previous carrying amount of $375 million on 1 October 20X6. The revaluation has already been recorded but depreciation for the year has not yet been charged. At 1 October 20X6 the buildings had a remaining life of 35 years.

Plant and equipment is to be depreciated at 20% per annum using the reducing balance method.

3 JK issued its 6% loan notes on 1 October 20X4. They were issued at their nominal value of $70 million. They will be repaid at a premium in 20Y4. The finance department have calculated that the loan notes have an effective rate of interest of 9%.

4 On 1 October 20X6, JK issued 5% convertible loan notes at their par value of $100 million. The loan notes are redeemable at par on 30 September 20Y0 or may be converted into 150 ordinary shares for every $100 of loan note. An equivalent loan note without the conversion option would have carried an interest rate of 8%. Interest of $5 million has been paid on 30 September 20X7.

The present value of $1 payable at the end of year, based on interest rates of 5% and 8% are:

End of year	5%	8%
1	0.95	0.93
2	0.91	0.86
3	0.86	0.79
4	0.82	0.73

5 The financial assets are held for trading purposes and represent investments in the equity shares of listed companies. These investments are classified as 'at fair value through profit or loss'. At 30 September 20X7 the fair value of these investments was estimated to be $150 million.

6 The balance on the income tax account in the trial balance is an overprovision arising as a result of the settlement of the previous year's tax charge. The directors have estimated the provision for income tax for the year to 30 September 20X7 at $24 million.

Required:

Prepare the statement of profit or loss and other comprehensive income of JK for the year ended 30 September 20X7 and a statement of financial position as at that date.

Test your understanding 8

1 On 1 January 20X0 Dunston Co issued $20 million of convertible loan stock, redeemable in three years' time for $22 million or convertible into 500,000 ordinary $1 shares. Dunston Co's treasury department has calculated that the present value of the cash flows, discounted at the interest rate on similar debt without the conversion option is $19,001,600.

What amounts should be shown in the statement of financial position for the debt at the date of issue?

A Debt element $19,001,600 and equity element $998,400

B Debt element $998,400 and equity element $19,001,600

C Debt element $20,000,000 and equity element $500,000

D Debt element $22,000,000 and equity element 0

2 An entity acquires a 6% $1,000 bond, a financial asset, for $970 at the beginning of Year 1. Interest is receivable annually in arrears. The bond is redeemable at the end of Year 3 at a premium of 3%. The financial asset is measured at amortised cost. The effective interest rate of the financial instrument has been calculated at 8.1%.

Calculate the closing statement of financial position figure at the end of Year 2. Work to the nearest $.

$__________

3 On 1 January 20X0, Aditi Co issued $30 million 5% convertible loan stock at par. This is redeemable at $30 million in three years' time or convertible into 1,000,000 ordinary $1 shares at the option of the holder.

The effective interest rate on a similar bond without the conversion option is 7%.

What amount should be shown as a liability (to the nearest thousand) on the statement of financial position for the convertible loan stock at the date of issue?

$__________ '000.

4 Sharp Co has 5% $1 redeemable preference shares in issue which will be redeemed in 5 years' time.

How should the preference share capital and preference dividend be presented in the financial statements of Sharp Co?

A Preference share capital as equity and preference dividend in the statement of changes in equity

B Preference share capital as equity and preference dividend in the statement of profit or loss

C Preference share capital as a liability and preference dividend in the statement of changes in equity.

D Preference share capital as a liability and preference dividend in the statement of profit or loss

5 McTagg purchased 1 million shares in Bauer Co, a listed company, for $4 million on 1 January 20X7. By the year end, 31 December 20X7, the fair value of a Bauer Co share had moved to $4.80. If McTagg were to dispose of the shares, broker fees of $50,000 would be incurred.

What is the correct treatment for shares at year end?

A Hold shares in investments at $4.75 million, with $750k gain being taken to the statement of profit or loss

B Hold shares in investments at $4.8 million, with $800k gain being taken to the statement of profit or loss

C Hold shares in investments at $4.8 million, with $800k gain shown in the statement of changes in equity

D Hold shares in investments at $4.75 million, with $750k gain shown in the statement of changes in equity

6 **In order to hold a debt instrument at amortised cost, which TWO of the following tests must be applied?**

A Fair value test

B Contractual cash flow characteristics test

C Investment appraisal test

D Business model test

Test your understanding answers

Test your understanding 1

1 When the loan notes are issued:

Dr Bank $20,000

Cr Loan notes $20,000

Statement of profit or loss

	1	2	3	4
Finance costs	(1,000)	(1,000)	(1,000)	(1,000)

Statement of financial position

	1	2	3	4
Non-current liabilities	20,000	20,000		
Current liabilities			20,000	0

Workings:

Year	Opening	Finance costs 5%	Cash paid 5%	Closing
1	20,000	1,000	(1,000)	20,000
2	20,000	1,000	(1,000)	20,000
3	20,000	1,000	(1,000)	20,000
4	20,000	1,000	(1,000)	
			(20,000)*	0

*The loan notes are repaid at par i.e. $20,000 at the end of year 4.

2 When the loan notes are issued:

Dr Bank $40,000

Cr Loan notes $40,000

Statement of profit or loss

	1	2	3
Finance costs	(3,600)	(3,924)	(4,276)

Statement of financial position

	1	2	3
Non-current liabilities	43,600		
Current liabilities		47,524	0

Workings:

Year	Opening	Finance costs 9%	Cash paid 0%	Closing
1	40,000	3,600	(0)	43,600
2	43,600	3,924	(0)	47,524
3	47,524	4,276	(0)	
			(51,800)	0

The loan notes are repaid at par i.e. $40,000, plus a premium of $11,800 at the end of year 3.

3 When the loan notes are issued:

Dr Bank $18,966

Cr Loan notes $18,966

Working:

Nominal value	20,000
Discount 2.5%	(500)
Issue costs	(534)
	18,966

Year 1

Statement of profit or loss

Finance cost	(1,328)

Statement of financial position

Non-current liabilities	19,494

Workings:

Year	Opening	Finance costs 7%	Cash paid 4%	Closing
1	18,966	1,328	(800)	19,494

Test your understanding 2

Annual payment = 40,000 × $1 × 8% = $3,200

Year ended 31 March	Opening balance	Finance cost @ 12%	Cash paid @ 8%	Closing balance
	$	$	$	$
20X8	40,000	4,800	(3,200)	41,600
20X9	41,600	4,992	(3,200)	43,392

	20X9	20X8
Statement of financial position	$	$
Non-current liability: preference shares	43,392	41,600
Statement of profit or loss		
Finance cost	(4,992)	(4,800)

Test your understanding 3

1 When the convertible bonds are issued:

	$000
Dr Bank	36,000
Cr Financial liability	29,542
Cr Equity	6,458

Year	Cash flow	Discount factor 9.1%	Present value
	$000	$000	$000
1	720	0.92	662
2	720	0.84	605
3	36,720	0.77	28,275
			29,542

Cash flow = 2% × 36,000 = 720

Statement of profit or loss

	1	2	3
Finance costs	(2,688)	(2,867)	(3,062)

Statement of financial position

	1	2	3
Equity:			
Equity option	6,458	6,458	6,458
Non-current liabilities	31,510	33,658	
Current liabilities			36,000

Workings:

Year	Opening	Finance costs 9.1%	Cash paid 2%	Closing
1	29,542	2,688	(720)	31,510
2	31,510	2,867	(720)	33,658
3	33,658	3,062	(720)	36,000

2 When the convertible bonds are issued:

Dr Bank $5,000,000

Cr Financial liability $4,734,000

Cr Equity $266,000

Year	Cash flow	Discount factor	Present value
1	200,000	0.94	188,000
2	200,000	0.89	178,000
3	5,200,000	0.84	4,368,000
			4,734,000

Cash flow = 4% × 5,000,000 = $200,000

Statement of profit or loss

	1	2	3
Finance costs	(284,040)	(289,082)	(294,428)

Statement of financial position

	1	2	3
Equity:			
Equity option	266,000	266,000	266,000
Non-current liabilities	4,818,040	4,907,122	
Current liabilities			5,000,000

Workings:

Year	Opening	Finance costs 6%	Cash paid 4%	Closing
1	4,734,000	284,040	(200,000)	4,818,040
2	4,818,040	289,082	(200,000)	4,907,122
3	4,907,122	294,428	(200,000)	5,000,000

Test your understanding 4

1 This financial instrument appears to be a debt instrument which passes both the business model test and the contractual cash flow characteristics test. It can be measured at amortised cost.

Statement of profit or loss

	1	2	3
Investment Income	600	612	625

Statement of financial position

	1	2	3
Non-current assets:			
Investments	5,100		0
Current assets:			
Investments		5,212	

Working:

Year	Opening	Investment income 12%	Cash received 10%	Closing
1	5,000	600	(500)	5,100
2	5,100	612	(500)	5,212
3	5,212	625	(500)	
			(5,337)	0

2 The investment should be measured at fair value through profit or loss.

Statement of profit or loss

Investment Income (10,000 × (4.90 – 4.20))	7,000

Statement of financial position

Current assets	
Investments (10,000 × 4.90)	49,000

3 The investment in these shares is considered to be a financial asset at fair value through other comprehensive income.

Statement of profit or loss and other comprehensive income

Other comprehensive income

Loss on investment	(8,000)

Statement of financial position

Non-current asset investments (20,000 × $3.40)	68,000
FVOCI reserve	(8,000)

Test your understanding 5 – Bland

(a) The business model is to hold the asset until redemption. Therefore, the debt instrument will be measured at amortised cost.

The asset is initially recognised at its fair value plus transaction costs of $9,144 ($9,000 + $144).

Interest income will be recognised in profit or loss using the effective rate of interest.

	b/f	**Interest at 11% (SPL)**	**Received $10,000 × 6%**	**c/f (SFP)**
	$	$	$	$
20X5	9,144	1,006	(600)	9,550
20X6	9,550	1,050	(600)	10,000
20X7	10,000	1,100	(600)	10,500

Note that the above table shows the balance at 31 December 20X7 prior to the bond's redemption on that date.

	20X5	20X6	20X7
	$	$	$
Statement of profit or loss			
Investment income	1,006	1,050	1,100
Statement of financial position			
Financial asset investment	9,550	10,000	–

(b) The business model is to hold the asset until redemption, but sales may be made to invest in other assets with higher returns. Therefore, the debt instrument will be measured at fair value through other comprehensive income.

The asset is initially recognised at its fair value plus transaction costs of $9,144 ($9,000 + $144).

Interest income will be recognised in profit or loss using the effective rate of interest, with exactly the same calculations as for amortised cost above.

At the end of each year the asset must be revalued to fair value. Any gain or loss will be recorded in other comprehensive income.

	b/f	Interest at 11%	Received	c/f	Gain/ Loss (balance)	Fair value
	$	$	$	$	$	$
20X5	9,144	1,006	(600)	9,550	1,450	11,000
20X6	11,000	1,050	(600)	11,450	(1,050)	10,400
20X7	10,400	1,100	(600)	10,900	(400)	10,500

Note that the amounts recognised in profit or loss as interest income must be the same as if the asset was simply held at amortised cost, so the interest income figures are the same as in part (a). Take great care when calculating the interest income.

In the year ended 31 December 20X5 a revaluation gain of $1,450 will be recognised in other comprehensive income. The asset will be held at $11,000 on the statement of financial position.

In the year ended 31 December 20X6 a revaluation loss of $1,050 will be recognised in other comprehensive income. The asset will be held at $10,400 on the statement of financial position.

In the year ended 31 December 20X7 a revaluation loss of $400 will be recognised in other comprehensive income.

	20X5	20X6	20X7
	$	$	$
Statement of profit or loss and other comprehensive income			
Investment income	1,006	1,050	1,100
Other comprehensive income:			
Gain/loss on investment	1,450	(1,050)	(400)
Statement of financial position			
Financial asset investment	11,000	10,400	–

Test your understanding 6

As the entity still bears the risk of slow payment and irrecoverable debts, the substance of the factoring is that of a loan on which finance charges will be made. The receivable should not have been derecognised nor should all of the difference between the gross receivable and the amount received from the factor have been treated as an administration cost. The required adjustments can be summarised as follows:

	Dr	Cr
	$000	$000
Receivables (to reinstate the balance)	12,000	
Loan from factor		9,600
Administration $(12,000 – 9,600)		2,400
Finance costs: accrued interest ($9.6 million 1.0%)	96	
Accruals		96
	12,096	12,096

Test your understanding 7

Statement of profit or loss and other comprehensive income for the year ended 30 September 20X7

	$000
Revenue	565,000
Cost of Sales **(W3)**	(392,437)
	–––––––
Gross profit	172,563
Distribution costs	(53,730)
Administrative expenses	(44,810)
	–––––––
Profit from operations	74,023
Finance costs **(W1 + W2)** (6,695 + 7,164)	(13,859)
Investment Income (150,000 – 130,000)	20,000
	–––––––
Profit before tax	80,164
Tax (– 2,150 + 24,000)	(21,850)
	–––––––
Profit for the year	58,314
	–––––––
Other comprehensive income:	
Profit for the year	58,314
Revaluation surplus	75,000
	–––––––
Comprehensive income	133,314
	–––––––

Statement of financial position as at 30 September 20X7

	$000	$000
Non-current assets		
Land and buildings (100,000 + 340,000) **(W5)**		440,000
Plant and equipment **(W5)**		161,748
		601,748
Current assets		
Inventory **(W4)**	61,320	
Receivables	48,670	
Financial assets (130,000 + 20,000)	150,000	
Cash	29,885	
		289,875
		891,623
Equity		
Share capital		100,000
Share premium		30,000
Conversion option **(W2)**		10,450
Revaluation surplus		145,000
Retained earnings (285,611 + 58,314)		343,925
		629,375
Non-current liabilities		
6% Loan notes **(W1)**	76,884	
5% Convertible loan notes **(W2)**	91,714	
		168,598
Current liabilities		
Payables	69,650	
Income tax	24,000	
		93,650
		891,623

Workings:

(W1) 6% Loan notes

Balance per TB $74,389

Interest paid in year per TB $4,200

Year	Opening	Finance costs 9%	Cash paid 6%	Closing
20X7	74,389	6,695	(4,200)	76,884

(W2) 5% Convertible Loan notes

Balance per TB $100,000

Interest paid in year per TB $5,000

Split proceeds of $100,000 into liability and equity.

To calculate liability, calculate present value of future cash flows

Year	Cash flow	Discount factor 8%	Present value
1	5,000	0.93	4,650
2	5,000	0.86	4,300
3	5,000	0.79	3,950
4	105,000	0.73	76,650
			89,550

Cash flow = 5% × 100,000 = $5,000

Therefore, when the convertible bonds are issued:

Dr Bank	100,000
Cr Financial Liability	89,550
Cr Equity (balance)	10,450

Equity balance will remain at 10,450.

Liability balance to be measured at amortised cost:

Year	Opening	Finance costs 8%	Cash paid 5%	Closing
20X7	89,550	7,164	(5,000)	91,714

(W3) Cost of Sales

	$
Per TB	339,000
Inventory write down **(W4)**	3,000
Depreciation – buildings	10,000
Depreciation – plant and equipment	40,437
	392,437

(W4) Inventory

Cost per TB		64,320
Damaged items		
Cost	25,000	
Net realisable value (30,000 – 8,000)	22,000	
Write down required		(3,000)
Inventory for SFP		61,320

(W5) Non-current assets

	Land	**Buildings**	**Plant & equipment**
Valuation/Cost per TB	100,000	350,000	265,585
Accumulated depreciation per TB			(63,400)
			202,185
Depreciation charge			
(350,000/35)		(10,000)	
(20% × 202,185)			(40,437)
Carrying amount	100,000	340,000	161,748

Test your understanding 8

1 **A** – The liability is as calculated per the question. The equity amount is the cash received less the liability amount.

2 **$1,009**

Year	Opening	Interest 8.1%%	Payment	Closing
1	970	79	(60)	989
2	989	80	(60)	**1,009**

3 **$28,425** – The liability element is found by calculating the present value of cash flows, discounted using the interest rate on a similar bond without the conversion option. The annual payment is $1.5 million ($30 million × 5%) so the present value of the payments is as follows:

Year	Payment	Discount	Present value ($000)
1	1,500	1/1.07	1,402
2	1,500	$1/1.07^2$	1,310
3	31,500	$1/1.07^3$	25,713
			28,425

4 **D** – Redeemable preference shares will be shown as a liability, with the payments being shown as finance costs.

5 **B** – The default category for equity investments is fair value through profit or loss so the investments should be revalued to fair value (not fair value less costs to sell), with the gain or loss taken to the statement of profit or loss.

6 **B and D**

Chapter

10

Foreign currency

Chapter learning objectives

Upon completion of this chapter you will be able to:

- define presentation and functional currencies
- record transactions that are in a foreign currency.

PER

One of the PER performance objectives (PO6) is to record and process transactions and events. You use the right accounting treatments for transactions and events. These should be both historical and prospective – and include non-routine transactions. Working though this chapter should help you understand how to demonstrate that objective.

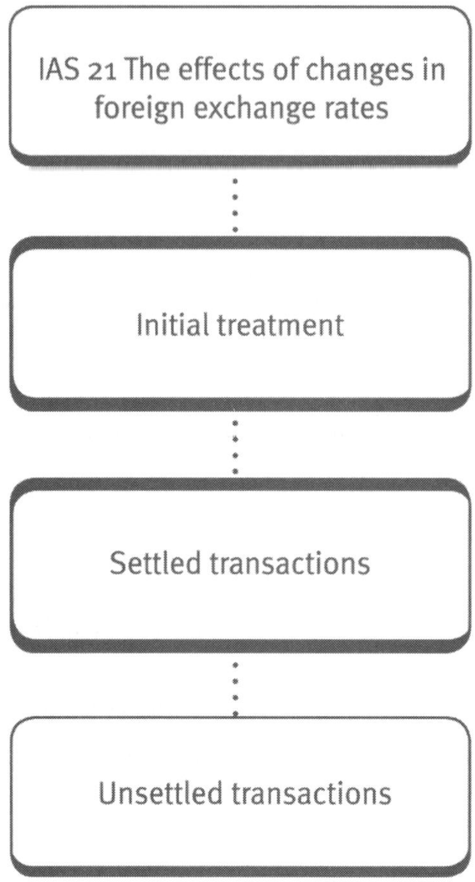

1 Objective of IAS 21

The objective of IAS 21 is to produce rules that an entity should follow in the translation of foreign currency activities. It is only individual transactions in foreign currency that are examinable in FR.

Definitions

Exchange rates

- Historic rate: rate in place at the date the transaction takes place, sometimes referred to as the spot rate.
- Closing rate: rate at the reporting date.
- Average rate: average rate throughout the accounting period.

Assets and liabilities

- Monetary items: items that can be easily converted into cash, e.g. receivables, payables, loans.
- Non-monetary items: items that give no right to receive or deliver cash, e.g. inventory, plant and machinery.

Currency

- Functional currency: **'the currency of the primary economic environment in which an entity operates'** (IAS 21, para 8). This will usually be the currency in which the majority of an entity's transactions take place.
- Presentation currency**: 'the currency in which the financial statements are presented'** (IAS 21, para 8).

Functional currency

IAS 21 says that an entity should consider the following primary factors when determining its functional currency:

- the currency that mainly influences sales prices for goods and services
- the currency of the country whose competitive forces and regulations mainly determine the sales price of goods and services
- the currency that mainly influences labour, materials and other costs of providing goods and services.

If the primary factors are inconclusive then the following secondary factors should also be considered:

- the currency in which funds from financing activities are generated
- the currency in which receipts from operating activities are retained.

2 Individual company – Translating transactions

Mechanics of translation

Initial transactions

- Translate using the historic rate prevailing at the transaction date.
- The average rate can also be used if it does not fluctuate significantly during the accounting period.

Settled transactions

If a transaction is settled (payment or receipt occurs) during the accounting period:

- Translate at the date of payment / receipt using the historic rate prevailing at that date.
- As this may be different to the initial transaction an exchange difference may arise, this is posted to the **statement of profit or loss (see Treatment of exchange differences below).**

Test your understanding 1

On 1 April 20X8 Collins Co, a company that uses the dollar ($) as its functional currency, buys goods from an overseas supplier, who uses Kromits (Kr) as its functional currency. The goods are priced at Kr54,000. Payment is made 2 months later on 31 May 20X8.

The prevailing exchange rates are:

1 April 20X8 Kr1.80 : $1

31 May 20X8 Kr1.75 : $1

Required:

Record the journal entries for these transactions.

Unsettled transactions

- If a transaction is still unsettled at the reporting date, there will be an outstanding asset or liability on the statement of financial position.
- If the asset/liability is a monetary item it should be retranslated at the closing rate.
- If the asset/liability is a non-monetary item it should remain at the historic rate.
- Exchange differences will arise on the retranslation of the monetary items, and these are also posted to the statement of profit or loss.

Test your understanding 2

On 1 January 20X6 Wilkie Co, a company that uses the dollar ($) as its functional currency, buys goods from an overseas supplier, who uses Dinar (D) as its functional currency. The goods are priced at D35,000. Payment is still outstanding at the reporting date of 31 March 20X6.

The prevailing exchange rates are:

1 January 20X6 D1.75 : $1

31 March 20X6 D1.90 : $1

Required:

Record the journal entries for these transactions.

Treatment of exchange differences

- If the exchange difference relates to trading transactions it is disclosed within other operating income/operating expenses.
- If the exchange difference relates to non-trading transactions it is disclosed within interest receivable and similar income/finance costs.

Test your understanding 3

ABC Co has a year end of 31 December 20X1 and uses the dollar ($) as its functional currency.

On 25 October 20X1 ABC Co buys goods from a Swedish supplier for Swedish Krona (SWK) 286,000.

Rates of exchange:

25 October 20X1 $1 = SWK 11.16

16 November 20X1 $1 = SWK 10.87

31 December 20X1 $1 = SWK 11.02

Required:

Show the accounting treatment for the above transactions if:

(a) A payment of SWK286,000 is made on 16 November 20X1.

(b) The amount owed remains outstanding at the year-end date.

Non-monetary Items

- **Cost model**

  Non-monetary items that are held at cost are initially translated at the historic rate and carried forward at this value. They are not retranslated.

3 Chapter summary

Initial treatments

Transactions are translated at historic rate.

Settled transactions

Settlement is translated at spot rate.

Unsettled transactions

Monetary items are retranslated at closing rate.

Non-monetary items remain translated at historic rate when cost was first measured.

Exchange gains/losses

Recorded in statement of profit or loss unless movement in fair value recorded in equity, in which case the exchange gain/loss is also taken to equity.

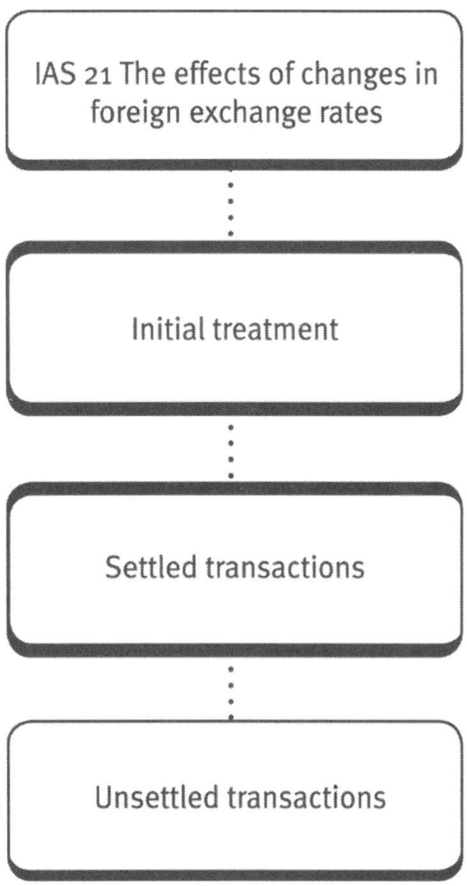

Test your understanding 4

Data for Questions 1 to 3

An entity based in the US sold goods overseas for Kr200,000 on 28 March 20X3 when the exchange rate was Kr0.65:$1.

The customer paid in April 20X3 when the rate was Kr0.70:$1.

The exchange rate at the year ended 30 June 20X3 was Kr0.75:$1.

1 **Prepare the journal entries to record the sale of the goods by the US entity.**

2 **Show the journal entries to record the payment in April 20X3.**

3 **If the amount was outstanding at the year-end, what would the gain or loss in the statement of profit or loss be?**

$ __________

4 An entity based in the US purchased goods for Kr200,000 on 28 March 20X3 when the exchange rate was Kr0.65: $1.

The exchange rate at the year ended 30 June 20X3 was Kr0.75:$1.

If the goods were unsold at the year-end, what should be the value of inventory?

$ __________

5 An entity bought land on credit for Kr100,000 when the exchange rate was 1Kr/$0.85. At the year end the entity had not paid its supplier. The exchange rate at the year-end was 1Kr/$0.92.

Which THREE of the following amounts would be recorded in the financial statements at year end?

A	Property, plant and equipment	$85,000
B	Trade payable	$85,000
C	Foreign exchange loss	$7,000
D	Property, plant and equipment	$92,000
E	Trade payable	$92,000
F	Foreign exchange loss	$Nil

Test your understanding answers

Test your understanding 1

Initial transaction

Translate at historic rate on 1 April, Kr54,000/1.8 = $30,000

Dr Purchases $30,000

Cr Payables $30,000

On settlement

Translate at historic rate on 31 May, Kr54,000/1.75 = $30,857

Dr Payables $30,000

Dr SPL – foreign exchange loss $857

Cr Cash $30,857

Test your understanding 2

Initial transaction

Translate at historic rate on 1 January 20X6, D35,000/1.75 = $20,000

Dr Purchases $20,000

Cr Payables $20,000

At the reporting date

Payables are monetary items, so retranslate at the closing rate on 31 March 20X6, reducing the payables balance to D35,000/1.90 = $18,421 and recognising a gain of $1,579 ($20,000 – $18,421) in the SPL.

Dr Payables $1,579

Cr SPL Exchange gain $1,579

Test your understanding 3

(a) **Original transaction**

25 October 20X1 Value = 286,000/11.16 = $25,627

Dr Purchases 25,627

Cr Payables 25,627

16 November 20X1 Payment 286,000/10.87 = $26,311

Dr Payables 25,627

Dr SPL **684 (Balancing figure, 26,311 – 25,627)**

Cr Cash 26,311

(b) If **the amount remains outstanding:**

31 December 20X1 Retranslate payable 286,000/11.02 = $25,953

Dr SPL **326 (25,953 – 25,627)**

Cr Payables 326

Note: The inventory would not be restated and would remain at the original transaction price of $25,627.

Test your understanding 4

1 **On the sale:**

Translate the sale at the spot rate prevailing on the transaction date.

Kr200,000/0.65 = $307,692

	$
Dr Receivables	307,692
Cr Revenue	307,692

2 **Loss on translation = $307,692 – $285,714 = $21,978**

The journal entries would be as follows:

Dr Bank (Kr200,000/0.70)	285,714
Cr Receivables (Original amount)	307,692
Dr SPL (Balancing figure)	21,978

3 **$41,025. The monetary item must be retranslated at the reporting date rate of exchange:**

Dollar value at the reporting date = Kr200,000/0.75 = $266,667

This results in a reduction in the receivables (and therefore a foreign exchange loss) of $41,025

For tutorial purposes the journal entry would be as follows: Loss on translation = $307,692 – $266,667 = $41,025

Cr Receivables	41,025
Dr SPL	41,025

4 **$307,692.** At the reporting date:

No adjustment will be made at year-end to the inventory because inventory is a non-monetary item.

For tutorial purposes the transactions would be recorded as follows:

Purchase:

Translate the sale at the spot rate prevailing on the transaction date.

Kr200,000/0.65 = $307,692 (Dr Purchases, Cr Payables)

Inventory would remain unchanged at the reporting date, $307,692.

The payables would be restated at the year-end.

Dollar value at the reporting date = Kr200,000/0.75 = $266,667

Gain on translation = 307,692 – 266,667 = 41,025

Dr Payables	41,025
Cr SPL	41,025

5 **A, C, E**

At acquisition:

Kr100,000 × 0.85 = $85,000

	$
Dr Non-current asset	85,000
Cr Payables	85,000

The land is a non-monetary asset and remains at $85,000 at the year end. Payables, as a monetary item, must be retranslated at the reporting date rate of exchange:

Value at the reporting date = Kr100,000 × 0.92 = $92,000

This results in an increase in the payables of $7,000

Loss on translation = $92,000 – $85,000 = $7,000

Cr Payables	7,000
Dr P/L (loss)	7,000

Chapter

11

Revenue

Chapter learning objectives

Upon completion of this chapter you will be able to:

- discuss the issues relating to the recognition of revenue
- understand the 5-step approach with regards to the recognition of revenue
- record revenue in relation to contracts satisfied at a point in time
- discuss how progress is recorded in relation to contracts satisfied over time
- record revenue in relation to contracts satisfied over time
- record assets and liabilities relating to revenue from contracts with customers.

PER

One of the PER performance objectives (PO6) is to record and process transactions and events. You use the right accounting treatments for transactions and events. These should be both historical and prospective – and include non-routine transactions. Working though this chapter should help you understand how to demonstrate that objective.

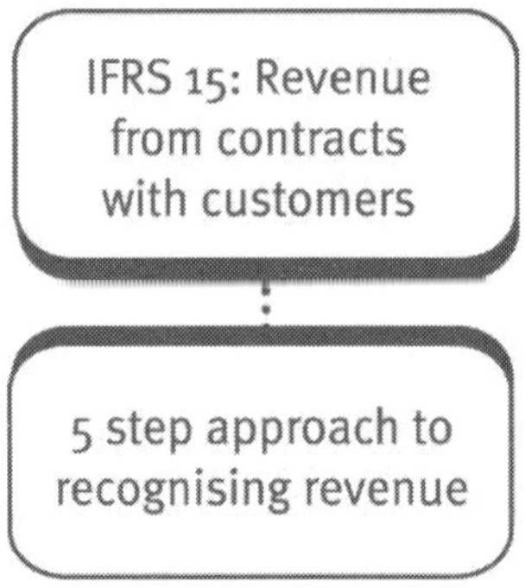

1 5-step approach

IFRS 15 – Revenue recognition: A five step process

An entity recognises revenue by applying the following five steps:

1. Identify the contract
2. Identify the separate performance obligations within a contract
3. Determine the transaction price
4. Allocate the transaction price to the performance obligations in the contract
5. Recognise revenue when (or as) a performance obligation is satisfied

The five steps will be considered in more detail in this section. However, the following illustration may help you to gain an understanding of the basic principles.

Illustration 1 – The five steps

On 1 December 20X1, Wade receives an order from a customer for a computer as well as 12 months of technical support. Wade delivers the computer (and transfers its legal title) to the customer on the same day.

The customer paid $420 on 1 December 20X1. The computer normally sells for $300 and the technical support for $120.

The 5 steps would be applied to this transaction as follows:

Step 1 – Identify the contract

There is an agreement between Wade and its customer for the provision of goods (the computer) and services (the technical support).

Step 2 – Identify the separate performance obligations within a contract

There are two performance obligations within the contract:

- The supply of a computer
- The supply of technical support

Step 3 – Determine the transaction price

The total transaction price is $420.

Step 4 – Allocate the transaction price to the performance obligations in the contract

Based on stand-alone sales prices, $300 should be allocated to the sale of the computer and $120 should be allocated to the sale of technical support.

Step 5 – Recognise revenue when (or as) a performance obligation is satisfied

Control over the computer has been passed to the customer so the full goods revenue of $300 should be recognised on 1 December 20X1.

The technical support is provided over time, so revenue from this should be recognised over time. In the year ended 31 December 20X1, revenue of $10 ($^1/_{12}$ × $120) should be recognised from the provision of technical support.

The five steps of revenue recognition will now be considered in more detail.

Step 1: Identify the contract

A contract is **'an agreement between two or more parties that creates enforceable rights and obligations'** (IFRS 15, Appendix A).

A contract can be agreed in writing, orally, or through other customary business practices.

An entity can only account for revenue if the contract meets the following criteria:

- **'the parties to the contract have approved the contract and are committed to perform their respective obligations**
- **the entity can identify each party's rights regarding the goods or services to be transferred**
- **the entity can identify the payment terms for the goods or services to be transferred**
- **the contract has commercial substance, and**
- **it is probable that the entity will collect the consideration to which it will be entitled in exchange for the goods or services that will be transferred to the customer'** (IFRS 15, para 9).

Illustration 2 – Identifying the contract

Mono Co has a year end of 31 March 20X6.

On 1 January 20X6, Mono Co signed a contract with a customer to supply them with an asset on 31 March 20X6 in return for payment of $360,000 on 30 September 20X6. Control of the asset would pass to the customer on 31 March 20X6.

By 31 March 20X6, Mono Co did not believe that it would probably be paid the $360,000. Therefore, the contract cannot be accounted for and no revenue should be recognised.

Step 2: Identifying the separate performance obligations within a contract

Performance obligations are promises to transfer distinct goods or services to a customer.

Some contracts contain more than one performance obligation. For example:

- An entity may enter into a contract with a customer to sell a car, which includes one year's free servicing and maintenance
- An entity might enter into a contract with a customer to provide 5 lectures, as well as to provide a textbook on the first day of the course.

The distinct performance obligations within a contract must be identified.

Performance obligations may not be limited to the goods or services that are explicitly stated in the contract. An entity's customary business practices, published policies or specific statements may create an expectation that the entity will transfer goods or service to the customer.

An entity must decide if the nature of a performance obligation is:

- to provide the specified goods or services itself (i.e. the entity is the principal), or
- to arrange for another party to provide the goods or service (i.e. the entity is an agent)

If an entity is an agent, then **revenue is recognised based on the fee or commission** to which it is entitled.

Illustration 3 – Agency sales

Hadrian Co's revenue includes $45,000 for goods it sold acting as an agent for Offa. Hadrian Co earned a commission of 10% on these sales and remitted the difference of $40,500 (included in cost of sales) to Offa.

How should the agency sale be treated in Hadrian's statement of profit or loss?

Solution

Hadrian should not have included $45,000 in its revenue because it is acting as the agent and not the principal. Only the commission element of $4,500 ($45,000 × 10%) can be recorded in revenue. The following adjustment is therefore required:

	$	
Dr Revenue	40,500	Reducing revenue to $4,500
Cr Cost of sales	40,500	Reducing cost of sales to nil

Step 3: Determining the transaction price

The transaction price is **the 'amount of consideration to which an entity expects to be entitled in exchange for transferring promised goods or services to a customer'** (IFRS 15, Appendix A).

Amounts collected on behalf of third parties (such as sales tax) are excluded.

The consideration promised in a contract with a customer may include fixed amounts, variable amounts, or both.

'When determining the transaction price, an entity shall consider the effects of all of the following:

- **variable consideration**
- **the existence of a significant financing component in the contract**
- **non-cash consideration**
- **consideration payable to a customer'** (IFRS 15, para 48).

Financing

In determining the transaction price, an entity must consider if the timing of payments provides the customer or the entity with a significant financing benefit.

If there is a significant financing component, then the consideration receivable needs to be discounted to present value using the rate at which the customer would be able to borrow.

The following may indicate the existence of a significant financing component (IFRS 15, para 61):

- a difference between the amount of promised consideration and the cash selling price of the promised goods or services
- a significant length of time between the transfer of the promised goods or services to the customer and the payment date.

Test your understanding 1 – Keema Co

Keema Co enters into a contract with a customer to supply furniture on 30 September 20X3. Control of the furniture transfers to the customer on that date. The price stated in the contract is $750,000 and is due for payment on 30 September 20X5.

Market rates of interest available to this particular customer are 7%.

Required:

Explain how this transaction should be accounted for in the financial statements of Keema Co for the year ended 30 September 20X3 and 20X4.

Consideration payable to a customer

If consideration is paid to a customer in exchange for a distinct good or service, then it is essentially a purchase transaction and should be accounted for in the same way as other purchases from suppliers.

Assuming that the consideration paid to a customer is not in exchange for a distinct good or service, an entity should account for it as a reduction of the transaction price.

Illustration 4 – Consideration payable to a customer

Golden Gate Co enters into a contract with a major chain of retail stores. The customer commits to buy at least $20m of products over the next 12 months. The terms of the contract require Golden Gate Co to make a payment of $1m to compensate the customer for changes that it will need to make to its retail stores to accommodate the products.

By 31 December 20X1, Golden Gate Co has transferred products with a sales value of $4m to the customer.

How much revenue should be recognised by Golden Gate Co in the year ended 31 December 20X1?

Solution

The payment made to the customer is not in exchange for a distinct good or service. Therefore, the $1m paid to the customer is a reduction of the transaction price.

The total transaction price is being reduced by 5% ($1m/$20m). Therefore, Golden Gate reduces the transaction price of each good by 5% as it is transferred.

By 31 December 20X1, Golden Gate should have recognised revenue of $3.8m ($4m × 95%).

Step 4: Allocate the transaction price

The total transaction price should be allocated to each performance obligation in proportion to stand-alone selling prices.

The best evidence of a stand-alone selling price is the observable price of a good or service when the entity sells that good or service separately in similar circumstances and to similar customers.

If a stand-alone selling price is not directly observable, then the entity estimates the stand-alone selling price.

Discounts

In relation to a bundled sale, any discount should generally be allocated across each component in the transaction. A discount should only be allocated to a specific component of the transaction if that component is regularly sold separately at a discount.

Test your understanding 2 – Shinji Co

Shinji Co sells a machine and one year's free technical support for $50,000. It usually sells the machine for $60,000 but does not sell technical support for this machine as a stand-alone product. Other support services offered by Shinji Co attract a mark-up of 50%. It is expected that the technical support will cost Shinji Co $10,000.

Required:

How should the transaction price be allocated between the machine and the technical support?

Step 5: Recognise revenue

Revenue is recognised **'when (or as) the entity satisfies a performance obligation by transferring a promised good or service to a customer'** (IFRS 15, para 31).

For each performance obligation identified, an entity must determine at contract inception whether it satisfies the performance obligation over time, or satisfies the performance obligation at a point in time.

Satisfying a performance obligation at a point in time

If a performance obligation is satisfied at a point in time then the entity must determine the point in time at which a customer obtains control of a promised asset.

Control of an asset refers to the ability to direct the use of, and obtain substantially all of the remaining benefits (inflows or savings in outflows) from, the asset. Control includes the ability to prevent other entities from obtaining benefits from an asset.

The following are indicators of the transfer of control:

- The entity has a present right to payment for the asset
- The customer has legal title to the asset
- The entity has transferred physical possession of the asset
- The customer has the significant risks and rewards of ownership of the asset
- The customer has accepted the asset.

Consignment inventory

This can raise the issue of **consignment inventory**, where one party legally owns the inventory but another party keeps the inventory on its premises. The key issue relates to which party has the majority of indicators of control.

e.g

Illustration 5 – Consignment inventory

On 1 January 20X3 Frod Motor Co, a car manufacturer, entered into an agreement to provide Dusty, a car retailer, with cars for resale.

The terms of the agreement were as follows:

Dusty pays the cost of insuring and maintaining the cars.

Dusty can display the cars in its showrooms and use them as demonstration models.

When a car is sold to a customer, Dusty pays Frod Motor Co the factory price prevailing at the time the car was originally delivered.

All cars remaining unsold 90 days after their original delivery must be purchased by Dusty at the factory price prevailing at the time of delivery.

Frod Motor Co can require Dusty to return the cars at any time within the 90-day period. In practice, this right has never been exercised.

Dusty can return unsold cars to Frod Motor Co at any time during the 90-day period, without penalty. In practice, this has never happened.

At 31 December 20X3 the agreement is still in force and Dusty holds several cars which were delivered less than 90 days earlier.

How should these cars be treated in the financial statements of Dusty for the year ended 31 December 20X3?

Solution

The key issue is whether Dusty has purchased the cars from Frod Motor Co or whether they are merely on loan.

In order to decide whether or not Dusty has purchased the cars we need to determine whether control has passed from Frod Motor Co to Dusty, in other words whether Dusty is receiving the benefits of holding the cars and is exposed to the risks inherent in those benefits.

Frod Motor Co can demand the return of the cars and Dusty is able to return them without paying a penalty. This suggests that Dusty does not have the automatic right to retain or to use them.

Dusty incurs the cost of insurance and maintenance, costs normally associated with holding inventories.

The purchase price is the price at the date the cars were first delivered. This suggests that the sale actually takes place at the delivery date, because it is Dusty that will benefit from any price rises and suffer if the price goes down.

It appears that both parties experience the risks and benefits. However, although the agreement provides for the return of the cars at either party's request, in practice this has never happened.

Conclusion: The cars are assets of Dusty and should be included in its statement of financial position. Therefore Frod Motor Co will recognise revenue when the cars are despatched to Dusty.

Repurchase agreements

A repurchase agreement is where an entity sells an asset but retains a right to repurchase the asset. This is often not recognised as a sale, but as a secured loan against the asset. Indications that this should not be recognised as a sale may include:

- Sale is below fair value
- Option to repurchase is below the expected fair value
- Entity continues to use the asset
- Entity continues to hold the majority of risks and rewards associated with ownership of the asset
- Sale is to a bank or financing company

Illustration 6 – Sale and repurchase

Ardglen sells its maturing inventory, with a cost of $1 million, to Alba, a bank, for its fair value of $1.5 million on 1 January 20X1. Ardglen has the option to repurchase the inventory on 31 December 20X8 for $2.2 million. Ardglen will continue to hold the inventory within its warehouse as normal throughout the period, and so is responsible for its maintenance and insurance. At 31 December 20X8 the inventory is expected to have a fair value of $4 million.

Giving reasons, show how Ardglen should record the above transaction during the year ended 31 December 20X1.

Solution

Alba faces the (minimal) risk of falling inventory retail values.

Ardglen continues to insure and maintain the inventory.

Ardglen will benefit from any increases in value, which seem highly likely to occur.

Ardglen should not derecognise the inventory but should continue to recognise it as an asset in the statement of financial position. This transaction is in substance a secured loan with effective interest of $0.7 million ($2.2 million – $1.5 million) over the eight-year period.

The receipt of 'sale proceeds' should therefore be recognised as a non-current liability loan, with interest charged each year on the outstanding amount. The effective interest rate is approximately 5%.

Note that any effective interest rates would always be provided within any FR exam question.

Bill-and-hold arrangements

A bill-and-hold arrangement is a contract under which an entity bills a customer for a product but the entity retains physical possession of the product until it is transferred to the customer at a point of time in the future.

For this to be recognised within revenue, the customer must have obtained control of the product, despite it physically remaining with the entity.

There may be a fee for custodial services, where the entity recognises a fee for holding the goods on behalf of the customer. This performance obligation would be satisfied over time, so any revenue would be recognised on this basis.

For a bill-and-hold arrangement to exist:

- The customer must have requested the arrangement
- The product must be identified as belonging to the customer
- The product must be ready for physical transfer to the customer
- The entity cannot have the ability to use the product or sell it to someone else.

Substance over form

Determining the substance of a transaction

Common features of transactions whose substance is not readily apparent are:

- the legal title to an asset may be separated from the principal benefits and risks associated with the asset (as with leases)
- a transaction may be linked with other transactions which means that the commercial effect of an individual transaction cannot be understood without an understanding of all of the transactions involved
- options may be included in a transaction where the terms of the option make it highly likely that the option will be exercised.

Test your understanding 3 – Johan

Johan entered into the following sale transactions during the year:

(a) On 1 April 20X6, Johan sold its factory to Cruyff, a finance company, for $800,000. Johan continued to use the factory and was responsible for the insurance and maintenance of the building. Johan has the right to repurchase the factory for $980,000 on 1 April 20X9, representing a 7% growth in value each year. At 1 April 20X6 the factory had a fair value of $1.5 million, with a carrying amount of $600,000. The fair value is expected to increase by April 20X9.

(b) On 31 March 20X7, Johan sells an oven plus spare parts to Marco for $220,000. The price was split between $200,000 for the oven and $20,000 for the spare parts. Johan delivered the machine on 31 March 20X7 but was asked to hold the spare parts by Marco, because Marco's factory was very close to Johan's warehouse. Johan expects to hold the spare parts for 2-4 years.

The parts are kept separately in the warehouse, cannot be used or sold by Johan, and are ready for immediate delivery or collection at Marco's request. Johan agreed to the transaction as it decided that holding costs would be insignificant.

Required:

Explain the financial reporting treatment for the issues for the year ended 31 March 20X7.

Satisfying a performance obligation over time

'An entity transfers control of a good or service over time and, therefore, satisfies a performance obligation and recognises revenue over time, if one of the following criteria is met:

A the customer simultaneously receives and consumes the benefits provided by the entity's performance as the entity performs

B the entity's performance creates or enhances an asset (for example, work in progress) that the customer controls as the asset is created or enhanced, or

C the entity's performance does not create an asset with an alternative use to the entity and the entity has an enforceable right to payment for performance completed to date' (IFRS 15, para 35).

In FR, a common application of this is likely to be a building company constructing an asset for a customer. As long as the building company is not able to use the asset, and has a right to payment for work to date, revenue would be recognised over time.

'For each performance obligation satisfied over time, an entity shall recognise revenue over time by measuring the progress towards complete satisfaction of that performance obligation'

(IFRS 15, para 39).

Appropriate methods of measuring progress include (IFRS 15, para B14 – B19):

- output methods (such as surveys of performance (for example the value of the work certified as completed so far compared to the overall contract price), or time elapsed (time spent on the contract compared to total duration)).
- input methods (such as costs incurred to date as a proportion of total expected costs).

Revenue will be recognised based on the amount of progress made compared to the total price.

Contract costs

IFRS 15 says that the following costs must be capitalised:

- The incremental costs of obtaining a contract.
- The costs of fulfilling a contract if they do not fall within the scope of another standard (such as IAS 2 *Inventories*) and the entity expects them to be recovered.

The capitalised costs will be amortised as revenue is recognised. This means that they will be expensed to cost of sales as the contract progresses.

These will be matched against revenue based on either the input or output method of measuring progress. This means cost of sales will be measured as the percentage of progress made × total costs.

For a contract with a customer where revenue is recognised over time, there are three important rules to be aware of:

1. If the expected outcome is a **profit:**
   - revenue and costs should be recognised according to the progress of the contract.
2. If the expected outcome is a **loss:**
   - the whole loss should be recognised immediately, recording a provision as an onerous contract.
3. If the expected outcome or progress is **unknown** (often due to it being in the very early stages of the contract):
   - Revenue should be recognised to the level of recoverable costs (usually costs spent to date).
   - Contract costs should be recognised as an expense in the period in which they are incurred.

   In the majority of cases, this will mean that revenue and cost of sales will both be stated at costs incurred to date, with no profit or loss recorded.

Contract revenue and costs

Contract revenue

Contract revenue comprises:

- the initial amount of revenue agreed in the contract
- variations in contract work and claims, to the extent that:
  - it is probable that they will result in revenue
  - they are capable of being reliably measured.

Claims are amounts that the contractor seeks to reclaim from the customer as reimbursement for costs not included in the contract price. They may arise due to errors in design or customer-caused delay.

- incentive payments (additional payments made to the contractor if performance standards are met or exceeded) when
  - the contract is sufficiently advanced that it is probable that the specified performance standards will be met or exceeded, and
  - the amount of the incentive can be measured reliably.

Contract revenue is reduced by the amount of any penalties arising from delays caused by the contractor in the completion of the contract.

Contract costs

Contract costs comprise:

- costs that relate directly to the specific contract
- costs that are attributable to contract activity in general and can be allocated to the contract
- such other costs as are specifically chargeable to the customer under the terms of the contract.

Costs that relate directly to a specific contract include:

- site labour costs, including site supervision
- costs of materials used in construction
- depreciation of plant and equipment used on the contract
- costs of moving plant, equipment and materials to and from the contract site
- costs of hiring plant and equipment
- costs of design and technical assistance that is directly related to the contract
- the estimated costs of rectification and guarantee work, including expected warranty costs
- claims from third parties.

Costs that may be attributable to contract activity in general and can be allocated to specific contracts include:

- insurance
- costs of design and technical assistance that are not directly related to a specific contract
- construction overheads.

Illustration 7 – Contract profit

The following information relates to a construction contract:

Contract price	$800,000
Costs to date	$320,000
Estimated costs to complete	$280,000
Estimated stage of completion	60%

(a) **What amounts of revenue, costs and profit should be recognised in the statement of profit or loss?**

(b) Take the same contract, but now assume that the business is not able to reliably estimate the outcome of the contract although it is believed that all costs incurred will be recoverable from the customer.

What amounts should be recognised for revenue, costs and profit in the statement of profit or loss?

Solution

		$
(a)	Revenue ($800,000 × 60%)	480,000
	Costs ((320,000 + 280,000) × 60%)	(360,000)
	Profit	$120,000
(b)	Revenue (same as costs)	320,000
	Costs	(320,000)
	Profit	Nil

Presentation in the statement of financial position

As well as revenue and expenses, there are likely to be contract assets or liabilities. These will depend on the amounts recorded in the statement of profit or loss compared to the cash received or the costs to date.

The detail of these is covered further in step 4 below.

In calculating the entries to be made for a contract where the performance obligation is satisfied over time, such as a building project for a customer, a 4-step approach can be helpful.

Step 1 – Calculate overall profit or loss

	$
Contract price	X
Less: Costs to date	(X)
Less: Costs to complete	(X)
Overall profit/loss	X/(X)

Step 2 – Determining the progress of a contract

There are two acceptable methods of measuring progress towards satisfying a performance obligation:

- Input methods – based on the inputs used. A commonly used measure looks at contract costs incurred to date as a percentage of total expected costs.
- Output methods – based on performance completed to date. This is commonly done based on the value of the work certified to date as a percentage of the total contract price.

  If revenue is earned equally over time (e.g. providing a monthly payroll service), then revenue would be recognised on a straight line basis over that period.

Where progress cannot be measured

Revenue should be recognised only to the extent of contract costs incurred that will probably be recoverable.

Step 3 – Statement of profit or loss (if profitable)

	$
Revenue (Total price × progress %)	
less revenue recognised in previous years	X
Cost of sales (Total costs × progress %)	
less cost of sales recognised in previous years	(X)
Profit	X

If a contract is in the second year, it is important to remember that any revenue/costs recognised in previous years should be deducted from the cumulative revenue/costs. This will give the figures to be recognised in the current year.

For example, if a contract is worth $10 million and it is 90% satisfied by the end of year 2, and was 50% satisfied by the end of year 1, then $9 million has been earned to date, of which $5 million would have been recognised in year 1. This means that $4 million would be recognised as revenue in year 2.

Step 4 – Statement or financial position

At the year end, there will either be a contract asset or liability, recorded in current assets or current liabilities. This will be calculated as shown below:

	$
Costs to date (Actual costs, not necessarily cost of sales)	X
Profit/loss to date	X/(X)
Less: Amount billed to date	(X)
Contract asset/liability	X/(X)

Note that these figures are **cumulative** and not annual.

If an item of property, plant and equipment is used in the contract, the asset will be held at carrying amount at the year-end. The depreciation will be charged to the statement of profit or loss according to the progress made towards satisfying the contract.

Contract asset/liability

IFRS 15 is not prescriptive about the treatment of contract assets/liabilities.

As alternatives to the term 'contract asset', IFRS 15 also allows the terms receivable and work-in-progress to be used. If revenue exceeds cash received, this could be included within trade receivables. If costs to date exceed cost of sales, this could be included within inventory, as work-in-progress.

If the cash received exceeds the revenue recognised to date, there will be a contract liability (effectively deferring the income).

If a contract is loss-making, there will be a provision recorded to recognise the full loss under the onerous contract, as per IAS 37 (see Chapter 15). This can either be termed as a contract liability or a provision.

Test your understanding 4 – Baker

On 1 January 20X1, Baker entered into a contract with a customer to construct a specialised building for consideration of $2m plus a bonus of $0.4m if the building is completed within 18 months. Estimated costs to construct the building were $1.5m. If the contract is terminated by the customer, Baker can demand payment for the costs incurred to date plus a mark-up of 30%. On 1 January 20X1, as a result of factors outside of its control, Baker was not sure whether the bonus would be achieved.

At 31 December 20X1 Baker had incurred costs of $1m. They were still unsure as to whether the bonus target would be met. Baker measures progress towards completion based on costs incurred.

At 31 December 20X1 Baker had received $1 million from the customer.

Required:

How should this transaction be accounted for in the year ended 31 December 20X1?

Test your understanding 5

On 1 January 20X1, Castle entered into a contract with a customer to construct a specialised building for consideration of $10m. Castle is not able to use the building themselves at any point during the construction.

At 31 December 20X1, Castle had incurred costs of $6m. Costs to complete are estimated at $6m. Castle measures progress towards completion based on costs incurred.

At 31 December 20X1 Castle had received $3 million from the customer.

Required:

How should this transaction be accounted for in the year ended 31 December 20X1?

Test your understanding 6

On 1 January 20X1 Amir entered into a contract with a customer to construct a stadium for consideration of $100m. The contract was expected to take 2 years to complete.

At 31 December 20X1 Amir had incurred costs of $24m. Costs to complete are estimated at $20m. In addition to these costs, Amir purchased plant to be used on the contract at a cost of $16m. This plant was purchased on 1 January 20X1 and will have no residual value at the end of the 2 year contract. Depreciation on the plant is to be allocated on a straight line basis across the contract.

Amir measures progress on contracts using an output method, based on the value of work certified to date.

At 31 December 20X1, the value of the work certified was $45 million, and the customer had paid $11.4m.

Required:

How should this transaction be accounted for in the year ended 31 December 20X1?

2 Chapter summary

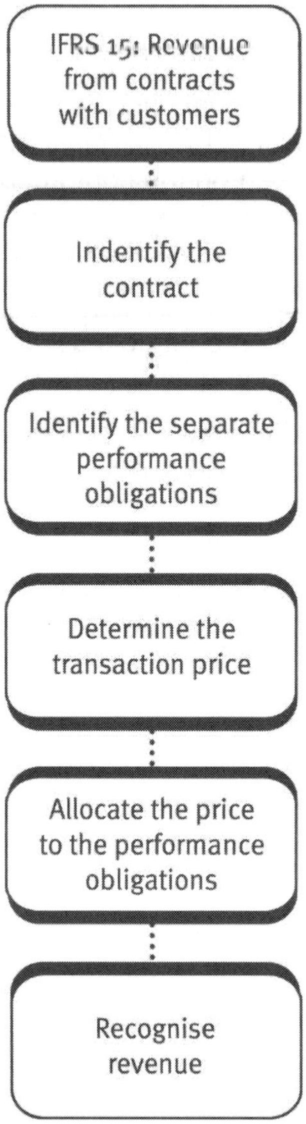

Test your understanding 7

Hardfloor Co fits out nightclubs. The projects generally take a number of months to complete. The company had three contracts in progress at the year ended 30 April 20X7, and details are as follows:

	J	K	L
	$000	$000	$000
Costs incurred to date	320	540	20
Costs to complete	40	90	220
Contract price	416	684	300
Work certified to date	312	456	–
Progress payments	250	480	–

Hardfloor Co accounts for profit on its construction contracts using the percentage of completion derived from the sales earned as work certified compared to the total sales value.

Calculate the effects of the above contracts upon the financial statements of Hardfloor Co for the year ended 30 April 20X7.

Test your understanding 8

Merryview specialises in long-term contracts. In each contract Merryview is entitled to receive payments reflecting the progress of the work, so revenue should be recognised over time.

One of its contracts, with Better Homes, is to build a complex of luxury flats. The price agreed for the contract is $10 million and its scheduled date of completion is 31 December 20X2. Details of the contract to 31 March 20X1 are:

Commencement date	1 July 20X0
Contract costs:	$000
Architects' and surveyors' fees	500
Materials delivered to site	2,800
Direct labour costs	3,500
Overheads are apportioned at 40% of direct labour costs	
Estimated cost to complete (excluding depreciation – see below)	14,800

Plant and machinery used exclusively on the contract cost $3,600,000 on 1 July 20X0. At the end of the contract it is expected to be transferred to a different contract at a value of $600,000. Depreciation is to be based on a time-apportioned basis. Better Homes made a progress payment of $12,800,000 to Merryview on 31 March 20X1.

At 31 March 20X2 the details for the construction contract have been summarised as:

	$000
Contract costs to date (i.e. since the start of the contract) excluding all depreciation	20,400
Estimated cost to complete (excluding depreciation)	6,600

A further progress payment of $16,200,000 was received from Better Homes on 31 March 20X2. Merryview accounts for profit on its construction contracts using the input method, measured using the percentage of the cost to date compared to the total estimated contract cost.

Required:

Prepare extracts from the financial statements of Merryview reflecting the impact of the contract with Better Homes for:

(i) the year to 31 March 20X1

(ii) the year to 31 March 20X2.

Test your understanding 9

1 The following information relates to a contract for the construction of a building for a customer. The builder has a right to regular payments as the work progresses.

	$
Contract price	5 million
Work certified to date	2 million
Costs to date	1.8 million
Estimated costs to complete	2.2 million

What is the revenue, cost of sales and gross profit that can be recognised, assuming that the company's policy is to measure progress using an output method, based on the work certified to date?

	Revenue	Cost of sales	Gross profit
A	$2 million	$1.8 million	$0.2 million
B	$2 million	$1.6 million	$0.4 million
C	$2 million	$1.55 million	$0.45 million
D	$2.25 million	$1.8 million	$0.45 million

2 The following information relates to a contract for the construction of a building for a customer. The builder has a right to regular payments as the work progresses. Progress is measured on an output basis, based on the work certified compared to the contract price.

	$000
Contract price	370
Work certified to date	320
Costs to date	360
Estimated costs to complete	50

What amounts should be shown in the statement of profit or loss for revenue and cost of sales?

	Revenue ($000)	Cost of sales ($000)
A	320	360
B	370	400
C	320	355
D	370	410

Data for Questions 3 and 4

CN started a three-year contract to build a new university campus on 1 April 20X7. The contract had a fixed price of $90 million. CN incurred costs at 31 March 20X8 of $77 million and estimated that a further $33 million would need to be spent to complete the contract. CN has a right to receive regular payments under the contract. To date, CN have received $55 million. CN uses an input method based on costs to calculate the progress of the contract.

3 **What revenue should be recorded for the year to 31 March 20X8?**

$ ___________

4 **What should be shown in CN's statement of financial position as at 31 March 20X8?**

	Current assets	Current liabilities
A	Trade receivables 6	Provision 6
B	Trade receivables 8	Provision 20
C	Trade receivables 6	Provision 20
D	Trade receivables 8	Provision 6

5 **Which of the following is not one of the 5 steps for recognising revenue according to IFRS 15 *Revenue from Contracts with Customers*?**

A Identify the contract

B Assess the likelihood of economic benefits

C Determine the contract price

D Allocate the transaction price to the performance obligations in the contract.

6 Daphne is an agent who works on behalf of Celeste, a famous singer. Daphne has just collected $1 million from a promoter for ticket sales for a recent show by Celeste. Daphne earns commission of 10% in relation to Celeste's work.

What is the correct double entry for the receipt of the $1 million?

A	Dr Cash $1 million	Cr Trade payables $1 million
	Dr Trade Receivables $100,000	Cr Revenue $100,000
B	Dr Cash $1 million	Cr Revenue $1 million
	Dr COS $900,000	Cr Trade payables $900,000
C	Dr COS $900,000	Cr Revenue $1 million
	Dr Cash $100,000	
D	Dr Cash $1 million	Cr Revenue $100,000
		Cr Trade payables $900,000

7 Coal Co sold a specialised piece of equipment to Oil Co on 1 September 20X7 for a total price of $4m, which incorporated both the sale of equipment and support service. Due to the specialised nature of the equipment, Coal Co had additionally agreed to provide a support service for two years to 31 August 20X9. The cost to Coal Co of providing this service will be $300,000 per annum. Coal Co usually earns a gross margin of 20% on such contracts.

What revenue should be included in the statement of profit or loss of Coal Co for the year ended 31 December 20X7?

$______________ '000

8 Almeyda entered into a sale and repurchase agreement for its head office on 1 January 20X1, selling it to a bank for $4 million. At this date the head office had a fair value of $6 million and a carrying amount of $3.8 million. Almeyda will continue to use the head office for the next 2 years and has the option to buy it back for $4.84 million, based on an effective interest rate of 10% per year over the next 2 years. Property prices are expected to increase over the next 2 years.

What is the net amount to be shown in the statement of profit or loss for the year ended 31 December 20X1?

A $400,000 expense

B $200,000 income

C $200,000 expense

D $300,000 expense

Test your understanding answers

Test your understanding 1 – Keema Co

Due to the length of time between the transfer of control of the asset and the payment date, this contract includes a significant financing component.

The consideration must be adjusted for the impact of the financing transaction. A discount rate should be used that reflects the rate available to the customer i.e. 7%.

Revenue should be recognised when the performance obligation is satisfied. This is achieved when control of the furniture passes to the customer.

Revenue and a corresponding receivable should be recognised at \$655,079 (\$750,000 × $1/1.07^2$) on 30 September 20X3.

Each year, the discount on the receivable will be unwound by 7%, recognising the increase as finance income, and increasing the value of the receivable (debit receivable, credit finance income).

In the financial statements for the year ended 30 September 20X4 Keema Co will recognise finance income of \$45,856 and a receivable of \$700,935, as follows:

	$
1 October 20X3 b/f	655,079
20X4 Finance income @ 7%	45,856
30 September 20X4 Receivable balance	700,935

Test your understanding 2 – Shinji Co

The selling price of the machine is \$60,000 based on observable evidence.

There is no observable selling price for the technical support. Therefore the stand-alone selling price needs to be estimated. One approach for this is to use the expected costs plus a margin. Based on this the selling price of the service would be \$15,000 (\$10,000 × 150%).

The total stand-alone selling price of the machine and support is \$75,000 (\$60,000 + \$15,000). However, total consideration receivable is only \$50,000. This means that the customer is receiving a discount for purchasing a bundle of goods and services of 33% (\$25,000/\$75,000).

IFRS 15 says that an entity must consider whether the discount relates to the whole bundle or to a particular performance obligation. In the absence of additional information, it is assumed here that it relates to the whole bundle.

So we can use a discount of 33% on the stand-alone prices or alternatively the actual prices for each element could be calculated based on a proportion of the stand-alone prices.

	Stand-alone price		Actual price
	$		$
Machine	60,000	Less 33% =	40,000
Support	15,000	Less 33% =	10,000
	75,000		50,000

The alternative method would calculate the price of the machine based on the machine's proportion of total stand-alone price, so

$50,000 × 60,000/75,000 = $40,000

The revenue will be recognised as and when the performance obligations are satisfied.

Test your understanding 3 – Johan

(a) The scenario indicates that control of the factory has not passed to Cruyff. Johan has retained use of the factory, as well as responsibility for maintaining and insuring it.

In addition to this, the sale has been made at a value significantly lower than the market value. The option to repurchase is also significantly below the market value. Therefore, this should not be treated as a sale.

The factory should not be removed from the financial statements of Johan. The $800,000 should be treated as a loan, with 7% interest recorded on it each year. Therefore, for the year ended 31 March 20X7 $56,000 ($800,000 × 7%) should be recorded in finance costs.

(b) This is a bill-and-hold arrangement. Even though Johan retains physical possession of the parts, Marco retains control. This can be seen in the fact that Johan cannot use or sell the goods and must release them immediately upon Marco's request.

In this arrangement there are potentially three performance obligations. These will be the provision of the oven and the spare parts, and the storage of the spare parts. However, the storage of the parts is deemed insignificant.

The performance obligations to provide the machine and the spare parts appear to be met on 31 March 20X7, so the full $220,000 revenue can be recognised on this date.

If the cost to store the parts had been deemed to be significant, and therefore part of the transaction price, the price related to this performance obligation would be separately recognised over the expected period of holding the parts.

Test your understanding 4 – Baker

Constructing the building is a single performance obligation.

The bonus is variable consideration. It is excluded from the transaction price because it is not highly probable that a significant reversal in the amount of cumulative revenue recognised will not occur.

The construction of the building should be accounted for as an obligation settled over time.

Baker should recognise revenue based on progress towards satisfaction of the construction of the building.

1 **Overall contract**

	$000
Price	2,000
Costs to date	(1,000)
Costs to complete	(500)
Overall profit	500

2 **Progress**

An input method is used to calculate the progress, being costs to date compared to total costs.

1,000/1,500 = 66.7% (or 2/3)

3 **Statement of profit or loss**

	$000
Revenue (2,000 × 2/3)	1,333
Cost of sales (1,500 × 2/3)	(1,000)
Profit	333

4 **Statement of financial position**

	$000
Costs to date	1,000
Profit to date	333
Less: Billed to date	(1000)
Contract asset	**333**

Test your understanding 5

The construction of the building should be accounted for as an obligation settled over time.

Castle should recognise revenue based on progress towards satisfaction of the construction of the building.

1 **Overall contract**

	$000
Price	10,000
Costs to date	(6,000)
Costs to complete	(6,000)
Overall **loss**	(2,000)

As the contract is loss making, Castle must provide for the full loss immediately.

2 **Progress**

An input method is used to calculate the progress, being costs to date compared to total costs.

6,000/12,000 = 50%

3 **Statement of profit or loss**

	$000
Revenue (10,000 × 50%	5,000
Cost of sales (12,000 × 50%)	(6,000)
Cost of sales (provision to recognise the full loss)	(1,000)
Loss	(2,000)

Revenue and expenses should be recorded based on the progress to date. However, doing this would only recognise 50% of the loss. Therefore a provision is made in order to recognise the full loss of $2 million immediately.

4 **Statement of financial position**

	$000
Costs to date	6,000
Loss to date	(2,000)
Less: Amount billed to date	(3,000)
Contract asset	**1,000**

Test your understanding 6

1 **Overall contract**

	$000
Price	100,000
Costs to date	(24,000)
Costs to complete	(20,000)
Plant cost	(16,000)
Overall profit	40,000

2 **Progress**

An output method is used to calculate the progress, being work certified to date compared to the total contract price

45,000/100,000 = 45%

3 **Statement of profit or loss**

	$000
Revenue ($100,000 × 45%)	45,000
Cost of sales (Total costs of $60,000 × 45%)	(27,000)
Profit	18,000

4 **Statement of financial position**

	$000	
Non-current assets		
Property, plant & equipment	8,000	**(W1)**
Current assets		
Contract asset	38,600	**(W2)**

Alternatively, the current asset could be split between receivables and inventory, rather than being held as a contract asset:

Current assets		
Inventory (work-in-progress)	5,000	**(W3)**
Trade receivable	33,600	(45,000 revenue less 11,400 cash received **(W4)**)

Workings:

(W1) Property, plant & equipment

The plant cost $16 million and should be depreciated over the 2 year period. Therefore by the year end, the depreciation is $8 million, and the carrying amount is also $8 million.

(W2) Contract asset

	$000
Costs to date ($24m + $8m depreciation)	32,000
Profit to date	18,000
Less: Amount billed to date	(11,400)
Contract asset	38,600

(W3) Inventory

As the costs to date (costs spent to date plus depreciation to date) exceed the cost of sales, the difference will be treated as work-in-progress within inventory.

Costs to date: $24m + $8m depreciation = $32m

Cost of sales: $27m

Therefore WIP = $32m – $27m = **$5m**.

(W4) Receivable

Revenue – $45 million. Cash received = $11.4 million.
Therefore receivable = $33.6 million

Test your understanding 7

1 **Overall contract**

	J	K	L
	$000	$000	$000
Revenue	416	684	300
Costs to date	(320)	(540)	(20)
Costs to complete	(40)	(90)	(220)
Total profit	56	54	60

2 **Progress**

Contract	**% complete calculated as:** **Work certified / Contract price**
J	312/416 = 75%
K	456/684 = 66.67%
L	–/300 = Nothing certified

3 **Statement of profit or loss**

Note: For contract L, revenue should be recognised to level of recoverable costs as the progress is unknown.

	J	K	L
	$000	$000	$000
Revenue			
(Price × progress %)	312	456	20
Cost of sales			
(Total costs × progress%)	(270)	(420)	(20)
Gross profit	42	36	–

4 **Statement of financial position**

	Contract J	Contract K	Contract L
	$000	$000	$000
Costs to date	320	540	20
Profit/loss to date	42	36	–
Less: billed to date	(250)	(480)	–
Contract asset	112	96	20

Test your understanding 8

1 **Overall contract**

	31 March 20X1	31 March 20X2
	$000	$000
Price	**40,000**	**40,000**
Costs to date:		20,400
Architects' and surveyors' fees	500	
Materials used	2,800	
Direct labour	3,500	
Overheads (40% of 3,500)	1,400	
Depreciation		
($3m/30 months × 9 months)	900	
($3m/30 months × 21 months)		2,100
Total costs to date	**9,100**	**22,500**

	31 March 20X1 $000	31 March 20X2 $000
Costs to complete:		
Excluding depreciation	14,800	6,600
Depreciation ($3m/30 months × 21 months)	2,100	
Depreciation ($3m/30 months × 9 months)		900
Total costs	**26,000**	**30,000**
Total profit	**14,000**	**10,000**

2 **Progress**

$$\frac{\textbf{Costs to date}}{\textbf{Total costs}}$$

20X1	9,100/26,000 = 35%
20X2	22,500/30,000 = 75%

3 **Statement of profit or loss**

	31 March 20X1 $000	31 March 20X2 $000	
Revenue (40,000 × 35%)	14,000	16,000	((40,000×75%) –14,000)
Cost of sales (26,000 × 35%)	(9,100)	(13,400)	((30,000×75%) – 9,100)
Gross profit	4,900	2,600	

4 **Statement of financial position**

31 March 20X1		
Non-current assets		(Cost 3,600 less 900 depreciation)
Property, plant and equipment	2,700	
Current assets		
Contract asset	1,200	(See below)

	$000	
31 March 20X2		
Non-current assets		
Property, plant and equipment	1,500	(Cost 3,600 less 2,100 depreciation)
Current assets		
Contract asset	1,000	(See below)

Working for contract asset:

	20X1	**20X2**
	$000	$000
Costs to date (cumulative)	9,100	22,500
Profit to date (cumulative)	4,900	7,500
Less: Amount billed to date (cumulative)	(12,800)	(29,000)
Contract asset	1,200	1,000

	$000	
31 March 20X2		
Non-current assets		
Property, plant and equipment	1,500	(Cost 3,600 less 2,100 depreciation)
Current assets		
Contract asset	1,000	(See below)

Working for contract asset:

	20X1	**20X2**
	$000	$000
Costs to date (cumulative)	9,100	22,500
Profit to date (cumulative)	4,900	7,500
Less: Amount billed to date (cumulative)	(12,800)	(29,000)
Contract asset	1,200	1,000

Test your understanding 9

1 **B**

Step 1 – Overall	$m
Total revenue	5.0
Costs to date	(1.8)
Costs to complete	(2.2)
Total profit	1.0

Step 2 – Progress

Progress = 2 million/5 million = 40%

Step 3 – Statement of profit or loss	
Revenue (40% × 5)	2
Cost of sales (40% × 4)	(1.6)
Gross profit	0.4

2 **A**

Step 1 – Overall	$000
Total revenue	370
Costs to date	(360)
Costs to complete	(50)
Total loss	(40)

Step 2 – Progress

Work certified/Price = 320/370 = 86%

Step 3 – Statement of profit or loss	
Revenue (86% × 370)	320
Cost of sales (86% × 410 total costs)	(355)
Cost of sales (provision for the full loss)	(5)
Total loss	(40)

We must recognise the whole of the loss in order to be prudent – hence cost of sales will be the balancing item between revenue and loss.

3 **$63 million**

Step 1 – Overall	$m
Price	90
Costs to date	(77)
Costs to complete	(33)
Total loss	(20)

Step 2 – Progress

Costs to date/Total costs = 77/110 = 70%

Step 3 – Statement of profit or loss	
Revenue (70% × 90)	63
Cost of sales (70% × 110 total costs)	(77)
Cost of sales (provision for the full loss)	(6)
Total loss	(20)

The revenue to be recognised will be 70% × total revenue of $90 million = $63 million.

The contract makes an overall loss of $20 million which must be recognised immediately in order to be prudent.

4 **D**

Step 4 – Statement of financial position	
Current assets	
Trade receivables	
(63 revenue – 55 cash received)	8
Current liabilities	
Provision (to recognise full loss)	6

5 **B** – While assessing the likelihood of economic benefits is part of identifying the contract, it is not listed as one of the five steps.

6 **D** – As an agent, Daphne should only record the commission of $100,000 in revenue. As the cash has been received, Daphne must record that in cash and create a payable for $900,000 to remit the balance to Celeste.

7 **$3,375,000** – There are two performance obligations here. The revenue from the sale of the equipment should be recognised at a point in time, and the revenue in relation to the support should be recognised over time. The service element costs $300,000 a year. As Coal Co makes a margin of 20%, this would be sold for $375,000 per year ($300,000 × 100/80). Therefore the total revenue for the service for 2 years = $375,000 × 2 = $750,000. The revenue on the goods = $4m – $750,000 = $3,250,000.

The revenue in relation to the service is recognised over 2 years. By 31 December 20X7, 4 months of the service has been performed so can be recognised in revenue ($375,000 × 4/12 = $125,000).

Therefore the total revenue = $3,250,000 + $125,000 = $3,375,000

8 **A** – This transaction should be treated as a loan secured on the property. Therefore the only entry into the statement of profit or loss for the year will be $400,000 finance cost ($4m × 10%).

Chapter

12

Leases

Chapter learning objectives

Upon completion of this chapter you will be able to:

- account for right-of-use assets and lease liabilities in the records of the lessee
- explain the exemption from the recognition criteria for leases in the records of the lessee
- account for sale and leaseback agreements.

PER

One of the PER performance objectives (PO6) is to record and process transactions and events. You use the right accounting treatments for transactions and events. These should be both historical and prospective – and include non-routine transactions. Working though this chapter should help you understand how to demonstrate that objective.

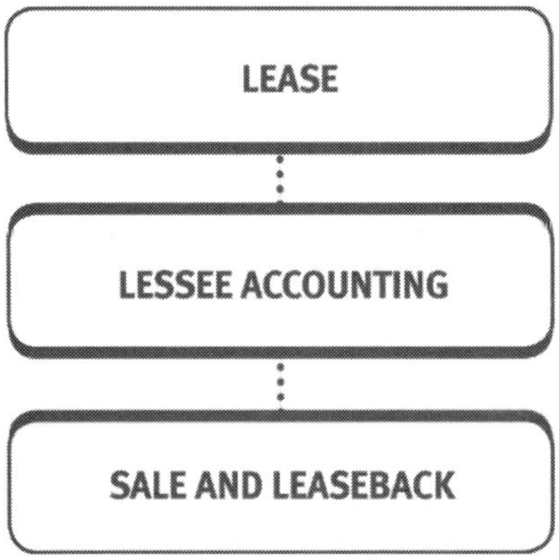

1 Leases: Definitions (IFRS 16, Appendix A)

'A lease is a contract, or part of a contract, that conveys the right to use an asset (the underlying asset) for a period of time in exchange for consideration.'

The **lessor** is the **'entity that provides the right to use an underlying asset in exchange for consideration.'**

The **lessee** is the **'entity that obtains the right to use an underlying asset in exchange for consideration.'**

A **right-of-use asset 'represents the lessee's rights to use an underlying asset for the lease term.'**

2 Lessee accounting

Basic principle

At the commencement of the lease, the lessee should recognise a lease liability and a right-of-use asset.

Initial measurement

The liability (IFRS 16, para 26)

The lease liability is initially measured at the present value of the lease payments that have not yet been paid.

Lease payments should include the following (IFRS 16, para 27):

- Fixed payments
- Amounts expected to be payable under residual value guarantees
- Options to purchase the asset that are reasonably certain to be exercised
- Termination penalties, if the lease term reflects the expectation that these will be incurred.

A residual value guarantee is when the lessor is guaranteed that the underlying asset at the end of the lease term will not be worth less than a specified amount.

The discount rate should be the rate implicit in the lease. If this cannot be determined, then the entity should use its incremental borrowing rate (the rate at which it could borrow funds to purchase a similar asset).

The right-of-use asset

The right-of-use asset is initially recognised at cost.

The initial cost of the right-of-use asset comprises (IFRS 16, para 24):

- The amount of the initial measurement of the lease liability (see above)
- Lease payments made at or before the commencement date
- Any initial direct costs
- The estimated costs of removing or dismantling the underlying asset as per the conditions of the lease.

The lease term

To calculate the initial value of the liability and right-of-use asset, the lessee must consider the length of the lease term. The lease term comprises (IFRS 16, Appendix A):

- Non-cancellable periods
- Periods covered by an option to extend the lease if reasonably certain to be exercised
- Periods covered by an option to terminate the lease if these are reasonably certain not to be exercised.

Test your understanding 1 – Dynamic

On 1 January 20X1, Dynamic entered into a two year lease for a lorry. The contract contains an option to extend the lease term for a further year. Dynamic believes that it is reasonably certain to exercise this option. Lorries have a useful life of ten years.

Lease payments are $10,000 per year for the initial term and $15,000 per year for the option period. All payments are due at the end of the year. To obtain the lease, Dynamic incurs initial direct costs of $3,000. The interest rate within the lease is not readily determinable. Dynamic's incremental rate of borrowing is 5%.

Required:

Calculate the initial carrying amount of the lease liability and the right-of-use asset and provide the double entries needed to record these amounts in Dynamic's financial records.

Subsequent measurement

The liability

The carrying amount of the lease liability is increased by the interest charge, calculated as the outstanding liability multiplied by the discount rate of interest. This interest is also recorded in the statement of profit or loss:

Dr Finance costs (SPL)	X
Cr Lease liability (SFP)	X

The carrying amount of the lease liability is reduced by cash repayments:

Dr Lease liability	X
Cr Cash	X

To work out the interest and year end liabilities, a lease liability table is often used (see illustration below). The layout of the table will depend on whether payments are made at the end of the year (in arrears) or at the start of the year (in advance).

Payments in arrears

Year	Balance b/f	Interest	Payment	Balance c/f
1	X	X	(X)	X
2	X	X	(X)	X
				(NCL)

Payments in advance

Year	Balance b/f	Payment	Subtotal	Interest	Balance c/f
1	X	(X)	X	X	X
2	X	(X)	X	X	X
			(NCL)		

On the statement of financial position the total liability at the end of year 1 is split between its non-current and current elements. For payments made in advance or arrears the non-current liability (NCL) is represented by the balance outstanding immediately after the payment in year 2. The difference between the total liability at the year-end and the non-current liability will be the current liability. Note that where payments are made in advance the non-current liability is not the balance outstanding at the end of year 2, as this includes the interest charge for year 2.

The right-of-use asset

The right-of-use asset is measured using the cost model (unless another measurement model is chosen). This means that the asset is measured at its initial cost less accumulated depreciation and impairment losses.

Depreciation is calculated as follows:

- If ownership of the asset transfers to the lessee at the end of the lease term then depreciation should be charged over the asset's useful life,
- Otherwise, depreciation is charged over the shorter of the useful life and the lease term (as defined previously).

e.g

Illustration 1 – Lease payments in arrears

Riyad enters into an agreement to lease an asset. The terms of the lease are as follows.

1 Primary period is for four years from 1 January 20X2 with a rental of $2,000 pa payable on 31 December each year.

2 The present value of the lease payments is $5,710

3 The interest rate implicit in the lease is 15%.

What figures will be shown in the financial statements for the year ended 31 December 20X2?

Solution

A **non-current right-of-use asset** is recorded at an initial value of $5,710.

Annual **depreciation charge = 1/4 × $5,710 = $1,428.**

A liability is initially recorded at $5,710.

The total finance charge for the lease is calculated as the difference between the total payments of $8,000 and the initial value of $5,710 = $2,290. The allocation of this to each rental period is calculated using the implicit interest rate on a lease liability table as follows:

Period	Liability b/f	Interest @ 15%	Payment	Liability c/f
20X2	5,710	857	(2,000)	4,567
20X3	4,567	685	(2,000)	3,252
20X4	3,252	488	(2,000)	1,740
20X5	1,740	260	(2,000)	–
		2,290	8,000	

The format above will be used whenever the payments under a lease are made in arrears. If the payments are due in advance, the rental paid is deducted from the capital sum at the start of the period before the interest is calculated.

Extracts from financial statements for the year to 31 December 20X2

Statement of profit or loss

	$
Depreciation	(1,428)
Finance cost	(857)

Statement of financial position

Non-current assets	
Right-of-use asset (5,710 – 1,428)	4,282
Non-current liabilities	
Lease	3,252
Current liabilities	
Lease	1,315

Test your understanding 2 – Dynamic (continued)

This question follows on from the previous TYU.

Required:

Prepare extracts from Dynamic's financial statements in respect of the lease agreement for the year ended 31 December 20X1.

Short-life and low value assets

If the lease is short-term (less than 12 months at the inception date) or of a low value then a simplified treatment is allowed.

In these cases, the lessee can choose to recognise the lease payments in profit or loss on a straight line basis. No lease liability or right-of-use asset would therefore be recognised.

Low value assets

IFRS 16 *Leases* does not specify a particular monetary amount below which an asset would be considered 'low value', although the basis for conclusion indicates a value of $5,000 as a guide

The standard also gives the following examples of low value assets:

- tablets
- small personal computers
- telephones
- small items of furniture.

The assessment of whether an asset qualifies as having a 'low value' must be made based on its value when new. Therefore, a car would not qualify as a low value asset, even if it was very old at the commencement of the lease.

Illustration 2 – Low value assets

On 1 April 20X6 Taggart acquires telephones for its sales force under a two year lease agreement. The terms of the lease require an initial payment of $2,000, followed by two payments of $8,000 each on 31 March 20X7 and 31 March 20X8.

Show the impact of this lease arrangement on the financial statements of Taggart for the year ended 31 December 20X6.

Solution

IFRS 16 *Leases* permits a simplified treatment for assets with a lease period of 12 months or less, or of low value. Although the standard does not give a numerical definition of 'low value' it does give examples of the types of assets that may be included, and this includes telephones. The simplified treatment allows the lease payments to be charged as an expense over the lease period, applying the accruals concept.

$$\text{Annual lease rental expense} = \frac{\text{Total rentals payable}}{\text{Total lease period}} = \frac{\$2,000 + \$8,000 + \$8,000}{2 \text{ years}}$$

$$= \$9,000 \text{ per annum}$$

Expense to 31 December 20X6	=	$9,000 × 9/12	= $6,750

The expense in this period of $6,750 is not the same as the payment of $2,000 so we need to accrue an additional expense of $4,750.

Financial statements extract:

Statement of profit or loss for the year ended 31 December 20X6

	$
Lease rental expense	(6,750)

Statement of financial position 31 December 20X6

	$
Current liabilities	
Accrual	4,750

Mid-year entry into a lease

If a company enters into a lease part-way through the year, the depreciation and interest will need to be time-apportioned.

The liability table is likely to need extra columns to split the table between pre- and post-payment.

e.g

Illustration 3 – Mid-year entry into a lease

Shaeen Ltd entered into an agreement to lease an item of plant on 1 October 20X8. The lease required four annual payments of $200,000 each, commencing on 1 October 20X8. The plant has a useful life of four years and is to be scrapped at the end of this period. The present value of the lease payments is $700,000. The implicit interest rate within the lease is 10%.

Prepare extracts of the financial statements in respect of the leased asset for the year ended 31 March 20X9.

Solution

Statement of profit or loss extract	$
Depreciation **(W1)**	(87,500)
Finance costs **(W2)**	(25,000)
Statement of financial position extract	
Non-current assets	
Right-of-use asset (700,000 – 87,500)	612,500
Non-current liabilities	
Lease (W3)	350,000
Current liabilities	
Lease (525,000 – 350,000)	175,000

Workings

(W1) Depreciation

Depreciated over 4 years

Expense = 700,000/4 years × 6/12 = $87,500

(W2) Lease

Year-end	Bal b/f	Interest @10% × 6/12	Initial balance	Paid	Balance @ 1 Oct	Interest @10% × 6/12	Bal c/f
31.3.X9	–		700,000	(200,000)	500,000	25,000	525,000
31.3.Y0	525,000	25,000		(200,000)	350,000		

Note that there is no interest charged in the first half of the first year and that the interest charged in the first half of the second year reflects the interest on the balance at 1 October. Once calculated, the split for non-current and current liabilities works as normal.

3 Sale and leaseback

If an entity (the seller-lessee) transfers an asset to another entity (the buyer-lessor) and then leases it back from the buyer, the seller-lessee must assess whether the transfer should be accounted for as a sale.

For this purpose, the seller must apply IFRS 15 *Revenue from Contracts with Customers* to decide whether a performance obligation has been satisfied. This normally occurs when the buyer obtains control of the asset. Control of an asset refers to the ability to obtain substantially all of the remaining benefits.

Transfer is not a sale

If the transfer is not a sale then the seller-lessee continues to recognise the transferred asset and will recognise a financial liability equal to the transfer proceeds.

In simple terms, the transfer proceeds are treated as a loan. The detailed accounting treatment of financial assets and financial liabilities is covered in Chapter 9.

Transfer is a sale

If the transfer does qualify as a sale then the seller-lessee must measure the right-of-use asset as the proportion of the previous carrying amount that relates to the rights retained.

- This means that the seller-lessee will recognise a profit or loss based only on the rights transferred to the buyer-lessor.

Test your understanding 3 – Painting

On 1 January 20X1, Painting sells an item of machinery to Collage for its fair value of $3 million. The asset had a carrying amount of $1.2 million prior to the sale. This sale represents the satisfaction of a performance obligation, in accordance with IFRS 15 *Revenue from Contracts with Customers.* Painting enters into a contract with Collage for the right to use the asset for the next five years. Annual payments of $500,000 are due at the end of each year. The interest rate implicit in the lease is 10%.

The present value of the annual lease payments is £1.9 million. The remaining useful life of the machine is much greater than the lease term.

Required:

Explain how Painting will account for the transaction on 1 January 20X1.

4 Chapter summary

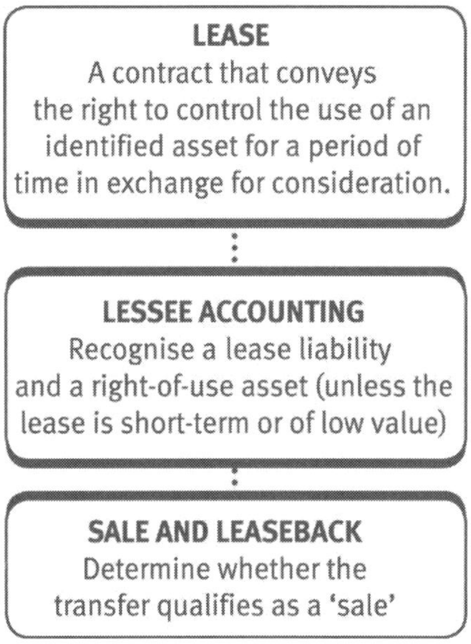

Test your understanding 4 – Fryatt

Leases

The following trial balance relates to Fryatt at 31 May 20X7:

	Dr	Cr
	$	$
Revenue		630,000
Cost of sales	324,000	
Distribution costs	19,800	
Administration expenses	15,600	
Loan interest paid	6,800	
Property – cost	240,000	
Property – depreciation at 1 June 20X6		40,000
Plant and equipment – cost	140,000	
Plant and equipment – depreciation at 1 June 20X6		48,600
Trade receivables	51,200	
Inventory – 31 May 20X7	19,600	
Bank	4,300	
Trade payables		35,200
Ordinary shares $1		25,000
Share premium		7,000
Bank Loan (repayable 31 December 20X9)		20,000
Retained earnings at 1 June 20X6		15,500
	821,300	821,300

The following notes are relevant:

1 Owned plant and equipment is to be depreciated on the reducing balance basis at a rate of 20% per annum. The property cost includes land at a cost of $60,000. The building is depreciated over 30 years on a straight line basis. All depreciation is charged to cost of sales.

2 On 1 June 20X6 Fryatt commenced using an item of plant and machinery under a lease agreement, with three annual payments of $29,000. The first payment was made on 31 May 20X7 and has been charged to cost of sales. The present value of the lease payments at 1 June 20X6 was $72,000. Under the terms of the lease Fryatt has the option to extend the lease indefinitely at a reduced rental at the end of the 3 years. The plant has an estimated useful life of six years, with a negligible value at the end of this period. The rate of interest implicit in the lease is 10%.

3 The directors have estimated the provision for income tax for the year to 31 May 20X7 at $7,200.

Required:

Prepare the statement of profit or loss for Fryatt for the year to 31 May 20X7 and a statement of financial position at that date, in a form suitable for presentation to the shareholders and in accordance with the requirements of IFRS Standards.

Test your understanding 5 – MCQ

1 An entity leases a computer with legal title of the asset passing after two years. The entity usually depreciates computers over three years. The entity also leases a machine for seven years but legal title does not pass to the entity at the end of the agreement. The entity usually depreciates machinery over ten years.

Over what period of time should the computer and machine be depreciated?

	Computer	Machine
A	2 years	7 years
B	2 years	10 years
C	3 years	7 years
D	3 years	10 years

2 An entity leases a motor vehicle. The present value of the minimum lease payments is $27,355 and the rate implicit in the lease is 10%. The terms of the lease require three annual rentals to be paid of $10,000 each at the start of each year.

At the end of the first year of the lease what amount will be shown for the lease liability in the company's statement of financial position under the headings of current liabilities and non-current liabilities?

	Current liabilities	Non-current liabilities
A	$9,091	$10,000
B	$10,000	$10,900
C	$10,900	$10,000
D	$10,000	$9,091

3 IFRS 16 *Leases* permits a simplified treatment for certain assets.

For which of the following leases would the simplified treatment not be permitted?

A Motor car with cost of $10,000, leased for 9 months

B Telephone with cost of $500, leased for 24 months

C Motor car with original cost of $10,000, current fair value of $500, leased for 24 months

D Desk with cost of $750, leased for 24 months

4 On 1 April 20X7 Chan sells an item of plant to a finance company and leases it back for a period of five years, at the end of which the fair value of the plant is estimated to be nil.

Which of the following represents the correct accounting treatment for this transaction?

A Recognise the profit on disposal in the current year, capitalise the new lease at the present value of the lease payments

B Spread the profit on disposal over five years, capitalise the new lease at the present value of the lease payments

C Ignore the disposal, treat the sale proceeds as a financial liability

D Revalue the plant to the value of the sale proceeds, treat the sale proceeds as a financial liability

5 CS acquired a machine via a lease agreement on 1 January 20X7. The lease was for a five-year term with rentals of $20,000 per year payable in arrears. The present value of the lease rentals was $80,000 and the annual interest rate implicit in the lease was 7.93%.

Calculate the non-current liability and current liability figures to be shown in CS's statement of financial position at 31 December 20X8.

Non-current liability ________________

Current liability ________________

Test your understanding answers

Test your understanding 1 – Dynamic

The lease term is three years. This is because the option to extend the lease is reasonably certain to be exercised.

The lease liability is calculated as follows:

Date	Cash flow ($)	Discount rate	Present value ($)
31/12/X1	10,000	1/1.05	9,524
31/12/X2	10,000	$1/1.05^2$	9,070
31/12/X3	15,000	$1/1.05^3$	12,958
			31,552

The initial cost of the right-of-use asset is calculated as follows:

	$
Initial liability value	31,552
Direct costs	3,000
	34,552

The double entries to record this are as follows:

Dr Right-of-use asset	$31,552
Cr Lease liability	$31,552
Dr Right-of-use asset	$3,000
Cr Cash	$3,000

Test your understanding 2 – Dynamic (continued)

Statement of profit or loss	**$**
Depreciation **(W1)**	(11,517)
Finance costs (**W2)**	(1,578)

Statement of financial position	**$**
Non-current assets	
Right-of-use asset (34,552 – 11,517)	23,035
Non-current liabilities	
Lease **(W2)**	14,287
Current liabilities	
Lease **(W2)**	8,843

(W1) The right-of-use asset is depreciated over the three year lease term, because it is shorter than the useful life. This gives a charge of $11,517 ($34,552/3 years).

Cr Right-of-use asset (SFP)	$11,517
Cr Right-of-use asset (SFP)	$11,517

(W2) Lease liability table

Year-ended	**Opening**	**Interest (5%)**	**Payments**	**Closing**
	$	$	$	$
31/12/X1	31,552	1,578	(10,000)	23,130
31/12/X2	23,130	1,157	(10,000)	14,287

The total lease liability at 31 December 20X1 is $23,130, of which $14,287 is non-current and $8,843 (23,130 – 14,287) is current.

Test your understanding 3 – Painting

Painting must remove the carrying amount of the machine from its statement of financial position. It should instead recognise a right-of-use asset. This right-of-use asset will be measured as the proportion of the previous carrying amount that relates to the rights retained by Painting:

(1.9m/3m) × $1.2 million = $0.76 million.

The entry required is as follows:

Dr Cash	$3.00m
Dr Right-of-use asset	$0.76m
Cr Machine	$1.20m
Cr Lease liability	$1.90m
Cr Profit or loss (bal. fig.)	$0.66m

Note: The gain in profit or loss is the proportion of the overall $1.8 million gain on disposal ($3m – $1.2m) that relates to the rights transferred to Collage. This can be calculated as follows:

((3m – 1.9m)/3m) × $1.8m = $0.66 million.

The right-of-use asset and the lease liability will then be accounted for using normal lessee accounting rules.

Test your understanding 4 – Fryatt

Statement of Profit or Loss for the year ended 31 May 20X7

	$
Revenue	630,000
Cost of Sales **(W1)**	(331,280)
Gross profit	298,720
Distribution costs	(19,800)
Administrative expenses	(15,600)
Profit from operations	263,320
Finance costs (6,800 + 7,200 **(W3)**)	(14,000)
Profit before tax	249,320
Tax	(7,200)
Profit for the year	242,120

Statement of Financial Position as at 31 May 20X7

	$	$
Non-current Assets		
Property **(60,000 + 134,000 (W2)**)		194,000
Plant and Equipment **(W2)**		73,120
Right-of-use asset **(W2)**		60,000
		327,120
Current Assets		
Inventory	19,600	
Receivables	51,200	
Bank	4,300	
		75,100
		402,220
Equity		
Share capital		25,000
Share premium		7,000
Retained earnings (b/f 15,500 + Profit 242,120)		257,620
		289,620
Non-current Liabilities		
Bank loan		20,000
Lease **(W3)**		26,220
Current Liabilities		
Trade payables	35,200	
Lease (50,200 – 26,220) **(W3)**	23,980	
Income tax	7,200	
		66,380
		402,220

Workings:

(W1) Cost of sales

Per TB	324,000
Depreciation: plant & equipment **(W2)**	18,280
Depreciation: building **(W2)**	6,000
Depreciation: right-of-use-asset **(W2)**	12,000
Remove lease payment	(29,000)
	331,280

(W2) Non-current assets

	Land	**Building**	**Plant & equipment**	**Right-of-use**
Cost per TB/Lease	60,000	180,000	140,000	72,000
Accumulated depreciation		(40,000)	(48,600)	
			91,400	
Depreciation expense (180,000/30)		(6,000)		
(91,400 × 20%)			(18,280)	
(72,000/6)				(12,000)
	60,000	134,000	73,120	60,000

(W3) Lease

Year end	**b/f**	**Interest @10%**	**Payment**	**c/f**
31 May 20X7	72,000	7,200	(29,000)	50,200
31 May 20X8	50,200	5,020	(29,000)	26,220

Test your understanding 5 – MCQ

1 **C** – Assets should usually be depreciated over the lease term. However, the ownership of the computer transfers at the end of the lease, so the computer will be depreciated over its useful life of 3 years.

2 **D**

Year	Opening	Payment	Sub-total	Interest 10%	Closing
1	27,355	(10,000)	17,355	1,736	19,091
2	19,091	(10,000)	9,091	909	10,000

3 **C** – The simplified treatment under IFRS 16 *Leases* is permitted for assets of low-value or where the lease period is for less than 12 months. The standard does not specify a monetary amount for low-value but within the basis for conclusion indicates $5,000 or below as a guide. Low-value is based on original cost.

4 **C** – The sale cannot be recognised. Chan is physically retaining the asset for the remainder of its life and therefore control has not been transferred. The cash received as 'sale proceeds' effectively represents a loan, and would be accounted for as a financial liability.

5 Non-current liability – **$35,697**

Current liability – **$15,908**

Working:

Year	Opening	Interest @ 7.93%	Payment	Closing
20X7	80,000	6,344	(20,000)	66,344
20X8	66,344	5,261	(20,000)	51,605
20X9	51,605	4,092	(20,000)	35,697

The total liability at the end of 20X8 = $51,605

The non-current liability = $35,697 (amount still owing in one year's time)

The current liability = $15,908 ($51,605 – $35,697)

Chapter

13

Taxation

Chapter learning objectives

Upon completion of this chapter you will be able to:

- account for income taxes in accordance with IAS 12 *Income Taxes*
- record entries relating to income taxes in the accounting records
- explain the effect of temporary differences on accounting and taxable profit
- calculate and record deferred tax amounts in the financial statements.

PER

One of the PER performance objectives (PO6) is to record and process transactions and events. You use the right accounting treatments for transactions and events. These should be both historical and prospective – and include non-routine transactions. Working though this chapter should help you understand how to demonstrate that objective.

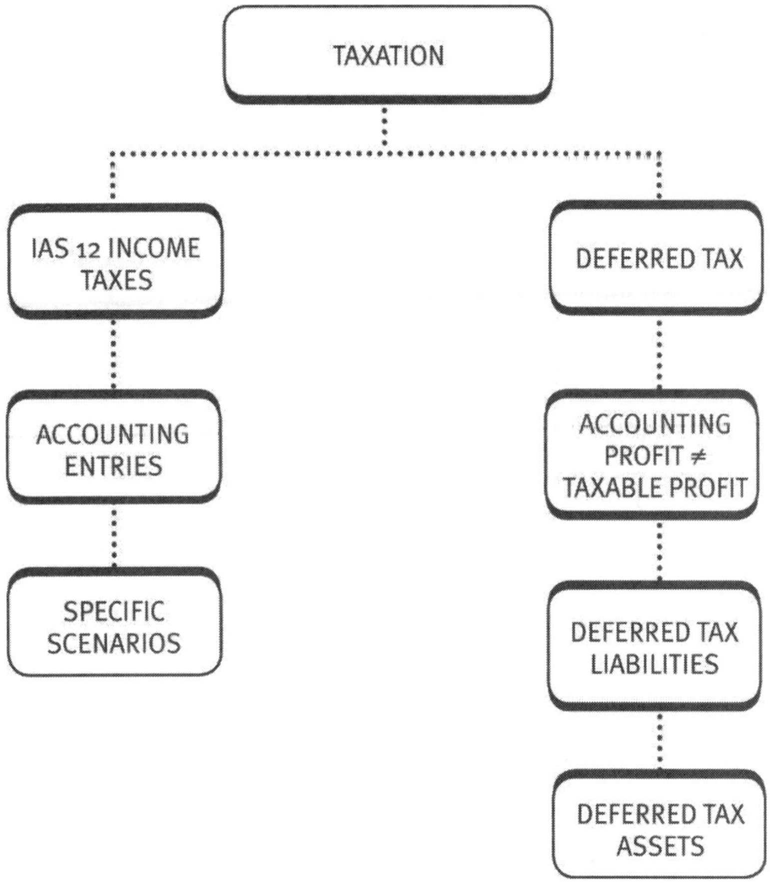

1 IAS 12 Income Taxes

IAS 12 *Income Taxes* states that there are two elements of tax that will need to be accounted for:

1 **Current tax** (the amount of tax payable/recoverable in respect of the taxable profit/loss for a period).

2 **Deferred tax** (an accounting adjustment aimed to match the tax effects of transactions to the relevant accounting period).

The figure for tax on profits is an estimate of the amount that will be eventually paid (or received) and will appear in current liabilities (or assets) in the statement of financial position.

To introduce tax payable by the company:

Dr Income tax expense (in statement of profit or loss)

Cr Income tax payable (in statement of financial position as current liability)

Note therefore that the balance on the statement of financial position for taxation will be only the current year's provision.

Under/over provisions

Any under or over-provision from the prior year is dealt with in the current year's tax charge. This **does not** affect the year-end tax liability. All we need to do is take the under- or over-provided amount to the statement of profit or loss.

- an under-provision increases the tax charge
- an over-provision decreases the tax charge.

Under/over-provisions

Note that any under- or over-provision within an exam question will simply be the balance for income tax on the trial balance.

The taxation account will only have two entries in a year: balance brought forward and payment. If the payment is the same as the balance brought forward then the balance on the trial balance will be zero. If the payment is not the same as the balance brought forward then there will be a balance on the trial balance which will represent the under- or over-provision.

A debit balance will represent an under-provision and should be charged to the statement of profit or loss.

A credit balance will represent an over-provision and should be credited to the statement of profit or loss.

Illustration 1

Simple has estimated its income tax liability for the year ended 31 December 20X8 at $180,000. In the previous year the income tax liability had been estimated as $150,000.

Required:

Calculate the tax expense that will be shown in the statement of profit and loss for the year ended 31 December 20X8 if the amount that was actually agreed and settled with the tax authorities in respect of 20X7 was:

(a) $165,000

(b) $140,000.

Solution

(a) **Under provision**

Statement of profit or loss charge:

	$
Year end estimate	180,000
Under provision re: 20X7 ($165,000 – 150,000)	15,000
Income tax expense	195,000

(b) **Over provision**

Statement of profit or loss charge

	$
Year end estimate	180,000
Over provision re: 20X7 ($150,000 – 140,000)	(10,000)
Income tax expense	170,000

2 Deferred tax

What is deferred tax?

Deferred tax is:

- the estimated **future** tax consequences of transactions and events recognised in the financial statements of the **current** and **previous** periods.

Deferred taxation is a basis of allocating tax charges to particular accounting periods. The key to deferred taxation lies in the two quite different concepts of profit:

- the **accounting profit** (or the **reported profit**), which is the figure of profit before tax, reported to the shareholders in the published accounts
- the **taxable profit,** which is the figure of profit on which the taxation authorities base their tax calculations.

Accounting profit and taxable profit

The difference between accounting profit and taxable profit is caused by:

- permanent differences
- temporary differences.

The accounting problem

One important reason why deferred tax should be recognised is that profit for tax purposes may differ from the profit shown by the financial statements. Such a difference may be caused by permanent or temporary factors. For example, if an expense in the statement of profit or loss is not allowed for tax purposes (e.g. entertaining expenses), a **permanent difference** arises, and the tax expense increases as a result.

A **temporary difference** arises when an expense is allowed for both tax and accounting purposes, but within different accounting periods. For example, if relief for capital expenditure is given at a faster rate for tax purposes than the depreciation in the financial statements, the tax charge will be lower in the earlier years than it would have been if based on the accounting profit, but in subsequent years the tax charge will be higher, as shown by TYU 1 below.

Temporary differences

'Temporary differences are differences between the carrying amount of an asset or liability in the statement of financial position and its tax base' *(IAS 12, para 5)* An asset or liability's tax base is the amount attributed to that asset or liability for tax purposes.

Examples of temporary differences include:

- certain types of income and expenditure that are taxed on a cash, rather than accruals, basis, e.g. certain provisions
- the difference between a non-current asset's depreciation charged and the tax allowances (tax depreciation) given. This is the most common practical example of a temporary difference.

For your examination non-current assets are the most likely source of temporary differences.

Reasons for recognising deferred tax

- The accruals concept requires its recognition.
- The deferred tax is a liability (or asset) which will eventually be settled.
- The overstatement of profit caused by failing to allow for deferred tax liabilities can lead to:
  - over-optimistic dividend payments based on inflated profits
  - distortion of earnings per share (EPS) and of the price/earnings (P/E) ratio, both important indicators of a company's performance
  - shareholders being misled.

IAS 12 and deferred tax

The fundamental principle of IAS 12 is that:

- An entity should recognise a deferred tax liability or asset whenever the recovery or settlement of the carrying amount of an asset or liability would make future tax payments larger or smaller than they would be if such recovery or settlement were to have no tax consequences.
- Deferred tax is calculated using the liability method, in which deferred tax is calculated by reference to the tax base of an asset or liability compared to its carrying amount.

Accounting entries for deferred tax

In the FR examination you may have to calculate the temporary difference, which is likely to be the difference between a non-current asset's

Carrying amount	X
Tax base	(X)
Temporary difference	X

Deferred tax = temporary difference × tax rate

It is the movement on deferred tax that will need to be accounted for:

Increase in deferred tax provision:	Dr Income tax expense/OCI	X
	Cr Deferred tax (SFP)	X
Reduction in deferred tax provision:	Dr Deferred tax (SFP)	X
	Cr Income tax expense/OCI	X

Deferred tax assets

A deductible temporary difference arises where the **tax base of an asset exceeds its carrying amount.**

'A deferred tax asset shall be recognised for all deductible temporary differences to the extent that it is probable that taxable profit will be available against which the deductible temporary difference can be utilised' *(IAS 12, para 24).*

If a deferred tax asset arises from an entity making losses previously, the entity must be able to demonstrate that sufficient forecasted profits will be available to utilise the asset in order to recognise it.

Test your understanding 1

Deferred taxation

A company's financial statements show profit before tax of $1,000 in each of years 1, 2 and 3. This profit is stated after charging depreciation of $200 per annum, due to the purchase of an asset costing $600 in year 1 which is being depreciated over its 3-year useful life on a straight line basis.

The tax allowances granted for the asset are:

Year 1	$240
Year 2	$210
Year 3	$150

Income tax is calculated as 30% of taxable profits.

Apart from the above depreciation and tax allowances there are no other differences between the accounting and taxable profits.

Required:

(a) Ignoring deferred tax, prepare statement of profit or loss extracts for each of years 1, 2 and 3.

(b) Accounting for deferred tax, prepare statement of profit or loss and statement of financial position extracts for each of years 1, 2 and 3.

Deferred tax liabilities

IAS 12 requires:

- a deferred tax liability to be recognised for all taxable temporary differences, with minor exceptions. A taxable temporary difference arises where the carrying amount of an asset is greater than its tax base
- the liability to be calculated and provided in full
- no discounting of the liability.

Revaluation of non-current assets

As seen in Chapter 2, it is permissible to revalue non-current assets to represent their fair value. When a revaluation takes place the carrying amount of the asset will change but the tax base will remain unaffected.

The difference between the carrying amount of a revalued asset and its tax base is an example of a temporary difference and will give rise to a deferred tax liability or asset, which will be taken to the revaluation surplus (via other comprehensive income), rather than the statement of profit or loss.

Application to scenarios

Revaluation of non-current assets

Deferred tax should be recognised on revaluation gains even where there is no intention to sell the asset or rollover relief is available on the gain.

The revaluation of non-current assets results in taxable temporary differences, and so a deferred tax liability. This is charged as a component of other comprehensive income (alongside the revaluation gain itself). It is therefore disclosed either in the statement of profit or loss and other comprehensive income or in a separate statement showing other comprehensive income.

Tax losses

Where unused tax losses are carried forward, a deferred tax asset can be recognised to the extent that taxable profits will be available in the future to offset the losses.

If an entity does not expect to have taxable profits in the future it cannot recognise the asset in its own accounts.

If, however, the entity is part of a group and may surrender tax losses to other group companies, a deferred tax asset may be recognised in the consolidated accounts.

The asset is equal to the tax losses expected to be utilised multiplied by the tax rate.

Test your understanding 2

On 1 January 20X8 Simone Co decided to revalue its land for the first time. A qualified property valuer reported that the market value of the land on that date was $80,000. The land was originally purchased 6 years ago for $65,000.

The required provision for income tax for the year ended 31 December 20X8 is $19,400. The difference between the carrying amounts of the net assets of Simone (including the revaluation of the land above) and their (lower) tax base at 31 December 20X8 is $27,000. The opening balance on the deferred tax account was $2,600. Simone's rate of income tax is 25%.

Required:

Prepare extracts of the financial statements to show the effect of the above transactions.

3 Summary

Tax usually forms part of a published accounts question in the exam and you may find it helpful to use the following standard workings:

Income tax

Year end estimate (given in question)	X
Under/(over) provision (figure from trial balance)	X/(X)
Increase/(decrease) in deferred tax (see below)	X/(X)
Charge to statement of profit or loss	X

Deferred tax

Balance b/f per trial balance	X
Balance c/f (to SFP) (Temporary difference × tax rate)	X
Increase/decrease in deferred tax (to either statement of profit or loss or equity)	X/(X)

Test your understanding 3

The following trial balance relates to Molly Co at 31 December 20X1:

	$	$
Revenue	50,000	
Purchases	20,000	
Distribution costs	10,400	
Administration expenses	15,550	
Loan interest paid	400	
Non-current assets (carrying amount)	35,000	
Income tax		500
Deferred tax at 1 January 20X1		8,000
Interim dividend paid	1,600	
Trade receivables and payables	10,450	29,000
Inventory as at 1 January 20X1	8,000	
Cash and cash equivalents	8,100	
Ordinary shares $0.50		8,000
Share premium		3,000
10% Loan notes		8,000
Retained earnings at 1 January 20X1		3,000
	109,500	109,500

The following is to be taken into account:

1 Land that cost $5,000 is to be revalued to $11,000. Ignore deferred tax on the revaluation.

2 The balance on the income tax account represents an over-provision of tax for the previous year.

3 The income tax for the current year is estimated at $3,000. The deferred tax provision is to be increased to $8,600.

4 Closing inventory is valued at $16,000 at cost for the year. Included in this amount is inventory that cost $8,000 but during the inventory count it was identified that these goods had become damaged and as result the selling price was reduced. The goods are now believed to have a selling price of $4,500 after incurring rectification costs of $500.

Required:

Prepare Molly Co's statement of profit or loss and other comprehensive income, statement of financial position and statement of changes in equity for the year-ended 31 December 20X1.

Test your understanding 4

The following trial balance relates to Weiser at 31 December 20X8:

	$000	$000
Revenue		190,000
Cost of sales	130,000	
Distribution costs	7,100	
Administrative expenses	23,200	
Loan interest	400	
Building – cost (note (i))	25,000	
Accumulated depreciation at 1 January 20X8		5,000
Plant and equipment at cost (note (i))	22,250	
Accumulated depreciation at 1 January 20X8		7,250
Inventory	27,400	
Trade receivables	16,500	
Trade payables		13,500
Bank		1,100
Equity shares of 50 cents each		30,000
Retained earnings 1 January 20X8		4,150
Deferred tax		1,350
Current tax	500	
	252,350	252,350

The following information is relevant:

(i) The directors had the building valued at $24 million on 1 January 20X8 by an independent surveyor. The directors wish to incorporate this value into the financial statements. The building was originally purchased 4 years ago and is being depreciated over its original useful life of 20 years which has not changed as a result of the revaluation. Weiser does not make a transfer to retained earnings in respect of excess amortisation. The revaluation gain will create a deferred tax liability (see note (ii)).

Plant and equipment is being depreciated at 20% per annum on a reducing balance basis. All depreciation/amortisation should be charged to cost of sales.

(ii) A provision for income tax for the year ended 31 December 20X8 of $12 million is required. At 31 December 20X8, the tax base of Weiser's net assets was $7 million less than their carrying amounts. This excludes the gain on the revaluation of the building. The income tax rate of Weiser is 30%.

Required:

Prepare Weiser's statement of profit or loss and other comprehensive income, a statement of changes in equity for the year ended 31 December 20X8, and a statement of financial position as at that date.

4 Chapter summary

TAXATION

IAS 12 Income taxes

ACCOUNTING ENTRIES

Dr income tax expense

Cr income tax payable.

UNDER- AND OVER-PROVISIONS

Tax charge is based on estimates; under- or over-provisions dealt with in following year:

Tax charge

Current year charge + last year's under-provision

Or

Current year charge – last year's over-provision.

DEFERRED TAX

the estimated **future** tax consequences of transactions and events recognised in the financial statements of the **current** and **previous** periods.

ACCOUNTING PROFIT ≠ TAXABLE PROFIT

Due to

- permanent differences
- temporary differences.

DEFERRED TAX LIABILITIES

- recognise for all taxable temporary differences, with minor exceptions
- the liability is to be calculated using full provision
- no discounting is permitted.

DEFERRED TAX ASSETS

- recognise for all deductible temporary differences if probable that taxable profit will be available
- no discounting is permitted.

Test your understanding 5

1 The following information has been extracted from the accounting records of Clara Co:

Estimated income tax for the year ended 30 September 20X0	$75,000
Income tax paid for the year ended 30 September 20X0	$80,000
Estimated income tax for the year ended 30 September 20X1	$83,000

Select the figures that will be shown as an expense in the statement of profit or loss for the year ended 30 September 20X1 and as a liability in the statement of financial position as at that date in respect of income tax.

Expense $000	**Liability** $000
83	83
88	88

2 Tamsin Co's accounting records show the following:

Income tax payable on current year profits	$60,000
Over-provision in relation to the previous year	$4,500
Opening provision for deferred tax	$2,600
Closing provision for deferred tax	$3,200

What is the income tax expense that will be shown in the statement of profit or loss for the year?

$____________

3 A piece of machinery cost $500. Tax depreciation to date has amounted to $220 and depreciation charged in the financial statements to date is $100. The rate of income tax is 30%.

What is the deferred tax liability in relation to this asset?

$____________

4 WS prepares its financial statements to 30 June. The following profits (before tax) were recorded from 20X1 to 20X3:

20X1 $100,000

20X2 $120,000

20X3 $110,000

The entity provides for tax at a rate of 30% and incorporates this figure in the year-end accounts. The actual amounts of tax paid in respect of 20X1 and 20X2 were $28,900 and $37,200.

Required:

Prepare extracts from the statement of profit or loss and statement of financial position of WS for each of the 3 years, showing the tax charge and tax liability.

Test your understanding answers

Test your understanding 1

(a) **Statement of profit or loss (extracts)**

	1	2	3
Profit before tax	1,000	1,000	1,000
Income tax expense	(288)	(297)	(315)
Profit after tax	712	703	685

Workings:

(W1)

	1	2	3
Accounting profits	1,000	1,000	1,000
Depreciation	200	200	200
Capital allowance	(240)	(210)	(150)
Taxable profits	960	990	1,050
Income Tax @ 30%	288	297	315

(b) **Statement of profit or loss (extracts)**

	1	2	3
Profit before tax	1,000	1,000	1,000
Income tax expense	(300)	(300)	(300)
Profit after tax	700	700	700

Statement of financial position (extracts)

	1	2	3
Non-current liabilities			
Deferred tax	12	15	0
Current liabilities			
Taxation	288	297	315

Workings:

(W1) as before

	1	**2**	**3**
Accounting profits	1,000	1,000	1,000
Depreciation	200	200	200
Capital allowance	(240)	(210)	(150)
Taxable profits	960	990	1,050
Income Tax @ 30%	288	297	315

(W2) Temporary differences and deferred tax

	1	**2**	**3**
Carrying amount	400	200	Nil
	(600 – 200)	(600 – 200 – 200)	(600 – 200 – 200-200)
Tax base	360	150	Nil
	(600 – 240)	(600 – 240 – 210)	(600 – 240 – 210 – 150)
Temporary difference	40	50	0
Deferred tax provision @ 30%	12	15	0
Increase (Decrease)	12	3	(15)

(W3) Income tax expense

	1	**2**	**3**
Income tax	288	297	315
Deferred tax	12	3	(15)
Income tax expense	300	300	300

Test your understanding 2

Statement of profit or loss and other comprehensive income (extract)

	$	$
Income tax expense **(W2)**		19,800
Other comprehensive income:		
Revaluation gain (80,000 – 65,000)	15,000	
Deferred tax (15,000 × 25%)	(3,750)	
		11,250

Statement of financial position (extract)

	$
Non-current assets	
Land	80,000
Equity	
Revaluation surplus (as above)	11,250
Non-current liabilities	
Deferred tax **(W1)**	6,750
Current liabilities	
Income tax payable	19,400

Statement of changes in equity (extract)

	$
Revaluation gain (80,000 – 65,000)	15,000
Deferred tax on revaluation (15,000 × 25%)	(3,750)
	11,250

(W1) Deferred tax

	$
Balance c/f (27,000 × 25%)	6,750
Less balance b/f	(2,600)
Increase in deferred tax	4,150

Tutorial note: Of the total increase in deferred tax, $3,750 ($15,000 × 25%) relates to the revaluation surplus and should be reported in other comprehensive income. The remainder should be charged to the statement of profit or loss.

(W2) Income tax expense

	$
Year end estimate	19,400
Increase in deferred tax (4,150 **(W1)** – 3,750 tax on revaluation)	400
	19,800

Test your understanding 3

Molly Co: Statement of profit or loss and other comprehensive income for the year ended 31 December 20X1

Revenue	50,000
Cost of sales **(W1)**	(16,000)
Gross profit	34,000
Distribution costs	(10,400)
Administration expenses	(15,550)
Profit from operations	8,050
Finance cost **(W2)**	(800)
Profit before tax	7,250
Income tax expense **(W3)**	(3,100)
Profit for year	4,150
Other comprehensive income:	
Revaluation gain **(W4)**	6,000
Total comprehensive income	10,150

Molly Co: Statement of financial position as at 31 December 20X1

	$	$
Non-current assets		
Property, plant and equipment **(W4)**		41,000
Current assets		
Inventories **(W5)**	12,000	
Trade receivables	10,450	
Cash and cash equivalents	8,100	
		30,550
Total assets		71,550

Equity and liabilities		
Capital and reserves		
Share capital $0.50	8,000	
Share premium	3,000	
Revaluation surplus	6,000	
Retained earnings	5,550	
		22,550
Non-current liabilities		
10% Loan	8,000	
Deferred taxation	8,600	
		16,600
Current liabilities		
Trade payables	29,000	
Loan interest payable (W2)	400	
Income tax	3,000	
		32,400
		71,550

Molly Co: Statement of changes in equity for the year ended 31 December 20X1

	Share capital $	Share premium $	Reval'n surplus $	Retained earnings $	Total $
Balance at 1 January 20X1	8,000	3,000	–	3,000	14,000
Net profit for the year (SPL)				4,150	4,150
Dividends paid				(1,600)	(1,600)
Revaluation of land **(W4)**			6,000	–	6,000
Balance at 31 December 20X1	8,000	3,000	6,000	5,550	22,550

Workings:

(W1)

Cost of sales	$
Purchases	20,000
Opening inventory	8,000
Closing inventory **(W5)**	(12,000)
	16,000

(W2)

Loan interest due (10% × $8,000) = $800 (charge to SPL)

Amount paid (TB) $400, therefore accrual required for $400

(W3)

Income tax	$
Trial balance over-provision	(500)
Current year estimate	3,000
Increase in deferred tax provision (8,600 – 8,000)	600
	3,100

(W4)

Property, plant & equipment	$
Trial balance carrying amount	35,000
Increase in valuation of land ($5,000 to $11,000)	6,000
	41,000

(W5)

Inventory	$
Closing inventory at cost	16,000
Damaged inventory at cost	(8,000)
Damaged inventory at NRV ($4,500 – $500)	4,000
	12,000

Inventory is valued at the lower of cost or net realisable value (NRV).

Test your understanding 4

Statement of profit or loss and other comprehensive income for the year ended 31 December 20X8

	$000
Revenue	190,000
Cost of sales (130,000 + 1,500 **(W1)** + 3,000 **(W3)**)	(134,500)
Gross profit	55,500
Distribution costs	(7,100)
Administrative expenses	(23,200)
Profit from operations	25,200
Finance costs	(400)
Profit before tax	24,800
Taxation	(13,250)
Profit for the year	11,550
Other comprehensive income:	
Revaluation of property **(W1)**	4,000
Transfer to deferred tax **(W4)**	(1,200)
	2,800
	14,350

Statement of changes in equity for the year ended 31 December 20X8

	Share capital	Reval'n surplus	Retained earnings	Total
	$000	$000	$000	$000
Balance at 1 January 20X8	30,000	nil	4,150	34,150
Total comprehensive income		2,800	11,550	14,350
Balance at 31 December 20X8	30,000	2,800	15,700	48,500

Statement of financial position as at 31 December 20X8

	$000	$000
Non-current assets		
Building (25,000 – 5,000 + 4,000 **(W1)** – 1,500 **(W1)**)		22,500
Plant and equipment (22,250 – 7,250 – 3,000 **(W2)**)		12,000
		34,500
Current assets		
Inventory	27,400	
Receivables	16,500	
		43,900
		78,400
Equity		
Share capital		30,000
Retained earnings		15,700
Revaluation surplus		2,800
		48,500
Non-current liabilities		
Deferred tax **(W4)**		3,300
Current liabilities		
Trade payables	13,500	
Bank	1,100	
Taxation	12,000	
		26,600
		78,400

Workings:

(W1) Building

	$000
Revaluation:	
Carrying amount at 1 January 20X8 (25,000 – 5,000)	20,000
Valuation	24,000
Gain on revaluation	4,000
Depreciation:	
24,000/16 years remaining	1,500

(W2) Plant and equipment

	$000
Depreciation charge:	
(22,250 – 7,250) × 20%	3,000

(W3) Tax expense

	$000
Year-end estimate	12,000
Under provision	500
Increase in deferred tax **(W4)**	750
	13,250

(W4) Deferred tax

	$000
b/f per trial balance	1,350
c/f (7,000 + 4,000) × 30%)	3,300
Increase in deferred tax	1,950

Tutorial note: The increase in deferred tax must be split between the revaluation surplus $1,200 (4,000 × 30%) and the balance taken to the statement of profit or loss $750 (ß).

Test your understanding 5

1 **Statement of profit or loss (extract)**

	$
Current tax for year ended 30 September 20X1	83,000
Under-provision for year ended 30 September 20X0 (80,000 – 75,000)	5,000
Income tax expense	88,000

Statement of financial position (extract)

Income tax payable	83,000

2 **$56,100**

Statement of profit or loss (extract)

	$
Current tax	60,000
Over-provision	(4,500)
Deferred tax (3,200 – 2,600)	600
	56,100

3 **$36** – Deferred tax liability = temporary difference × tax rate = ($220 – $100) × 30% = $36.

4 **Statement of profit or loss (extract)**

	20X1	**20X2**	**20X3**
	$	$	$
Income tax expense **(W1)**	(30,000)	(34,900)	(34,200)

Statements of financial position (extract)

	20X1	**20X2**	**20X3**
	$	$	$
Current liabilities			
Income tax payable (profits × 30%)	30,000	36,000	33,000

(W1) Income tax expense

	20X1	**20X2**	**20X3**
	$	$	$
Current tax estimate	30,000	36,000	33,000
Under/(over) provision **(W2)**	0	(1,100)	1,200
Income tax expense	30,000	34,900	34,200

(W2) Under/over provisions

	20X1	20X2	20X3
	$	$	$
Current tax estimate	30,000	36,000	33,000
Amount paid	28,900	37,200	?
Under/(over) provision	(1,100)	1,200	34,200

Remember these under/(over) provisions will not have an effect on the current year accounts but the following year accounts due to the timing of payments.

Chapter

14

Earnings per share

Chapter learning objectives

Upon completion of this chapter you will be able to:

- define basic earnings per share (EPS)
- calculate EPS with a bonus issue during the year
- calculate EPS with an issue at full market value during the year
- calculate EPS with a rights issue during the year
- explain the relevance of diluted EPS (DEPS)
- calculate DEPS involving convertible debt
- calculate DEPS involving share options (warrants)
- explain the importance of EPS as a stock market indicator
- explain why the trend in EPS may be a more accurate indicator of performance than a company's profit trend
- explain the limitations of EPS as a performance measure.

PER

One of the PER performance objectives (PO6) is to record and process transactions and events. You use the right accounting treatments for transactions and events. These should be both historical and prospective – and include non-routine transactions. Working though this chapter should help you understand how to demonstrate that objective.

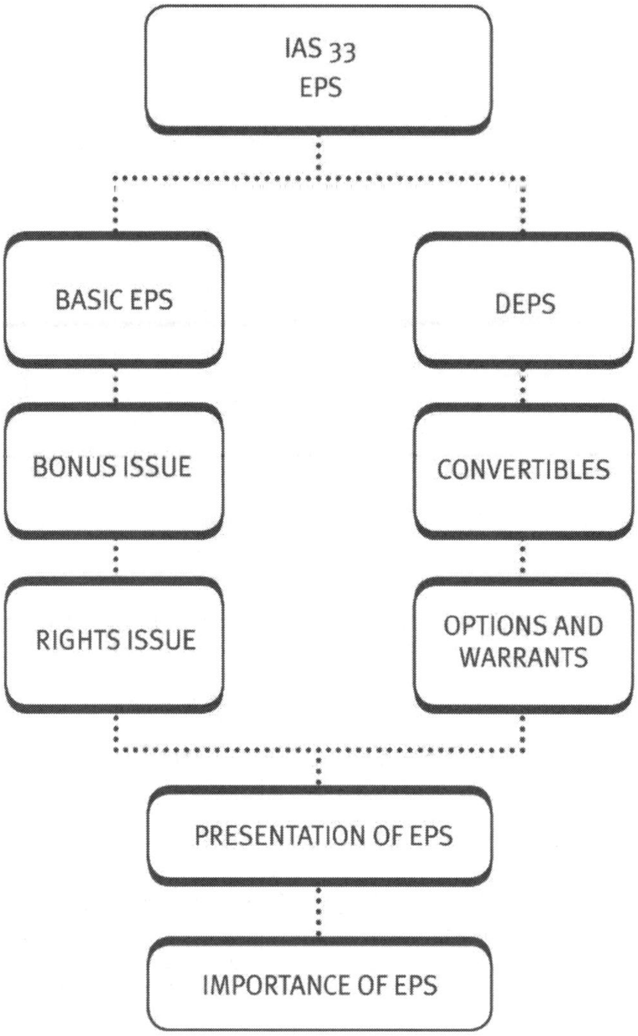

1 Introduction

Earnings per share (EPS) is widely regarded as the most important indicator of a company's performance. It is important that users of the financial statements:

- are able to compare the EPS of different entities and
- are able to compare the EPS of the same entity in different accounting periods.

IAS 33 *Earnings per Share* achieves comparability by:

- defining earnings
- prescribing methods for determining the number of shares to be included in the calculation of EPS
- requiring standard presentation and disclosures.

The scope of IAS 33

IAS 33 applies to entities whose ordinary shares are publicly traded.

Publicly traded entities which present both parent and consolidated financial statements are only required to present EPS based on the consolidated figures.

2 Basic EPS

The basic EPS calculation is simply:

$$\frac{\text{Earnings}}{\text{Shares}}$$

This should be expressed as cents per share to 1 decimal place.

- Earnings: group profit after tax, less non-controlling interests (see group chapters) and irredeemable preference share dividends.
- Shares: weighted average number of ordinary shares in issue during the period.

Issue of shares at full market price

Earnings should be apportioned over the weighted average equity share capital (i.e. taking account of the date any new shares are issued during the year).

Illustration 1 – Full market share issue

An entity, with a year-end of 31 December 20X8, issued 200,000 shares at full market price of $3 on 1 July 20X8.

Relevant information

	20X8	**20X7**
Profit attributable to the ordinary shareholders for the year ending 31 December	$550,000	$460,000
Number of ordinary shares in issue at 31 December	1,000,000	800,000

Required:

Calculate the EPS for each of the years.

Solution

Calculation of EPS

20X7 Earnings per share = $\frac{\$460,000}{800,000}$ = 57,5¢

Issue at full market price

Date	Actual number of shares	Fraction of year	Total
1 Jan 20X8 b/f	800,000	6/12	400,000
1 July 20X8 Issue	200,000		
1 July 20X8 c/f	1,000,000	6/12	500,000
Number of shares in EPS calculation			900,000

20X8 Earnings per share = $\frac{\$550,000}{900,000}$ = 61.1¢

Since the 200,000 shares have only generated additional resources towards the earning of profits for half a year, the number of new shares is adjusted proportionately. Note that the approach is to use the earnings figure for the period without adjustment, but divide by the average number of shares weighted on a time basis.

Test your understanding 1

Gerard's earnings for the year ended 31 December 20X4 are $2,208,000. On 1 January 20X4, the issued share capital of Gerard was 8,280,000 ordinary shares of $1 each. The company issued 3,312,000 shares at full market value on 30 June 20X4.

Calculate the EPS for Gerard for 20X4.

Bonus issue

A bonus issue (or capitalisation issue or scrip issue):

- does not provide additional resources to the issuer
- means that the shareholder owns the same proportion of the business before and after the issue.

In the calculation of EPS:

- in the current year, the bonus shares are deemed to have been issued at the start of the year
- comparative figures are restated to allow for the proportional increase in share capital caused by the bonus issue. Doing this treats the bonus issue as if it had always been in existence.
- **Note:** If you have an issue of shares at full market price and a bonus issue, you apply a bonus fraction from the start of the year **up to** the date of the bonus issue. For example, if the bonus issue was 1 share for every 5 owned, the bonus fraction would be 6/5 (as everyone who had 5 shares now has 6).

e.g

Illustration 2 – Bonus share issue

Consider:

- Mr A owns 5,000 shares in Company B which has an issued capital of 100,000 shares. Mr A therefore owns 5% of Company B.
- Company B makes a 1 for 1 bonus issue.
- Mr A now owns 10,000 shares and Company B has 200,000 shares in issue. Mr A still owns 5% of Company B.

The shares issued as a result of the bonus issue are deemed to have been issued at the start of the earliest reporting period, regardless of the actual date when the bonus issue took place. To ensure that the EPS for the year of the bonus issue remains comparable with the EPS of previous years, comparative figures for earlier years are restated using the same increased figure.

e.g

Illustration 3 – Bonus share issue

An entity makes a bonus issue of one new share for every five existing shares held on 1 July 20X8.

	20X8	**20X7**
Profit attributable to the ordinary shareholders for the year ending 31 December	$550,000	$460,000
Number of ordinary shares in issue at 31 December	1,200,000	1,000,000

Calculate the EPS in 20X8 accounts.

Solution

Calculation of EPS in 20X8 accounts.

20X7 comparative	$\frac{\$460,000}{1,200,000}$	= 38.3¢
20X8	$\frac{\$550,000}{1,200,000}$	= 45.8¢

In the 20X7 accounts, the EPS for the year would have appeared as 46¢ ($460,000 ÷ 1,000,000). In the example above, the computation has been reworked in full. However, to make the changes required it would be simpler to adjust the original EPS figure.

Since the old calculation was based on dividing by 1,000,000 while the new is determined by using 1,200,000, it would be necessary to multiply the EPS by the first and divide by the second.

The fraction to apply is, therefore:

$$\frac{1,000,000}{1,200,000} \text{ or } \frac{5}{6}$$

Consequently:

$$46¢ \times \frac{5}{6} = 38.3¢$$

Test your understanding 2

Dorabella had the following capital and reserves on 1 April 20X1:

	$000
Share capital ($1 ordinary shares)	7,000
Share premium	900
Revaluation surplus	500
Retained earnings	9,000
Shareholders' funds	17,400

Dorabella makes a bonus issue of one share for every seven held, on 31 August 20X2.

Dorabella's results are as follows:	**20X3**	**20X2**
	$000	$000
Profit after tax	1,150	750

Calculate EPS for the year ending 31 March 20X3, together with the comparative EPS for 20X2 that would be presented in the 20X3 accounts.

Bonus and market issues combined

If a question gives both a bonus issue and an issue of shares at full price:

- Apply the bonus fraction from the start of the year up until the date of the bonus issue
- Time apportion the number of shares to reflect the cash being received from the market issue.

Test your understanding 3

An entity had 1 million shares in issue on 1 January 20X1. They issued 200,000 shares at market value on 1 April 20X1, followed by a 1 for 5 bonus issue on 1 August 20X1, with a further 300,000 issued at market value on 1 October 20X1.

If profit for the year ending 31 December 20X1 is $220,000, what is the basic earnings per share?

Rights issue

Rights issues present special problems:

- they contribute additional resources
- they are normally priced below full market price.

Therefore they combine the characteristics of issues at full market price and bonus issues, and the calculation of shares in issue reflects this

1 adjust for bonus element in rights issue, by multiplying capital in issue before the rights issue by the following fraction:

$$\frac{\text{Market price before issue}}{\text{Theoretical ex rights price}}$$

2 calculate the weighted average capital in the issue as above.

Calculating EPS when there has been a rights issue can be done using a four-step process:

Step 1 – Calculate theoretical ex-rights price (TERP)

Start with the number of shares previously held by an individual at their market price. Then add in the number of new shares purchased at the rights price. You can then find the TERP by dividing the total value of these shares by the number held.

For example, if there was a 1 for 3 rights issue for $3, and the market price before this was $5:

3 shares @ $5 market price = $15

1 new share @ $3 rights price = $3

Therefore a shareholder now has 4 shares with a value of $18. The TERP is now $18/4 = **$4.50**

Step 2 – Bonus fraction

$$\frac{\text{Market price before issue}}{\text{Theoretical ex rights price}}$$

In this example, the bonus fraction would therefore be **5/4.5**

Step 3 – Weighted average number of shares

Draw up the usual table to calculate the weighted average number of shares. When doing this, the bonus fraction would be applied from the start of the year **up to** the date of the rights issue, but not afterwards.

Step 4 – Earnings per share (EPS)

You can now calculate earnings per share in the usual way:

$$\frac{\text{Profit after tax}}{\text{Weighted average number of shares}}$$

It is important to note that if you are asked to restate the prior year EPS, then this is simply the prior year's EPS multiplied by the inverse of the bonus fraction. This calculation effectively increases the number of shares in the previous year's calculation.

e.g

Illustration 4 – Rights issue

An entity issued one new share for every two existing shares held by way of a rights issue at $1.50 per share on 1 July 20X8. Pre-issue market price was $3 per share.

Relevant information

	20X8	**20X7**
Profit attributable to the ordinary shareholders for the year ending 31 December	$550,000	$460,000
Number of ordinary shares in issue at 31 December	1,200,000	800,000

Solution

Step 1 – Theoretical ex-rights price (TERP)

	No. of shares	**Price $**	**Value $**
Prior to rights issue	2	3.00	6.00
Taking up rights	1	1.50	1.50
	3		7.50

TERP = $7.50/3 = $2.50

Step 2 – Bonus fraction

Market price before issue/TERP = $3/$2.5

Step 3 – Weighted average number of shares

	No.	Bonus fraction	Time	Shares
1 January 20X8 b/f	800,000	3/2.5	6/12	480,000
Rights issue	400,000			
1 July	1,200,000		6/12	600,000
				1,080,000

Step 4 – EPS

20X8 EPS

$$\text{EPS} = \frac{\$550{,}000}{1{,}080{,}000} = 50.9¢ \text{ per share}$$

20X7 EPS

Last year, reported EPS: $460,000 ÷ 800,000 = 57.5¢

20X7 Restated EPS

57.5¢ × 2.5/3 = 47.9¢

Proof that free element is included within rights fraction:

The market value is now $2.50. The company has issued 400,000 shares at $1.50, raising $600,000.

At the market value of $2.50, $600,000 would only buy 240,000 shares ($600,000/$2.50).

Therefore 160,000 share have been issued for free (400,000 issued, but cash only received for 240,000)

800,000 × 3/2.5 = 960,000. Therefore by applying the rights fraction of 3/2.5 from the start of the year, we are accounting for the free 160,000 shares immediately.

Test your understanding 4

On 31 December 20X1, the issued share capital consisted of 4,000,000 ordinary shares of 25¢ each. On 1 July 20X2 the entity made a rights issue in the proportion of 1 for 4 at 50¢ per share and the shares were quoted immediately before the issue at $1. Its trading results for the last two years were as follows:

	Year ended 31 December	
	20X2	**20X1**
	$	$
Profit after tax	425,000	320,000

Show the calculation of basic EPS to be presented in the financial statements for the year ended 31 December 20X2 (including comparative).

3 Diluted earnings per share (DEPS)

Introduction

Equity share capital may increase in the future due to circumstances which exist now. When it occurs, this increase in shares will reduce, or dilute, the earnings per share. The provision of a diluted EPS figure attempts to alert shareholders to the potential impact on EPS of these additional shares.

Examples of dilutive factors are:

- the conversion terms for convertible bonds/convertible loans etc.
- the exercise price for options and the subscription price for warrants.

Basic principles of calculation

To deal with potential ordinary shares, adjust the basic earnings and number of shares assuming convertibles, options, etc. had converted to equity shares on the first day of the accounting period, or on the date of issue, if later.

DEPS is calculated as follows:

$$\frac{\text{Earnings + notional extra earnings}}{\text{Number of shares + notional extra shares}}$$

Importance of DEPS

The basic EPS figure calculated as above could be misleading to users if at some future time the number of shares in issue will increase without a proportionate increase in resources. For example, if an entity has issued bonds convertible at a later date into ordinary shares, on conversion the number of ordinary shares will rise but no fresh capital will be received by the entity. However earnings will rise by the savings in interest no longer payable on the bonds. Often the earnings increase is less, proportionately, than the increase in the shares in issue. This effect is referred to as 'dilution' and the shares to be issued are called 'dilutive potential ordinary shares'.

IAS 33 therefore requires an entity to disclose the DEPS, as well as the basic EPS, calculated using current earnings but assuming that the maximum future dilution has already happened. Existing shareholders can look at the DEPS to see the effect on current profitability of commitments already entered into. **'For the purpose of calculating DEPS, the number of ordinary shares shall be the weighted average number of ordinary shares calculated as for basic EPS, plus the weighted average number of ordinary shares that would be issued on the conversion of all the dilutive potential ordinary shares into ordinary shares. Dilutive potential ordinary shares shall be deemed to have been converted into ordinary shares at the beginning of the period or, if later, the date of the issue of the potential ordinary shares'** *(IAS 33, para 36)*

Convertible instruments

The principles of convertible bonds and convertible preference shares are similar and will be dealt with together.

If the convertible bonds/preference shares had been converted:

- the interest/dividend would be saved therefore earnings would be higher
- the additional earnings would be subject to tax
- the number of shares would increase.

Illustration 5 – Convertible instruments

On 1 April 20X1, an entity issued a convertible loan note of $1,250,000. The loan note carries an effective interest rate of 8%. Each $100 nominal of the loan stock will be convertible in 20X6/20X9 into the number of ordinary shares set out below:

- On 31 December 20X6 124 shares.
- On 31 December 20X7 120 shares.
- On 31 December 20X8 115 shares.
- On 31 December 20X9 110 shares.

Up to 20X6, the maximum number of shares issuable after the end of the financial year will be at the rate of 124 shares per $100 on $1,250,000 debt, which is 1,550,000 shares. With 4,000,000 already in issue, the total would become 5,550,000. In the DEPS calculation always assume that the maximum possible number of shares will be issued.

Relevant information

Issued share capital:

- $500,000 in 10% cumulative irredeemable preference shares of $1.
- $1,000,000 in ordinary shares of 25c = 4,000,000 shares.
- The rate of tax is 30%.

Trading results for the years ended 31 December were as follows:

	20X2	**20X1**
	$	$
Profit before interest and tax	1,100,000	991,818
Interest on 8% convertible loan note	(100,000)	(75,000)
Profit before tax	1,000,000	916,818
Income tax	(300,000)	(275,045)
Profit after tax	700,000	641,773

Solution

Calculation of EPS

	20X2	20X1
Basic EPS	$	$
Profit after tax	700,000	641,773
Less: Preference dividend	(50,000)	(50,000)
Earnings	650,000	591,773
EPS based on 4,000,000 shares	16.3¢	14.8¢
DEPS		
Earnings as above	650,000	591,773
Add: Interest on the convertible loan note	100,000	75,000
Less: Income tax @ 30%	(30,000)	(22,500)
	70,000	52,500
Adjusted earnings	720,000	644,273
EPS based on 5,550,000 shares (20X1 – 5,162,500)	13.0¢	12.5¢

The weighted average number of shares issued and issuable for 20X1 would have been the issued 4,000,000 plus nine months' worth of the potential shares, i.e. 4,000,000 + ($^9/_{12}$ × 1,550,000) = 5,162,500.

Convertible preference shares are dealt with on the same basis except that they often do not qualify for tax relief, so there is no tax adjustment.

Test your understanding 5

A company had 8.28 million shares in issue at the start of the year and made no new issue of shares during the year ended 31 December 20X4, but on that date it had in issue $2,300,000 convertible loan stock 20X6-20X9. The loan stock carries an effective rate of 10%. Assume an income tax rate of 30%. The earnings for the year were $2,208,000.

This loan stock will be convertible into ordinary $1 shares as follows.

20X6	90 $1 shares for $100 nominal value loan stock
20X7	85 $1 shares for $100 nominal value loan stock
20X8	80 $1 shares for $100 nominal value loan stock
20X9	75 $1 shares for $100 nominal value loan stock

Calculate the diluted earnings per share for the year ended 31 December 20X4.

Options and warrants to subscribe for shares

An option or warrant gives the holder the right to buy shares at some time in the future at a predetermined price.

Cash is received by the entity at the time the option is exercised, and the DEPS calculation must allow for this.

The total number of shares issued on the exercise of the **option** or **warrant** is split into two:

- the number of shares that would have been issued if the cash received had been used to buy shares at fair value (using the average price of the shares during the period)
- the remainder, which are treated like a **bonus issue** (i.e. as having been issued for no consideration).

The number of shares issued for no consideration is added to the number of shares when calculating the DEPS.

A formula for DEPS with an option can be used to work out the number of free shares:

$$\text{No. of options} \times \frac{\text{Fair value} - \text{exercise price}}{\text{Fair value}}$$

Illustration 6 – Options

On 1 January 20X7, a company has 4 million ordinary shares in issue and issues options for a further million shares. The profit for the year is $500,000.

During the year to 31 December 20X7 the average fair value of one ordinary share was $3 and the exercise price for the shares under option was $2.

Calculate basic EPS and DEPS for the year ended 31 December 20X7.

Solution

Basic EPS = $\frac{\$500,000}{4,000,000}$ = 12.5¢

Options or warrants

	$
Earnings	500,000
Number of shares	
Basic	4,000,000
Options **(W1)**	333,333
	4,333,333

The DEPS is therefore $\frac{\$500,000}{4,333,333}$ = 11.5¢

(W1) Number of shares at option price

Options = 1,000,000 × $2

= $2,000,000

At fair value $\frac{\$2,000,000}{\$3}$ = 666,667

Number issued free = 1,000,000 – 666,667 = 333,333

Or, using formula, number of free shares:

1,0000 × (3 – 2)/3 = 333,333

Test your understanding 6

A company had 8.28 million shares in issue at the start of the year and made no issue of shares during the year ended 31 December 20X4, but on that date there were outstanding options to purchase 920,000 ordinary $1 shares at $1.70 per share. The average fair value of ordinary shares was $1.80. Earnings for the year ended 31 December 20X4 were $2,208,000.

Calculate the diluted earnings per share for the year ended 31 December 20X4.

4 The importance of EPS

Price earnings ratio

The EPS figure is used to compute the major stock market indicator of performance, the price earnings ratio (P/E ratio). The calculation is as follows:

$$\text{P/E ratio} = \frac{\text{Market value of share}}{\text{EPS}}$$

Trend in EPS

Although EPS is based on profit on ordinary activities after taxation, the trend in EPS may be a more accurate performance indicator than the trend in profit.

EPS measures performance from the perspective of investors and potential investors and shows the amount of earnings available to each ordinary shareholder, so that it indicates the potential return on individual investments.

Illustration 7 – Trend in EPS

The stock market places great emphasis on a company's P/E ratio and therefore a standard form of measurement of EPS is required.

Where an entity has increased its profits after issuing a large number of new ordinary shares, comparing the reported profits from year to year would not give a true picture. However, a more accurate indication of profitability would be obtained by examining the trend of EPS reported for each accounting period.

Limitations of EPS

EPS is used primarily as a measure of profitability, so an increasing EPS is seen as a good sign. EPS is also used to calculate the price earnings ratio which is dealt with below.

The limitations of EPS may be listed as follows.

- In times of rising prices EPS will increase as profits increase. Thus any improvement in EPS should be viewed in the context of the effect of price level changes on the company's profits, as apparent growth in earnings may not be real.
- Where there is a new share issue for cash, say half way through the year, the new shares are included for half the year on the grounds that earnings will also increase for half of the year. However, in practice a new project funded by that cash does not begin generating normal returns immediately, so a new share issue is often initially accompanied by a decrease in EPS.
- EPS is dependent on an earnings figure which is subject to many areas of judgement. Some elements of that earnings figure, such as movements on provisions, are particularly sensitive to different judgements.
- An earnings figure should never be used as a single key performance measure. This is to take far too simplistic an approach to performance analysis.
- EPS cannot be used as a basis of comparison between companies, as the number of shares in issue in any particular company is not related to the amount of capital employed. For example, two companies may have the same amount of capital employed but one company has 100,000 $1 shares in issue and reserves of $4,900,000. Another company may have 5 million 50¢ shares in issue and reserves of $2,500,000. If earnings are the same, EPS is different.
- An entity's earnings are affected by the choice of its accounting policies. Therefore it may not always be appropriate to compare the EPS of different companies.
- EPS is an historical figure based on historical accounts, and therefore it does not necessarily have predictive value.
- DEPS is only an additional measure of past performance despite looking at future potential shares.

Importance of DEPS

DEPS is important for the following reasons:

- it shows what the current year's EPS would be if all the dilutive potential ordinary shares in issue had been converted
- it can be used to assess trends in past performance
- in theory, it serves as a warning to equity shareholders that the return on their investment may fall in future periods.

DEPS as an additional past performance measure

DEPS as currently required by IAS 33 is not intended to be forward looking but is an additional past performance measure. For example, when calculating DEPS where there are warrants or options, fair value is based on the average price of an ordinary share over the reporting period, rather than the market price at the period end. Therefore, DEPS is only of limited use as a prediction of future EPS.

5 Chapter summary

IAS 33 EPS

Basic EPS

Earnings
Shares

Earnings = group PAT, less Non-controlling interests and irredeemable preference share dividends

Shares = weighted average number of ordinary shares outstanding during the period.

Bonus issue

- shares are deemed to have been issued at the start of the year
- comparative EPS is restated using the same higher share figure.

Rights issue

Weighted average capital:

- adjust for bonus element in rights issue
- calculate the weighted average capital in the issue.

DEPS

Alerts shareholders to the potential impact on EPS of:

- the conversion terms for convertible bonds
- the conversion terms for convertible preference shares
- the exercise price for options and the subscription price for warrants.

=

Earnings + notional extra earnings
Number of shares + notional extra shares

Convertibles

If convertible bonds/preference shares had been converted:

- interest/dividend would be saved therefore earnings would be higher
- number of shares would increase.

Options and warrants

On exercise:

- DEPS calculation must allow for cash received
- no effect on the earnings. therefore no adjustment to earnings is required.

Test your understanding 7

On 1 January the issued share capital of Pillbox was 12 million preference shares of $1 each and 10 million ordinary shares of $1 each. Assume where appropriate that the income tax rate is 30%. The earnings for the year ended 31 December were $5,950,000.

Calculate the EPS for (a) – (d) and DEPS for (e) and (f) separately in respect of the year ended 31 December for each of the following circumstances, on the basis that:

(a) there was no change in the issued share capital of the company during the year ended 31 December

(b) the company made a bonus issue on 1 October of one ordinary share for every four shares in issue at 30 September

(c) the company issued 1 share for every 10 on 1 August at full market value of $4

(d) the company made a rights issue of $1 ordinary shares on 1 October in the proportion of 1 of every 3 shares held, at a price of $3. The middle market price for the shares on the last day of quotation cum rights was $4 per share

(e) the company made no new issue of shares during the year ended 31 December, but on that date it had in issue $2,600,000 10% convertible bonds. These bonds will be convertible into ordinary $1 shares as follows:

20X6	90	$1 shares for $100 nominal value bonds
20X7	85	$1 shares for $100 nominal value bonds
20X8	80	$1 shares for $100 nominal value bonds
20X9	75	$1 shares for $100 nominal value bonds

(f) the company made no issue of shares during the year ended 31 December, but on that date there were outstanding options to purchase 74,000 ordinary $1 shares at $2.50 per share. Share price during the year was $4.

Test your understanding 8

1 In the year ended 31 December 20X6, there were 12 million ordinary shares in issue and the earnings per share was calculated as 33.3¢ per share. In the year ended 31 December 20X7 the earnings available for ordinary shareholders amounted to $5 million.

On 30 September 20X7 the company made a one for four bonus issue.

What is the EPS for the year ended 31 December 20X7 and the restated EPS for the year ended 31 December 20X6?

	20X7	**20X6**
A	33.3¢	33.3¢
B	41.7¢	33.3¢
C	39.2¢	26.6¢
D	33.3¢	26.6¢

2 In the year ended 31 December 20X6, there were 12 million ordinary shares in issue and that the earnings available for ordinary shareholders was $4 million. In the year ended 31 December 20X7 the earnings available for ordinary shareholders amounted to $5 million.

On 31 March 20X7 the company issued two million extra shares for cash.

What is the EPS for the year ended 31 December 20X7 and year ended 31 December 20X6?

	20X7	**20X6**
A	33.3¢	33.3¢
B	41.7¢	33.3¢
C	37¢	33.3¢
D	37¢	29.6¢

3 In the year ended 31 December 20X6, there were 12 million ordinary shares in issue and the earnings per share was calculated as 33.3¢ per share. In the year ended 31 December 20X7 the earnings available for ordinary shareholders amounted to $5 million. The company made a one for five rights issue on 30 June 20X7 at a price of $1.50 and the cum rights price on the last day before the rights was $2.

What is the EPS for the year ended 31 December 20X7 and the restated EPS for the year ended 31 December 20X6?

	20X7	**20X6**
A	37.2¢	32¢
B	37.9¢	32¢
C	34.7¢	27.8¢
D	37.2¢	33.3¢

4 In the year ended 31 December 20X7, there were 12 million ordinary shares in issue, and the earnings available for ordinary shareholders amounted to $5 million. There are 1 million 10% $1 convertible loan notes in issue, convertible at the rate of 3 ordinary shares for every $4 of loan notes in the year ended 31 December 20X7. The rate of tax is 30%.

What is the fully diluted EPS for the year ended 31 December 20X7?

A 41.7¢

B 39.8¢

C 39.5¢

D 37.2¢

5 In the year ended 31 December 20X7 there were 12 million ordinary shares in issue, and the earnings available for ordinary shareholders amounted to $5 million. There are 1 million options in issue, with a fair value and exercise price of $2 and $1.50 respectively.

What is the fully diluted EPS for the year ended 31 December 20X7?

A 41.7¢

B 40.8¢

C 39.5¢

D 37.2¢

Test your understanding answers

Test your understanding 1

Issue at full market price

Date	Number of shares	Fraction of year	Total
1 Jan 20X4 b/f	8,280,000	6/12	4,140,000
New issue	3,312,000		
30 June 20X4 c/f	11,592,000	6/12	5,796,000
Number of shares in EPS calculation			9,936,000

The earnings per share for 20X4 would now be calculated as:

$$\frac{\$2,208,000}{9,936,000} = 22.2¢$$

Test your understanding 2

The number of shares to be used in the EPS calculation for both years is 7,000,000 + 1,000,000 = 8,000,000.

The EPS for 20X2 is 750,000/8,000,000 = 9.4¢

The EPS for 20X3 is 1,150,000/8,000,000 = 14.4¢

Alternatively adjust last year's actual EPS

20X2 10.7¢ (750,000/7,000,000) × 7/8 = 9.4¢.

Test your understanding 3

Date	Number of shares	Bonus fraction	Fraction of year	Total
1 Jan b/f	1,000,000	6/5	3/12	300,000
Issue	200,000			
1 Apr b/f	1,200,000	6/5	4/12	480,000
1 for 5 bonus	240,000			
1 Aug b/f	1,440,000		2/12	240,000
Issue	300,000			
1 Oct b/f	1,740,000		3/12	435,000
Number of shares in EPS calculation				1,455,000

The earnings per share for 20X1 would now be calculated as:

$\frac{\$220,000}{1,455,000} = 15.1¢$

Test your understanding 4

Step 1 – Theoretical ex-rights price (TERP)

	Number	Price $	Value $
Prior to rights issue	4	1.00	4.00
Taking up rights	1	0.50	0.50
	5		4.50

TERP = $4.50/5 = 90¢

Step 2 – Bonus fraction

Market price before issue/TERP = $1/$0.9

Step 3 – Weighted average number of shares

	No.	Bonus fraction	Time	Weighted average
1 January b/f	4,000,000	1/0.9	6/12	2,222,222
1 for 4 rights	1,000,000			
1 July b/f	5,000,000		6/12	2,500,000
				4,722,222

Step 4 – EPS

20X2 EPS

$$\text{EPS} = \frac{\$425{,}000}{4{,}722{,}222} = 9.0¢ \text{ per share}$$

20X1 EPS

Last year, reported EPS: $320,000 ÷ 4,000,000 = 8.0¢

20X1 Restated EPS

8.0 × 0.9/1 = **7.2¢**

Test your understanding 5

If this loan stock was converted to shares the impact on earnings would be as follows.

	$	$
Basic earnings		2,208,000
Add notional interest saved		
($2,300,000 × 10%)	230,000	
Less: Tax relief $230,000 × 30%	(69,000)	
		161,000
Revised earnings		2,369,000

Number of shares if loan converted

Basic number of shares	8,280,000
Maximum notional extra shares	
$2,300,000 \times \frac{90}{100}$	2,070,000
Revised number of shares	10,350,000

$$DEPS = \frac{\$2,369,000}{10,350,000} = 22.9¢$$

Test your understanding 6

	$
Earnings	2,208,000
Number of shares	
Basic	8,280,000
Options **(W1)**	51,111
	8,331,111

$$\text{The DEPS is therefore: } = \frac{\$2,208,000}{8,331,111} = 26.5¢$$

(W1) Number of shares at option price

Options = 920,000 × $1.70 = $1,564,000

$$\text{At fair value: } \frac{\$1,564,000}{\$1.80} = 868,889$$

Number issued free = 920,000 – 868,889 = 51,111

(W1) (Alternative)

Alternatively, number of free shares using formula:

920,000 × (1.8 – 1.7)/1.8 = 51,111

Test your understanding 7

(a) EPS (basic) = 59.5¢

Earnings	$5,950
Shares	10,000

(b) EPS (basic) = 47.6¢

Earnings	$5,950
Shares (10m × 5/4)	12,500

(c) EPS (basic) = 57.1¢

Earnings	$5,950
Shares **(W1)**	10,416

(W1) Weighted average number of shares ('000)

	No.	**Time**	**Shares**
1 January	10,000	7/12	5,833
1 for 10 issue	1,000		
1 August	11,000	5/12	4,583
			10,416

(d) 52.5¢

Step 1 – Theoretical ex-rights price (TERP)

Number of shares	**Price $**	**Value $**
3	4.00	12.00
1	3.00	3.00
4	**(Balancing fig) 3.75**	15.00

TERP = 3.75

Step 2 – Bonus fraction

Market price before issue/TERP = $4/$3.75

Step 3 – Weighted average number of shares

	Number	Bonus fraction	Time	Shares
1 January	10m	4/3.75	9/12	8m
1 July	13.33m		3/12	3.33m
				11.33m

Step 4 – EPS

$5.95m/11.33m = **52.5¢**

(e) EPS (fully diluted) = 49.7¢

Earnings (5.95m + (10% × 2.6m × 70%))	$6,132
Shares (10m + (90/100 × 2.6m))	12,340

(f) EPS (fully diluted) = 59.3¢

Earnings	$5,950
Shares (10m + ((4 – 2.50)/4 × 74,000)	10,028

Alternative calculation for (f):

Cash received from options = $185,000 (74,000 × $2.50)

At market value, this would buy 46,250 shares ($185,000/$4).

Therefore 27,750 shares have been issued for free, as only 46,250 have been paid for but 74,000 have been issued.

These 'free' shares would be added to the 10m shares as shown in the above working to give the diluted EPS.

Alternative working for free shares (using formula, as above):

74,000 × (4 – 2.50)/4 = 27,750

Test your understanding 8

1 **D**

The weighted average number of shares for 20X7 is 15m (12m plus bonus issues of 1/4 = extra 3m)

20X7 EPS = \$5m/15m = \$0.333.

20X6 re-stated EPS = 33.3c × 4/5 = 26.6¢

2 **C**

EPS 20X6 = \$4m/12m = 33.3¢

EPS 20X7 = \$5m/13.5m (W1) = 37¢

(W1) Weighted average number of shares

	No.	**Time**	**Shares**
1 January	12m	3/12	3m
Issue	2m		
1 April	14m	9/12	10.5m
			13.5m

3 **A**

Step 1 – Theoretical ex-rights price (TERP)

Number of shares	**Price \$**	**Value \$**
5	2.00	10.00
1	1.50	1.50
6	**(Balancing fig) 1.92**	11.50

TERP = 1.92

Step 2 – Bonus fraction

Market price before issue/TERP = \$2/\$1.92

Step 3 – Weighted average number of shares

	No.	Bonus fraction	Time	Shares
1 January	12m	2/1.92	6/12	6.25m
1 for 5 rights	2.4m			
1 July	14.4m		6/12	7.2m
				13.45m

Step 4 – EPS

\$5m/13.45m = 37.2¢

20X6 re-stated = 33.3¢ × 1.92/2 = 32¢

4 **B**

For diluted EPS:

$$\frac{\text{Earnings + notional extra earnings}}{\text{Number of shares + notional extra shares}}$$

Notional extra earnings = \$100,000 interest saved less \$30,000 additional tax = \$70,000

Notional extra shares = \$1m × 3/4 = 750,000 shares

$$\frac{\$5\text{m} + \$70{,}000}{12\text{m} + 750{,}000}$$

= 39.8¢

5 **B**

If the options are exercised, then \$1.5m cash will be raised.

At market value, \$1.5m would buy 750,000 shares (\$1.5m/\$2), meaning 250,000 shares have been issued for free.

DEPS = \$5m/12.25m (12m + 250,000 free shares) = **40.8¢**

Working for free shares using the formula method:

1,000,000 × (2 – 1.5)/2 = 250,000

Chapter

15

IAS 37 and IAS 10

Chapter learning objectives

Upon completion of this chapter you will be able to:

- explain why an accounting standard on provisions is necessary
- distinguish between legal and constructive obligations
- explain in what circumstances a provision may be made
- explain in what circumstances a provision may not be made
- show how provisions are accounted for
- explain how provisions should be measured
- define contingent liabilities and contingent assets
- explain the accounting treatment of contingent liabilities and contingent assets
- identify and account for warranties/guarantees
- identify and account for onerous contracts
- identify and account for environmental and similar provisions
- identify and account for provisions for future repairs and refurbishments.
- explain the period covered by IAS 10 *Events after the Reporting Period*
- explain the difference between adjusting and non-adjusting events
- identify the correct accounting treatment for events occurring after the year end.

PER

One of the PER performance objectives (PO6) is to record and process transactions and events. You use the right accounting treatments for transactions and events. These should be both historical and prospective – and include non-routine transactions. Working though this chapter should help you understand how to demonstrate that objective.

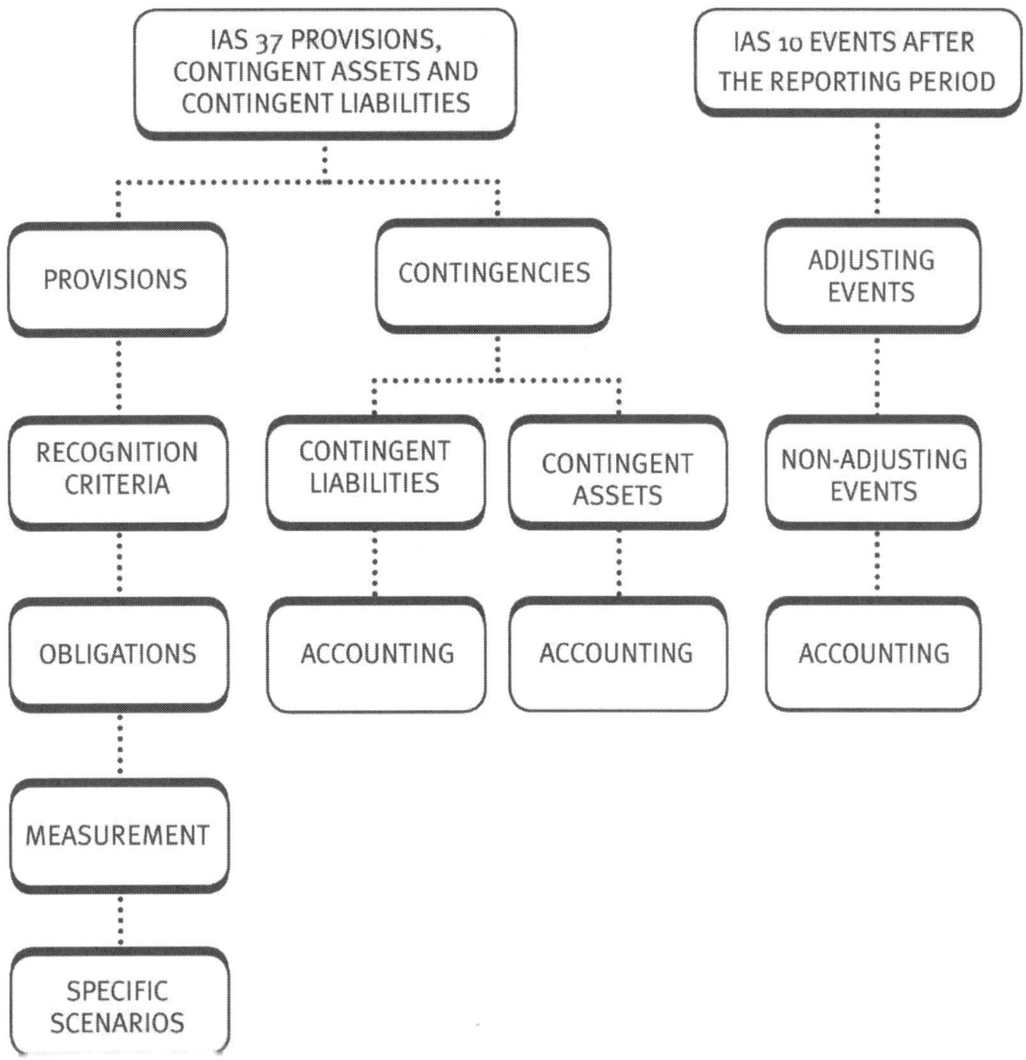

1 Provisions

The problem

Until the issue of IAS 37 *Provisions, Contingent Liabilities and Contingent Assets*, there was no accounting standard covering the general topic of provisions. This led to various problems.

- Provisions were often recognised as a result of an intention to make expenditure, rather than an obligation to do so.
- Several items could be aggregated into one large provision that was reported as an exceptional item (the 'big bath').
- Inadequate disclosure meant that in some cases it was difficult to ascertain the significance of the provisions and any movements in the year.

The historical problem of provisioning

The making of provisions was an area of accounting abuse prior to the introduction of any relevant accounting standard. Users of financial statements found it very difficult to understand profit figures arrived at after the charging or releasing of provisions at management's discretion. A common example was on the appointment of a new management team to a business.

- On appointment the new management would set up large provisions for reorganisations (depressing profits), saying they were needed as a result of the actions of the previous management – such depressed profits could therefore be blamed on that previous management team.
- One or more years later the new management would 'discover' that not all those provisions were necessary, so they would be written back (enhancing profits), probably without any disclosure. So the profits under the new management would look impressive, when in reality they had been created by the release of provisions charged in an earlier period.

Objective of IAS 37

The objective of IAS 37 *Provisions, Contingent Liabilities and Contingent Assets* is to ensure that:

- **'appropriate recognition criteria and measurement bases are applied to provisions, contingent liabilities and contingent assets, and that**
- **sufficient information is disclosed in the notes to the financial statements to enable users to understand their nature, timing and amount.'** IAS 37 Objective

What is a provision?

'A provision is a liability of uncertain timing or amount' (IAS 37, para 10).

'A liability is a present obligation of the entity arising from past events, the settlement of which is expected to result in an outflow from the entity of resources embodying economic benefits' (Framework para 4.4 (b)).

Recognition of a provision

'A provision shall be recognised when:

- **an entity has a present obligation (legal or constructive) as a result of a past event,**
- **a reliable estimate can be made of the amount of the obligation, and**
- **it is probable that an outflow of resources embodying economic benefits will be required to settle the obligation**

If these conditions are not met, no provision shall be recognised' (IAS 37, para 14).

1 **A present obligation as a result of a past event**

The obligation needs to exist because of events which have already occurred at the year-end and give rise to a potential outflow of economic resources. This obligation can either be:

(a) Legal/contractual

(b) Constructive – This is where the company establish a valid expectation through a course of past practice, regardless of whether there is a legal requirement to perform the task or not.

Recognition

An **intention** to make a payment is not enough on its own to justify a provision. There must be an actual **obligation** to make a payment.

This is important in the accounting for repairs or refurbishments known to be required in future. As an example, if a property lease includes requirement that the premises are repainted every five years and the future cost is estimated at, say, $100,000, the lessee would probably prefer to spread this cost over the five years, by charging $20,000 against profits each year. In this way there will be a provision of $100,000 in five years' time and profits have been equally affected each year.

IAS 37 does not permit this approach, because there is no obligation to incur this cost until the five years have elapsed. Over the first four years this is a future obligation which can be avoided by the simple means of selling the lease to someone else! IAS 37 requires the full cost to be recognised in the fifth year. The lessee will probably not like the way profits are unaffected by this cost over four years but then suffer a major hit in the fifth.

Illustration 1 – Refunds

A retail store has a policy of refunding purchases by dissatisfied customers, even though it is under no legal obligation to do so. Its policy of making refunds is generally known.

Should a provision be made at the year end?

Solution

- The policy is well known and creates a valid expectation.
- There is a constructive obligation.
- It is probable some refunds will be made.
- These can be measured using expected values.

Conclusion: A provision is required.

2 **A reliable estimate can be made**

Provisions should be recognised at the best estimate. If the provision relates to one event, such as the potential liability from a court case, this should be measured using the **most likely outcome**. If the provision is made up of numerous events, such as a provision to make repairs on goods within a year of sale, then the provision should be measured using **expected values**.

Illustration 2 – Expected values

An entity sells goods with a warranty covering customers for the cost of repairs of any defects that are discovered within the first two months after purchase. Past experience suggests that 88% of the goods sold will have no defects, 7% will have minor defects and 5% will have major defects. If minor defects were detected in all products sold, the cost of repairs would be $24,000. If major defects were detected in all products sold, the cost would be $200,000.

What amount of provision should be made?

Solution

The expected value of the cost of repairs is $11,680 [(7% × 24,000) + (5% × 200,000)].

e.g

Illustration 3 – Best estimate

An entity has to rectify a serious fault in an item of plant that it has constructed for a customer. The individual most likely outcome is that the repair will succeed at the first attempt at a cost of $400,000, but there is a chance that a further attempt will be necessary, increasing the total cost to $500,000.

What amount of provision should be recognised?

Solution

A provision for $400,000 is recognised.

This is because the best estimate of the liability is its most likely outcome, not the worst-case scenario.

3 **There is a probable outflow of economic resources**

If the likelihood of the event is not probable, no provision should be made. If there is a possible liability, then the company should record a contingent liability instead.

'A contingent liability is:

- **a possible obligation that arises from past events and whose existence will be confirmed only by the occurrence or non-occurrence of one or more uncertain future events not wholly within the control of the entity, or**
- **a present obligation that arises from past events but is not recognised because:**
  - **it is not probable that an outflow of resources embodying economic benefits will be required to settle the obligation, or**
  - **the amount of the obligation cannot be measured with sufficient reliability'** (IAS 37, para 10).

A contingent liability is disclosed as a note to the accounts only, no entries are made into the financial statements other than this disclosure.

Similar to a contingent liability, a company may also have a contingent asset to disclose.

'A contingent asset is a possible asset that arises from past events and whose existence will be confirmed only by the occurrence or non-occurrence of one or more uncertain future events not wholly within the control of the entity' (IAS 37 para 10).

Summary

The accounting treatment can be summarised in a table:

Degree of probability	Outflow	Inflow
Virtually certain	Recognise liability	Recognise asset
Probable	Recognise provision	Disclose contingent asset
Possible	Disclose contingent liability	Ignore
Remote	Ignore	Ignore

Warranty provisions

Introduction

A warranty is often given in manufacturing and retailing businesses. There is either a legal or constructive obligation to make good or replace faulty products.

Warranty provisions

A provision is required at the time of the sale rather than the time of the repair/replacement as the making of the sale is the past event which gives rise to an obligation.

This requires the seller to analyse past experience so that they can estimate:

- how many claims will be made – if manufacturing techniques improve, there may be fewer claims in the future than there have been in the past
- how much each repair will cost – as technology becomes more complex, each repair may cost more.

The provision set up at the time of sale:

- is the number of repairs expected in the future multiplied by the expected cost of each repair
- should be reviewed at the end of each accounting period in the light of further experience.

Guarantees

In some instances (particularly in groups) one entity will make a guarantee on behalf of another to pay off a loan, etc. if the other entity is unable to do so.

A provision should be made for this guarantee if it is probable that the payment will have to be made.

It may otherwise require disclosure as a contingent liability.

Future operating losses/future repairs

No provision may be made for future operating losses or repairs because they arise in the future and can be avoided (close the division that is making losses or sell the asset that may need repair) and therefore no obligation exists.

Onerous contracts

'An onerous contract is a contract in which the unavoidable costs of meeting the obligations under the contract exceed the economic benefits expected to be received under it' (IAS 37, para 10).

The signing of the contract is the past event giving rise to the obligation to make the payments and those payments, discounted if the effect is material, will be the measure of the excess of cost over the benefits.

A provision for this net cost should be recognised as an expense in the statement of profit or loss in the period when the contract becomes onerous. In subsequent periods, this provision will be increased by the unwinding of the discount (recognised as a finance charge) and reduced by any payments made.

Environmental provisions

A provision will be made for future environmental costs if there is either a legal or constructive obligation to carry out the work

This will be discounted to present value at a pre-tax market rate.

Test your understanding 1

Environmental provision

Rowsley is a company that carries out many different activities. It is proud of its reputation as a 'caring' organisation and has adopted various ethical policies towards its employees and the wider community in which it operates. As part of its annual financial statements, the company publishes details of its environmental policies, which include setting performance targets for activities such as recycling, controlling emissions of noxious substances and limiting use of non-renewable resources.

The company has an overseas operation that is involved in mining precious metals. These activities cause significant damage to the environment, including deforestation. The company incurred capital costs of $100 million in respect of the mine and it is expected that the mine will be abandoned in eight years' time. The mine is situated in a country where there is no environmental legislation obliging companies to rectify environmental damage, and it is very unlikely that any such legislation will be enacted within the next eight years. It has been estimated that the cost of cleaning the site and re-planting the trees will be $25 million if the replanting were successful at the first attempt, but it will probably be necessary to make a further attempt, which will increase the cost by a further $5 million. The company's cost of capital is 10%.

Discuss whether a provision for the cost of cleaning the site should be made and prepare extracts of the financial statements.

Restructuring provisions

'A restructuring is a programme that is planned and controlled by management, and materially changes either:

- **the scope of a business undertaken by an entity, or**
- **the manner in which that business is conducted'** (IAS 37, para 10).

A provision may only be made if:

- a detailed, formal and approved plan exists, and
- the plan has been announced to those affected.

The provision should:

- include direct expenditure arising from restructuring
- exclude costs associated with ongoing activities.

Restructuring provisions – Further detail

Any provision may only be made if a present obligation exists.

In the context of a restructuring, a detailed, formal and approved plan must exist. This in itself is not enough to create a provision, because management may change its mind.

A provision should only be made if the plan has also been announced to those affected. This creates a constructive obligation, because management is now very unlikely to change its mind.

The restructuring provision may only include direct expenditure arising from the restructuring, which is both necessarily entailed by the restructuring, and not associated with the ongoing activities of the entity.

It should therefore include costs such as redundancies and write-downs on property plant and equipment.

Costs associated with retraining or relocating staff, marketing or investment in new systems and distribution networks may not be included in the provision, because they relate to the future conduct of the business.

e.g

Illustration 4 – Restructuring provisions

On 14 June 20X5 a decision was made by the board of an entity to close down a division. The decision was not communicated at that time to any of those affected and no other steps were taken to implement the decision by the year end of 30 June 20X5. The division was closed in September 20X5.

Should a provision be made at 30 June 20X5 for the cost of closing down the division?

Solution

- No constructive obligation exists.
- This is a board decision, which can be reversed.
- No provision can be made.

Illustration 5 – Contingencies

A common example of contingencies arises in connection with legal action.

If A sues B because it believes that it has incurred losses as a result of B's faulty products, then B may be liable for damages. Whether or not the damages will actually be paid depends on the outcome of the case.

Solution

Until the outcome of the case is known, B has a contingent **liability** and A has a contingent **asset.**

Accounting for contingent liabilities

Contingent liabilities:

- should not be recognised in the statement of financial position
- should be disclosed in a note unless the possibility of a transfer of economic benefits is remote.

Accounting for contingent assets

Contingent assets should not generally be recognised, but if the possibility of inflows of economic benefits is probable, they should be disclosed.

If a gain is virtually certain, it falls within the definition of an asset and should be recognised as such, not as a contingent asset.

Illustration 6 – Contingent liability

During the year to 31 March 20X9, a customer commenced legal proceedings against a company, claiming that one of the food products that it manufactures had caused several members of his family to become seriously ill. The company's lawyers have advised that this action will probably not succeed.

Should the company disclose this in its financial statements?

Solution

- Legal advice is that the claim is unlikely to succeed.
- It is unlikely that the company has a present obligation to compensate the customer and therefore no provision should be recognised.
- There is, however, a contingent liability.
- Unless the possibility of a transfer of economic benefits is remote, the financial statements should disclose a brief description of the nature of the contingent liability, an estimate of its financial effect and an indication of the uncertainties relating to the amount or timing of any outflow.

2 IAS 10 Events after the Reporting Period

Events after the reporting period

Events after the reporting period are those events, both favourable and unfavourable, which occur between the reporting date and the date on which the financial statements are approved for issue by the board of directors.

Adjusting and non-adjusting events

Adjusting events are events after the reporting date that provide additional evidence of conditions existing at the reporting date.

Non-adjusting events are events after the reporting date that concern conditions that arose after the reporting date.

Adjusting events

Examples of adjusting events include:

- irrecoverable debts arising after the reporting date, which may help to quantify the allowance for receivables as at the reporting date
- sale of inventory below cost, providing evidence of net realisable value
- amounts received or receivable in respect of insurance claims which were being negotiated at the reporting date
- the discovery of fraud or errors.

Non-adjusting events

Examples of non-adjusting events include:

- a major business combination after the reporting date
- the destruction of a major production plant by a fire after the reporting date
- abnormally large changes in asset prices or foreign exchange rates after the reporting date.

Accounting for adjusting and non-adjusting events

Adjusting events require the adjustment of amounts recognised in the financial statements.

Non-adjusting events should be disclosed by note if they are of such importance that non-disclosure would affect the ability of the users of the financial statements to make proper evaluations and decisions.

The note should disclose the nature of the event and an estimate of the financial effect, or a statement that such an estimate cannot be made.

Test your understanding 2

Anderson's year end is 31 December 20X7. The following events all occurred in January 20X8.

State whether the events below would be classed as adjusting or non-adjusting events.

Event	Adjusting	Non-adjusting
Insolvency of a customer	✓	
Loss of inventory due to a flood		✓
Completion of the purchase of another company		✓
Evidence showing that the net realisable value of inventory is below cost	✓	
A court case from August is settled by Anderson	✓	
The discovery of a fraud showing the financial statements were incorrect	✓	

Non-adjusting events

These are events arising after the reporting date but which do not concern situations existing at the reporting date. Such events will not, therefore, have any effect on items in the statement of financial position or statement of profit or loss being prepared.

However, where non-adjusting events after the reporting date are of such importance that non-disclosure would affect the ability of the users of the financial statements to make proper evaluations and decisions, an entity should disclose the following information for each non-adjusting event after the reporting date:

- the nature of the event
- an estimate of its financial effect, or a statement that such an estimate cannot be made.

Going concern

If an event after the reporting date indicates that the going concern assumption is inappropriate for the entity, then the statement of financial position should be prepared on a break-up basis.

Illustration 7 – Events after the reporting date

Shortly after the reporting date a major credit customer of an entity went into liquidation because of heavy trading losses and it is expected that little or none of the $12,500 debt will be recoverable. $10,000 of the debt relates to sales made prior to the year-end and $2,500 relates to sales made in the first two days of the new financial year.

In the 20X1 financial statements the whole debt has been written off, but one of the directors has pointed out that, as the liquidation is an event after the reporting date, the debt should not in fact be written off but disclosure should be made by note to this year's financial statements, and the debt written off in the 20X2 financial statements.

Advise whether the director is correct.

Solution

Under IAS 10 an event after the reporting date is an event which occurs between the financial period end and the date on which the financial statements are approved by the board of directors.

$10,000 of the receivable existed at the reporting date and the liquidation of the major customer provides more information about that receivable.

In accordance with IAS 10, this is an adjusting event which would require the debt existing at the reporting date to be written off in the 20X1 financial statements.

The remaining receivable did not exist at the reporting date and should therefore be written off in the 20X2 financial statements.

Proposed dividends

Equity dividends proposed before but approved and paid after the reporting date may not be included as liabilities at the reporting date.

We account for dividends on a cash basis so they are non-adjusting events after the reporting date and must be disclosed by note as required by IAS 1.

3 Chapter summary

IAS 37 PROVISIONS, CONTINGENT ASSETS AND CONTINGENT LIABILITIES

Provisions
= A liability of uncertain timing or amount.

Recognition criteria
- Present obligation
- Probable outflow of resources
- Reliable estimate.

Obligations
- Legal
- Constructive.

Measurement
- Expected values
- Best estimate.

Specific scenarios
- Warranties
- Guarantees
- Future operating losses
- Onerous contracts
- Environmental provisions
- Restructuring provisions

CONTINGENCIES

Contingent liabilities
= possible obligation.

Contingent assets
= possible asset.

Accounting

Flow is:	Outflow	Inflow
Virtually certain	Liability	Asset
Probable	Provide	Disclose
Possible	Disclose	Ignore
Remote	Ignore	Ignore

IAS 10 EVENTS AFTER THE REPORTING PERIOD
= events between the reporting date and date of approval of accounts

ADJUSTING EVENTS
= Events which provide additional evidence of conditions existing at the reporting date.

NON-ADJUSTING EVENTS
= Events which concern conditions that arose after the reporting date.

ACCOUNTING
Adjusting = adjust accounts
Non-adjusting = disclose.

Test your understanding 3

Randall is currently preparing its financial statements for the year ended 31 March 20X8. The board has met to discuss the following issues:

(i) Some of the products sold by Randall are sold with warranties enabling customers to return faulty goods within 2 years of purchase. Randall will either repair the product or refund the sales value to the customer.

During the year the sales value of products sold with such warranties totalled $300,000. Based on past experience it is anticipated that 20% of these products will be returned under the terms of the warranty.

Of the goods that are returned it is expected that 5% will be beyond repair and Randall will need to refund the full sales value to the customer.

The remaining 95% of returned goods will be able to be repaired. This will cost Randall, on average, 30% of the items sales price.

Some of the goods that have been sold this year have already been returned under the terms of the warranty. Randall has incurred costs of $5,000 in respect of these items.

As at 31 March 20X7, Randall's financial statements showed a provision of $14,000 in respect of warranty costs. This was made up of $4,000 in relation to goods sold during the year ended 31 March 20X6 and $10,000 in respect of goods sold during the year ended 31 March 20X7. The warranty in respect of items sold during the year ended 31 March 20X6 has expired as at 31 March 20X8. During the year ended 31 March 20X8, $3,000 of costs were incurred in respect of warranty claims made in relation to goods sold in the year ended 31 March 20X7.

(ii) A month before the year-end, a fire destroyed a significant proportion of Randall's inventories. Randall has since been negotiating compensation with their insurers. Initially, the insurers were of the view that Randall had not followed applicable legislation to protect against fire damage and were contesting the claim. Randall was confident that they had complied with the legislation and referred the matter to their solicitors. In April 20X8 the board of directors received a letter from the insurance company stating that they are satisfied that Randall did comply with appropriate legislation. The solicitors have advised the directors that it is now probable that they will receive compensation in the region of $50,000.

Explain how these matters should be dealt with in the financial statements of Randall in the year ended 31 March 20X8. (Your answer should quantify amounts where possible.)

Test your understanding 4

Sebastian Co is currently involved in four legal cases, all of them unrelated.

- In Case A, Sebastian Co is suing a supplier for $100,000.
- In Case B, Sebastian Co is suing a professional adviser for $200,000.
- In Case C, Sebastian Co is being sued by a customer for $300,000.
- In Case D, Sebastian Co is being sued by an investor for $400,000.

Sebastian Co has been advised by its lawyers that the probabilities of success in each case are as follows:

Case	**Likelihood of Sebastian Co winning the case**
A	10%
B	90%
C	98%
D	60%

State the accounting treatment for each of the four cases.

Test your understanding 5

1 Jackson Co's year end is 31 December 20X0. In February 20X1 a major customer went into liquidation and the directors believe that they will not be able to recover the $450,000 owed to them.

How should this item be treated in the financial statements of Jackson Co for the year ended 31 December 20X0?

A The $450,000 should be disclosed by note as an irrecoverable debt

B The financial statements are not affected at all

C The financial statements for 20X0 are not affected, but the balance should be written off in 20X1

D The financial statements should be adjusted to show the $450,000 as an irrecoverable debt

2 A former employee is claiming compensation of $50,000 from Harriot for wrongful dismissal. The company's solicitors have stated that they believe that the claim is unlikely to succeed. The legal costs relating to the claim are likely to be in the region of $5,000 and will be incurred regardless of whether or not the claim is successful.

How should these items be treated in the financial statements of Harriot?

A Provision should be made for $55,000

B Provision should be made for $50,000 and the legal costs should be disclosed by note

C Provision should be made for $5,000 and the compensation of $50,000 should be disclosed by note

D No provisions should be made but both items should be disclosed by note

3 Blacksmith has claimed compensation of $30,000 from another entity for breach of copyright. The solicitors of Blacksmith have advised the directors that their claim is likely to succeed.

How should this item be treated in the financial statements of Blacksmith?

A The item should not be included in the financial statements

B The item should be disclosed by note in the financial statements

C The financial statements should show an asset of $30,000

D The financial statements should show an asset of $30,000 and a note should be included explaining the item

4 **Which of the following items are non-adjusting items per IAS 10 *Events after the Reporting Period*?**

(i) Changes in the rates of foreign exchange

(ii) Destruction of machinery by fire

(iii) Net realisable value of inventory being lower than cost

(iv) Acquisition of a competitor's business

(v) Insolvency of a customer

A i, ii and iv

B iii and v

C i, iii and v

D ii, iii and v

5 **Which TWO of the following could be classified as adjusting events occurring after the end of the reporting period for the year ended 31 December 20X1:**

A A serious fire, occurring 1 month after the year-end, that damaged the sole production facility, causing production to cease for 3 months.

B One month after the year-end, a notification was received advising that a large receivables balance would not be paid as the customer was being wound up. No payments are expected from the customer.

C A large quantity of parts for a discontinued production line was discovered at the back of the warehouse during the year-end inventory count on 30 December. The parts have no value except a nominal scrap value and need to be written off.

D The entity took delivery of a new machine from the USA in the last week of the financial year. It was discovered almost immediately afterwards that the entity supplying the machine had filed for bankruptcy and would not be able to honour the warranties and repair contract on the new machine. Because the machine was so advanced, it was unlikely that any local entity could provide maintenance cover.

E An asset held for sale was held in current assets at $70,000 in the financial statements, but was sold for $65,000 after the year end.

6 X is currently defending two legal actions:

- An employee, who suffered severe acid burns as a result of an accident in X's factory, is suing for $20,000, claiming that the directors failed to provide adequate safety equipment. X's lawyers are contesting the claim, but have advised the directors that they will probably lose.
- A customer is suing for $50,000, claiming that X's hair-care products damaged her hair. X's lawyers are contesting this claim, and have advised that the claim is unlikely to succeed.

How much should X provide for these legal claims in its financial statements?

$__________

7 **Which of the following would require a liability to be created by BW at the end of its reporting period, 31 October 20X1:**

A The government introduced new laws on data protection which come into force on 1 January 20X2. BW's directors have agreed that this will require a large number of staff to be retrained. At 31 October 20X1, the directors were waiting on a report they had commissioned that would identify the actual training requirements.

B At the end of the reporting period, BW is negotiating with its insurance provider about the amount of an insurance claim that it had filed. On 20 November 20X1, the insurance provider agreed to pay $200,000.

C BW makes refunds to customers for any goods returned within 30 days of sale, and has done so for many years.

D A customer is suing BW for damages alleged to have been caused by BW's product. BW is contesting the claim and, at 31 October 20X1, the directors have been advised by BW's legal advisers that it is unlikely to lose the case.

8 DH has the following two legal claims outstanding:

– A legal action against DH claiming compensation of $700,000, filed in February 20X1. DH has been advised that it is probable that it will lose the case.

– A legal action taken by DH against another entity, claiming damages of $300,000, started in March 20W8. DH has been advised that it is probable that it will win the case.

How should DH report these legal actions in its financial statements for the year ended 30 April 20X1?

	Legal action against DH	Legal action taken by DH
A	Disclose by a note to the accounts	No disclosure
B	Make a provision	No disclosure
C	Make a provision	Disclose as a note
D	Make a provision	Accrue the income

Test your understanding answers

Test your understanding 1

- The initial costs of $100 million incurred on the mine should be capitalised in accordance with IAS 16.
- It is clear that there is no legal obligation to rectify the damage. However, through its published policies, the group has created expectations on the part of those affected that it will take action to do so.
- There is therefore a constructive obligation to rectify the damage and a transfer of economic benefits is probable.
- The company must recognise a provision for the best estimate of the cost.
- As the most likely outcome is that more than one attempt at replanting will be needed, the full amount of $30 million should be provided.
- The expenditure will take place sometime in the future, and so the provision should be discounted at a pre-tax rate that reflects current market assessments of the time value of money and the risks specific to the liability.
- The financial statements should disclose the carrying amount of the provision at the reporting date, a description of the nature of the obligation and the expected timing of the expenditure. The financial statements should also give an indication of the uncertainties about the amount and timing of the expenditure.

Accounting entries for the long-term environmental provision:

			$000
1	Dr	Non-current assets	13,995
	Cr	Provisions (non-current liability)	13,995
		Recognise provision at present value ($30,000 \times 1/1.1^8$)	
2	Dr	Depreciation expense	14,249
	Cr	Accumulated depreciation	14,249
		Annual depreciation charge ((100,000 + 13,995)/8 years)	
3	Dr	Finance costs	1,400
	Cr	Provisions (non-current liability)	1,400
		First year unwinding of the discount (13,995 × 10%)	

Statement of profit or loss (extract)

	$000
Depreciation	(14,249)
Finance costs:	
Unwinding of discount	(1,400)

Statement of financial position (extract)

Non-current assets	
Mine	
Cost: (100,000 + 13,995)	113,995
Accumulated depreciation	(14,249)
	99,746
Non-current liabilities	
Environmental provision (13,995 + 1,400)	15,395

Test your understanding 2

Event	
Insolvency of a receivable balance	**Adjusting**
Loss of inventory due to a flood	**Non-adjusting**
Completion of the purchase of another company	**Non-adjusting**
Evidence showing that the net realisable value of inventory is below cost	**Adjusting**
A court case from August is settled by Anderson	**Adjusting**
The discovery of a fraud showing the financial statements were incorrect	**Adjusting**

Test your understanding 3

(i) The sale of goods with a warranty represents a past event which gives rise to a present obligation to either refund or repair the products. It is probable that some of the goods will be returned under the warranty and Randall is able to use past experience to provide a reliable estimate of the amount of the obligation. Therefore, under the rules of IAS 37, Randall must make a provision at the year-end in respect of the costs to be incurred under the warranty.

From this year's sales of $300,000, goods with a sales value of $60,000 (20% × $300,000) are expected to be returned under the warranty.

Of these, $3,000 (5% × $60,000) will be beyond repair and the full sales value will need refunding to customers.

Of the remaining, $57,000 (95% × $60,000) it is anticipated that they can be repaired at a cost of $17,100 (30% × $57,000).

Thus Randall is expecting to incur total warranty costs of $20,100 in respect of goods sold during the year ended 31 March 20X8. $5,000 of these costs have already been incurred during the year and therefore Randall should only provide for an additional $15,100 at the year-end.

Of the opening provision of $14,000, $4,000 should be removed since the warranty has expired in relation to these goods. Of the remaining $10,000, $3,000 of costs have been incurred during the year in relation to these items and therefore Randall are only expecting to incur future costs of $7,000 in relation to these items as at 31 March 20X8.

Therefore the total provision required as at 31 March 20X8 is $22,100 ($15,100 + $7,000).

(ii) This situation represents a contingent asset in accordance with IAS 37. A possible asset, the insurance claim, has arisen as a result of a past event i.e. the fire damaging the inventory.

According to IAS 37, contingent assets should be ignored in the financial statements unless it is probable that there will be an inflow of benefits, in which case the matter may be disclosed by note.

As at the year-end, the insurers are contesting the claim and therefore it would seem that it was not probable that Randall would receive the compensation.

However, since the year-end, the insurers have indicated that they will no longer be contesting the claim, and so it now seems probable that Randall will receive the compensation.

This is an adjusting event, in accordance with IAS 10, since the negotiation of the insurance claim was underway at the year-end and the receipt of the letter after the year-end provides additional evidence.

Therefore, the directors of Randall can now disclose the insurance claim in the note to their financial statements.

Test your understanding 4

Case	Comment	Accounting treatment
A	Contingent gain which is possible	Not recognised
B	Contingent gain which is possible	Disclose as a note
C	Contingent liability which is remote (It is virtually certain that we will win)	Not recognised
D	Contingent liability which is possible (It is probable that we will win)	Disclose as a note

Disclosure of a note would state the nature of the contingency, elements of uncertainty and the financial effect of the case if the gain/loss should arise.

Test your understanding 5

1 **D** – The customer's financial difficulties would have existed at the year end, even if Jackson didn't know about this. Therefore this should be adjusted in the financial statements.

2 **C** – The defeat in the legal claim is only possible, so no provision should be required for this. However, the $5,000 fees will definitely be paid so a provision must be made for this amount.

3 **B** – This relates to a potential inflow, and inflows should only be recognised as an asset in the financial statements if they are virtually certain. If an inflow is probable, then it should be disclosed as a contingent asset.

4 **A** – Inventory valuation should be adjusted to ensure that the balance is recorded at the lower of cost and NRV. The insolvency of a customer should be adjusted for, as in issue 1.

5 **B and E** – The insolvency of a customer will be an adjusting event. The asset held for sale is now to be sold at a loss. As the company know this, the value of the asset held for sale should be adjusted to $65,000.

6 **$20,000** – The $20,000 should be provided, as it is probable that X will lose the case. The $50,000 claim only appears to represent a possible outflow, so this would be disclosed as a contingent liability.

7 **C** – This would represent a constructive obligation, as BW would have created an expectation through the past practice of giving refunds.

8 **C** – Whilst probable outflows must be recorded as provisions, probable inflows should only be disclosed as contingent assets.

Chapter

16

Statement of cash flows

Chapter learning objectives

Upon completion of this chapter you will be able to:

- prepare a statement of cash flows for a single entity using the indirect method in accordance with IAS 7
- compare the usefulness of cash flow information with that of a statement of profit or loss and other comprehensive income
- interpret a statement of cash flows to assess the performance and financial position of an entity
- indicate other information, including non-financial information, that may be of relevance to the assessment of an entity's performance.

PER

One of the PER performance objectives (PO7) is to prepare external financial reports. You take part in preparing and reviewing financial statements – and all accompanying information – and you do it in accordance with legal and regulatory requirements. Working though this chapter should help you understand how to demonstrate that objective.

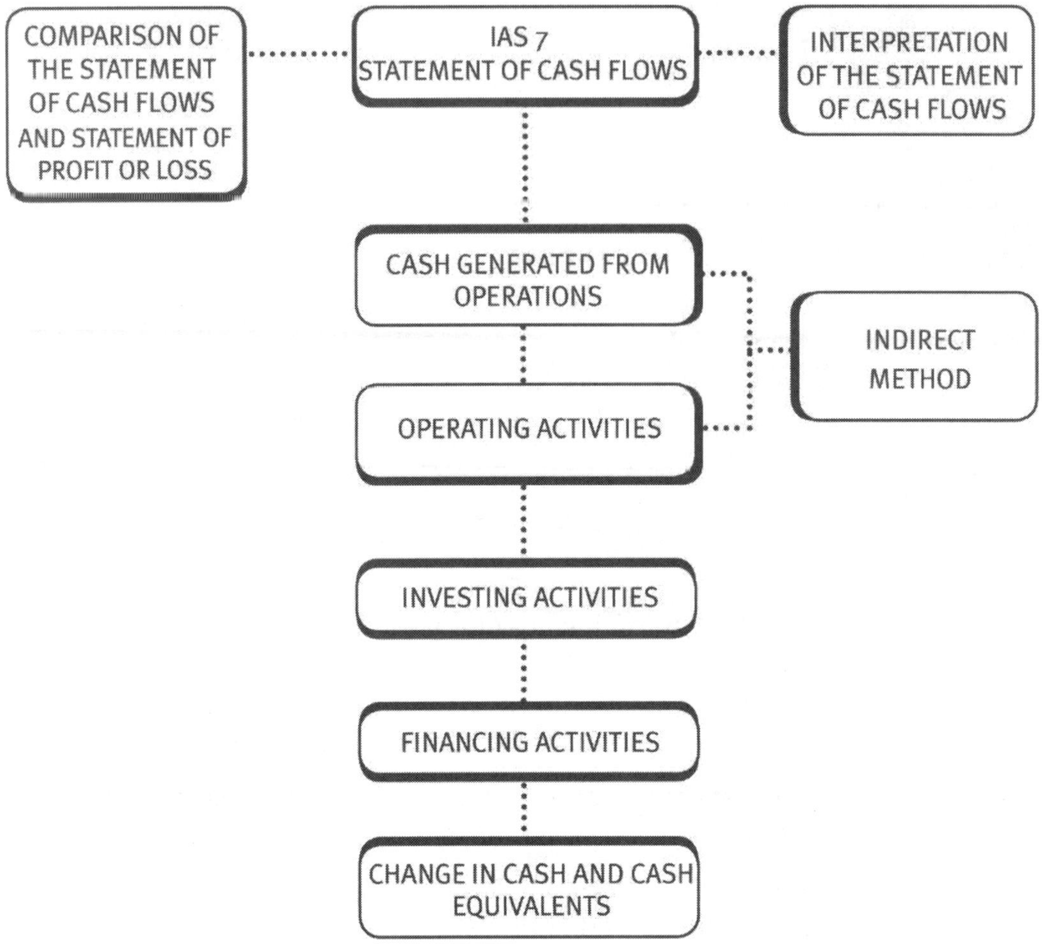

1 IAS 7 Statement of Cash Flows

Objective of the statement of cash flows

The objective of IAS 7 *Statement of Cash Flows* is:

- to ensure that all entities provide information about the historical changes in cash and cash equivalents by means of a statement of cash flows
- to classify cash flows (i.e. inflows and outflows of cash and cash equivalents) during the period between those arising from operating, investing and financing activities.

Usefulness of cash flow

Users of financial statements need information on the liquidity, viability and financial adaptability of entities. Deriving this information involves the user making assessments of the future cash flows of the entity. Future cash flows are regarded in financial management theory, and increasingly in practice in large companies, as the prime determinant of the worth of a business.

Although IAS 7 does not prescribe a format for statements of cash flows, it does require the cash flows to be classified into:

- operating activities
- investing activities
- financing activities.

This classification may require a particular transaction to be shown partly under one heading and partly under another. For example, when the cash repayment of a loan includes both interest and capital, the interest might be shown as an operating activity and the capital element as a financing activity.

The aggregation of the three types of cash flow leads to the overall movement in cash and cash equivalents, as defined below.

The objective of the standard headings is to ensure that cash flows are reported in a form that highlights the significant components of cash flow and facilitates comparison of the cash flow performance of different businesses.

Each cash flow should be classified according to the substance of the transaction that gives rise to it. The substance of a transaction determines the most appropriate standard heading under which to report cash flows that are not specified in the standard categories.

One reason why the statement of cash flows was considered necessary is that final profit figures are relatively easy to manipulate. There are many items in a statement of profit or loss whose measurement involves the use of judgement:

- inventory valuation
- depreciation
- allowance for receivables.

This makes it difficult to interpret a company's results with absolute confidence. A statement of cash flows showing merely inflows and outflows of cash is easier to understand and more difficult to manipulate.

Cash flows, including net present value adjustments, have always been a popular management accounting tool and the requirement to produce a statement of cash flows as part of the financial statements helps to form a basis for any future decision-making process.

Definitions

'Cash: Cash on hand (including overdrafts) and on demand deposits.

Cash equivalents: Short-term, highly liquid investments that are readily convertible to known amounts of cash and are subject to an insignificant risk of changes in value' (IAS 7, para 6).

Proforma statement of cash flows

It is often helpful to think of the statement of cash flows in two parts:

1 The calculation of cash generated from operations. There are two methods used for this: the direct method and the indirect method. The direct method is no longer included on the FR syllabus.

2 The statement of cash flows.

1 **Reconciliation from profit before tax to cash generated from operations ('the reconciliation')**

	$
Profit before tax	X
Adjustments for:	
Finance costs	X
Investment income	(X)
Depreciation	X
Profit on sale of non-current assets	(X)
Provisions increase/decrease	X(X)
Government grant amortisation	(X)
Increase/decrease in prepayments	(X)X
Increase/decrease in accruals	X(X)
Operating profit before working capital changes	X
Increase/decrease in inventories	(X)X
Increase/decrease in trade receivables	(X)X
Increase/decrease in trade payables	X(X)
Cash generated from operations	X

This method starts with profit before tax. Finance costs are added back and investment income is deducted in order to work back to profit from operations.

Any non-cash items are then adjusted for in order to find cash generated from operations (the cash version of profit from operations).

Non-cash expenses are added back to remove them (such as depreciation, loss on disposal).

Non-cash income items are deducted in order to remove them (such as profit on disposal, release of government grants).

Adjustments are also made to working capital, to remove the impact of credit sales/purchases. When adjusting for these items, consider whether the movements are good or bad for cash. For example, an increase in receivables is bad for cash, as it means this cash has not yet been collected from the customers.

Adjustments to profit before tax

Depreciation

- Depreciation is not a cash flow.
- Depreciation has to be added back to reported profit in deriving cash from operating activities.
- Capital expenditure will be recorded under 'investing activities' at the time of the cash outflow.

Profit/loss on disposal of non-current asset

When a non-current asset is disposed of:

- the cash inflow from sale is recorded under 'investing activities'
- a loss on disposal is added to profit in deriving cash from operating activities
- similarly, a profit on disposal is deducted from profit.

Change in receivables

- an increase in receivables is a deduction from profit in deriving cash from operating activities
- similarly, a decrease in receivables is an addition to profit.

Change in inventory

- An increase in inventory is a deduction from profit in deriving cash from operating activities
- similarly, a decrease in inventory is an addition to profit.

Change in payables

- an increase in payables is an addition to profit in deriving cash from operating activities
- similarly, a decrease in payables is a deduction from profit.

Working capital changes

Change in receivables

Recognition of a sale creates income, irrespective of the date of the cash receipt. If the cash has not been received by the reporting date, however, there is no cash inflow from operating activities for the current accounting period. Similarly, opening receivables represent sales of a previous accounting period, all of which should have been received as cash in the current period.

The change between opening and closing receivables will thus represent the adjustment required to move from reported revenue to net cash inflow from sales.

- An increase in receivables is a deduction from reported profit. Less sales from the previous period are being received in cash than are being carried forward to the next period.
- A decrease in receivables is an addition to reported profit.

Change in inventories

Inventory at the reporting date represents a purchase which has not actually been charged against current profits. However, as cash was spent on its purchase or a payable incurred, it does represent an actual or potential cash outflow.

Strictly, the amount of inventory paid for in cash should be calculated and profit adjusted by the movement in such inventories between the two reporting dates. A corresponding adjustment would be made to payables (see below) to the extent that the expense relating to such payables will not have been charged in the statement of profit or loss.

In practice, the overall movement in inventory is taken due to:

- the practical difficulties of determining how much inventory has not been paid for at the reporting date
- the advantages of showing an adjustment to profit which corresponds to movements in inventory as shown on the statement of financial position.

Change in payables

A purchase represents the incurring of expenditure and a charge or potential charge to the statement of profit or loss. It does not represent a cash outflow until paid. To the extent that a purchase results in a charge to the statement of profit or loss:

- an increase in payables between two reporting dates is an addition to reported profit
- a decrease in payables is a deduction from reported profit.

If the purchase does not result in a charge to the statement of profit or loss in the current year, the corresponding payable is not included in the reconciliation of profit to net cash inflow. For example, a payable in respect of a non-current asset is not included. As stated earlier, a payable for purchases which form part of inventory at the reporting date should not be included either, but in practice will be.

2 **Statement of cash flows**

Cash flows from operating activities:		
Cash generated from operations	X	
Interest paid	(X)	
Tax paid	(X)	
Net cash from operating activities		X(X)
Cash flows from investing activities:		
Purchases of property, plant and equipment	(X)	
Proceeds of sale of property, plant and equipment	X	
Proceeds from government grants	X	
Interest received	X	
Dividends received	X	
Net cash from investing activities		X(X)
Cash flows from financing activities:		
Proceeds from issue of shares	X	
Proceeds from long-term borrowings	X	
Payment of lease liabilities	(X)	
Dividends paid	(X)	
Net cash used in financing activities		X(X)
Net increase/decrease in cash and cash equivalents		X/(X)
Cash and cash equivalents at beginning of the period		X
		X

Analysis of cash and cash equivalents:	**This year**	**Last year**
	$	$
Cash on hand and balances with banks	X/(X)	X/(X)
Short-term investments	X	X
Cash and cash equivalents	X(X)	X(X)

Operating activities

Cash flows from operating activities typically include 3 items:

- Cash generated from operations. This is the total from the reconciliation in the first part.
- Interest paid
- Tax paid

To calculate interest and tax paid, workings may be required. These can be done using either columns or T accounts. Examples of these are shown below.

Interest paid:

Interest liability b/f	X
Finance cost per SPL	X
Interest liability c/f	(X)
Interest paid	(X)

Tax Paid:

Liabilities b/f (both current and deferred)	X
Tax charge per SPL	X
Deferred tax on revaluations of PPE	X
Liabilities c/f (both current and deferred)	(X)
Tax paid	(X)

Interest and income taxes

Interest and dividends

Interest paid is normally shown as part of operating activities.

Dividends paid are shown in the IAS 7 specimen format as part of financing activities, but may alternatively be shown under operating activities.

Income taxes

Cash flows arising from taxes on income should be separately disclosed as part of operating activities unless they can be specifically identified with financing and investing activities. It is reasonable to include income taxes as part of operating activities unless a question gives a clear indication to the contrary.

If income tax payments are allocated over more than one class of activity, the total should be disclosed by note.

Investing activities

Investing cash flows include:

- cash paid for property, plant and equipment and other non-current assets
- cash received on the sale of property, plant and equipment and other non-current assets
- cash paid for investments in or loans to other entities
- dividends received on investments.

To work out figures relating to property, plant and equipment a working will be required. This is because many items will affect the balance. These will include additions, disposals, revaluations and depreciation.

Balance b/f	X
Additions	X
Revaluation	X
Disposals	(X)
Depreciation	(X)
Balance c/f	X

Note: If the asset opening and closing cost is given as well as the opening and closing accumulated depreciation, you will need a working for the asset cost to calculate additions and a separate working for accumulated depreciation to calculate the depreciation expense.

Financing activities

Financing cash flows comprise receipts or repayments of principal from or to external providers of finance including:

- receipts from issuing shares or other equity instruments
- receipts from issuing debentures, loans, notes and bonds and from other long-term and short-term borrowings (other than overdrafts, which are normally included in cash and cash equivalents)
- repayments of amounts borrowed (other than overdrafts)
- the capital element of lease rental payments.

Again, workings can be set up for any of these items. Most commonly, the workings are needed for lease liabilities and retained earnings.

Lease liabilities paid

Liabilities b/f (both current and non-current)	X
New lease additions	X
Liabilities c/f (both current and non-current)	(X)
Lease liabilities paid	X

Dividends paid

Retained earnings b/f	X
Profit for the year	X
Retained earnings c/f	(X)
Dividends paid	X

Example 1 – Statement of cash flows

Jack plc

The draft statements of financial position as at 31 March 20X7 and 20X6 of Jack plc are shown below.

	20X7		20X6	
	$m	$m	$m	$m
Non-current assets:				
Intangible assets		450		410
Property, plant and equipment		2,480		1,830
		2,930		2,240
Current assets:				
Inventory	920		763	
Receivables	642		472	
Cash	–		34	
		1,562		1,269
		4,492		3,509
Share capital and reserves:				
Ordinary shares of $1 each		500		400
Retained earnings		1,071		1,732
Other components of equity:				
Share premium account	90		70	
Revaluation surplus	170		–	
		260		70
Non-current liabilities:				
8% loan note 20Y2	200		–	
10% redeemable preference shares	350		350	
Government grants	210		160	
Deferred tax	52		30	
Environmental provision	76		24	
		888		564

Current liabilities:				
Trade payables	680		518	
Accrued interest	4		–	
Bank overdraft	63		–	
Taxation	176		185	
Government grants	50		40	
		973		743
		4,492		3,509

The draft statement of profit or loss for Jack plc for the year to 31 March 20X7 is as follows.

	$m	$m
Revenue		3,665
Cost of sales:		
Depreciation	366	
Impairment of intangible	36	
Other costs	2,522	
		(2,924)
Gross profit for period		731
Other operating income – government grant		50
		781
Distribution costs	75	
Administration	56	
Environmental provision	67	
		(198)
		583
Finance cost – loan note interest	(12)	
Preference dividend	(35)	
		(47)
Profit before tax		536
Taxation		(177)
Profit for the period after tax		359

Jack plc – Other comprehensive income for the year ended 31 March 20X7

	$m
Profit for the year	359
Other comprehensive income	
Gain on property revaluation	170
Total comprehensive income for the year	**529**

The following information is relevant.

Tangible non-current assets

These include land which was revalued giving a surplus of $170 million during the period.

The company's motor vehicle haulage fleet was replaced during the year.

The fleet originally cost $42 million and had been written down to $11 million at the time of its replacement. The gross cost of the fleet replacement was $180 million and a trade-in allowance of $14 million was given for the old vehicles.

The company acquired some new plant on 1 July 20X6 at a cost of $120 million from Bromway. An arrangement was made on the same day for the liability for the plant to be settled by Jack plc issuing at par an 8% loan note dated 20Y2 to Bromway. The value by which the loan notes exceeded the liability for the plant was received from Bromway in cash.

Environmental provision

The provision represents an estimate of the cost of environmental improvements relating to the company's mining activities.

Ordinary share issue

During the year Jack plc made a bonus issue from the share premium account of one new share for every ten shares held. Later Jack plc made a further share issue for cash. A dividend of $220 million was paid during the year.

Preference dividend

The full preference dividend was paid during the year.

Prepare a statement of cash flows for Jack plc for the year to 31 March 20X7 in accordance with IAS 7 *Statements of Cash Flows*.

Solution

Statement of cash flows for the year ended 31 March 20X7

	$m	$m
Cash from operating activities:		
Profit before tax		536
Adjustments for:		
Finance cost		47
Depreciation		366
Impairment		36
Profit on disposal of vehicles (14 – 11)		(3)
Government grants		(50)
Non-cash environmental provision (67 – 15) **(W6)**		52
Increase in inventory		(157)
Increase in receivables		(170)
Increase in payables		162
Cash generated from operations		819
Less: Interest paid (12 – 4)		(8)
Less: Tax paid **(W1)**		(164)
Net cash from operating activities		647
Cash from investing activities:		
Payments to acquire non-current assets **(W2)**	(723)	
Government grant received **(W3)**	110	
Purchase of goodwill (450 – 410 + 36)	(76)	
		(689)
Cash from financing activities:		
Equity dividends paid	(220)	
Preference dividend	(35)	
Issue of ordinary shares (W4)	120	
Issue of debentures (W5)	80	
		(55)
Decrease in cash and cash equivalents (34 + 63)		(97)

Workings: Column format

(W1) Tax paid:

	£m
Liabilities b/f (185 + 30)	215
Tax charge per SPL	177
Liabilities c/f (176 + 52)	(228)
Tax paid	**164**

(W2) Property, plant & equipment

Balance b/f	1,830
Plant acquired in exchange for debentures	120
Trade in allowance	14
Revaluation	170
Disposals	(11)
Depreciation	(366)
Additions (ß)	**723**
Balance c/f	2,480

(W3) Government grant

Liabilities b/f (40 + 160)	200
Credited to SPorL	(50)
Grants received (ß)	**110**
Liabilities c/f (50 + 210)	260

(W4) Issue of ordinary shares:

Share premium carried forward	90
Share capital carried forward	500
Share capital brought forward	(400)
Share premium brought forward	(70)
Cash proceeds of issue	120

Note: Bonus issue is not cash, and as sourced from share premium may be ignored.

(W5) Issue of loan notes:

	$000
8% loan notes	
Total value issued	200
Exchanged for plant (non-cash)	(120)
Balance (i.e. cash received)	80

(W6) Environmental provision:

Balance b/f	24
Charge to SPL	67
Payments made (ß)	**(15)**
Balance c/f	76

Workings: T-account format

(W1) Taxation

	$m		$m
Tax paid in year (cash)	164	Taxation b/f	185
Taxation c/f	176	Deferred tax b/f	30
Deferred tax c/f	52	SPL charge	177
	392		392

(W2) Property, plant & equipment

	$m		$m
Balance brought forward	1,830	Depreciation	366
Revaluation	170	Disposal at book value	11
Trade-in allowance	14		
Plant exchanged for debentures	120		
(ß) Cash paid	723	Balance carried forward	2,480
	2,857		2,857

(W3) Government grant

	$m		$m
Credited in SPL	50	Balance brought forward:	
		(40 + 160)	200
Balance carried forward:		(ß) cash received	110
(50 + 210)	260		
	310		310

(W4) Share capital/share premium

	$m		$m
Bonus			
(Dr share premium)	40	Balances b/f (400 + 70)	470
		Bonus (Cr share capital)	40
Balances c/f (500 + 90)	590	(ß) cash received	120
	630		630

(W5) Loan

	$m		$m
		Balance b/f	–
		PPE	120
Balance c/f	200	(ß) cash received	80
	200		200

(W6) Environmental provision

	$m		$m
(ß) Cash payment	15	Balance brought forward	24
Balance carried forward	76	Charged in SPL	67
	91		91

Approach

It is often best to set up a page for the reconciliation, a page for the statement of cash flows, and a page for workings. Begin by putting profit from operations at the top of the reconciliation (profit before tax + finance costs – investment income).

Next, put the cash and cash equivalents at the start of the year and end of the year at the bottom of the statement of cash flows (remember to include overdrafts and short-term deposit accounts). The movement in cash equivalents can now be calculated.

From there, work down the statement of financial position. The movements in trade receivables, payables and inventory can be put into the reconciliation. You may want to set up workings for the remaining balances, either using columns or T accounts.

Then work through the statement of profit or loss, then the notes. Some of the information will need to go into the workings, but some can go straight into the reconciliation or statement of cash flows. A good rule to follow is:

- If an item is a non-cash item, include it on the reconciliation.
- If the item is cash paid or received, include it in the statement of cash flows.

Test your understanding 1

The financial statements of Hollywood are given below.

	30 September 20X3		**30 September 20X2**	
	$000	$000	$000	$000
Non-current assets:				
Property plant and equipment		634		510
Current assets:				
Inventory	420		460	
Trade receivables	390		320	
Interest receivable	4		9	
Investments	50		0	
Cash in bank	75		0	
Cash in hand	7		5	
		946		794
Total assets		1,580		1,304

Capital and reserves:				
Ordinary shares 50c each	363		300	
Share premium	89		92	
Revaluation surplus	50		0	
Retained profits	63		(70)	
		565		322
Non-current liabilities:				
10% loan notes	0		40	
5% loan notes	329		349	
		329		389
Current liabilities:				
Bank overdraft	0		70	
Trade payables	550		400	
Income tax	100		90	
Accruals	36		33	
		686		593
		1,580		1,304

Statement of profit or loss for the year to 30 September 20X3

	$000	$000
Revenue		2,900
Cost of sales		(1,734)
Gross profit		1,166
Administrative expenses	342	
Distribution costs	520	
		(862)
Profit from operations		304
Income from investments	5	
Finance cost	(19)	
		(14)
Profit before tax		290
Income tax expense		(104)
Profit for the year		186

Hollywood – Other comprehensive income for the year ended 30 September 20X3

	$000
Profit for the year	186
Other comprehensive income	
Gain on property revaluation	50
Total comprehensive income for the year	236

Additional information:

1 On 1 October 20X2, Hollywood issued 60,000 50c ordinary shares at a premium of 100%. The proceeds were used to finance the purchase and cancellation of all its 10% loan notes and some of its 5% loan notes, both at par. A bonus issue of one for ten shares held was made on 1 November 20X2. All shares in issue qualified for the bonus.

2 The current asset investment was a 30-day government bond.

3 Non-current tangible assets include certain properties which were revalued in the year.

4 Non-current tangible assets disposed of in the year had a carrying amount of $75,000. Cash received on disposal was $98,000.

5 Depreciation charged for the year was $87,000.

6 The accruals balance includes interest payable of $33,000 at 30 September 20X2 and $6,000 at 30 September 20X3.

7 Interim dividends paid during the year were $53,000.

Prepare a statement of cash flows for the year ended 30 September 20X3 and an analysis of cash and cash equivalents.

Test your understanding 2

Statement of cash flows

The following financial statements relate to BT for the year ended 31 May 20X7:

Statement of financial positions as at 31 May

	20X7		20X6	
	$m	$m	$m	$m
Non-current assets:				
Property, plant and equipment		572		496
Intangible		30		40
		602		536
Current assets:				
Inventory	140		155	
Receivables	130		110	
Investments	95		20	
Cash at bank	7		3	
		372		288
		974		824
Equity:				
$1 Equity shares	230		200	
Share premium	45		35	
Revaluation surplus	22		12	
Retained earnings	166		147	
		463		394
Non-current liabilities:				
Lease liability	49		30	
Loans	31		60	
Government grants	80		75	
Deferred tax	72		67	
Warranty provision	30		26	
		262		258

Current liabilities:				
Bank overdraft	8		20	
Trade payables	210		111	
Lease liability	5		3	
Income tax	14		10	
Interest payable	2		8	
Government grant	10		20	
		249		172
		974		824

Statement of profit or loss for the year ended 31 May 20X7

	$m
Revenue	312
Cost of sales	(187)
Gross profit	125
Distribution costs	(31)
Administrative expenses	(27)
Profit from operations	67
Finance costs	(17)
Investment income	3
Profit before tax	53
Income tax expense	(22)
Profit for the year	31

Movement on retained earnings

Balance b/f	147
Profit for the year	31
Dividends	(12)
Balance c/f	166

Notes:

Property, plant and equipment

During the year, assets with a carrying amount of $31 million were sold for $21 million. New assets acquired under leases totalled $28 million. Depreciation charged for the year totalled $37 million.

Government grant

Grant income of $55 million has been credited to operating expenses during the year.

Intangible non-current assets

There were no additions or disposals during the year.

Current asset investment

The current asset investment is an investment in 30-day government bonds.

Warranty provision

The warranty provision relates to costs that are expected to be incurred in repairing faulty goods that have been sold with a warranty. The provision is charged to cost of sales.

Shares

On 1 September 20X6 a 1 for 20 bonus issue was made, utilising share premium. On 1 February 20X7 a further share issue was made for cash.

Required:

Prepare a cash flow statement for BT for the year ended 31 May 20X7 in compliance with IAS 7.

2 Comparison of the statement of cash flows and statement of profit or loss

Advantages of the statement of cash flows

- It may assist users of financial statements in making judgements on the amount, timing and degree of certainty of future cash flows.
- It gives an indication of the relationship between profitability and cash-generating ability, and thus of the quality of the profit earned.
- Analysts and other users of financial information often, formally or informally, develop models to assess and compare the present value of the future cash flow of entities. Historical cash flow information could be useful to check the accuracy of past assessments.

- A statement of cash flows in conjunction with a statement of financial position provides information on liquidity, viability and adaptability. The statement of financial position is often used to obtain information on liquidity, but the information is incomplete for this purpose as the statement of financial position is drawn up at a particular point in time.
- Cash flows cannot be manipulated easily and are not affected by judgement or by accounting policies.

Limitations of the statement of cash flows

- Statements of cash flows are based on historical information and therefore do not provide complete information for assessing future cash flows.
- There is some scope for manipulation of cash flows, e.g. a business may delay paying suppliers until after the year end.
- Cash flow is necessary for survival in the short-term, but in order to survive in the long-term a business must be profitable. It is often necessary to sacrifice cash flow in the short-term in order to generate profits in the long-term (e.g. by investment in non-current assets). A huge cash balance is not a sign of good management if the cash could be invested elsewhere to generate profit.

Accruals versus cash flow

The accruals or matching concept applied in preparing a statement of profit or loss has the effect of smoothing cash flows for reporting purposes. This practice arose because interpreting basic cash flows can be very difficult and the accruals process has the advantage of helping users understand the underlying performance of a company.

For example an item of plant has an estimated useful life of five years and was purchased for $10,000.

Cash flow point of view

Outflow of cash in year 1 of $10,000 and no further outflows in the next four years.

Statement of profit or loss point of view

Applying the accruals concept would result in depreciation of $2,000 p.a. being charged (assuming straight-line depreciation).

It is important to realise that profit is affected by many subjective items. This has led to accusations of profit manipulation or creative accounting, hence the disillusionment in the usefulness of the statement of profit or loss.

Another example of the difficulty in interpreting cash flow is that counter-intuitively a negative overall cash flow is not always a bad thing. It could represent an investment in increasing capacity which would bode well for the future. Nor is a positive cash flow necessarily a good thing. This may be from the sale of non-current assets because of the need to raise cash urgently.

A statement of cash flows can provide information which is not available from statements of financial position and statements of profit or loss. However, statements of cash flows should normally be used in conjunction with statements of profit or loss and statements of financial position when making an assessment of future cash flows. Neither cash flow nor profit provides a complete picture of a company's performance when looked at in isolation.

3 Interpretation of statements of cash flow

The statement of cash flows should be reviewed after preparation. In particular, cash flows in the following areas should be reviewed:

- cash generation from trading operations
- dividend and interest payments
- capital expenditure
- financial investment
- management of financing
- net cash flow.

Interpreting cash flows

Cash generation from trading operations

The figure should be compared to the operating profit. The reconciliation note to the statement of cash flows is useful in this regard. Overtrading may be indicated by:

- high profits and low cash generation
- large increases in inventory, receivables and payables.

When discussing this area, comments should be made regarding working capital management, giving any potential reasons for movements in inventory, receivables and payables, discussing the impact this may have on cash flow and customer/supplier relations going forwards.

Dividend and interest pay-outs

These can be compared to cash generated from trading operations to see whether normal operations can sustain such payments. If cash generated from operations cannot cover these, the business may have problems continuing as a going concern.

If the cash generated from operations can cover these payments, then any cash left over is free cash, and comments should be made about what the business has done with this (such as buying assets, repaying debt, paying a dividend).

Investing activities

The nature and scale of a company's investment in non-current assets is clearly shown.

A simple test may be to compare investment and depreciation.

- If investment > depreciation, the company is investing at a greater rate than its current assets are wearing out – this suggests expansion.
- If investment = depreciation, the company is investing in new assets as existing ones wear out. The company appears stable.
- If investment < depreciation the non-current asset base of the company is not being maintained. This is potentially worrying as non-current assets are generators of profit.

As sales of non-current assets are largely one-off transactions, these should be looked at closely. A significant cash inflow may suggest that the company has needed to raise funds by selling assets. This is a concern as the cash receipt is unlikely to be repeated, and the business will now have fewer assets against which to secure future funding.

If the cash received from sale of non-current assets is relatively low, it may suggest that the company is selling older assets. This would be completely normal if additions were also high, as it suggests that older assets are being replaced by newer ones.

In terms of additions, the sources of finance should be considered, to see whether the company has funded these from cash generated from operations, or from debt/equity. If debt has been raised, this is not a huge problem, but regular repayments will need to be made.

Other items in investing activities are likely to include interest or dividends received. These should hopefully be regular cash flows which could be expected to continue into the future, unless the related investments are sold.

Financing

The current and future implications should be considered when looking at the financing section. If new loans have been received, then there will be higher interest going forwards, and regular repayments required. Conversely, if loans have been repaid, this will help cash flow in future periods.

If shares have been issued, there is no requirement for this to be repaid, and no interest. However, shareholders may expect regular dividends which could have to be paid indefinitely.

Cash flow

The statement clearly shows the end result in cash terms of the company's operations in the year. Do not overstate the importance of this figure alone, however. A decrease in cash in the year may be for very sound reasons (e.g. there was surplus cash last year) or may be mainly the result of timing (e.g. a new loan was raised just after the end of the accounting period).

To help in determining the future cash position, other areas of the published accounts should be considered as illustrated below.

Example 2 – Interpretation of cash flow

Look at the answer to the cash flow for Hollywood – what can we see?

Solution

- An operating profit of $290,000 becomes an operating cash inflow of $518,000, suggesting a high quality profit supported by cash.
- Other than the impact of depreciation, this inflow is largely due to working capital management, which should be considered in more detail:
  - Inventories have decreased, so releasing cash.
  - Payables and accruals have increased, so Hollywood is retaining cash for longer

  Although these movements have a positive impact on the cash flow statement, they may have the opposite effect on the business. A fall in inventories may result in stockouts and so lost business, whilst an increase in payables may lead to poor supplier relationships and so supply being cut off or penalties.
- Mandatory payments of interest and tax are easily covered by the cash generated from operations, leaving $378,000 free cash flow.

- The major source of cash inflow in the year is operating activities. As operating activities are, presumably, sustainable, this places Hollywood in a positive position.
- This operating cash inflow is supplemented by smaller cash inflows from the sale of non-current assets and a share issue. These cash flows are not sustainable year on year.
- The majority of the cash outflow has been on the purchase of non-current assets. This will benefit Hollywood in the long term as the assets are used to create profits.
- Spend on non-current assets exceeds the depreciation charge for the year which suggests that the company may be expanding.
- $60,000 has also been used to redeem loan notes. This, together with the share issue, will improve Hollywood's gearing position, making it a less risky investment.
- Overall the cash position has improved during the year, changing from a net overdraft position to a positive and high cash balance. Although this is a good trend, having cash sitting in a bank is not an efficient use of resources and Hollywood should address this by investing the cash.

4 Chapter summary

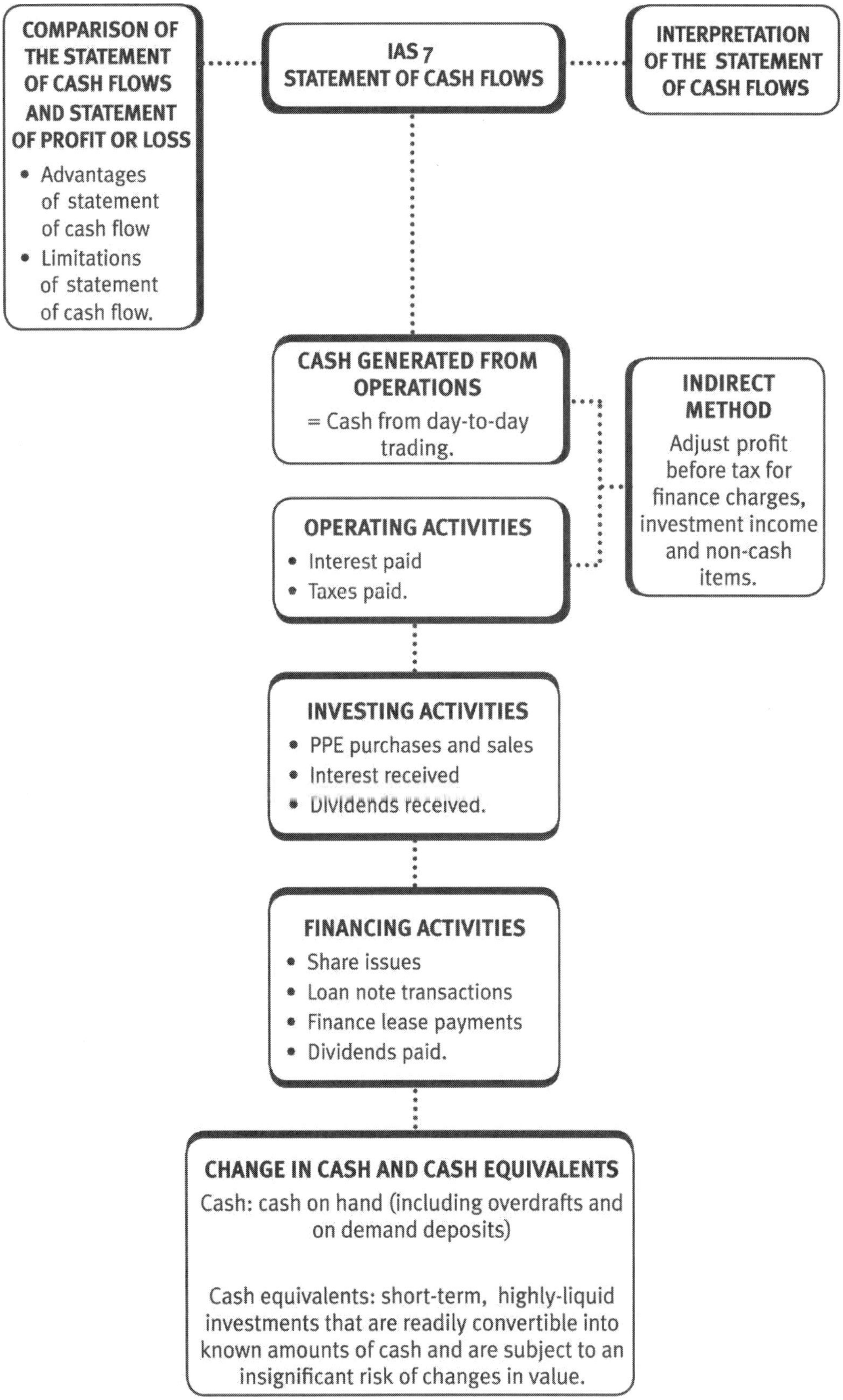

Test your understanding 3

Below are extracts from the financial statements of Poochie Ltd:

Statement of profit or loss for the year ended 31 March 20X1

	$
Revenue	30,650
Cost of sales	(26,000)
Gross profit	4,650
Distribution costs	(900)
Administrative expenses	(500)
Profit from operations	3,250
Investment income	680
Finance costs	(400)
Profit before tax	3,530
Income tax expense	(300)
Profit for the period	3,230

Statements of financial position

	31 March 20X1		31 March 20X0	
	$	$	$	$
Assets				
Non-current assets				
Property, plant and equipment	2,280		850	
Investments	2,500		2,500	
		4,780		3,350
Current assets				
Inventories	1,000		1,950	
Trade and other receivables	1,900		1,200	
Cash and cash equivalents	410		160	
		3,310		3,310
Total assets		8,090		6,660

Equity and liabilities				
Capital and reserves				
Share capital	1,000		900	
Share premium	500		350	
Retained earnings	3,410		1,300	
		4,910		2,630
Non-current liabilities				
Long term borrowings (including leases)		2,300		1,040
Current liabilities				
Trade and other payables	250		1,890	
Interest payable	230		100	
Taxation	400		1,000	
		880		2,990
Total equity and liabilities		8,090		6,660

Additional information:

- Profit from operations is after charging depreciation on the property, plant and equipment of $450.
- During the year ended 31 March 20X1, plant and machinery costing $80 and with accumulated depreciation of $60, was sold for $20.
- During the year ended 31 March 20X1, the company acquired property, plant and equipment costing $1,900, of which $900 was acquired by means of lease. Cash payments of $1,000 were made to purchase property, plant and equipment.
- $90 was paid under the lease.
- The receivables at the end of 20X1 includes $100 of interest receivable. There was no equivalent balance at the beginning of the year.
- Investment income of $680 is made up of $300 interest receivable and $380 dividends received.
- Dividends paid during the year were $1,200.

Required:

Prepare a statement of cash flows for Poochie Ltd for the year ended 31 March 20X1 in compliance with IAS 7 *Statement of Cash Flows*.

Test your understanding 4

CFQ is a large retailer, which has been established for many years. CFQ develops and manufactures products themselves, rather than buying them from wholesalers.

Extracts from CFQ's financial statements are shown below:

	20X1	**20X0**
	$000	$000
Property, plant and equipment	635,000	645,000
FVPL investments	93,000	107,000
Development costs	29,000	24,000

During 20X1, CFQ sold plant for $45 million, which had a carrying amount of $60 million at the date of disposal.

CFQ's statement of profit or loss included the following:

- Depreciation of property, plant and equipment $120 million
- Loss on FVPL investments $21 million
- Amortisation of development costs $8 million

Required:

(a) Prepare the cash flows from investing activities section of CFQ's statement of cash flows.

(b) Comment on what the investing activities show about CFQ as a business, highlighting any areas which may require further investigation.

Test your understanding 5

1 Barlow Ltd uses the 'indirect method' for the purpose of calculating net cash flow from operating activities in the statement of cash flows.

The following information is provided for the year ended 31 December 20X0:

	$
Profit before tax	5,600
Depreciation	956
Profit on sale of equipment	62
Increase in inventories	268
Increase in receivables	101
Increase in payables	322

What is the cash generated from operations?

A $6,571

B $6,541

C $6,447

D $5,803

2 Evans plc had the following balances in its statement of financial position as at 30 June 20X0 and 20X1:

	20X1	**20X0**
10% Debentures	$130,000	$150,000
Share capital	$120,000	$100,000
Share premium	$45,000	$35,000

How much will appear in the statement of cash flows for the year ended 30 June 20X1 under the heading 'cash flows from financing activities'?

$____________

3 At 1 January 20X0 Casey Ltd had property, plant and equipment with a carrying amount of $250,000. In the year ended 31 December 20X0 the company disposed of assets with a carrying amount of $45,000 for $50,000. The company revalued a building from $75,000 to $100,000 and charged depreciation for the year of $20,000. At the end of the year, the carrying amount of property, plant and equipment was $270,000.

How much will be reported in the statement of cash flows for the year ended 31 December 20X0 under the heading 'cash flows from investing activities'?

A $10,000 outflow

B $10,000 inflow

C $60,000 outflow

D $50,000 inflow

4 **Put the items below into the correct category in the statement of cash flows.**

	Operating activities	**Investing activities**	**Financing activities**
Purchase of non-current assets			
Dividends received			
Interest paid			
Borrowings repaid			

5 **How much interest was paid in the year?**

	$000
Interest accrued b/fwd	600
Interest charged to the statement of profit or loss	700
Interest accrued c/fwd	500

$__________

6 At 1 October 20X0, BK had the following balance:

Accrued interest payable $12,000 credit.

During the year ended 30 September 20X1, BK charged finance costs of $41,000 to its statement of profit or loss. The closing balance on the accrued interest payable account at 30 September 20X1 was $15,000 credit.

How much interest paid should BK show on its statement of cash flows for the year ended 30 September 20X1?

A $38,000

B $41,000

C $44,000

D $53,000

7 The following balances have been extracted from O'Brien's financial statements:

Taxation payable, balance at 31 March 20X0 $920,000

Taxation payable, balance at 31 March 20X1 $890,000.

Income tax expense in the statement of profit or loss for the year to 31 March 20X1 $850,000.

Deferred tax balance at 31 March 20X0 $200,000.

Deferred tax balance at 31 March 20X1 $250,000

How much should be included in the statement of cash flows for income tax paid in the year?

A $800,000

B $830,000

C $850,000

D $880,000

Test your understanding answers

Test your understanding 1

Statement of cash flows for Hollywood for the year ended 30 September 20X3

	$000	$000
Cash flows from operating activities:		
Profit before tax	290	
Adjustments for:		
Income from investments	(5)	
Interest expense	19	
Depreciation	87	
Profit on disposal of non-current asset (98 – 75)	(23)	
Operating profit before working capital changes	368	
Decreases in inventories	40	
Increase in trade receivables	(70)	
Increase in trade payables	150	
Increase in sundry accruals **(W1)**	30	
Cash generated from operations	518	
Cash flows from operating activities:		
Cash generated from operations (as above)	518	
Interest paid **(W2)**	(46)	
Income taxes paid **(W3)**	(94)	
Net cash from operating activities		378
Cash flows from investing activities:		
Purchase of tangible non-current assets **(W4)**	(236)	
Proceeds from sale of non-current assets	98	
Interest received **(W5)**	10	
Net cash used in investing activities		(128)

Cash flows from financing activities:

Proceeds from issue of share capital (60 × $1)	60	
Redemption of 10% loan notes	(40)	
Redemption of 5% loan notes	(20)	
Dividends paid	(53)	
Net cash used in financing activities		(53)
Net increase in cash and cash equivalents		197
Cash and cash equivalents at 1 October 20X2 (5 – 70)		(65)
Cash and cash equivalents at 30 September 20X3 (50 + 75 + 7 – 0)		132

Tutorial note: IAS 7 alternatively permits 'dividends paid' to be presented as an operating cash flow, so that presentation would be equally acceptable.

Analysis of cash and cash equivalents

	30 Sept 20X3	**30 Sept 20X2**
	$000	$000
Cash in bank	75	–
Cash in hand	7	5
Short term investments	50	–
Bank overdraft	–	(70)
Total cash and cash equivalents	132	(65)

Workings:

(W1) Movement in sundry accruals excluding interest payable

	$000
Accruals c/f (36 – 6)	30
Accruals b/f (33 – 33)	0
Therefore – Increase in accruals	30

Answers: Column format

(W2) Interest paid:

Interest liability b/f	33
Finance cost per SPL	19
Interest paid (Balancing figure)	**(46)**
Interest liability c/f	6

(W3) Tax paid:

Liability b/f	90
Tax charge per SPL	104
Tax paid (Balancing figure)	**(94)**
Liability c/f	100

(W4) PPE:

Balance b/f	510
Revaluation	50
Disposal	(75)
Depreciation	(87)
Additions (Balancing figure)	**236**
Balance c/f	634

(W5) Interest received:

Interest receivable b/f	9
Finance income per SPorL	5
Interest received (Balancing figure)	**(10)**
	4

Answers: T-account format

(W2) Interest paid

	$000		$000
Paid (balancing figure)	46	Balance b/f	33
Balance c/f	6	SPL charge	19
	52		52

(W3) Income taxes paid

	$000		$000
Paid (bal fig)	94	Bal b/f	90
Bal c/f	100	SPL charge	104
	194		194

(W4) Tangible non-current assets

	$000		$000
Bal b/f	510	Disposal	75
Revaluation	50	Depreciation	87
Paid (bal fig)	236	Bal c/f	634
	796		796

(W5) Interest received

	$000		$000
Balance b/f	9	Received (balancing figure)	10
SPL income	5	Bal c/f	4
	14		14

Test your understanding 2

BT

Reconciliation	$m	$m
Profit before tax	53	
Investment income	(3)	
Finance costs	17	
Loss on disposal of non-current assets (21 – 31)	10	
Government grant income	(55)	
Depreciation	37	
Amortisation (40 – 30)	10	
Decrease in inventory	15	
Increase in receivables	(20)	
Increase in payables	99	
Increase in provisions	4	
	167	

BT

Cash flows from operating activities	$m	$m
Cash generated from operations	167	
Finance costs paid **(W1)**	(23)	
Tax paid **(W2)**	(13)	
		131
Cash flows from investing activities		
Sale proceeds of tangible non-current assets	21	
Purchases of tangible non-current assets **(W3)**	(106)	
Investment income received	3	
Government gnats received **(W4)**	50	
		(32)

Cash flows from financing activities

Repayment of loans (60-31)	(29)	
Repayment of lease (W5)	(7)	
Issue of shares (20 + 20) (W6)	40	
Dividends paid	(12)	
		(8)
Increase in cash and cash equivalent		91
Cash and cash equivalent b/f (20 + 3 – 20)		3
Cash and cash equivalents c/f (95 + 7 – 8)		94

Answers: Column format

(W1) Interest paid

Interest liability b/f	8
Finance cost per SPL	17
Interest paid (Balancing figure)	**(23)**
Interest liability c/f	2

(W2) Tax paid

Liabilities b/f (both current and deferred)	77
Tax charge per SPL	22
Tax paid (Balancing figure)	**(13)**
Liabilities c/f (both current and deferred)	86

(W3) PPE

Balance b/f	496
Revaluation (22-12)	10
Disposal	(31)
Lease additions	28
Depreciation	(37)
Additions (Balancing figure)	**106**
Balance c/f	572

(W4) Government grants:

Grants b/f (20 + 75)	95
Released to SPL	(55)
Grant received (Balancing figure)	**50**
	——
Grants c/f (10+80)	90

(W5) Lease liabilities:

Liabilities b/f (3 + 30)	33
Lease additions	28
Liability repaid (Balancing figure)	**(7)**
	——
Liabilities c/f (5 + 49)	54

(W6) Share capital/share premium:

	Share capital	**Share premium**
Bal b/d	200	35
Bonus issue (1 for 20)	10	(10)
	——	——
	210	25
Cash issue (balance)	20	20
	——	——
Bal c/d	230	45
	——	——

Workings: T-account format

Finance costs

		Bal b/d	8
Bank (balance)	23	SPL charge	17
Bal c/d	2		
	——		——
	25		25
	——		——

Tax

		Bal b/d – IT	10
Bank (balance)	13	Bal b/d – DT	67
Bal c/d – IT	14		
Bal c/d – DT	72	SPL charge	22
	——		——
	99		99
	——		——

Tangible non-current assets

Bal b/d	496		
Leases	28	Depreciation	37
Revaluations	10	Disposal	31
Bank (balance)	106	Bal c/d	572
	640		640

Government Grant

		Bal c/d – CL	20
P or L charge	55	Bal c/d – NCL	75
Bal c/d – CL	10	Bank (balance)	50
Bal c/d – NCL	80		
	145		145

Leases

		Bal c/d – CL	3
Bank (balance)	7	Bal c/d – NCL	30
Bal c/d – CL	5	New leases	28
Bal c/d – NCL	49		
	61		61

Test your understanding 3

Poochie Ltd: Statement of cash flows for the year ended 31 March 20X1

	$
Reconciliation	
Profit before tax	3,530
Finance costs	400
Investment income	(680)
Depreciation	450
Operating profit before working capital changes	3,700
Decrease in inventories (1,950 – 1,000)	950
Increase in trade receivables (1,900 – 100 – 1,200)	(600)
Decrease in trade payables (1,890 – 250)	(1,640)
Cash generated from operations	2,410

Poochie Ltd: Statement of cash flows for the year ended 31 March 20X1

	$	$
Cash flows from operating activities		
Cash generated from operations	2,410	
Interest paid **(W1)**	(270)	
Income tax paid **(W2)**	(900)	
Net cash from operating activities		1,240
Cash flows from investing activities		
Purchase of property, plant and equipment **(W3)**	(1,000)	
Proceeds from sale of property, plant and equipment	20	
Interest received **(W4)**	200	
Dividends received	380	
Net cash from investing activities		(400)
Cash flow from financing activities		
Proceeds from issue of shares **(W5)**	250	
Proceeds from long-term borrowing **(W6)**	450	
Payment of lease	(90)	
Dividends paid	(1,200)	
	(1,200)	
Net cash from financing activities		(590)
Net increase in cash and cash equivalents		250
Cash and cash equivalents at beginning of period		160
Cash and cash equivalents at end of period		410

Answers: Column format

(W1) Interest paid:

Interest liability b/f	100
Finance cost per SPL	400
Interest paid (Balancing figure)	**(270)**
Interest liability c/f	230

(W2) Tax paid:

Liability b/f	1,000
Tax charge per SPL	300
Tax paid (Balancing figure)	**(900)**
Liability c/f	400

(W3) Property, plant and equipment:

Balance b/f	850
Depreciation	(450)
Disposal (80 – 60)	(20)
Lease additions	900
Additions (Balancing figure)	**1,000**
Balance c/f	2,280

(W4) Interest receivable

Balance b/f	–
SPorL income	300
Interest received (Balancing figure)	**(200)**
Balance c/f	100

(W5) Share capital/share premium

Balance b/f (900 + 350)	1,250
Share issue (Balancing figure)	**250**
Balance c/f (1,000 + 500)	1,500

(W6) Long-term borrowings

Liability b/f	1,040
Lease additions	900
Repayment of lease	(90)
Loan received (Balancing figure)	**450**
Liability c/f	2,300

Workings: T-account format

(W1) Interest payable

Bank (ß)	270	Bal b/d	100
Bal c/d	230	SPL	400
	500		500

(W2) Tax

Bank (ß)	900	Bal b/d	1,000
Bal c/d	400	SPL	300
	1,300		1,300

(W3) Property, plant and equipment

Bal b/d	850	Dep'n	450
Lease	900	Disposal (80 – 60)	20
Bank (ß)	1,000	Bal c/d	2,280
	2,750		2,750

(W4) Interest receivable

Bal b/d	–	Bank (ß)	200
SPL	300	Bal c/d	100
	300		300

Receivables b/d = $1,200

Receivables c/d = $1,800 ($1,900 – $100 interest receivable)

Increase in receivables = $600

(W5) Share issue = ($1,000 + $500) – ($900 + $350) = $2504

(W6) Long-term borrowings

Bank: repayment of lease	90	Bal b/d	1,040
		Bank (ß)	450
Bal c/d	2,300	New lease: PP&E	900
	2,390		2,390

Assets acquired under lease of $900 should be debited to the PPE account **(W3)** and credited to the liability account **(W6).**

The payment for the lease of $90 should be credited to the bank and debited to the liability account **(W6).** This payment of $90 is the only cash item to appear on the statement of cash flow for the lease.

Test your understanding 4

(a) **Cash flows from investing activities**

	$000
Purchase of property, plant and equipment **(W1)**	(170,000)
Proceeds from sale of property, plant and equipment	45,000
Purchase of investments **(W2)**	(7,000)
Development costs capitalised **(W3)**	(13,000)
Net cash from investing activities	(145,000)

(b) CFQ appears to be a growing business. This can be seen by the large purchase of property, plant and equipment.

It would be useful to assess what assets have been purchased by CFQ. This could represent new premises, suggesting that CFQ are opening new stores. It could also represent new plant and equipment, which may mean that CFQ have developed new product lines or are expanding the level of production.

The sale of plant has been made at a significant loss. The reason for this disposal should be investigated. If this is because CFQ have changed the method of production and these are surplus assets, then selling plant appears reasonable.

The large loss on disposal is a concern. This may mean that CFQ are under-depreciating assets. Alternatively, it may be that the machine was a specialised piece of equipment which had a lower sale value than value in use.

The loss on disposal, coupled with the fair value loss on investments will both have had significant impacts on the profit of CFQ for the year. However, neither of these represents a cash outflow so will not negatively affect CFQ's liquidity.

The investment value may well be linked to the local economy, or may be shares in an underperforming company. The reasons for the loss should be investigated, as should the details of the new investment. If the new investment is in the same area as the existing ones, this may also be at risk of falling in the future.

The development costs capitalised provide another indication of CFQ being a growing entity. This suggests that CFQ are looking to develop new products or processes, which will hopefully lead to increased revenues in the future.

It would be helpful to see the rest of the cash flow, in order to ascertain where the funding for this expansion has come from, whether CFQ had existing cash reserves, or had to raise further finance. If this finance has been raised from debt or equity, it may put pressure on future cash flows in the form of interest, repayments or dividend payments.

Conclusion

Overall, CFQ appear to be growing, shown in the increased PPE and development costs.

It is worth noting that the loss on disposal and investments make up a total expense of $36 million, so it would be useful to see a full statement of profit or loss. This would enable us to assess what impact this has had on the overall profit or loss for the year.

Workings: Column format

(W1) Property, plant and equipment:

	$000
Balance b/f	645,000
Disposal	(60,000)
Depreciation	(120,000)
Additions (Balancing figure)	**170,000**
Balance c/f	635,000

(W2) Investments:

	$000
Balance b/f	107,000
Fair value loss	(21,000)
Purchase of investments (Balancing figure)	**7,000**
Balance c/f	93,000

(W3) Development costs:

	$000
Balance b/f	24,000
Amortisation	(8,000)
Additions (Balancing figure)	**13,000**
Balance c/f	29,000

Workings: T-account format

(W1) Property, plant and equipment

	$000		$000
Balance b/f	645,000	Depreciation	120,000
		Disposal	60,000
Additions (balancing figure)	**170,000**	Balance c/f	635,000
	815,000		2,390

(W2) Investments

	$000		$000
Balance b/f	107,000	Fair value loss	21,000
Purchase (balance)	**7,000**	Balance c/f	93,000
	114,000		114,000
		Bal b/d	

(W3) Development costs

	$000		$000
Balance b/f	24,000	Amortisation	8,000
Additions (ß)	**13,000**	Balance c/f	29,000
	37,000		37,000

Test your understanding 5

1 **C**

Cash flows from operating activities	$
Profit before tax	5,600
Adjustments for:	
Depreciation	956
Profit on disposal	(62)
Increase in inventories	(268)
Increase in receivables	(101)
Increase in payables	322
Cash inflow from operations	6,447

2 **Net inflow of $10,000** (see below)

Repayment of debentures (150,000 – 130,000)	(20,000)
Issue of shares ((120,000 – 100,000) + (45,000 – 35,000))	30,000
Net inflow	10,000

3 **A**

Property, plant and equipment

	$		$
Bal b/d	250,000	Disposals	45,000
Revaluation	25,000	Depreciation	20,000
Additions (ß)	60,000		
		Bal c/d	270,00
	335,000		335,000

Purchase of property, plant and equipment	(60,000)
Proceeds from sale of property, plant and equipment	50,000
Net outflow	(10,000)

4

	Operating activities	Investing activities	Financing activities
Purchase of non-current assets		X	
Dividends received		X	
Interest paid	X		
Borrowings repaid			X

5 **$800** (600 + 700 – 500)

6 **A** – (12 + 41 – 15)

7 **B** – (920 + 800 – 890)

Movement on deferred tax = $50,000

Statement of profit or loss charge $850,000 – $50,000 = $800,000 relates to current tax

Chapter

17

Principles of consolidated financial statements

Chapter learning objectives

Upon completion of this chapter you will be able to:

- describe the concept of a group as a single economic unit
- explain the objective of consolidated financial statements
- explain and apply the definition of a subsidiary according to IFRS 10
- identify circumstances in which a group is required to prepare consolidated financial statements and those when it can claim exemption
- explain why directors may not wish to consolidate a subsidiary
- list the circumstances where it is permitted not to consolidate a subsidiary
- explain the need for using coterminous year ends and uniform accounting policies when preparing consolidated financial statements
- explain why it is necessary to eliminate intra-group transactions.

PER

One of the PER performance objectives (PO7) is to prepare external financial reports. You take part in preparing and reviewing financial statements – and all accompanying information – and you do it in accordance with legal and regulatory requirements. Working though this chapter should help you understand how to demonstrate that objective.

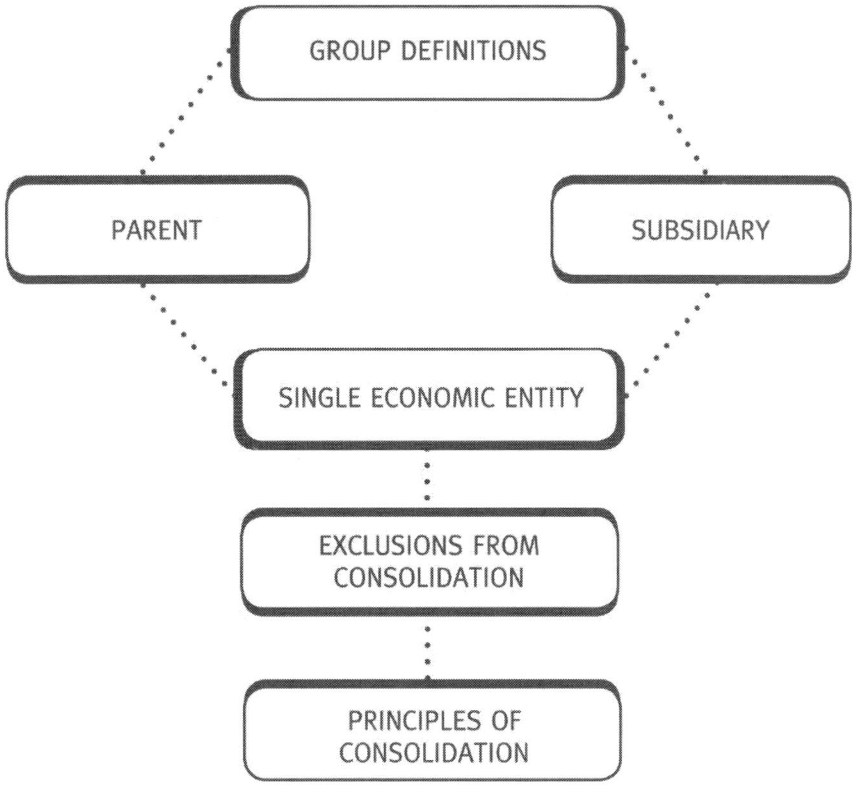

1 The concept of group accounts

What is a group?

If one company owns more than 50% of the ordinary shares of another company:

- this will usually give the first company 'control' of the second company
- the first company (the parent company, P) has enough voting power to appoint all the directors of the second company (the subsidiary company, S)
- P is able to manage S as if it were merely a department of P, rather than a separate entity
- in strict legal terms P and S remain distinct, but in economic substance they can be regarded as a single unit (a 'group').

Group concept

Although from the legal point of view, every company is a separate entity, from the economic point of view companies may not be separate.

In particular, when one company owns enough shares in another company to have a majority of votes at that company's annual general meeting (AGM), the first company may appoint all the directors of, and decide what dividends should be paid by, the second company.

This degree of control enables the first company to manage the trading activities and future plans of the second company as if it were merely a department of the first company.

International accounting standards recognise this situation, and require a parent company to produce consolidated financial statements showing the position and results of the whole group.

Group accounts

The key principle underlying group accounts is the need to reflect the economic substance of the relationship.

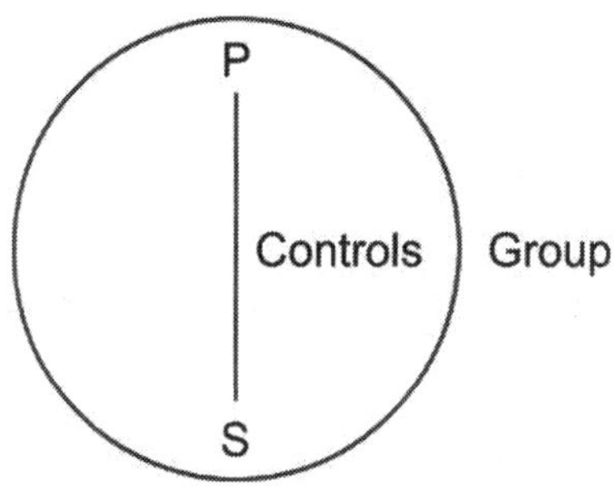

- P is an individual legal entity.
- S is an individual legal entity.

P controls S and therefore they form a single economic entity – the Group.

The single economic entity concept

The purpose of consolidated accounts is to:

- present financial information about a parent undertaking and its subsidiary undertakings as a single economic unit
- show the economic resources controlled by the group
- show the obligations of the group, and
- show the results the group achieves with its resources.

Business combinations consolidate the results and net assets of group members so as to display the group's affairs as those of a single economic entity. As already mentioned, this conflicts with the strict legal position that each company is a distinct entity. Applying the single entity concept is a good example of the accounting principle of showing economic substance over legal form.

Consolidated financial statements under the single entity concept

This is by far the most common form of group accounts. Consolidated financial statements are prepared by replacing the cost of investment with the individual assets and liabilities underlying that investment. If the subsidiary is only partly owned, all the assets and liabilities of the subsidiary are still consolidated, but the non-controlling shareholders' interest in those net assets is also presented.

The **single economic unit concept** focuses on the existence of the group as an economic unit rather than looking at it only through the eyes of the dominant shareholder group. It concentrates on the resources controlled by the entity.

This will mean that intra-group transactions will need to be removed, meaning that no income, expenses, assets or liabilities are included that have arisen from transactions between entities within the group.

Group financial statements

Group financial statements could be prepared in various ways, but in normal circumstances the best way of showing the results of a group is to imagine that all the transactions of the group had been carried out by a single equivalent entity and to prepare a statement of financial position, a statement of profit or loss and a statement showing other comprehensive income for that entity.

Such statements are called consolidated financial statements. Note that consolidated statements of cash flow are outside the FR syllabus.

There are three IFRS Standards within the FR syllabus relevant to the preparation of consolidated financial statements:

- IFRS 3 *Business Combinations* (revised January 2008)
- IFRS 10 *Consolidated Financial Statements* (issued May 2011)
- IAS 28 *Investments in Associates and Joint Ventures* (revised May 2011).

Each company in a group prepares its own accounting records and annual financial statements in the usual way. From the individual entities' financial statements, the parent prepares consolidated financial statements.

In addition to the above accounting standards dealing with the preparation of consolidated financial statements, the IASB has now issued:

- IFRS 12 *Disclosure of Interests in Other Entities* (not examinable in FR).

2 Definitions

IFRS 10 *Consolidated Financial Statements* uses the following definitions in Appendix A:

- **'parent – an entity that controls one or more entities'**
- **'subsidiary – an entity that is controlled by another entity'** (known as the parent)
- **'control of an investee – an investor controls an investee when the investor is exposed, or has rights, to variable returns from its involvement with the investee and has the ability to affect those returns through its power over the investee.'**

Requirements for consolidated financial statements

IFRS 10 outlines the circumstances in which a group is required to prepare consolidated financial statements.

Consolidated financial statements should be prepared when the parent company has control over the subsidiary (for examination purposes control is usually established based on ownership of more than 50% of voting power).

Control is identified by IFRS 10 as the sole basis for consolidation and comprises the following three elements:

- **'power over the investee**
- **exposure, or rights, to variable returns from its involvement with the investee**
- **the ability to use its power over the investee to affect the amount of the investor's returns'** (IFRS 10, para 7)

IFRS 10 adopts a principles-based approach to determining whether or not control is exercised in a given situation, which may require the exercise of judgement. One outcome is that it should lead to more consistent judgements being made, with the consequence of greater comparability of financial reporting information.

IFRS 10 states that investors should periodically consider whether control over an investee has been gained or lost and goes on to consider that a range of circumstances may need to be considered when determining whether or not an investor has power over an investee, such as:

- exercise of the majority of voting rights in an investee
- contractual arrangements between the investor and other parties holding less than 50% of the voting shares, with all other equity interests held by a numerically large, dispersed and unconnected group
- potential voting rights (such as share options or convertible loans) may result in an investor gaining or losing control at some specific date.

Exemption from preparation of group financial statements

A parent need not present consolidated financial statements if and only if:

- the parent itself is a wholly owned subsidiary or a partially-owned subsidiary and its owners, including those not otherwise entitled to vote, have been informed about, and do not object to, the parent not preparing consolidated financial statements
- the parent's debt or equity instruments are not traded in a public market
- the parent did not file its financial statements with a securities commission or other regulatory organisation for the purpose of issuing any class of instruments in a public market
- the ultimate parent company produces consolidated financial statements that comply with IFRS Standards and are available for public use.

3 IAS 27 Separate Financial Statements

When exemption from the preparation of financial statements is permitted, IAS 27 *Separate Financial Statements* requires that the following disclosures are made:

- the fact that consolidated financial statements have not been presented
- a list of significant investments (subsidiaries, associates etc.) including percentage shareholding, principal place of business and country of incorporation
- the bases on which those investments listed above have been accounted for in its separate financial statements.

Reasons for wanting to exclude a subsidiary

The directors of a parent company may not wish to consolidate some subsidiaries due to:

- poor performance of the subsidiary
- poor financial position of the subsidiary
- differing activities of the subsidiary from the rest of the group.

These reasons are not permitted under IFRS Standards.

Excluded subsidiaries

IFRS 10 and IAS 27 (revised) do not specify any other circumstances when subsidiaries must be excluded from consolidation. However, there may be specific circumstances that merit particular consideration as follows:

Reason for exclusion	Accounting treatment
Subsidiary held for resale	Held as current asset investment at the lower of carrying amount and fair value less costs to sell.
Materiality	Accounting standards do not apply to immaterial items. Therefore an immaterial item need not be consolidated.

Subsidiary held for resale

If on acquisition a subsidiary meets the criteria to be classified as 'held for sale' in accordance with IFRS 5, then it must still be included in the consolidation but accounted for in accordance with that standard. The parent's interest will be presented separately as a single figure on the face of the consolidated statement of financial position, rather than being consolidated as a subsidiary.

This might occur when a parent has acquired a group with one or more subsidiaries that do not fit into its long-term strategic plans and are therefore likely to be sold. In these circumstances the parent has clearly not acquired the investment with a view to long-term control of the activities, hence the logic of the exclusion.

Materiality

If a subsidiary is excluded on the grounds of immateriality, the case must be reviewed from year to year, and the parent would need to consider each subsidiary to be excluded on this basis, both individually and collectively. Ideally, a parent should consolidate all subsidiaries which it controls in all accounting periods, rather than report changes in the corporate structure from one period to the next.

Non-coterminous year ends

Some companies in the group may have differing accounting dates. In practice such companies will often prepare financial statements up to the group accounting date for consolidation purposes.

For the purpose of consolidation, IFRS 10 states that where the reporting date for a parent is different from that of a subsidiary, the subsidiary should prepare additional financial information as of the same date as the financial statements of the parent unless it is impracticable to do so.

If it is impracticable to do so, IFRS 10 allows use of subsidiary financial statements made up to a date of not more than three months earlier or later than the parent's reporting date, with due adjustment for significant transactions or other events between the dates.

Uniform accounting policies

'If a member of a group uses accounting policies other than those adopted in the consolidated financial statements for like transactions and events in similar circumstances, appropriate adjustments are made to that group member's financial statements in preparing the consolidated financial statements to ensure conformity with the group's accounting policies' (IFRS 10, para B87).

4 Chapter summary

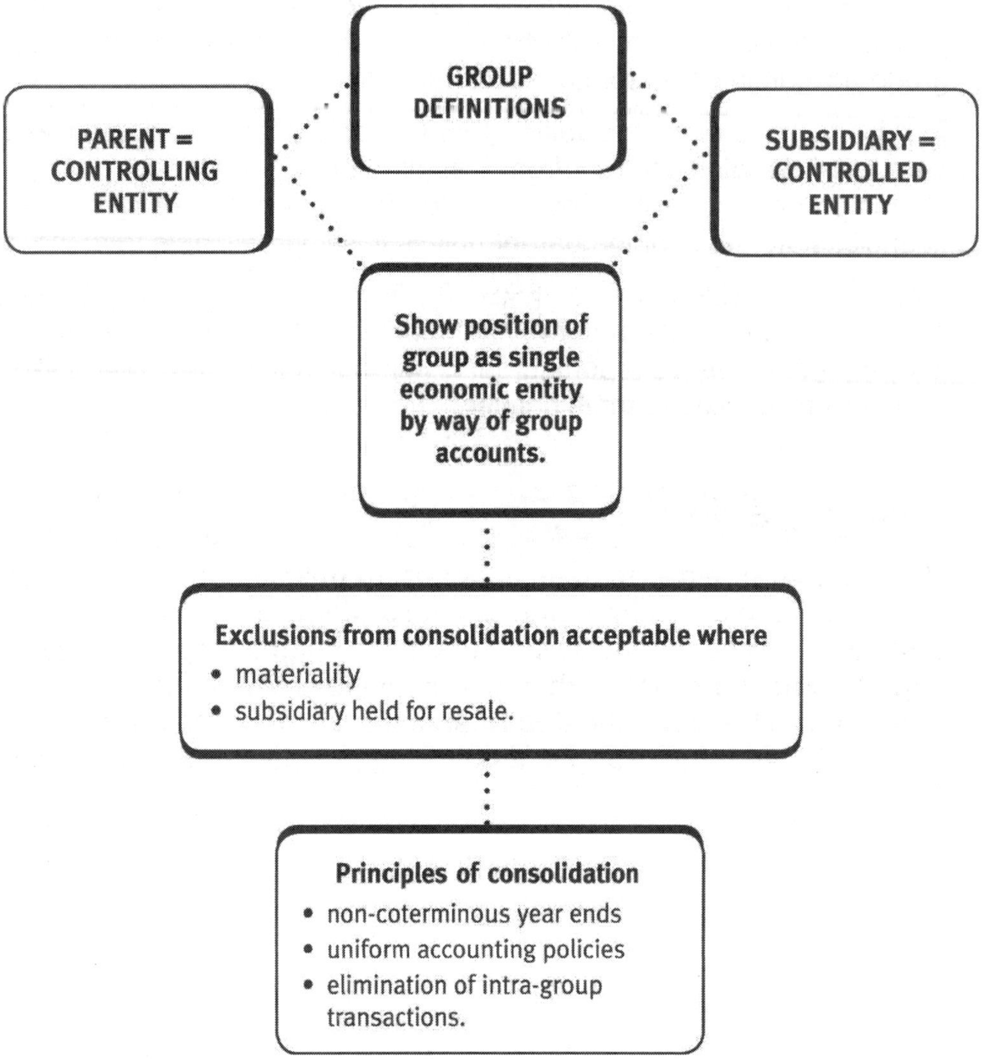

Test your understanding 1

1 **Which of the following definitions is not included within the definition of control per IFRS 10?**

A Having power over the investee

B Having exposure, or rights, to variable returns from its investment with the investee

C Having the majority of shares in the investee

D Having the ability to use its power over the investee to affect the amount of the investor's returns

2 **Which of the following situations is unlikely to represent control over an investee?**

A Owning 55% and being able to elect 4 of the 7 directors

B Owning 51 %, but the constitution requires that decisions need the unanimous consent of shareholders

C Having currently exercisable options which would take the shareholding of the company to 55%

D Owning 40% of the shares, but having the majority of voting rights within the company

3 **Which of the following is NOT a condition which must be met for the parent to be exempt from producing consolidated financial statements?**

A The activities of the subsidiary are significantly different to the rest of the group and to consolidate them would prejudice the overall group position

B The ultimate parent company produces consolidated financial statements that comply with IFRS Standards and are publicly available

C The parent's debt or equity instruments are not traded in a public market

D The parent itself is a wholly-owned subsidiary or a partially-owned subsidiary whose owners do not object to the parent not producing consolidated financial statements

4 **Which of the following statements regarding consolidated financial statements is correct?**

A For consolidation, it may be acceptable to use financial statements of the subsidiary if the year-end differs from the parent by 2 months

B For consolidation, all companies within the group must have the same year-end

C All companies within a group must have the same accounting policy in their individual financial statements

D Only 100% subsidiaries need to be consolidated

Test your understanding answers

Test your understanding 1

1 **C** – While having the majority of shares may be a situation which leads to control, it does not feature in the definition of control per IFRS 10.

2 **B** – The fact that unanimous consent is required would suggest that there is no control over the investee.

3 **A** – The activities of the subsidiary are irrelevant when making the decision as to whether to produce consolidated financial statements or not.

4 **A** – IFRS 10 states that where the reporting date for a parent is different from that of a subsidiary, the subsidiary should prepare additional financial information as of the same date as the financial statements of the parent unless it is impracticable to do so.

If it is impracticable to do so, IFRS 10 allows use of subsidiary financial statements made up to a date of not more than three months earlier or later than the parent's reporting date, with due adjustment for significant transactions or other events between the dates.

The companies do not have to have the same policies in their individual financial statements, but adjustments will be made to prepare the consolidated financial statements using the group policies.

All subsidiaries need to be consolidated, not just 100% owned ones.

Chapter

18

Consolidated statement of financial position

Chapter learning objectives

Upon completion of this chapter you will be able to:

- prepare a consolidated statement of financial position for a simple group (parent and one subsidiary)
- deal with non-controlling interests (at fair value or proportionate share of net assets)
- describe and apply the required accounting treatment of consolidated goodwill
- account for impairment of goodwill
- explain and account for the consolidation of other reserves (e.g. share premium and revaluation surplus)
- account for the effects of intra-group trading in the statement of financial position
- explain why it is necessary to use fair values when preparing consolidated financial statements
- account for the effects of fair value adjustments.

PER

One of the PER performance objectives (PO7) is to prepare external financial reports. You take part in preparing and reviewing financial statements – and all accompanying information – and you do it in accordance with legal and regulatory requirements. Working though this chapter should help you understand how to demonstrate that objective.

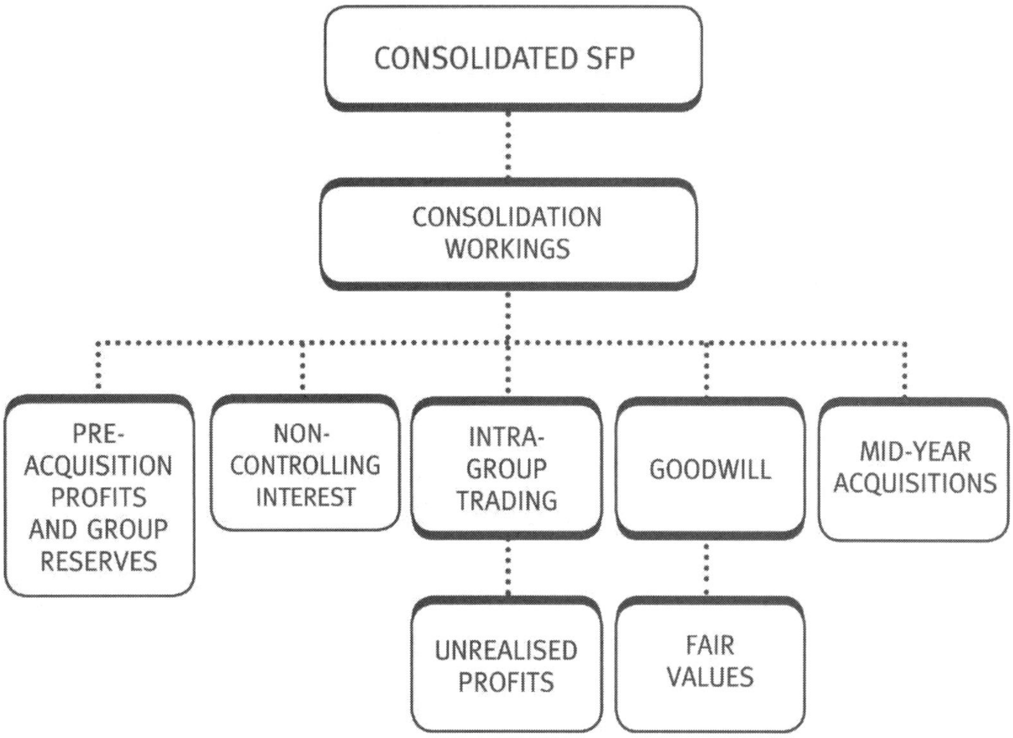

1 Principles of the consolidated statement of financial position

Basic principle

The basic principle of a consolidated statement of financial position is that it shows all assets and liabilities of the parent and subsidiary.

Intra-group items are excluded, e.g. receivables and payables shown in the consolidated statement of financial position only include amounts owed from/to third parties.

Method of preparing a consolidated statement of financial position

1 The investment in the subsidiary (S) shown in the parent's (P's) statement of financial position is replaced by the net assets of S.

2 The cost of the investment in S is effectively cancelled with the ordinary share capital and reserves of the subsidiary, leaving goodwill as a balance.

This produces a consolidated statement of financial position showing:

- the net assets of the whole group (P + S)
- the share capital of the group which always equals the share capital of P only and
- the retained earnings, comprising profits earned by the group (i.e. all of P's historical profits + post-acquisition profits made by S).

Illustration 1 – Principles of the consolidated statement of financial position

Statements of financial position at 31 December 20X4

	P	S
	$000	$000
Non-current assets	60	50
Investment in S at cost	50	
Current assets	40	40
	150	90
Ordinary share capital ($1 shares)	100	40
Retained earnings	30	10
Current liabilities	20	40
	150	90

P acquired 100% of the shares in S on 31 December 20X4 at a cost of $50,000.

Prepare the consolidated statement of financial position at 31 December 20X4.

Solution

Approach

1 The balance on 'investment in S at cost' in P's statement of financial position will be replaced by the underlying assets and liabilities which the investment represents, i.e. the assets and liabilities of S.

2 The cost of the investment in the subsidiary is effectively cancelled with the ordinary share capital and reserves of S. This is normally achieved in consolidation workings (discussed in more detail below). However, in this simple example, it can be seen that the relevant figures are equal and opposite ($50,000), and therefore cancel directly.

This leaves a consolidated statement of financial position showing:

- the net assets of the whole group (P + S)
- the share capital of the group, which equals the share capital of P only, $100,000
- retained earnings comprising profits made by the group. S is purchased on the reporting date, therefore there are no post-acquisition earnings of S to include in the group reserves. So the consolidated retained earnings will only include the $30,000 retained earnings of the parent.

By adding the net assets of each company, and cancelling the investment in S against the share capital and reserves of S, we arrive at the consolidated statement of financial position given below.

P consolidated statement of financial position at 31 December 20X4

	$000
Non-current assets (60,000 + 50,000)	110
Current assets (40,000 + 40,000)	80
	190
Share capital ($1 ordinary shares)	100
Retained earnings	30
Current liabilities (20,000 + 40,000)	60
	190

Note: Under no circumstances will any share capital of any subsidiary ever be included in the figure of share capital in the consolidated statement of financial position.

The mechanics of consolidation

A standard group accounting question will provide the financial statements of P and S and will require the preparation of consolidated financial statements.

The best approach is to use a set of standard workings.

(W1) Establish the group structure

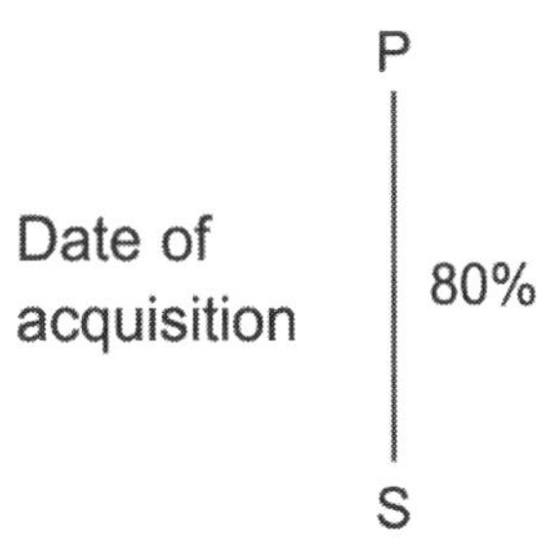

This indicates that P owns 80% of the ordinary shares of S and when they were acquired.

Working 1 will show:

– How much of the subsidiary is owned by P

– How long P has had control over S

This will be useful for working out the share of S's results since acquisition.

(W2) Net assets of subsidiary

	At the date of acquisition	At the reporting date	Post-acquisition
	$	$	$
Share capital	X	X	
Reserves:			
Share premium	X	X	–
Retained earnings	X	X	X
Revaluation surplus	X	X	X
	X	X	X

Working 2 shows the value of S's net assets at various points in time, giving an approximation of the fair value of S.

- The first column shows the fair value of S at acquisition, which can be used to calculate goodwill (in Working 3)
- The second column shows the fair value of S's net assets at the year-end
- The final column shows the post-acquisition movement in S's net assets. This increase or decrease will be split between the 2 parties that own S (the parent and the non-controlling interest), according to their % ownership.
- **Note:** If there is a post-acquisition revaluation surplus, the group share of the post-acquisition revaluation would be part of the group revaluation surplus and not taken to retained earnings.

(W3) Goodwill

	$
Parent holding (investment) at fair value	X
Non-controlling interest at acquisition *	X
	X
Less: Fair value of net assets at acquisition **(W2)**	(X)
Goodwill on acquisition	X
Impairment	(X)
	X

* Non-controlling interest (NCI)

If fair value method adopted:

NCI value = fair value of NCI's holding at acquisition (number of shares NCI own × subsidiary share price).

If proportion of net assets method adopted:

NCI value = NCI % × fair value of net assets at acquisition (from **W2**).

If goodwill is positive, treat it as a non-current asset on the statement of financial position.

If goodwill is negative, it is regarded as a gain on a bargain purchase and is included as a gain within retained earnings in Working 5.

(W4) Non-controlling interest (NCI)

NCI value at acquisition (as in **(W3)**)	X
NCI share of post-acquisition reserves **(W2)**	X
NCI share of impairment (fair value method only)	(X)
	X

This shows the value of the subsidiary that is not owned by the parent at year-end.

(W5) Group retained earnings

	$
P's retained earnings (100%)	X
P's % of S's post-acquisition retained earnings	X
Less: P's share of impairment **(W3)**	(X)
	X

This shows the retained earnings that are attributable to the parent's shareholders.

Goodwill

Goodwill on acquisition

In Example 1 both the cost of the shares in S and the net assets of S were $50,000. This will not always be the case.

The value of a company will normally exceed the value of its net assets. The difference is **goodwill.** This goodwill represents assets not shown in the statement of financial position of the acquired company such as the reputation of the business.

Goodwill on acquisition is calculated by comparing the value of the subsidiary acquired to its net assets.

Where 100% of the subsidiary is acquired, the calculation is therefore:

	$
Cost of investment (= value of the subsidiary)	X
Less: net assets of subsidiary	(X)
Goodwill	X

Where less than 100% of the subsidiary is acquired, the value of the subsidiary comprises two elements:

- The value acquired by the parent
- The value of the part not acquired by the parent, known as the non-controlling interest

There are 2 methods by which goodwill may be calculated:

(i) Proportion of net assets method

(ii) Fair value method.

The proportion of net assets method calculates the value of goodwill attributable to the parent only, while the fair value method calculates the goodwill attributable to both the parent and non-controlling interest.

IFRS 3 Business Combinations

IFRS 3 governs accounting for all business combinations other than joint ventures and a number of other unusual arrangements not included within the FR syllabus. The definition of goodwill is:

'Goodwill is an asset representing the future economic benefits arising from other assets acquired in a business combination that are not individually identified and separately recognised' (IFRS 3, Appendix A).

Goodwill is calculated as the excess of the consideration transferred and amount of any non-controlling interest over the net of the identifiable assets acquired and liabilities assumed at the acquisition date.

Treatment of goodwill

Positive goodwill

- Capitalised as an intangible non-current asset.
- Tested annually for possible impairments.
- Amortisation of goodwill is not permitted by the IFRS Standard.

Impairment of positive goodwill

If goodwill is considered to have been impaired during the post-acquisition period this must be reflected within the group financial statements. Accounting for the impairment differs according to the policy followed to value the non-controlling interests, reflecting the ownership of the goodwill.

Proportion of net assets method:

Dr Group reserves **(W5)**

Cr Goodwill **(W3)**

Fair value method:

Dr Group reserves (% of impairment attributable to the parent – **(W5)**)

Dr NCI (% of impairment attributable to NCI – **(W4)**)

Cr Goodwill **(W3)**

Negative goodwill

- Arises where the cost of the investment is less than the value of net assets purchased.
- IFRS 3 does not refer to this as negative goodwill (instead it is referred to as a bargain purchase), however this is a commonly used term.
- Most likely reason for negative goodwill is a misstatement of the fair values of assets and liabilities. The standard therefore requires that the goodwill calculation is reviewed to ensure that the correct fair values have been included.
- After such a review, any negative goodwill remaining is credited directly to the statement of profit or loss, or retained earnings (W5) if we are only considering the statement of financial position.

Pre- and post-acquisition reserves

Pre- and post-acquisition profits

Pre-acquisition profits are the reserves which exist in a subsidiary at the date when it is acquired. They are capitalised at the date of acquisition by including them in the goodwill calculation (W3).

Post-acquisition profits are profits made and included in the retained earnings of the subsidiary following acquisition. They are apportioned between the group retained earnings (W5) and the NCI (W4).

Group reserves

When looking at the reserves of S at the year-end, e.g. revaluation surplus, a distinction must be made between:

- those reserves of S which existed at the date of acquisition (pre acquisition reserves) and
- the increase in the reserves of S which arose after acquisition (post-acquisition reserves).

As with retained earnings, only P's share of post-acquisition reserves of S is included in the group reserves in the statement of financial position, with the NCI's share added to the NCI.

If there is a post-acquisition revaluation surplus in the subsidiary, then P's share of this is added to the revaluation surplus in the consolidated statement of financial position.

Non-controlling interests

What is a non-controlling interest?

In some situations a parent may not own all of the shares in the subsidiary, e.g. if P owns a controlling 80% interest in the ordinary shares of S, there is a non-controlling interest of 20%.

Note, however, that P still controls S.

Accounting treatment of a non-controlling interest

As P controls S:

- in the consolidated statement of financial position, include all of the net assets of S (to show control).
- show the net assets of S which belong to the non-controlling interest within the equity section of the consolidated statement of financial position (calculated in (W4)).

Test your understanding 1

The following statements of financial position have been prepared at 31 December 20X8.

	Dickens	Jones
	$	$
Non-current assets:		
Property, plant & equipment	85,000	18,000
Investment: Shares in Jones	60,000	
Current assets	160,000	84,000
	305,000	102,000
Equity:		
Ordinary $1 shares	65,000	20,000
Share premium	35,000	10,000
Retained earnings	70,000	25,000
	170,000	55,000
Current liabilities	135,000	47,000
	305,000	102,000

Dickens acquired 16,000 ordinary $1 shares in Jones on 1 January 20X8, when Jones' retained earnings stood at $20,000 and its share premium was $10,000. On this date, the fair value of the 20% non-controlling shareholding in Jones was $12,500.

The Dickens Group uses the fair value method to value the non-controlling interest.

Prepare the consolidated statement of financial position of Dickens as at 31 December 20X8.

Test your understanding 2

Jack acquired 60% of the ordinary share capital of Daniel on 31 December 20X6 for $240,000. At this date the net assets of Daniel were $360,000.

What goodwill arises on the acquisition

(i) if the non-controlling interest (NCI) is valued using the proportion of net assets method?

(ii) if the NCI is valued using the fair value method and the fair value of the NCI on the acquisition date is $150,000?

2 Fair values

Fair value of consideration and net assets

To ensure that an accurate figure is calculated for goodwill:

- the consideration paid for a subsidiary must be accounted for at fair value
- the subsidiary's identifiable assets and liabilities acquired must be accounted for at their fair values.

IFRS 13 *Fair Value Measurement* (Chapter 8) defines fair value as:

'the price that would be received to sell an asset or paid to transfer a liability in an orderly transaction between market participants at the measurement date' (IFRS 13, para 9).

Fair values

In order to account for an acquisition, the acquiring company must measure the cost of what it is accounting for, which will normally comprise:

- the cost of the investment in its own statement of financial position
- the amount to be allocated between the identifiable net assets of the subsidiary, the non-controlling interest and goodwill in the consolidated financial statements.

The subsidiary's identifiable assets and liabilities are included in the consolidated accounts at their fair values for the following reasons:

- Consolidated accounts are prepared from the perspective of the group, rather than from the perspectives of the individual companies. The book values of the subsidiary's assets and liabilities are largely irrelevant, because the consolidated accounts must reflect their cost to the group (i.e. to the parent), rather than their original cost to the subsidiary. The cost to the group is their fair value at the date of acquisition.
- Purchased goodwill is the difference between the value of an acquired entity and the aggregate of the fair values of that entity's identifiable assets and liabilities. If fair values are not used, the value of goodwill will be meaningless.

Identifiable assets and liabilities recognised in the financial statements are those of the acquired entity that existed at the date of acquisition.

Assets and liabilities are measured at fair values, reflecting conditions at the date of acquisition.

The following do not affect fair values at the date of acquisition and are therefore dealt with as post-acquisition items.

- Changes resulting from the acquirer's intentions or future actions.
- Changes resulting from post-acquisition events.
- Provisions for future operating losses or reorganisation costs incurred as a result of the acquisition.

Calculation of cost of investment

The cost of acquisition includes the following elements:

- cash paid at the date of acquisition
- fair value of any other consideration i.e. deferred/contingent considerations and share exchanges (see below).

Incidental costs of acquisition such as legal, accounting, valuation and other professional fees should be written off as expenses through profit or loss as incurred. The issue costs of debt or equity associated with the acquisition should be recognised in accordance with IFRS 9/IAS 32 (see Chapter 10).

Deferred and contingent consideration

In some situations part or all of the purchase consideration is deferred until a later date – deferred consideration.

- Deferred consideration (i.e. a promise to pay an agreed sum on a predetermined date in the future) should be measured at fair value at the date of the acquisition, taking into account the time value of money.
- The fair value of any deferred consideration is calculated by discounting the amounts payable to present value at acquisition.
- Any contingent consideration should be included at **fair value**, which will be **given in the exam**. (A contingent consideration is an agreement to settle in the future provided certain conditions attached to the agreement are met. These conditions vary depending on the terms of the settlement).

There are two ways to discount the deferred amount to fair value at the acquisition date:

1 You may need to apply the discount fraction to the deferred amount, where r is the interest rate and n the number of years to settlement

$$\frac{1}{(1 + r)^{n}}$$

2 The examiner **may give you the discount factor** of the payment based on a given cost of capital. (For example, $1 receivable in three years' time based on a cost of capital of 10% = $0.75). You would then apply this factor to the deferred amount to calculate the fair value.

Each year the discount is then unwound by 'charging' interest on the outstanding liability. This increases the deferred liability each year (to increase to future cash liability) and the discount is treated as a finance cost.

This is also applied to any contingent consideration, as the fair value given will be at the present value.

As it is based on uncertain events, the fair value of the contingent consideration at acquisition could be different to the actual consideration transferred.

Any differences are normally treated as a change in accounting estimate and adjusted prospectively in accordance with IAS 8 (See Chapter 8).

Therefore the contingent consideration liability will be increased or decreased at the year end, with the movement taken to profit or loss and shown in retained earnings.

Contingent share exchange

Where contingent consideration involves the issue of shares, there is no liability (obligation to transfer economic benefits). This potential share issue should be recognised as part of equity under a separate caption representing shares to be issued.

Share exchange

Often the parent will issue shares in itself in return for the shares acquired in the subsidiary. The share price **at acquisition** should be used to record the fair value of the shares.

e.g

Illustration 2 – Cost of investment

Jack acquired 24 million $1 shares (80%) of the ordinary shares of Becky by offering a share-for-share exchange of two shares for every three shares acquired in Becky, and a cash payment of $1 per share payable three years later. Jack's shares have a nominal value of $1 and a current market value of $2. The cost of capital is 10% and the value of $1 receivable in 3 years' time can be taken as $0.75.

(i) **Calculate the cost of investment and show the journals to record it in Jack's financial statements.**

(ii) **Show how the discount would be unwound.**

Solution

(i) **Cost of investment**

	$
Deferred cash (at present value)	
24m × $1 × 0.75	18m
Share exchange	
24m × 2/3 × $2	32m
	50m

$50m is the cost of investment for the purposes of the calculation of goodwill.

Journals in Jack's individual accounts:

Dr	Cost of investment in subsidiary	$50m
Cr	Non-current liabilities – deferred consideration	$18m
Cr	Share capital (16 million shares issued × $1 nominal value)	$16m
Cr	Share premium (16 million shares issued × $1 premium element)	$16m

(ii) **Unwinding the discount**

Initial liability of $18m × 10% = $1.8m

Dr	Finance cost	$1.8m
Cr	Non-current liabilities – deferred consideration	$1.8m

For the next three years the discount will be unwound, taking the interest to finance cost until the full $24 million payment is made in Year 3.

Test your understanding 3

Cost of investment

The statements of financial position of P and S as at 30 June 20X8 are given below:

	P	S
	$	$
Property, plant & equipment	15,000	9,500
Investments	5,000	
Current assets	7,500	5,000
	27,500	14,500
Share capital $1	6,000	5,000
Share premium	4,000	
Retained earnings	12,500	7,200
	22,500	12,200
Non-current liabilities	1,000	500
Current liabilities	4,000	1,800
	27,500	14,500

P acquired 60% of S on 1 July 20X7 when the retained earnings of S were $5,800. P paid $5,000 in cash. P also issued 2 $1 shares for every 5 acquired in S and agreed to pay a further $2,000 in 3 years' time. The market value of P's shares at 1 July 20X7 was $1.80. P has only recorded the cash paid in respect of the investment in S. Current interest rates are 6%.

The P group uses the fair value method to value the non-controlling interest. At the date of acquisition the fair value of the non-controlling interest was $5,750.

Required:

Prepare the consolidated statement of financial position of P group as at 30 June 20X8.

Fair value of net assets acquired

IFRS 3 requires that the subsidiary's assets and liabilities are recorded at their fair value for the purposes of the calculation of goodwill and production of consolidated accounts.

Adjustments will therefore be required where the subsidiary's financial statements do not reflect the fair value of assets and liabilities.

How to include fair values in consolidation workings

1 Adjust **W2** to bring the net assets to fair value at acquisition date, taking into account any subsequent effect this will have on the year end position.

This will ensure that the fair value of net assets is carried through to the goodwill and non-controlling interest calculations.

	At acquisition	At reporting date	Post-acquisition
	$000	$000	$000
Share capital + reserves	X	X	X
Fair value adjustments	X	X	–
Fair value depreciation adjustments		(X)	(X)
	X	X	X

2 At the reporting date make the adjustment on the face of the statement of financial position when adding together assets and liabilities.

Fair value adjustments could include adjustments to recognised assets, such as property. There may also be intangible assets that are not recognised in the subsidiary's financial statements due to being internally generated. These will be recognised within the consolidated financial statements, as the parent is now purchasing these assets as part of buying the subsidiary, and a reliable measure of cost is therefore available.

In addition to this, any contingent liabilities in the subsidiary need to be recognised as liabilities in the consolidated financial statements if a fair value is assigned to them. As contingent liabilities will only be a disclosure note in the subsidiary's individual financial statements, the adjustment to be made in the consolidated financial statements will be to reduce the net assets in **W2** and to include a liability in the statement of financial position.

There may also be an adjustment necessary to the value of inventory at the acquisition date. The subsidiary will be carrying the inventory at the lower of cost and net realisable value, but its fair value will be replacement cost. If such an adjustment is necessary, take care to evaluate whether any adjustment is needed at the reporting date. If the entire inventory at the acquisition date has been sold by the reporting date then no further adjustment will be necessary in the reporting date column.

Test your understanding 4

Peppermint acquired 80% of the share capital of Spearmint two years ago, when the reserves of Spearmint stood at $125,000. Peppermint paid initial cash consideration of $1 million. Additionally Peppermint issued 200,000 shares with a nominal value of $1 and a market value at the acquisition date of $1.80. It was also agreed that Peppermint would pay a further $500,000 in three years' time. Current interest rates are 10% pa. The appropriate discount factor for $1 receivable three years from now is 0.75. The shares and deferred consideration have not yet been recorded.

Below are the statements of financial position of Peppermint and Spearmint as at 31 December 20X4:

	Peppermint	Spearmint
	$000	$000
Non-current assets		
Property, plant & equipment	5,500	1,500
Investment in Spearmint at cost	1,000	
Current assets		
Inventory	550	100
Receivables	400	200
Cash	200	50
	7,650	1,850
Equity		
Share capital	2,000	500
Retained earnings	1,400	300
	3,400	800
Non-current liabilities	3,000	400
Current liabilities	1,250	650
	7,650	1,850

Further information:

(i) At acquisition the fair values of Spearmint's plant exceeded its book value by $200,000. The plant had a remaining useful life of five years at this date.

(ii) For many years Spearmint has been selling some of its products under the brand name of 'Mintfresh'. At the date of acquisition the directors of Peppermint valued this brand at $250,000 with a remaining life of 10 years. The brand is not included in Spearmint's statement of financial position.

(iii) The consolidated goodwill has been impaired by $258,000.

(iv) The Peppermint Group values the non-controlling interest using the fair value method. At the date of acquisition the fair value of the 20% non-controlling interest was $380,000.

Prepare the consolidated statement of financial position as at 31 December 20X4.

3 Post-acquisition revaluations

If there is a **post-acquisition revaluation** in the subsidiary's non-current assets, the full amount of the gain should be added to non-current assets. The parent's share of the gain is taken to the revaluation surplus, with the NCI share of the gain being taken to NCI in W4.

e.g

Illustration 3 – Post-acquisition revaluations

P has owned 80% of S for many years. During the current year, P and S both revalue their properties for the first time. Both properties increase by $100,000.

The revaluations will be shown as follows:

		$000	$000
Dr	Property, plant & equipment	200	
Cr	Revaluation surplus (via OCI) ($100,000 + (80% × $100,000))		180
Cr	Non-controlling interest (20% × $100,000)		20

Uniform accounting policies

All group companies should have the same accounting policies.

If a group member uses different accounting policies, its financial statements must be adjusted to achieve consistency before they are consolidated.

This is achieved by:

1. adjusting the relevant asset or liability balance in the subsidiary's individual statement of financial position prior to adding across on a line by line basis, and
2. adjusting **W2** to reflect the impact of the different policy on the subsidiary's net assets.

4 Intra-group trading

Types of intra-group trading

P and S may well trade with each other leading to the following potential problem areas:

- current accounts between P and S
- loans held by one company in the other
- dividends and loan interest
- unrealised profits on sales of inventory
- unrealised profits on sales of non-current assets

Current accounts

If P and S trade with each other than this will probably be done on credit. Note that these intra-group transactions are usually recorded within a single account in each entity, known as the current account. This will lead to:

- a receivables (current) account in one entity's SFP
- a payables (current) account in the other entity's SFP.

These are amounts owing within the group rather than outside the group and therefore they must not appear in the consolidated statement of financial position.

They are therefore cancelled against each other on consolidation, by deducting from the relevant lines on the SFP.

Cash/goods in transit

At the year end, the current accounts may not agree, owing to the existence of in-transit items such as goods or cash.

The usual rules are as follows:

- If there are goods or cash in transit, adjust the statement of financial position as if the goods or cash had been received:
  - cash in transit adjusting entry is:
    - Dr Cash
    - Cr Receivables
  - goods in transit adjusting entry is:
    - Dr Inventory
    - Cr Payables

  This adjustment is for the purpose of consolidation only.
- Once in agreement, the current accounts may be cancelled as normal.
- This means that reconciled current account balance amounts are removed from both receivables and payables in the consolidated statement of financial position.

e.g

Illustration 4 – Inter-company current accounts

Current accounts and cash in transit

Draft statements of financial position for Plant and Shrub on 31 March 20X7 are as follows.

	Plant	**Shrub**
	$000	$000
Non-current assets		
Property, plant & equipment	100	140
Investment in S at cost	180	
Current assets		
Inventory	30	35
Trade receivables	20	10
Cash	10	5
	340	190

Equity and liabilities		
Share capital: Ordinary $1 shares	200	100
Share premium	10	30
Retained earnings	40	20
	250	150
Non-current liabilities: 10% loan notes	65	–
Current liabilities	25	40
	340	190

Notes:

Plant bought 80,000 shares in Shrub in 20X1 when Shrub's reserves included a share premium of $30,000 and retained earnings of $5,000.

Plant's records show $6,000 owing to Shrub, but Shrub's records show $8,000 owed by Plant. The difference is explained as cash in transit.

No impairment of goodwill has occurred to date.

Plant uses the proportion of net assets method to value the non-controlling interest.

Prepare Plant's consolidated statement of financial position as at 31 March 20X7.

Solution

Plant Group consolidated statement of financial position as at 31 March 20X7

	$000	$000
Assets		
Non-current assets:		
Intangible assets – goodwill (W3)		72
Property, plant & equipment (100 + 140)		240
		312
Current assets		
Inventory (30 + 35)	65	
Trade receivables (20 + 10 – 2 (CIT) – 6 (inter-co))	22	
Cash (10 + 5 + 2 (CIT))	17	
		104
		416
Equity and liabilities		
Share capital		200
Share premium		10
Retained earnings **(W5)**		52
Non-controlling interest **(W4)**		30
		292
Non-current liabilities: 10% loan notes		65
Current liabilities (25 + 40 – 6(inter-co))		59
		416

Workings:

Note: Cash in transit (CIT)

The $2,000 cash in transit should be adjusted for in order to reconcile the intra-group balance.

Assume that the cash has been received and therefore:

- increase Shrub's cash balance by $2,000 to $7,000
- decrease Shrub's receivables balance by $2,000 to $6,000

The outstanding intercompany balance requiring cancelling is therefore $6,000.

(W1) Group structure

P

20X1 | 80%

S

(W2) Net assets of Shrub

	Acquisition	**Reporting date**	**Post-acquisition**
	$000	$000	$000
Share capital	100	100	–
Share premium	30	30	–
Retained earnings	5	20	15
	135	150	15

(W3) Goodwill

	$000
Parent investment at fair value	180
NCI value at acquisition (20% × 135 (W2))	27
	207
Less: Fair value of net assets at acquisition (W2)	(135)
Goodwill on acquisition	72

(W4) Non-controlling interest

	$000
NCI value at acquisition (as in (W3))	27
NCI share of post-acquisition reserves (20% × 15 (W2))	3
	30

(W5) Group retained earnings

	$000
Plant retained earnings	40
80% of Shrub's post-acquisition retained earnings (80% × 15 (W2))	12
	52

Test your understanding 5

Fair value adjustments/intra-group balances

Statements of financial position of P and S as at 30 June 20X8 are given below:

	P	S
	$	$
Non-current assets:		
Land	4,500	2,500
Plant & equipment	2,400	1,750
Investments	8,000	
	14,900	4,250

	P	S
	$	$
Current assets:		
Inventory	3,200	900
Receivables	1,400	650
Bank	600	150
	5,200	1,700
	20,100	5,950
Ordinary share capital 50c	5,000	1,000
Retained earnings	8,300	3,150
	13,300	4,150
Non-current liabilities: 8% loan stock	4,000	500
Current liabilities	2,800	1,300
	20,100	5,950

(i) P acquired 75% of S on 1 July 20X5 when the balance on S's retained earnings was $1,150. P paid $3,500 for its investment in the share capital of S. At the same time, P invested in 60% of S's 8% loan stock.

(ii) At the reporting date P's payables included an amount due to S of $400. This did not agree to the corresponding amount in S's financial statements of $500. The difference is explained as cash in transit.

(iii) At the date of acquisition it was determined that S's land, carried at cost of $2,500 had a fair value of $3,750. S's plant was determined to have a fair value of $500 in excess of its carrying amount and had a remaining life of 5 years at this time. These values had not been recorded by S.

(iv) The P group uses the fair value method to value the non-controlling interest. For this purpose the subsidiary share price at the date of acquisition should be used. The subsidiary share price at acquisition was $2.20 per share.

(v) Goodwill has become impaired by $100.

Required:

Prepare the consolidated statement of financial position of the P group as at 30 June 20X8.

5 Unrealised profit

Profits made by entities within a group on transactions with other group entities are:

- recognised in the accounts of the individual entities concerned, but
- in terms of the group as a whole, such profits are unrealised and must be eliminated from the consolidated financial statements.

Unrealised profit may arise within a group on:

- inventory where entities trade with one another
- non-current assets where one group entity has transferred an asset to another.

The key is that we need to remove this profit by creating a Provision for Unrealised Profit (PUP)

Intra-group trading and unrealised profit in inventory

When one group entity sells goods to another a number of adjustments may be needed.

- Current accounts must be cancelled (see earlier in this chapter).
- Where goods are still held by a group entity, any unrealised profit must be cancelled.
- Inventory must be included at cost to the group (i.e. original cost to the entity which then sold it).

PUP

Where goods have been sold by one group entity to another at a profit, and some of these goods are still in the purchaser's inventory at the year-end, then the profit on these goods is unrealised from the viewpoint of the group as a whole.

This is because we treat the group as if it is a single entity. No one can make a profit by trading with themselves. Until the goods are sold to an outside party there is no **realised** profit from the group perspective.

For example, for a parent Pineapple and its subsidiary Satsuma, if Pineapple purchased goods for $400 and then sold these goods onto Satsuma during the year for $500, Pineapple would record a profit of $100 in their own individual financial statements. If these goods were still held in inventory by Satsuma at the year-end the statement of financial position of Satsuma would include closing inventory at the cost to Satsuma i.e. $500.

This situation results in two problems within the group:

1 The profit made by Pineapple is unrealised. The profit will only become realised by the group when sold on to a third party customer.

2 The value in Satsuma's inventory ($500) is not the cost of the inventory to the group, as the cost to the group was the purchase price of the goods from the external third party supplier i.e. $400.

An adjustment will need to be made so that the single entity concept can be upheld i.e. the group should report external profits, external assets and external liabilities only.

Adjustments for unrealised profit in inventory

The process to adjust for unrealised profit is:

1 Determine the value of closing inventory held by an individual entity which has been purchased from another entity in the group.

2 Using mark-up or margin, calculate the value of profit included within closing inventory.

3 Make the adjustments. These will depend on the seller.

If the seller is the parent, the profit element is included in the parent's retained earnings and belongs to the group.

Adjustment required:

Dr Group retained earnings (deduct the profit in **W5**)

Cr Group inventory (deduct from inventory on the face of the SFP)

If the seller is the subsidiary, the profit element is included in the subsidiary's retained earnings and relates partly to the group, partly to any non-controlling interest (NCI).

Adjustment required:

Dr Subsidiary retained earnings (deduct the profit in **W2** – in reporting date column)

Cr Group inventory (deduct from inventory on the face of the SFP)

By adjusting W2, the PUP will automatically be shared between the parent and the NCI.

Test your understanding 6

Health (H) bought 90% of the equity share capital of Safety (S), two years ago on 1 January 20X2 when the retained earnings of Safety stood at $5,000. Statements of financial position at the year end of 31 December 20X3 are as follows.

	Health		Safety	
	$000	$000	$000	$000
Non-current assets:				
Property, plant & equipment		100		30
Investment in Safety at cost		34		
		134		30
Current assets:				
Inventory	90		20	
Receivables	110		25	
Bank	10		5	
		210		50
		344		80
Equity:				
Share capital			15	5
Retained earnings			159	31
			174	36
Non-current liabilities:			120	28
Current liabilities			50	16
			344	80

Safety transferred goods to Health at a transfer price of $18,000 at a mark-up of 50%. Two-thirds of these goods remained in inventory at the year end. The current account in Health and Safety stood at $22,000 on that day. Goodwill has suffered an impairment of $10,000.

Health uses the fair value method to value the non-controlling interest. The fair value of the non-controlling interest at acquisition was $4,000.

Prepare the consolidated statement of financial position at 31 December 20X3.

Non-current assets

If one group entity sells non-current assets to another, adjustments must be made to recreate the situation that would have existed if the sale had not occurred:

- There would have been no profit on the sale.
- Depreciation would have been based on the original cost of the asset to the group.

Non-current asset PUP

Any profit on sale that is made by the selling entity is unrealised and eliminated as with inventory.

Unlike inventory, which is usually sold shortly after the reporting date, goods that become non-current assets of the receiving entity are likely to be included in the consolidated statement of financial position for a number of years.

Where there is unrealised profit on non-current assets the necessary provision for unrealised profit will reduce as the non-current asset is depreciated. Therefore it must be recalculated at the end of each period in which the asset appears in the consolidated statement of financial position.

Adjustments for unrealised profit in non-current assets

The easiest way to calculate the adjustment required is to compare the carrying amount of the asset now with the carrying amount that it would have been if the transfer had never occurred:

	With transfer	Without transfer	PUP adjustment
Carrying amount at date of transfer	X	X	(X)
Depreciation to reporting date	(X)	(X)	X
Carrying amount at reporting date	X	X	(X)

The net PUP amount should be deducted when adding across the parent and subsidiary's non-current assets. The profit on transfer should be deducted from the reserves of the selling company (Subsidiary W2, Parent W5). The difference in depreciation, i.e. the excess depreciation charged against the buying entity's profit, should be added to the reserves of the buying company (Subsidiary W2, Parent W5).

The adjustment to the subsidiary's reserves in W2 will then affect the post-acquisition profit, and effectively be shared between the parent and non-controlling interest.

e.g

Illustration 5 – Unrealised profit in non-current assets

P acquired 80% of S a number of years ago. P transferred an item of plant to S for $6,000 on 1 January 20X1. The plant originally cost P $10,000 and had an original useful life of 5 years when purchased 3 years ago. The useful life of the asset has not changed as a result of the transfer.

What is the unrealised profit on the transaction and how should this be treated within the financial statements at 31 December 20X1?

Solution

	Without transfer	**With transfer**	**Difference**
	$	$	$
Cost	10,000		
Depreciation (3 years)	(6,000)		
Carrying amount	4,000	6,000	2,000
Depreciation ($^1/_2$)	(2,000)	(3,000)	(1,000)
Carrying amount	2,000	3,000	1,000

The overall adjustment would be $1,000 at the reporting date, comprising $2,000 of initial profit less $1,000 of excess depreciation. To adjust the financial statements using standard workings:

Dr Consolidated retained earnings **(W5)**	$2,000
Cr Property, plant and equipment (**on SFP**)	$1,000
Cr Subsidiary earnings **(W2 Reporting date column)**	$1,000

The impact of the subsidiary earnings adjustment above in W2 is that non-controlling interest will be credited with $200 (20% × $1,000) and consolidated retained earnings will be credited with $800 (80% × $1,000).

If S had sold the plant to P, then the adjustment would have been:

Dr Subsidiary earnings (**W2 Reporting date column**)	$2,000
Cr Property, plant and equipment (**on SFP**)	$1,000
Cr Consolidated retained earnings (**W5**)	$1,000

The impact of the subsidiary earnings adjustment above in W2 is that non-controlling interest will be debited with $400 (20% × $2,000) and consolidated retained earnings will be debited with $1,600 (80% × $2,000).

6 Mid-year acquisitions

Calculation of reserves at date of acquisition

If a parent acquires a subsidiary mid-year, the net assets at the date of acquisition must be calculated based on the net assets at the start of the subsidiary's financial year plus the profits of up to the date of acquisition.

To calculate this it is normally assumed that S's profit after tax accrues evenly over time. However, there may be exceptions to this. The most common one of these is an intra-group loan from the parent to the subsidiary at the date of acquisition.

If this is the case, the subsidiary will have incurred loan interest in the post-acquisition period that would not have been charged in the pre-acquisition period.

e.g

Illustration 6 – Mid-year acquisition

P acquired 80% of S on 1 July 20X1. S's retained earnings at 31 December 20X1 are $15,000 and S's profit for the year was $8,000. Immediately after acquisition, P made a loan to S of $40,000 which carried interest at 10%.

What were S's retained earnings at acquisition?

Solution

Normally, to find S's retained earnings at acquisition, S's profit could be time apportioned to find the post-acquisition profit. If the intra-group loan didn't exist, then S's post-acquisition profit would be $4,000 (6/12 × $8,000). This would make retained earnings at acquisition $11,000 ($15,000 at year end less post-acquisition profits of $4,000).

However, the intra-group loan skews the results of S. While S has made a profit of $8,000, there is a $2,000 interest cost ($40,000 × 10% × 6/12) in the post-acquisition period which would not have existed in the first six months.

	Total profit	**Pre-acq'n**	**Post-acq'n**
	$000	$000	$000
Profit for year	8,000		
Add back interest cost	2,000		
Pre-interest profit	10,000	5,000	5,000
Less interest (all post acq'n)	(2,000)		(2,000)
Correct profit split	8,000	5,000	3,000

Therefore retained earnings at acquisition will be $12,000 ($15,000 less $3,000 post-acquisition) and the post-acquisition profits to go to consolidated retained earnings are $3,000.

Test your understanding 7

Consolidated statement of financial position

On 1 May 20X7 Karl bought 60% of Susan paying $76,000 cash. The summarised statements of financial position for the two entities as at 30 November 20X7 are:

	Karl	Susan
	$	$
Non-current assets		
Property, plant & equipment	138,000	115,000
Investments	98,000	–
Current assets		
Inventory	15,000	17,000
Receivables	19,000	20,000
Cash	2,000	–
	272,000	152,000
Share capital	50,000	40,000
Retained earnings	189,000	69,000
	239,000	109,000
Non-current liabilities: 8% Loan notes	–	20,000
Current liabilities	33,000	23,000
	272,000	152,000

The following information is relevant:

(i) The inventory of Karl includes $8,000 of goods purchased for cash from Susan at cost plus 25%.

(ii) On 1 June 20X7 Karl transferred an item of plant to Susan for $15,000. Its carrying amount at that date was $10,000, and its remaining useful life was 5 years.

(iii) Karl values the non-controlling interest using the fair value method. At the date of acquisition the fair value of the 40% non-controlling interest was $50,000.

(iv) An impairment loss of $1,000 is to be charged against goodwill at the year-end.

(v) Susan earned a profit of $9,000 in the year ended 30 November 20X7.

(vii) The loan note in Susan's books represents monies borrowed from Karl on 30 November 20X7.

(vii) Included in Karl's receivables is $4,000 relating to inventory sold to Susan during the year. Susan raised a cheque for $2,500 and sent it to Karl on 29 November 20X7. Karl did not receive this cheque until 4 December 20X7.

Required:

Prepare the consolidated statement of financial position as at 30 November 20X7.

Analysis of a company within a group

The FR examination may contain a question involving the analysis of a company which is part of a group. Whilst intra-group transactions will be removed from the consolidated financial statements, these will not be removed from the individual financial statements. Therefore extra attention must be paid to transactions which may not be at market value, or may be lost if the company is removed from the group. This can include:

- Intra-group loans – these may be at low interest, which may change if the company is removed from the group
- Intra-group receivables/payables – these can be done to manipulate an entity's cash position prior to a sale.
- Inventory/Non-current assets – Assets could have been sold at inflated prices between the group. The unrealised profits will be removed from the consolidated financial statements, but the item will remain at the inflated cost in the individual statements of financial position.
- Shared costs/assets – The company may share assets with others in the group, which would be lost if the company were removed from the group. Any additional assets (such as office space) that would be required if the company became a standalone entity should be taken into consideration.

7 Chapter summary

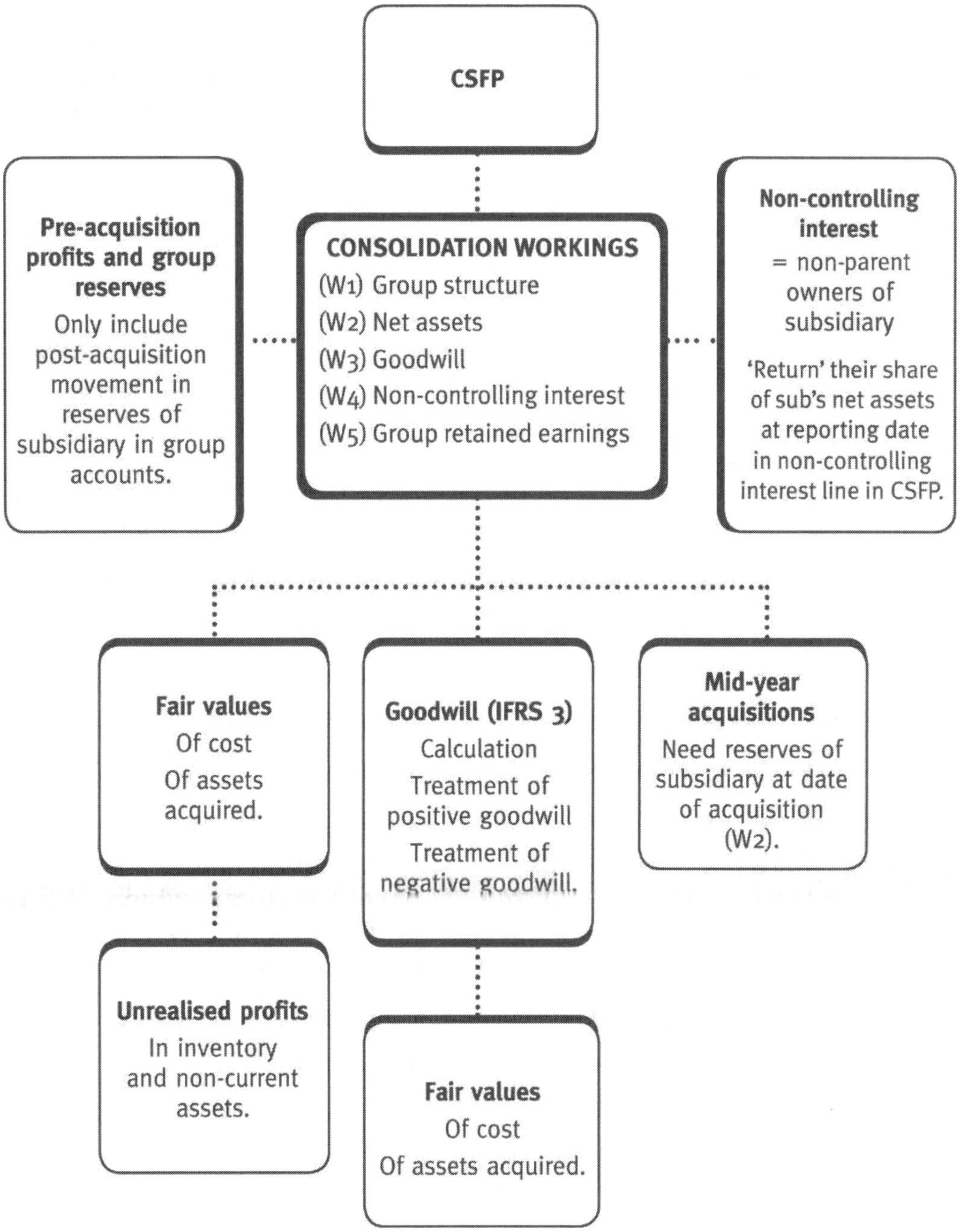

Test your understanding 8

1 LPD buys goods from its 75% owned subsidiary QPR. QPR earns a mark-up of 25% on such transactions. At the group's year end, 30 June 20X1 LPD had not yet taken delivery of goods, at a sales value of $100,000, which were despatched by QPR on 29 June 20X1.

What would be the net increase in inventory in the consolidated statement of financial position of the LPD group at 30 June 20X1?

$_________

2 STV owns 80% of the ordinary share capital of its subsidiary TUW. At the group's year end, 28 February 20X1, STV's payables include $3,600 in respect of inventories sold by TUW. TUW's receivables include $6,700 in respect of inventories sold to STV. Two days before the year end STV sent a payment of $3,100 to TUW that was not recorded by the latter until two days after the year end.

Which of the following adjustments would be necessary to adjust for the cash in transit?

A $2,325 to be added to cash

B $3,100 to be added to payables

C $3,100 to be added to inventories

D $3,100 to be added to cash

3 **Where the purchase price of an acquisition is less than the aggregate fair value of the net assets acquired, which ONE of the following accounting treatments of the difference is required by IFRS 3 *Business Combinations*?**

A Deduction from goodwill in the consolidated statement of financial position

B Immediate recognition as a gain in the statement of changes in equity

C Recognition in the statement of comprehensive income over its useful life

D Immediate recognition as a gain in profit or loss.

4 On 30 September 20X1 GHI purchased 100% of the ordinary share capital of JKL for $1.8 million. The carrying amount of JKL's net assets at the date of acquisition was $1.35 million. A valuation exercise showed that the fair value of JKL's property, plant and equipment at that date was $100,000 greater than its carrying amount.

What is the goodwill on acquisition?

$________

5 Paul acquired 75% of the share capital of Simon on 1 January 20X1. On this date, the net assets of Simon were $80,000. The non-controlling interest was calculated using fair value, which was calculated as $40,000 at the date of acquisition. At 1 January 20X3 the net assets of Simon were $120,000 and goodwill had been impaired by $10,000.

What was the value of the non-controlling interest at 1 January 20X3?

A $50,000

B $47,500

C $107,500

D $87,500

6 Peter acquired 90% of the share capital of Saul on 1 January 20X2. At this date, the fair value of Saul's net assets was $100,000 and goodwill was correctly calculated at $30,000. At 1 January 20X5, the fair value of the net assets of Saul was $140,000 and goodwill had been impaired by $20,000. At the same date, Peter's retained earnings were $70,000. The non-controlling interest is valued using the fair value method.

What is the total group retained earnings at 1 January 20X5?

A $60,000

B $75,000

C $88,000

D $100,000

Test your understanding answers

Test your understanding 1

Dickens: Consolidated statement of financial position as at 31 December 20X8

Non-current assets	$
Goodwill (W3)	22,500
Property, plant and equipment (85,000 + 18,000)	103,000
Current assets (160,000 + 84,000)	244,000
	369,500
Equity	
Share capital	65,000
Share premium	35,000
Group retained earnings (W5)	74,000
Non-controlling interest (W4)	13,500
	187,500
Current liabilities (135,000 + 47,000)	182,000
	369,500

(W1) Group structure

(percentage of shares purchased 16,000/20,000 = 80%)

D

1 Jan X8 | 80%

J

(W2) Net assets of Jones

	Acquisition	Reporting date	Post-acquisition
	$	$	$
Share capital	20,000	20,000	–
Share premium	10,000	10,000	–
Retained earnings	20,000	25,000	5,000
	50,000	55,000	5,000

(W3) Goodwill

Parent holding (investment) at fair value	60,000
NCI value at acquisition	12,500
	72,500
Less: Fair value of net assets at acquisition	(50,000)
Goodwill on acquisition	22,500

(W4) Non-controlling interests

NCI value at acquisition (as in **(W3)**)	12,500
NCI share of post-acquisition reserves (20% × 5,000 **(W2)**)	1,000
	13,500

(W5) Group retained earnings

Dickens	70,000
80% Jones post-acquisition profit (80% × 5,000 **(W2)**)	4,000
	74,000

Test your understanding 2

	(i) Proportional	(ii) Fair value
	$000	$000
Parent holding at fair value	240	240
Non-controlling interest		
$360,000 × 40%	144	
at fair value		150
Net assets	(360)	(360)
Goodwill	24	30

Test your understanding 3

Consolidated statement of financial position as at 30 June 20X8

Non-current assets	$
Goodwill **(W3)**	3,790
Property, plant & equipment (15,000 + 9,500)	24,500
Investments (5,000 – 5,000)	–
Current Assets (7,500 + 5,000)	12,500
	40,790
Share capital (6,000 + 1,200)	7,200
Share premium (4,000 + 960)	4,960
Retained earnings **(W5)**	13,239
Non-controlling Interest **(W4)**	6,310
	31,709
Non-current liabilities (1,000 + 500 + 1,680 +101)	3,281
Current liabilities (4,000 + 1,800)	5,800
	40,790

Workings:

(W1) Group structure

P

| 60%

S

1 July 20x7 i.e. 1 yr

(W2) Net assets

	Acquisition	Reporting date	Post-acquisition
	$	$	$
Share capital	5,000	5,000	–
Retained earnings	5,800	7,200	1,400
	10,800	12,200	1,400

(W3) Goodwill

Parent holding (investment) at fair value	
Cash paid	5,000
Share exchange (60% × 5,000 × 2/5 × $1.80)	2,160
Deferred consideration (2,000 × 1/1.08^3)	1,680
	8,840
NCI value at acquisition	5,750
	14,590
Less: Fair value of net assets at acquisition **(W2)**	(10,800)
Goodwill on acquisition	3,790

Shares

P has issued 1,200 shares valued at $1.80 each. These have not yet been recorded and so an adjustment is required to:

Cr	Share capital (1,200 × $1)	1,200
Cr	Share premium (1,200 × $0.80)	960

Deferred consideration

P has a liability to pay $2,000 in 3 years' time which has not yet been recorded. The liability is being measured at its present value of $1,680 at the date of acquisition and so the adjustment required is:

Cr	Non-current liabilities	$1,680

The statement of financial position date is 1 year after the date of acquisition and so the present value of the liability will have increased by 6% (i.e. it is unwound by 6%) by the statement of financial position date. An adjustment is therefore required to reflect this increase:

Dr	Finance cost i.e. Retained earnings of P (6% × 1,680)	$101
Cr	Deferred consideration i.e. Non-current liabilities	$101

(W4) Non-controlling interests

NCI value at acquisition (as in **(W3)**)	5,750
NCI share of post-acquisition reserves (40% × 1,400 **(W2)**)	560
	6,310

(W5) Retained earnings

P retained earnings	12,500
Deferred consideration finance cost	(101)
S (60% × 1,400 **(W2)**)	840
	13,239

Test your understanding 4

Peppermint: Consolidated statement of financial position at 31 December 20X4

	$000
Goodwill **(W3)**	782
Brand name (250 – 50 **(W2)**)	200
Property, plant & equipment (5,500 + 1,500 + 200 – 80 **(W2)**)	7,120
Current assets:	
Inventory (550 + 100)	650
Receivables (400 + 200)	600
Cash (200 + 50)	250
	9,602
Share capital (2,000 + 200)	2,200
Share premium (0 + 160)	160
Retained earnings **(W5)**	1,151
	3,511
Non-controlling interest **(W4)**	337
	3,848
Non-current liabilities (3,000 + 400)	3,400
Current liabilities (1,250 + 650)	1,900
Deferred consideration (375 + 79 **(W6)**)	454
	9,602

Workings:

(W1) Group structure

Peppermint

2 years ago | 80%

Spearmint

(W2) Net assets of Spearmint

	Acquisition	Reporting date	Post-acquisition
	$000	$000	$000
Share capital	500	500	–
Retained earnings	125	300	175
Fair value: Plant	200	200	–
Depreciation adjustment (200 × 2/5)	–	(80)	(80)
Fair value: Brand	250	250	–
Amortisation adjustment (250 × 2/10)	–	(50)	(50)
	1,075	1,120	45

(W3) Goodwill

Parent holding (investment) at fair value:	
Cash paid	1,000
Share exchange (200 × $1.80)	360
Deferred consideration ($500 × 0.75)	375
	1,735
NCI value at acquisition	380
	2,115
Less:	
Fair value of net assets at acquisition **(W2)**	(1,075)
Goodwill on acquisition	1,040
Impairment	(258)
Carrying goodwill	782

Peppermint has not yet recorded the share consideration or the deferred consideration. The journals required to record these are:

		$000
Dr	Investment	360
Cr	Share capital (200 × $1)	200
Cr	Share premium (200 × $0.80)	160
and Dr	Investment	375
Cr	Deferred consideration	375

The cost of the investment debit is used in the goodwill calculation (W3). The credit entries need to be recorded on the face of the SFP.

(W4) Non-controlling interest

NCI value at acquisition (as in (W3))	380
NCI share of post-acquisition reserves (20% × 45 (W2))	9
NCI share of impairment (20% × 258)	(52)
	337

(W5) Group retained earnings

Peppermint retained earnings	1,400
Unwind discount (W6)	(79)
Spearmint (80% × 45)	36
Impairment of goodwill (W3) (80% × 258)	(206)
	1,151

(W6) Unwinding of discount

Present value of deferred consideration at reporting date (see below)	454
Present value of deferred consideration at acquisition	(375)
	79

At acquisition, Peppermint should record a liability of 375, being the present value of the future cash flow at that date.

The reporting date is two years after acquisition, and therefore the liability in Peppermint's SFP at this date is 375×1.10^2.

So, Peppermint needs to:

Dr	Retained earnings (Finance costs in SPL)	79
Cr	Deferred consideration liability	79

Test your understanding 5

Consolidated statement of financial position as at 30 June 20X8

Non-current assets	$
Goodwill **(W3)**	600
Land (4,500 + 2,500 + 1,250 (W2))	8,250
Plant & equipment (2,400 + 1,750 + 500 – 300 (W2))	4,350
Investments (8,000 – 3,500 – (60% × 500))	4,200
	17,400
Current assets	
Inventory (3,200 + 900)	4,100
Receivables (1,400 + 650 – 100 (CIT) – 400 (inter-co))	1,500
Bank (600 + 150 + 100 (CIT))	850
	6,500
	23,900
Equity	
Share capital	5,000
Retained earnings **(W5)**	9,500
Non-controlling interest **(W4)**	1,500
	16,000
Non-current liabilities (4,000 + 500 – (60% × 500))	4,200
Current liabilities (2,800 + 1,300 – 400)	3,700
	23,900

Workings:

(W1) Group structure

P

75%

S

1 July 20X5 i.e. 3 yrs

(W2) Net assets

	Acquisition	Reporting date	Post-acquisition
	$	$	$
Share capital	1,000	1,000	–
Retained earnings	1,150	3,150	2,000
Fair value: land	1,250	1,250	–
Fair value: plant	500	500	–
Depreciation adjustment (500 × 3/5)	–	(300)	(300)
	3,900	5,600	1,700

(W3) Goodwill

Parent holding (investment) at fair value	3,500
NCI value at acquisition ((2,000 shares × 25%) × $2.20)	1,100
	4,600
Less: Fair value of net assets at acquisition **(W2)**	(3,900)
Goodwill on acquisition	700
Impairment	(100)
Goodwill per SFP	600

(W4) Non-controlling interest

NCI value at acquisition (as in **(W3)**)	1,100
NCI share of post-acquisition reserves **(W2)** (25% × 1,700)	425
Less: NCI share of impairment (25% × 100)	(25)
	1,500

(W5) Group retained earnings

100% P	8,300
75% of S post-acq retained earnings **(W2)** (75% × 1,700)	1,275
75% Impairment (75% × 100)	(75)
	9,500

Test your understanding 6

Health consolidated statement of financial position
31 December 20X3

Non current assets		$000
Goodwill **(W3)**		18
Property, plant & equipment (100 + 30)		130
		148
Current Assets		
Inventory (90 + 20 – 4 **(W6)**)	106	
Receivables (110 + 25 – 22 intra-group receivable)	113	
Bank (10 + 5)	15	
		234
		382
Equity		
Share capital		15.0
Group retained earnings **(W5)**		169.8
NCI **(W4)**		5.2
		190
Non-current liabilities (120 + 28)		148
Current liabilities (50 + 16 – 22 intra-group payable)		44
		382

Working paper:

(W1) Group structure

H

| 90% 01/01/X2 2 years ago

S

(W2) Net assets

	Acquisition	Reporting date	Post-acquisition
	$000	$000	$000
Share capital	5	5	–
Retained earnings	5	31	26
PUP **(W6)**		(4)	(4)
	10	32	22

(W3) Goodwill

Parent holding (investment) at fair value	34
NCI value at acquisition	4
	38
Less:	
Fair value of net assets at acquisition **(W2)**	(10)
Goodwill on acquisition	28
Impairment	(10)
Goodwill per SFP	18

(W4) Non-controlling interest

NCI value at acquisition **(W3)**	4
NCI share of post-acquisition reserves (10% × 22 **(W2)**)	2.2
Less: NCI share of impairment (10% × $10)	(1)
	5.2

(W5) Group reserves

100% Health	159
90% Safety post-acquisition (90% × 22 **(W2)**)	19.8
Impairment **(W3)** (90% × $10)	(9)
	169.8

(W6) PUP ($000)

Sales × mark-up fraction × remaining inventory

18 × 50/150 × 2/3 = **4**

Test your understanding 7

Karl consolidated statement of financial position as at 30 November 20X7

	$
Non-current assets	
Goodwill **(W3)**	21,250
Property, plant and equipment	
(138,000 + 115,000 – 4,500 **(W7)**)	248,500
Investments	
(98,000 – 76,000 – 20,000)	2,000
Current Assets	
Inventory	
(15,000 + 17,000 – 1,600 **(W6)**)	30,400
Receivables	
(19,000 + 20,000 – 2,500 (CIT) – 1,500 (intra-group))	35,000
Cash	
(2,000 + 2,500 (CIT))	4,500
	341,650
Share capital	50,000
Group retained earnings **(W5)**	185,890
Non-controlling Interest **(W4)**	51,260
	287,150
Non-current liabilities	
(20,000 – 20,000)	–
Current liabilities	
(33,000 + 23,000 – 1,500 (intra-group))	54,500
	341,650

Workings:

(W1) Group structure

K
|
| 60%
|
S
1 May 2007 i.e. 7 months

(W2) Net assets

	Acq'n	Reporting date	Post-acquisition
	$	$	$
Share capital	40,000	40,000	–
Retained earnings	63,750	69,000	5,250
PUP (W6)	–	(1,600)	(1,600)
PUP (W7)	–	500	500
	103,750	107,900	4,150

Retained earnings at reporting date	69,000
Post-acq profit (7/12 × 9,000)	(5,250)
Retained earnings at acquisition (balance)	63,750

(W3) Goodwill

Parent holding (investment) at fair value	76,000
NCI value at acquisition	50,000
	126,000
Less:	
Fair value of net assets at acquisition **(W2)**	(103,750)
Goodwill on acquisition	22,250
Impairment	(1,000)
Goodwill per SFP	21,250

(W4) Non-controlling interest

NCI value at acquisition (as in **(W3)**)	50,000
NCI share of post-acquisition reserves **(W2)** (40% × $4,150)	1,600
Less: NCI share of impairment **(W3)** (40% × $1,000)	(400)
Carrying goodwill	51,260

(W5) Retained earnings

100% Karl	189,000
PUP **(W7)**	(5,000)
60% Susan post-acquisition profit (60% × 4,150 **(W2)**)	2,490
Impairment – group share (60% × 1,000 **(W3)**)	(600)
	185,890

(W6) PUP – Inventory

Profit in inventory $8,000 × 25/125 = 1,600

(W7) PUP – Plant

	With transfer	Without transfer	PUP
Carrying amount at transfer	15,000	10,000	5,000
Depreciation (× $^1/_5$ × $^6/_{12}$)	(1,500)	(1,000)	(500)
Carrying amount at year-end	13,500	9,000	4,500

The net adjustment of $4,500 is split between:

Parent retained earnings – original profit **(W5)**	(5,000)
Subsidiary retained earnings – excess depreciation **(W2)**	500

Test your understanding 8

1 **$80,000 increase** – Goods in transit are valued at $100,000 but we must remove the PUP element.

PUP is calculated as $100,000 × 25/125 = $20,000. Hence we increase inventory by $100,000 but remove the PUP of $20,000.

The net value of goods in transit to the group is $80,000.

2 **D** – The double entry is: Dr Cash $3,100, Cr Receivables $3,100. The remaining $3,600 would then be cancelled from receivables and payables.

3 **D**

4 **$350,000**

	$
Cost of investment	1,800,000
Fair value of net assets acquired (1,350,000 + 100,000)	(1,450,000)
Goodwill on acquisition	**350,000**

5 **B**

	$
NCI Value at acquisition	40,000
NCI share of post-acquisition profit (25% × ($120,000 – $80,000)	10,000
NCI share of impairment (25% × $10,000)	(2,500)
NCI at 1 January 20X3	**47,500**

6 **C – $88,000**

	$
100% × Peter's retained earnings	70,000
90% × Saul's post-acquisition net assets (90% × ($140,000 – $100,000)	36,000
90% × Goodwill impairment (90% × $20,000)	(18,000)
Total retained earnings	**88,000**

Chapter

19

Consolidated statement of profit or loss

Chapter learning objectives

Upon completion of this chapter you will be able to:

- prepare a consolidated statement of profit or loss for a simple group and a non-controlling interest
- account for the effects of intra-group trading in the statement of profit or loss
- prepare a consolidated statement of profit or loss for a simple group with an acquisition in the period and non-controlling interest
- account for impairment of goodwill
- prepare a consolidated statement of profit or loss and other comprehensive income.

PER

One of the PER performance objectives (PO7) is to prepare external financial reports. You take part in preparing and reviewing financial statements – and all accompanying information – and you do it in accordance with legal and regulatory requirements. Working though this chapter should help you understand how to demonstrate that objective.

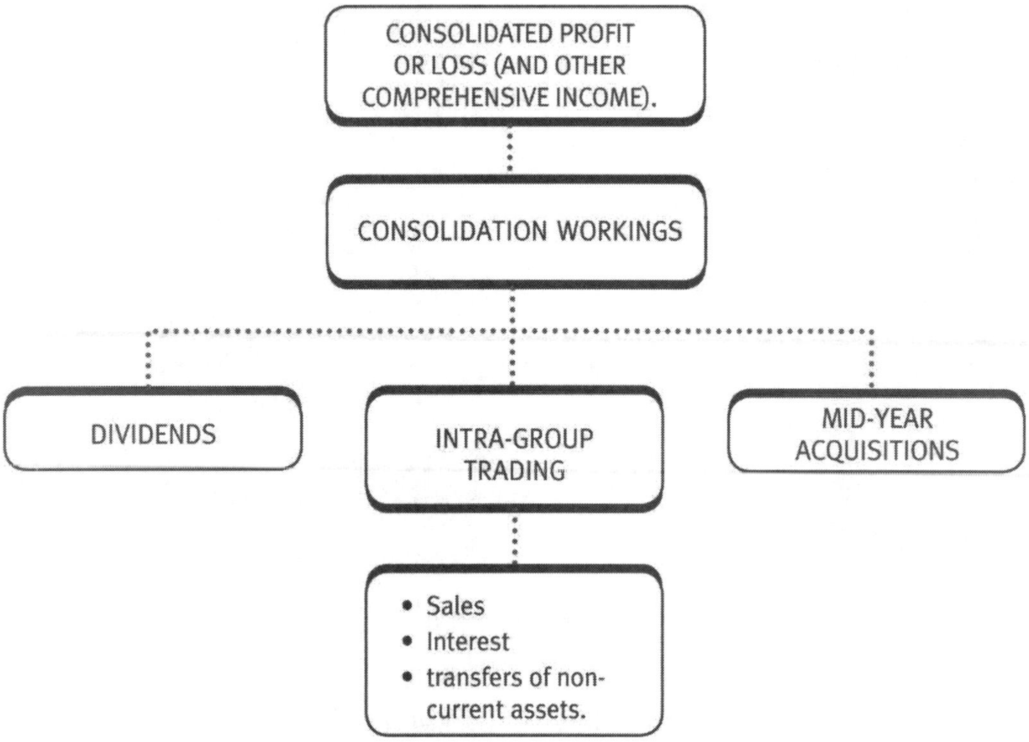

1 Principles of the consolidated statement of profit or loss

Basic principle

The consolidated statement of profit or loss shows the profit generated by all resources disclosed in the related consolidated statement of financial position, i.e. the net assets of the parent entity (P) and its subsidiary (S).

The consolidated statement of profit or loss follows these basic principles:

- From revenue down to profit for the year include all of P's income and expenses plus all of S's income and expenses (reflecting P's control of S).
- After profit for the year show split of profit between amounts attributable to the parent's shareholders and those attributable to the non-controlling interest (to reflect ownership).

The mechanics of consolidation

As with the statement of financial position, it is common to use a standard approach when producing a consolidated statement of profit or loss:

- group structure diagram
- proforma statement of profit or loss, combining income and expense for both parent and subsidiary
- workings for any adjustments detailed in the question, e.g. PUP, fair value depreciation etc.
- non-controlling interest (NCI) share of profit (see below)

Non-controlling interest

This is calculated as:

Subsidiary's profit after tax	X
Less:	
Fair value depreciation	(X)
PUP (where subsidiary is seller)	(X)
Impairment (if using the fair value method)	(X)
Adjusted subsidiary profit	X
Non-controlling interest (× NCI%)	X

2 Intra-group trading

Sales and purchases

The effect of intra-group trading must be eliminated from the consolidated statement of profit or loss.

Such trading will be included in the sales revenue of one group entity and the purchases of another.

- Consolidated sales revenue = P's revenue + S's revenue – intra-group sales.
- Consolidated cost of sales (COS) = P's COS + S's COS – intra-group sales.

Interest

If there is a loan outstanding between group entities the effect of any loan interest received and paid must be eliminated from the consolidated statement of profit or loss.

The relevant amount of interest should be deducted from group investment income and group finance costs.

If there is a mid-year acquisition, be careful with the finance costs, as the finance costs may include interest on a loan from the parent which has only arisen in the post-acquisition period.

For example, if the subsidiary's finance costs were $400,000 and the parent has owned the subsidiary for six months, the finance costs to be consolidated would normally be $200,000 ($400,000 × 6/12).

However, if, on acquisition, the parent loaned the subsidiary $2m at 10% interest, there will be $100,000 of finance cost in the second six months that would not appear in the first six months.

The interest charge without the parent loan interest would be $300,000. Six months of this would be $150,000, and this is the figure that would be included within the consolidated statement of profit or loss.

Dividends

A payment of a dividend by S to P will need to be removed from investment income in the statement of profit or loss. The effect of this on the consolidated statement of profit or loss is that any dividend income shown in the consolidated statement of profit or loss must arise from investments other than those in subsidiaries or associates (covered in Chapter 20).

Note that only dividends paid by P to its own shareholders appear in the consolidated financial statements. These are shown within the consolidated statement of changes in equity which you will not be required to prepare for the FR examination.

e.g

Illustration 1 – Basic consolidated profit or loss

The statements of profit or loss for Paddle and Skip for the year ended 31 August 20X4 are shown below. Paddle acquired 75% of the ordinary share capital of Skip several years ago.

	Paddle	**Skip**
	$000	$000
Revenue	2,400	800
Cost of sales and expenses	(2,160)	(720)
Trading profit	240	80
Investment income:		
Dividend received from Skip	3	
Profit before tax	243	80
Income tax expense	(115)	(40)
Profit for the year	128	40

Prepare Paddle's consolidated statement of profit or loss for the year ended 31 August 20X4.

Solution

Paddle consolidated statement of profit or loss for the year ended 31 August 20X4

	$000
Revenue	
(2,400 + 800)	3,200
Cost of sales and expenses	
(2,160 + 720)	(2,800)
Profit before tax	320
Income tax expense(115 + 40)	(155)
Profit for the year	165
Profit attributable to:	
Owners of parent (165 – NCI)	155
Non-controlling interest **(W1)**	10

(W1) Non-controlling interest

NCI share of subsidiary profit for the year

25% × $40 = $10

Provision for unrealised profit

Inventory

If any goods sold intra-group are included in closing inventory, their value must be adjusted to the cost to the group (as in the CSFP).

The adjustment for unrealised profit should be shown as an increase to cost of sales, returning closing inventory back to true cost to group and eliminating the unrealised profit.

Unrealised profit in inventory

In the previous chapter we dealt with the treatment of unrealised trading profits in the consolidated SFP, reducing inventory and retained earnings. In producing the consolidated statement of profit or loss, we need to understand the impact of this adjustment.

If, in a certain year:

- A buys an inventory item for $60
- A sells it to its subsidiary B for $80

If B still holds the item at the reporting date, then the statements of profit or loss of the two companies will include, in respect of these events:

	A	B
	$	$
Revenue	80	–
Cost of sales	(60)	–
Profit	20	–

Note that B's sales and cost of sales are nil because the goods are still held at the year end. As far as the group is concerned the $20 is an unrealised profit. In the consolidated statement of profit or loss, we must

1 eliminate sales and purchases of $80 as these are intra-group transactions

2 eliminate the unrealised profit of $20 in A (the seller) by increasing the cost of sales.

These adjustments would completely remove the impact of the above transaction.

If B had sold the item for $95 by the reporting date, the statements of profit or loss of the two companies would have shown:

	A	B
	$	$
Revenue	80	95
Cost of sales	(60)	(80)
Profit	20	15

As the goods have now been sold outside the group both companies have realised their profits and so there is no need to adjust the profit. However, a single equivalent company would show in its statement of profit or loss:

	$
Revenue	95
Cost of sales	(60)
Profit	35

In this case, we need eliminate only the $80 from sales revenue and the $80 from cost of sales in order to establish the correct revenue and cost of sales figures. No adjustment would be required for unrealised profit since all profits are now realised.

Effect on non-controlling interests

If the unrealised profit originally arose in the subsidiary, the non-controlling interest must be adjusted for its share of the unrealised profit. To achieve this, in the first instance all the unrealised profit must be eliminated as above to determine the correct amount of profit earned by the group trading as if it were a single entity. The NCI's share is then calculated by reference to the reduced amount of the subsidiary's profit. PUP is added on to the group cost of sales and the NCI's share is removed in the NCI working.

e.g

Illustration 2 – Unrealised profit in CSPL

On 1 January 20X9 Zebedee acquired 60% of the ordinary shares of Xavier.

The following statements of profit or loss have been produced by Zebedee and Xavier for the year ended 31 December 20X9.

	Zebedee	**Xavier**
	$000	$000
Revenue	1,260	520
Cost of sales	(420)	(210)
Gross profit	840	310
Distribution costs	(180)	(60)
Administration expenses	(120)	(90)
Profit from operations	540	160
Investment income from Xavier	36	
Profit before tax	576	160
Income tax expense	(130)	(26)
Profit for the year	446	134

During the year ended 31 December 20X9 Zebedee sold $84,000 worth of goods to Xavier. These goods had cost Zebedee $56,000. On 31 December 20X9 Xavier still had $36,000 worth of these goods in inventories (held at cost to Xavier).

Prepare the consolidated statement of profit or loss to incorporate Zebedee and Xavier for the year ended 31 December 20X9.

Solution

Consolidated statement of profit or loss for the year ended 31 December 20X9

	$000
Revenue	
(1,260 + 520 – 84 intra-group)	1,696
Cost of sales	
(420 + 210 – 84 intra-group + 12 **(W2)**)	(558)
Gross profit	1,138
Distribution costs (180 + 60)	(240)
Administrative expenses (120 + 90)	(210)
Profit before tax	688
Income tax expense (130 + 26)	(156)
Profit for the year	532
Profit attributable to:	
Owners of parent (532 – NCI)	478.4
Non-controlling interests **(W3)**	53.6

Workings:

(W1) Group structure

Zebedee

1 Jan X9 | 60%

Xavier

(W2) Unrealised profit in inventory

	$000
Selling price	84
Cost	(56)
Total profit	28

Closing inventory held by Xavier = 36

Profit included in closing inventory = 28 × 36/84 = **12**

(W3) Non-controlling interest

	$000
NCI share of Xavier profit = 40% × 134	**53.6**

Transfers of non-current assets

If one group company sells a non-current asset to another group company the following adjustments are needed in the statement of profit or loss to account for the unrealised profit and the additional depreciation.

- Any profit or loss arising on the transfer must be removed from the consolidated statement of profit or loss included in the seller's profit
- The depreciation charge for the buyer must be adjusted so that it is based on the cost of the asset to the group.

Unrealised profit on non-current assets

Non-current assets may be sold between group companies. If the selling price of such an asset is the same as the carrying amount in the books of the seller at the time of the sale, then no adjustments are necessary as the buyer will account for (and depreciate) the asset by reference to its original cost to the group.

If, however the seller makes a profit on the sale, the buyer will account for the asset at a value higher than the depreciated cost to the group. The profit made by the seller is gradually realised over the asset's remaining life by the buyer's depreciation charges being calculated on a value higher than original cost to the group. So at the time when the buyer has fully depreciated the acquired asset, the whole of the seller's profit has been realised and no adjustments are necessary.

However, as long as the buyer is still depreciating the acquired asset, the amount of the seller's unrealised profit must be eliminated from both earnings and the carrying amount of the asset. Adjustments are needed on the statement of financial position in order to return to the situation if the sale had not taken place:

- any remaining unrealised profit or loss arising on the transfer is eliminated by removing the profit on transfer from the seller and removing the excess depreciation from the buyer
- the asset's cost and accumulated depreciation are adjusted so that they are based on the cost of the asset to the group.

Similar adjustments are necessary in the statement of profit or loss, to remove the profit on the sale from the seller and the excess depreciation from the buyer. Note that the profit will only need to be removed in the year of sale, and the depreciation adjustment will need to be time-apportioned if the sale takes place part-way through the current year.

3 Other CSPL adjustments

Impairment of goodwill

Once any impairment has been identified during the year, the charge for the year will be passed through the consolidated statement of profit or loss. This will usually be through operating expenses, but always follow any instructions from the examiner.

If non-controlling interests have been valued at fair value, a portion of the impairment expense must be removed from the non-controlling interest's share of profit.

Fair values

If a depreciating non-current asset of the subsidiary has been revalued as part of a fair value exercise when calculating goodwill, this will result in an adjustment to the consolidated statement of profit or loss.

The subsidiary's own statement of profit or loss will include depreciation based on the carrying amount of the asset in the subsidiary's individual statement of financial position.

The consolidated statement of profit or loss must include a depreciation charge based on the fair value of the asset, as included in the consolidated SFP.

Extra depreciation must therefore be calculated and charged to an appropriate cost category (usually cost of sales, but in line with examiner requirements).

Test your understanding 1

Set out below are the draft statements of profit or loss of Prunes and its subsidiary company Sultanas for the year ended 31 December 20X7.

On 1 January 20X6 Prunes purchased 75,000 of Sultanas' total share capital of 100,000 $1 ordinary shares.

Statements of profit or loss for the year ended 31 December 20X7

	Prunes	**Sultanas**
	$000	$000
Revenue	600	300
Cost of sales	(360)	(140)
Gross profit	240	160
Operating expenses	(93)	(45)
Profit from operations	147	115
Finance costs	–	(3)
Profit before tax	147	112
Income tax expense	(50)	(32)
Profit for the year	97	80

The following additional information is relevant:

(i) During the year Sultanas sold goods to Prunes for $20,000, making a mark-up of one third. Only 20% of these goods were sold before the end of the year, the rest were still in inventory.

(ii) Goodwill has been subject to an impairment review at the end of each year since acquisition and the review at the end of the current year revealed a further impairment of $5,000. Impairment is to be recognised as an operating cost.

(iii) At the date of acquisition a fair value adjustment was made and this has resulted in an additional depreciation charge for the current year of $15,000. It is group policy that all depreciation is charged to cost of sales.

(iv) Prunes values the non-controlling interest using the fair value method.

Prepare the consolidated statement of profit or loss for the year ended 31 December 20X7 for the Prunes group.

Test your understanding 2

Given below are the statements of profit or loss for Paris and its subsidiary London for the year ended 31 December 20X5.

	Paris	**London**
	$000	$000
Revenue	3,200	2,560
Cost of sales	(2,200)	(1,480)
Gross profit	1,000	1,080
Distribution costs	(160)	(120)
Administrative expenses	(400)	(80)
Profit from operations	440	880
Investment income	160	–
Profit before tax	600	880
Taxation	(400)	(480)
Profit for the year	200	400

Additional information:

(i) Paris paid $1.5 million on 31 December 20X1 for 80% of London's 800,000 ordinary shares.

(ii) Goodwill impairments at 1 January 20X5 amounted to $152,000. A further impairment of $40,000 was found to be necessary at the year-end. Impairments are included within administrative expenses.

(iii) Paris made sales to London at a selling price of $600,000 during the year. Not all of the goods had been sold externally by the year-end. The profit element included in London's closing inventory was $30,000.

(iv) Additional fair value depreciation for the current year amounted to $10,000. All depreciation should be charged to cost of sales.

(v) London paid an interim dividend during the year of $200,000.

(vi) Paris values the non-controlling interest using the fair value method.

Prepare a consolidated statement of profit or loss for the year ended 31 December 20X5 for the Paris group.

4 Mid-year acquisitions

Mid-year acquisition procedure

If a subsidiary is acquired part way through the year, then the subsidiary's results should only be consolidated from the date of acquisition, i.e. the date on which control is obtained.

In practice this will require:

- Identification of the net assets of S at the date of acquisition in order to calculate goodwill.
- Time apportionment of the results of S in the year of acquisition. For this purpose, unless indicated otherwise, assume that revenue and expenses accrue evenly.
- After time-apportioning S's results, deduction of post-acquisition intra-group items as normal.

e.g

Illustration 3 – Mid-year acquisition

The following statements of profit or loss were prepared for the year ended 31 March 20X9.

	Ethos	Pathos
	$000	$000
Revenue	303,600	217,700
Cost of sales	(143,800)	(102,200)
Gross profit	159,800	115,500
Operating expenses	(71,200)	(51,300)
Profit from operations	88,600	64,200
Investment income	2,800	1,200
Profit before tax	91,400	65,400
Income tax expense	(46,200)	(32,600)
Profit for the year	45,200	32,800

On 30 November 20X8 Ethos acquired 75% of the issued ordinary capital of Pathos. No dividends were paid by either company during the year. The investment income is from quoted investments and has been correctly accounted for.

The profits of both entities are deemed to accrue evenly over the year.

Prepare the consolidated statement of profit or loss for the year ended 31 March 20X9 for the Ethos group.

Solution

Ethos: Consolidated statement of profit or loss for the year ended 31 March 20X9

	$000
Revenue 303,600 + (217,700 × 4/12))	376,167
Cost of sales (143,800 + (102,200 × 4/12))	(177,867)
Gross profit	198,300
Operating expenses (71,200 + (51,300 × 4/12))	(88,300)
Profit from operations	110,000
Investment income (2,800 + (1,200 × 4/12))	3,200
Profit before tax	113,200
Income tax expense (46,200 + (32,600 × 4/12))	(57,067)
Profit for the year	56,133

Profit attributable to:	
Owners of parent (balance)	53,400
Non-controlling interest (25% × ($32,800 × 4/12)	2,733

Ethos acquired 75% of the issued ordinary capital of Pathos on 30 November 20X8. This is the date on which control passed and hence the date from which the results of Pathos should be reflected in the consolidated statement of profit or loss.

All profits earned by Pathos in the four months since that date are post-acquisition profits.

The previous eight months' profit from 1 April 20X8 to 30 November 20X9 are all pre-acquisition and would be included within the reserves at acquisition for the calculation of goodwill.

Test your understanding 3

Pepper bought 70% of Salt on 1 July 20X6. The following are the statements of profit or loss of Pepper and Salt for the year ended 31 March 20X7:

	Pepper	**Salt**
	$000	$000
Revenue	31,200	10,400
Cost of sales	(17,800)	(5,600)
Gross profit	13,400	4,800
Operating expenses	(8,500)	(3,200)
Profit from operations	4,900	1,600
Investment income	2,000	–
Profit before tax	6,900	1,600
Income tax expense	(2,100)	(500)
Profit for the year	4,800	1,100

The following information is available:

(i) On 1 July 20X6, an item of plant in the books of Salt had a fair value of $5,000 in excess of its carrying amount. At this time, the plant had a remaining life of 10 years. Depreciation is charged to cost of sales.

(ii) During the post-acquisition period Salt sold goods to Pepper for $4,400. Of this amount, $500 was included in the inventory of Pepper at the year-end. Salt earns a 35% margin on its sales.

(iii) Goodwill amounting to $800 arose on the acquisition of Salt, which had been measured using the fair value method. Goodwill is to be impaired by 10% at the year-end. Impairment losses should be charged to operating expenses.

(iv) Salt paid a dividend of $500 on 1 January 20X7.

Required:

Prepare the consolidated statement of profit or loss for the year ended 31 March 20X7 for the Pepper group.

5 The consolidated statement of profit or loss and other comprehensive income

The consolidated statement of profit or loss **and** other comprehensive income may be asked for in the exam instead of simply a consolidated statement of profit or loss. The consolidated statement of profit or loss is the starting point and the other comprehensive income items are then recorded (a proforma statement of profit or loss and other comprehensive income is included in Chapters 1 and 23).

The items that you may need to consider in the FR syllabus for items of other comprehensive income include revaluations gains or losses and fair value through other comprehensive income gains or losses (Chapter 9). To demonstrate how these items should be dealt with, we will take TYU 3 and add items of comprehensive income to illustrate this.

e.g **Illustration 4**

The answer to Test Your Understanding 3 shows the consolidated statement of profit or loss for the Pepper group.

Additional information:

Salt's land increased in value by $500 over its value at the date of acquisition and there was a loss on its financial assets held at fair value through other comprehensive income (per IFRS 9, Chapter 9) for the year of $100. All items are deemed to accrue evenly over time except where otherwise indicated.

Consolidated statement of profit or loss and other comprehensive income for the Pepper group for the year ended 31 March 20X7

	$000
Revenue	34,600
Cost of sales	(18,150)
Gross profit	16,450
Operating expenses	(10,980)
Profit from operations	5,470
Investment income	1,650
Profit before tax	7,120
Income tax expense	(2,475)
Profit for the year	4,645
Other comprehensive income:	
Gain on revaluation of land	500
Loss on financial assets (100 × 9/12)	(75)
Total comprehensive income	5,070
Profit attributable to:	
Owners of parent (as in TYU 3 solution)	4,587
NCI (as in TYU 3 solution)	58
	4,645
Total comprehensive income attributable to:	
Owners of parent (balancing figure)	4,884
NCI (58 + (500 – (100 × 9/12) × 30%))	186
	5,070

Test your understanding 4

Papilla acquired 70% of Satago three years ago, when Satago's retained earnings were $430,000.

The financial statements of each company for the year ended 31 March 20X7 are as follows:

Statements of financial position as at 31 March 20X7

	P	S
	$000	$000
Non-current assets		
Property, plant and equipment	900	400
Investment in S at cost	700	–
Current assets	300	600
	1,900	1,000
Share capital ($1)	200	150
Share premium	50	–
Retained earnings	1,350	700
	1,600	850
Non-current liabilities	100	90
Current liabilities	200	60
	1,900	1,000

Statements of profit or loss for the year ended 31 March 20X7

	P	S
	$000	$000
Revenue	1,000	260
Cost of sales	(750)	(80)
Gross profit	250	180
Operating expenses	(60)	(35)
Profit from operations	190	145
Finance costs	(25)	(15)
Investment income	20	–
Profit before tax	185	130
Income tax expense	(100)	(30)
Profit for the year	85	100

You are provided with the following additional information:

(i) Satago had plant in its statement of financial position at the date of acquisition with a carrying amount of $100,000 but a fair value of $120,000. The plant had a remaining life of 10 years at acquisition. Depreciation is charged to cost of sales.

(ii) The Papilla group values the non-controlling interest at fair value. The fair value of the non-controlling interest at the date of acquisition was $250,000. Goodwill has been impaired by a total of 30% of its value at the reporting date, of which one third related to the current year.

(iii) At the start of the year Papilla transferred a machine to Satago for $15,000. The asset had a remaining useful life of 3 years at the date of transfer. It had a carrying amount of $12,000 in the books of Papilla at the date of transfer.

(iv) During the year Satago sold some goods to Papilla for $60,000 at a mark-up of 20%. 40% of the goods remained unsold at the year-end. At the year-end, Satago's books showed a receivables balance of $6,000 as being due from Papilla. This disagreed with the payables balance of $1,000 in Papilla's books due to Papilla having sent a cheque to Satago shortly before the year end which Satago had not yet received.

(v) Satago paid a dividend of $20,000 on 1 March 20X7.

Required:

Prepare the consolidated statement of financial position and consolidated statement of profit or loss for the year ended 31 March 20X7 for the Papilla group.

Analysis of a company within a group

The FR examination may contain a question involving the analysis of a company which is part of a group. Whilst intra-group transactions will be removed from the consolidated financial statements, these will not be removed from the individual financial statements. Therefore extra attention must be paid to transactions which may not be at market value, or may be lost if the company is removed from the group. This can include:

- Intra-group loans – these may be at low interest, which may change if the company is removed from the group, so the finance cost or investment income may have been manipulated
- Intra-group sales/purchases – these can be invoiced to artificially inflate revenue, or may be invoiced above or below market prices, which would not be maintained if the company were removed from the group

- Unrealised profits – Assets could have been sold at inflated prices within the group. The unrealised profits will be removed from the consolidated financial statements, but the profit will remain in the seller's individual statement of profit or loss.
- Shared costs/assets – The company may share assets with others in the group, an arrangement which would be lost if the company were removed from the group. Any additional costs that would be associated with the company as a standalone entity should also be taken into consideration.

6 Chapter summary

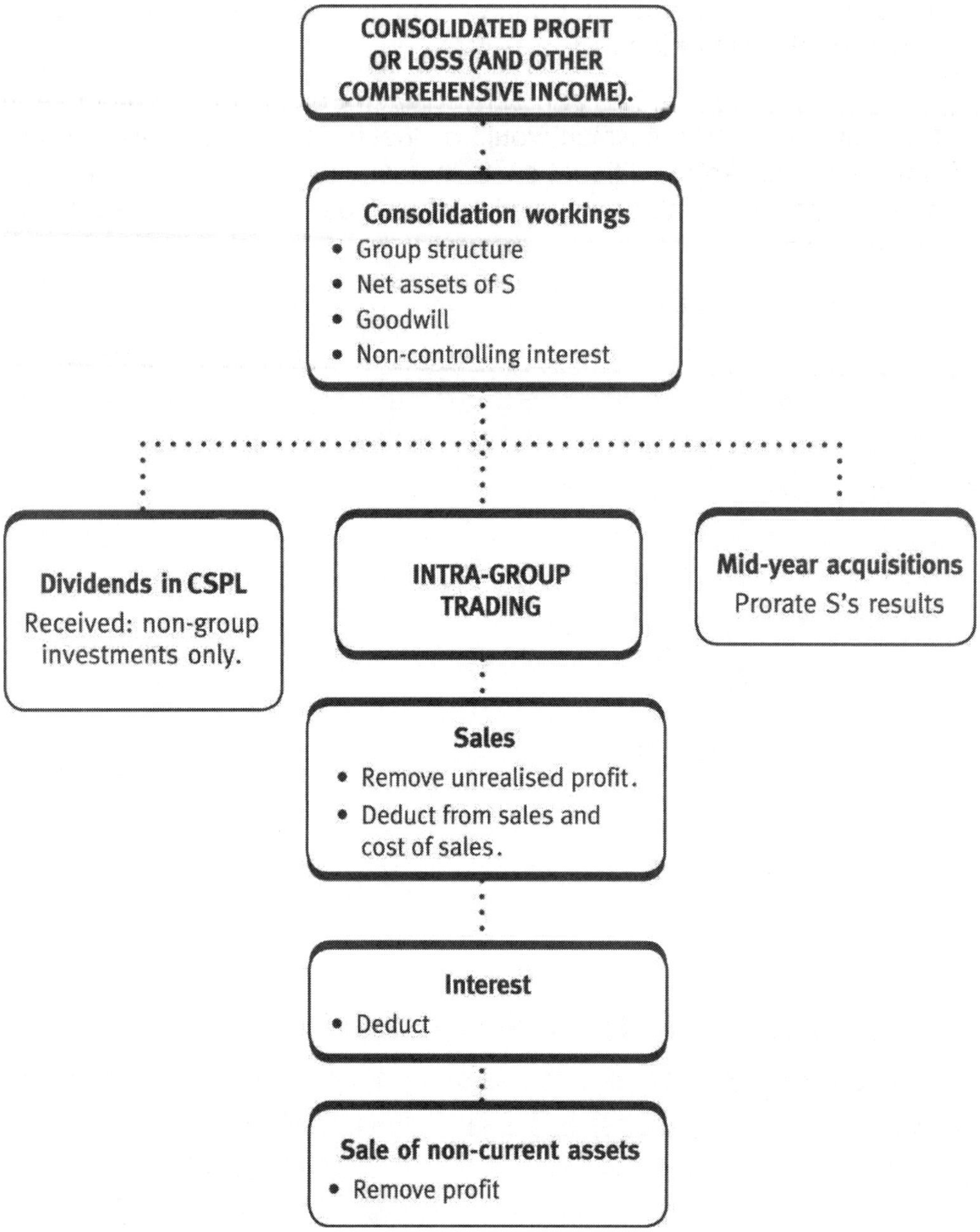

Test your understanding 5

1 The following figures relate to Barlow and its subsidiary Noon for the year ended 31 December 20X5.

	Barlow	**Noon**
Revenue	$600,000	$300,000
Cost of sales	$400,000	$200,000
Gross profit	$200,000	$100,000

During the year Barlow sold goods to Noon for $20,000, making a profit of $5,000. These goods were all sold by Noon before the year end.

Select the amounts to be recorded for total revenue and gross profit in the consolidated statement of profit or loss for Barlow for the year ended 31 December 20X5. Answers do not need to be selected from the same row.

Revenue	**Gross profit**
$000	**$000**
880	295
900	300

2 Pic Co acquired 80% of the ordinary shares of Nic Co on 31 December 20X4 when Nic Co's retained earnings were $20,000. At 31 December 20X5, Nic Co's retained earnings stood at $25,000. Neither entity has paid any dividend or made any other reserve transfers.

Calculate the non-controlling interest in the consolidated statement of profit or loss for the year ended 31 December 20X5.

$____________

3 Posh has owned 90% of Spice for many years. During the year, Posh sold goods to Spice for $50,000. These goods had originally cost Posh $40,000. Spice had not sold any of these goods by the year-end. The cost of sales figures for the two companies were as follows:

Posh $320,000, Spice $170,000.

At what value will cost of sales appear at in the consolidated statement of profit or loss?

A $500,000

B $480,000

C $450,000

D $430,000

4 During the current year, P sold goods to S for $520 at a mark-up of 30% on cost. At the year-end, S had sold all of these goods on to a fellow subsidiary, making no profit on the transaction. The fellow subsidiary still held all the goods in inventory at the year-end.

What is the PUP adjustment in the group accounts?

A Nil

B $156

C $120

D $145

5 Pink owns 75% of Scarlet. During 20X5, Scarlet sold goods to Pink for $75,000 at a profit margin of 25%.

How much will revenue be reduced by in the consolidated statement of profit or loss at the end of 20X5 if all of the goods remain in inventory at the year end?

A $75,000

B $18,750

C $14,063

D Nil

6 Cameron acquired a 60% holding in Clegg many years ago. At 31 December 20X9 Cameron held inventories with a carrying amount of $10,000, purchased from Clegg at cost plus 20%.

What is the effect of the above transaction on the consolidated statement of profit or loss for the year ended 31 December 20X9?

A Profit attributable to Owners of Cameron plc – Reduce by $1,000

Profit attributable to Non-controlling interest – Reduce by $667

B Profit attributable to Owners of Cameron plc – Reduce by $1,200

Profit attributable to Non-controlling interest – Reduce by $800

C Profit attributable to Owners of Cameron plc – Reduce by $1,667

Profit attributable to Non-controlling interest – No effect

D Profit attributable to Owners of Cameron plc – Reduce by $2,000

Profit attributable to Non-controlling interest – No effect

Test your understanding answers

Test your understanding 1

Prunes: Consolidated statement of profit or loss for the year ended 31 December 20X7

	$000
Revenue (600 + 300 – 20)	880
Cost of sales (360 + 140 – 20 + 4 **(W2)** + 15 (FV dep'n))	(499)
Gross profit	381
Operating expenses (93 + 45 + 5 (impairment))	(143)
Profit from operations	238
Finance costs	(3)
Profit before tax	235
Income tax expense (50 + 32)	(82)
Profit for the year	153
Attributable to:	
Owners of parent (153 – 14)	139
Non-controlling interest **(W3)**	14
	153

Workings:

(W1) Group structure

Prunes has owned 75% of Sultanas for 2 years.

(W2) Unrealised profit

	$000
(80% × 20) × 33%/133%	4

(W3) Non-controlling interest

	$000
Subsidiary profit for the year	80
Less:	
PUP	(4)
Impairment	(5)
Fair value depreciation	(15)
	56
NCI @ 25%	14

Test your understanding 2

Paris: Consolidated statement of profit or loss for the year ended 31 December 20X7

	$000
Revenue (3,200 + 2,560 – 600)	5,160
Cost of sales	
(2,200 + 1,480 – 600 + 30 (PUP) + 10 (FV dep'n))	(3,120)
Gross profit	2,040
Investment income (external only)	–
Distribution costs (160 + 120)	(280)
Administrative expenses (400 + 80 + 40)	(520)
Profit before tax	1,240
Income tax expense (400 + 480)	(880)
Profit for the year	360

Attributable to:	$000
Owners of parent	290
Non-controlling interest (W2)	70
	360

Workings:

(W1) Group structure

Paris

31 Dec X1 | 80%

London

(W2) Non-controlling interest

	$000
Subsidiary profit after tax	400
Less:	
Impairment	(40)
Fair value depreciation	(10)
	350
NCI share @ 20%	70

Test your understanding 3

Consolidated statement of profit or loss for the Pepper group for the year ended 31 March 20X7

	$
Revenue (31,200 + (9/12 × 10,400) – 4,400 **(W4)**)	34,600
Cost of Sales (17,800 + (9/12 × 5,600) + 375 **(W3)** – 4,400 **(W4)** + 175 **(W4)**)	(18,150)
Gross profit	16,450
Operating expenses (8,500 + (9/12 × 3,200) + 80 **(W5)**)	(10,980)
Profit from operations	5,470
Investment Income (2,000 – 350 **(W6)**)	1,650
Profit before tax	7,120
Income tax expense (2,100 + (9/12 × 500)	(2,475)
Profit for the year	4,645

Profit attributable to:	
Owners of parent (4,645 – 58)	4,587
NCI **(W2)**	58
	4,645

(W1) Group structure

P
| 70%
S

1 July 20x6 i.e. 9 months

(W2) Non-controlling Interests

	$
Subsidiary profit for the year (9/12 × $1,100)	825
Less:	
Fair value depreciation **(W3)**	(375)
PUP **(W4)**	(175)
Impairment **(W5)**	(80)
	195
NCI @ 30%	58

(W3) Fair value depreciation

FV Adjustment = $5,000

Depreciation Adjustment $5,000 × 1/10 × 9/12 = $375

(W4) Inter-company sales/PUP

Inter-co sales of $4,400 need eliminating from revenue and cost of sales.

PUP in inventory 35% × $500 = $175

The PUP will increase cost of sales and, since the subsidiary sold the goods, will reduce the NCI's share of profits.

(W5) Impairment

Impairment $800 × 10% = $80

(W6) Dividend

The subsidiary paid a dividend of $500 and so the parent will have recorded investment income of 70% × 500 = $350. As an intra-group transaction this needs eliminating.

Test your understanding 4

Papilla consolidated statement of financial position as at 31 March 20X7

	$000
Non-current assets	
Goodwill **(W3)**	245
Property, plant and equipment	
(900 + 400 + 20 – 6 – 2 (PUP))	1,312
Current assets (300 + 600 – 4 (PUP) – 6 + 5 intra-group)	895
	2,452
Share capital	200
Share premium	50
Retained earnings **(W5)**	1,456.2
	1,706.2
Non-controlling interest **(W4)**	296.8
	2,003
Non-current liabilities (100 + 90)	190
Current liabilities (200 + 60 – 1 intra-group)	259
	2,452

Consolidated statement of profit or loss for the year ended 31 March 20X7

	$000
Revenue (1,000 + 260 – 60)	1,200
Cost of Sales	
(750 + 80 – 60 + 2(Dep'n) + 4(PUP) + 2(PUP)	(778)
Gross profit	422
Operating expenses (60 + 35 + 35 (Impairment))	(130)
Profit from operations	292
Finance costs (25 + 15)	(40)
Investment Income (20 – (70% × 20))	6
Profit before tax	258
Income tax expense (100 + 30)	(130)
Profit after tax	128

Attributable to:	
Owners of parent (balance)	110
Non-controlling interest **(W4)**	18
	128

Workings:

(W1) Group structure

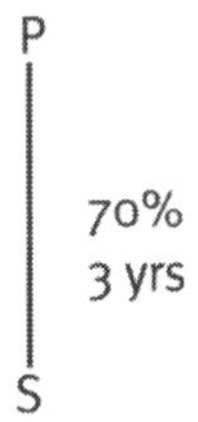

(W2) Net assets

	Acq'n	**SFP**	**Post**
	$000	$000	$000
Share capital	150	150	–
Retained earnings	430	700	270
FV adjustment machine	20	20	–
FV depreciation			
(20/10 × 3 years)		(6)	(6)
PUP **(W6)**		1	1
PUP **(W7)**	–	(4)	(4)
	600	861	261

(W3) Goodwill

Parent holding (investment) at fair value	700
NCI value at acquisition	250
	950
Less: Fair value of net assets at acquisition **(W2)**	(600)
	350
Impairment (30% × 350)	(105)
	245

Note: Of the total impairment of $105,000, one third i.e. $35,000 is to be charged to this years consolidated statement of profit or loss.

(W4) NCI – CSFP

NCI value at acquisition (as in **(W3)**)	250
NCI share of post-acquisition reserves **(W2)** (30% × 261)	78.3
NCI share of impairment **(W3)** (30% × 105)	(31.5)
	296.8

NCI – CSPL

Profit after tax	100
Dep'n (20 × 1/10)	(2)
PUP **(W6)**	1
PUP **(W7)**	(4)
Impairment **(W3)**	(35)
	60
NCI @ 30%	18

(W5) Group retained earnings

Parent retained earnings	1,350
PUP **(W6)**	(3)
Subsidiary post-acquisition profit (70% × 261)	182.7
Impairment (70% × 105)	(73.5)
	1,456.2

(W6) PUP – Non-current asset

Carrying amount in SFP (15 – (15 × 1/3 yrs))	10
Carrying amount without transfer should be (12 – (12 × 1/3 yrs))	(8)
PUP	2

Note that because both the profit and depreciation are included within cost of sales, we may adjust the net amount in cost of sales, although the depreciation element will affect the NCI calculation in W4. The full profit of $3,000 is adjusted in W5, the excess depreciation of $1,000 is adjusted in W2.

(W7) PUP – Inventory

Profit on sale (20/120 × 60)	10
Profit in inventory (40% × 10)	4

Test your understanding 5

1 Revenue = $600k + $300k – $20k intra-group sale = **$880k**

Cost of sales = $400k + $200k – $20k intra-group sale = $580k.

Therefore gross profit = $880k – $580k = **$300k**

2 **$1,000** – Non-controlling interest is calculated as the NCI% × Nic's profit for the year.

The change in retained earnings between the 2 years will be the profit for the year.

3 **C** – Cost of sales = $320k + $170k – $50k + $10k PUP = **$450k**

4 **C** – The unrealised profit = $520 × 30/130 = $120. As these items have been sold to another subsidiary, these remain in the group and the entire profit should be removed.

5 **A** – The full amount of the sale is always removed from revenue, regardless of the profit made or the amount left in inventory.

6 **A** – The total unrealised profit relating to the inventory = $10,000 × 20/120 = $1,667.

As the PUP relates to goods sold by the subsidiary, then this profit will be split between the parent's shareholders (taking 60% of the loss) and the NCI (taking 40%).

Chapter

20

Associates

Chapter learning objectives

Upon completion of this chapter you will be able to:

- define an associate
- explain the principles and reasoning for the use of equity accounting
- prepare a consolidated statement of financial position to include a single subsidiary and an associate
- prepare a consolidated statement of profit or loss to include a single subsidiary and an associate.

PER

One of the PER performance objectives (PO7) is to prepare external financial reports. You take part in preparing and reviewing financial statements – and all accompanying information – and you do it in accordance with legal and regulatory requirements. Working though this chapter should help you understand how to demonstrate that objective.

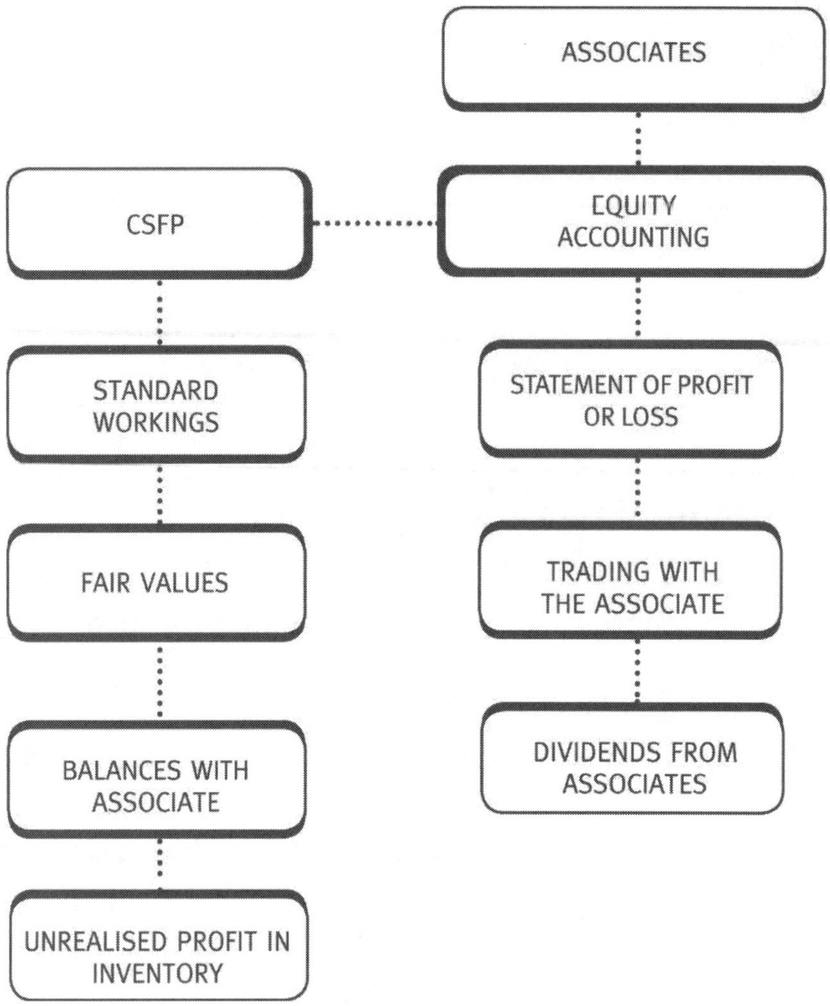

1 IAS 28 Investments in Associates and Joint Ventures

Definition of an associate

IAS 28 defines an **associate** as:

'An entity over which the investor has significant influence' (IAS 28, para 3).

'Significant influence is the power to participate in the financial and operating policy decisions of the investee but is not control or joint control over those policies' (IAS 28, para 3).

Significant influence is assumed with a shareholding of 20% to 50%.

Principles of equity accounting and reasoning behind it

Equity accounting is a method of accounting whereby the investment is initially recorded at cost and adjusted thereafter for the post-acquisition change in the investor's share of the net assets of the associate.

The effect of this is that the consolidated statement of financial position includes:

- 100% of the assets and liabilities of the parent and subsidiary company on a line by line basis
- an 'investment in associate' line within non-current assets which includes the cost of the investment plus the group share of post-acquisition reserves.

The consolidated statement of profit or loss includes:

- 100% of the income and expenses of the parent and subsidiary company on a line by line basis
- single line 'share of profit of associates' which includes the group share of any associate's profit after tax.

Equity method exemption

Accounting for associates according to IAS 28

The equity method of accounting is normally used to account for associates in the consolidated financial statements.

The equity method should not be used if:

- the investment is classified as held for sale in accordance with IFRS 5 or
- the parent is exempted from having to prepare consolidated accounts on the grounds that it is itself a wholly, or partially, owned subsidiary of another company (IFRS 10).

2 Associates in the consolidated statement of financial position

Preparing the consolidated statement of financial position (CSFP) including an associate

The CSFP is prepared on a normal line-by-line basis following the acquisition method for the parent and subsidiary.

The associate is included as a non-current asset investment calculated as:

	$000
Cost of investment	X
Share of post-acquisition profits	X
Less: Impairment losses	(X)
Less: PUP	(X)
	X

The group share of the associate's post-acquisition profits or losses, the impairment of associate investment and the PUP will also be included in the group retained earnings calculation (W5).

Standard workings

The calculations for an associate (A) can be incorporated into standard CSFP workings as follows.

(W1) Group structure

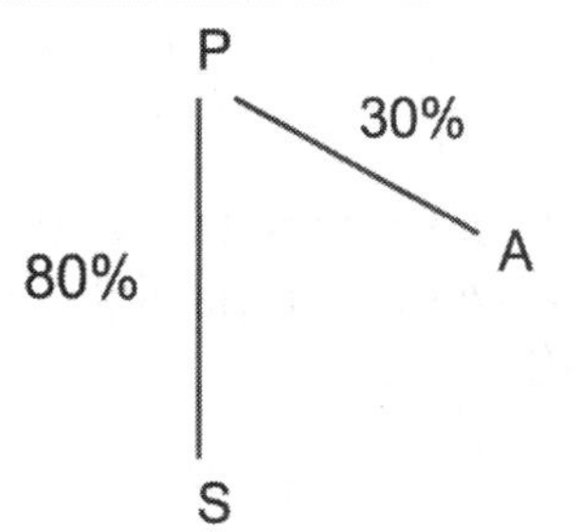

This indicates that

P owns 80% of the ordinary shares of S

P also owns 30% of the shares in A

(W2) Net assets of subsidiary

	At the date of acquisition	At the reporting date	Post-acquisition
	$	$	$
Share capital	X	X	–
Reserves:			
Share premium	X	X	–
Retained earnings	X	X	
Fair value adjustment	X	X	X
Fair value depreciation		(X)	(X)
PUP (where S is seller)		(X)	(X)
	X	X	X

(W3) Goodwill – Subsidiary

Parent holding (investment) at fair value	X
NCI value at acquisition	X
	X
Less:	
Fair value of net assets at acquisition **(W2)**	(X)
Goodwill at acquisition	X
Impairment	(X)
Goodwill per SFP	X

(W4) Non-controlling interest (NCI)

NCI value at acquisition **(W3)**	X
NCI share of subsidiary post-acquisition reserves **(W2)**	X
NCI share of impairment **(W3)** (fair value method only)	(X)
	X

(W5) Group retained earnings

	$
Parent retained earnings (100%)	X
Parent share of sub's post-acquisition retained earnings	X
Parent share of associate post-acquisition retained earnings	X
Less: Impairment losses to date (Subsidiary)	(X)
Less: Impairment losses to date (Associate)	(X)
Less: PUP (where P sells to S)	(X)
Less: PUP (where P sells to A or A sells to P)	(X)
	X

(W6) Investment in associate company

	$
Cost of investment	X
Parent share of post-acquisition profits **(W5)**	X
Less: Impairment **(W5)**	(X)
Less: PURP **(W5)**	(X)
	X

e.g

Illustration 1 – Associates in CSFP

Below are the statements of financial position of three companies as at 31 December 20X9.

	Dipsy	**Laa Laa**	**Po**
	$000	$000	$000
Non-current assets:			
Property, plant & equipment	1,120	980	840
Investments			
672,000 shares in Laa Laa	644	–	–
168,000 shares in Po	224	–	–
	1,988	980	840

Current assets:			
Inventory	380	640	190
Receivables	190	310	100
Bank	35	58	46
	605	1,008	336
	2,593	1,988	1,176
Equity:			
$1 ordinary shares	1,120	840	560
Retained earnings	1,232	602	448
	2,352	1,442	1,008
Current liabilities:			
Trade payables	150	480	136
Taxation	91	66	32
	2,593	1,988	1,176

You are also given the following information:

1 Dipsy acquired its shares in Laa Laa on 1 January 20X9 when Laa Laa had retained losses of $56,000.

2 Dipsy acquired its shares in Po on 1 January 20X9 when Po had retained earnings of $140,000.

3 An impairment test at the year-end shows that goodwill for Laa Laa remains unimpaired but the investment in Po has become impaired by $2,800.

4 The Dipsy Group values the non-controlling interest using the fair value method. The fair value of the non-controlling interest in Laa Laa on 1 January 20X9 was $160,000.

Prepare the consolidated statement of financial position of Dipsy for the year ended 31 December 20X9.

Solution

Dipsy: Consolidated statement of financial position as at 31 December 20X9

	$000	$000
Non-current assets:		
Goodwill **(W3)**		20.0
Property, plant & equipment (1,120 + 980)		2,100.0
Investment in associate **(W6)**		313.6
		2,433.6
Current assets:		
Inventory (380 + 640)	1,020.0	
Receivables (190 + 310)	500.0	
Receivables (35 + 58)	93.0	
		1,613.0
		4,046.6
Equity:		
$1 ordinary shares		1,120.0
Retained earnings **(W5)**		1,848.0
		2,968.0
Non-controlling interest **(W4)**		291.6
		3,259.6
Current liabilities:		
Trade payables (150 + 480)	630.0	
Taxation (91 + 66)	157.0	
		787.0
		4,046.6

Workings:

(W1) Group structure

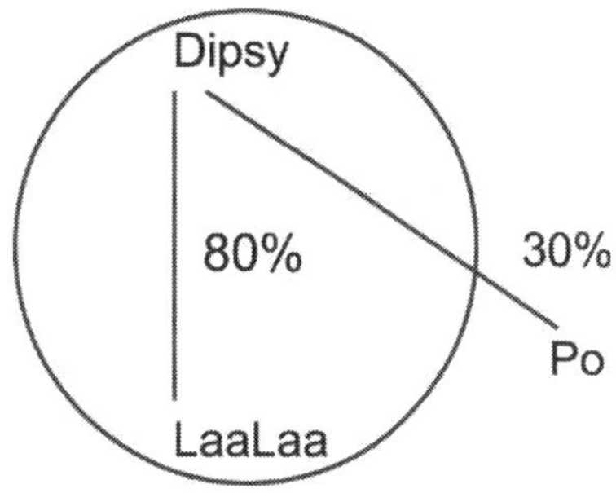

(W2) Net assets – Laa Laa

	Acquisition	Reporting date	Post-acquisition
	$000	$000	$000
Share capital	840	840	–
Retained earnings	(56)	602	658
	784	1,442	658

Note that Laa Laa has retained losses at the date of acquisition rather than the more usual retained earnings or profits.

(W3) Goodwill

	$000
Cost of investment	644
Fair value of NCI	160
	804
Less:	
100% net assets at acquisition	(784)
Total goodwill	20

(W4) Non-controlling interest

	$000
Fair value of NCI at acquisition	160.0
20% post-acquisition profit (20% × 658 **(W2)**)	131.6
	291.6

(W5) Group retained earnings

	$000
Dipsy (100%)	1,232.0
80% Laa Laa post-acquisition profit 80% × 658 **(W2)**	526.4
30% Po post-acquisition profit 30% × 448 – 140	92.4
Less: Impairments to date	(2.8)
	1,848.0

(W6) Investment in associate

	$000
Cost of investment	224.0
Post-acquisition profits **(W5)**	92.4
Less: Impairment **(W5)**	(2.8)
	313.6

Fair values and the associate

If the fair value of the associate's net assets at acquisition are materially different from their book value the net assets should be adjusted in the same way as for a subsidiary.

Balances with the associate

Generally the associate is considered to be outside the group. Therefore balances between group companies and the associate will remain in the consolidated statement of financial position.

So if a group company trades with the associate, the resulting payables and receivables will remain in the consolidated statement of financial position.

Unrealised profit in inventory

Unrealised profits on trading between group and associate must be eliminated **to the extent of the investor's interest** (i.e. % owned by parent).

Adjustment must be made for unrealised profit in inventory as follows.

1 Determine the value of closing inventory which is the result of a sale to or from the associate.

2 Use mark-up/margin to calculate the profit earned by the selling company.

3 Make the required adjustments as below:

Dr Share of profit of associate in SPL (Group retained earnings **(W5)** in CSOFP)

Cr Investment in associate (**W6**)

Test your understanding 1

Below are the statements of financial position of three entities as at 30 September 20X8

	P	S	A
	$000	$000	$000
Non-current assets			
Property, plant and equipment	14,000	7,500	3,000
Investments	10,000	–	–
	24,000	7,500	3,000
Current assets	6,000	3,000	1,500
	30,000	**10,500**	**4,500**
Equity			
Share capital			
($1 ordinary shares)	10,000	1,000	500
Retained earnings	7,500	5,500	2,500
	17,500	6,500	3,000
Non-current liabilities	8,000	1,250	500
Current liabilities	4,500	2,750	1,000
	30,000	**10,500**	**4,500**

Further information:

(i) P acquired 75% of the equity share capital of S several years ago, paying $5 million in cash. At this time the balance on S's retained earnings was $3 million.

(ii) P acquired 30% of the equity share capital of A on 1 October 20X6, paying $750,000 in cash. At 1 October 20X6 the balance on A's retained earnings was $1.5 million.

(iii) During the year, P sold goods to A for $1 million at a mark-up of 25%. At the year-end, A still held one quarter of these goods in inventory.

(iv) As a result of this trading, P was owed $250,000 by A at the reporting date. This agrees with the amount included in A's trade payables.

(v) At 30 September 20X8, it was determined that the investment in the associate was impaired by $35,000.

(vi) Non-controlling interests are valued using the fair value method. The fair value of the non-controlling interest in S at the date of acquisition was $1.6 million.

Required:

Prepare P's consolidated statement of financial position as at 30 September 20X8.

Test your understanding 2

P acquired 80% of S on 1 December 20X4 paying $4.25 in cash per share. At this date the balance on S's retained earnings was $870,000. On 1 March 20X7 P acquired 30% of A's ordinary shares. The consideration was settled by a share exchange of 4 new shares in P for every 3 shares acquired in A. The share price of P at the date of acquisition was $5. P has not yet recorded the acquisition of A in its books.

The statements of financial position of the three companies as at 30 November 20X7 are as follows:

	P	S	A
	$000	$000	$000
Non-current assets			
Property	1,300	850	900
Plant & equipment	450	210	150
Investments	1,825	–	–
Current assets			
Inventory	550	230	200
Receivables	300	340	400
Cash	120	50	140
	4,545	1,680	1,790
Share capital $1	1,800	500	250
Share premium	250	80	–
Retained earnings	1,145	400	1,200
	3,195	980	1,450

Non-current liabilities			
10% Loan notes	500	300	–
Current liabilities			
Payables	520	330	250
Taxation	330	70	90
	4,545	1,680	1,790

The following information is relevant:

(i) As at 1 December 20X4, plant in the books of S was determined to have a fair value of $50,000 in excess of its carrying amount. The plant had a remaining life of 5 years at this date.

(ii) During the post-acquisition period, S sold goods to P for $400,000 at a mark-up of 25%. P had a quarter of these goods still in inventory at the year-end.

(iii) In September 20X4 A sold goods to P for $150,000. These goods had cost A $100,000. P had $90,000 (at cost to P) in inventory at the year-end.

(iv) As a result of the above inter-company sales, P's books showed $50,000 and $20,000 as owing to S and A respectively at the year-end. These balances agreed with the amounts recorded in S's and A's books.

(v) Non-controlling interests are measured using the fair value method. The fair value of the non-controlling interest in S at the date of acquisition was $368,000. Goodwill has impaired by $150,000 at the reporting date. An impairment review found the investment in the associate to be impaired by $15,000 at the year-end.

(vi) A's profit after tax for the year is $600,000.

Required:

Prepare P's consolidated statement of financial position as at 30 November 20X7.

Test your understanding 3

The summarised statements of financial position of Bacup, Townley and Rishworth as at 31 March 20X7 are as follows:

	Bacup	Townley	Rishworth
	$000	$000	$000
Non-current assets:			
Property, plant & equipment	3,820	4,425	500
Development expenditure	–	200	–
Investments	1,600	–	–
	5,420	4,625	500
Current assets:			
Inventory	2,740	1,280	250
Receivables	1,960	980	164
Cash	1,260	–	86
	5,960	2,260	500
Total assets	11,380	6,885	1,000
Equity:			
Ordinary shares of 25 cents each	4,000	500	200
Reserves:			
Share premium	800	125	
Retained earnings			
– 1 April 20X6	2,300	380	450
– year to 31 March 20X7	1,760	400	150
	8,860	1,405	800
Current liabilities:			
Trade payables	2,120	3,070	142
Bank overdraft	–	2,260	–
Taxation	400	150	58
	2,520	5,480	200
Total equity and liabilities	11,380	6,885	1,000

The following information is relevant:

(i) **Investments**

Bacup acquired 1.6 million shares in Townley on 1 April 20X6 paying 75 cents per share. On 1 October 20X6 Bacup acquired 40% of the share capital of Rishworth for $400,000.

(ii) **Development expenditure**

Development expenditure is to be written off as incurred as it does not meet the criteria for capitalisation in IAS 38. The development expenditure in the statement of financial position of Townley relates to a project that was commenced on 1 April 20X5. At the date of acquisition the value of the capitalised expenditure was $80,000. None of the development expenditure of Townley has yet been amortised.

(iii) **Intra-group trading**

The inventory of Bacup includes goods at a transfer price of $200,000 purchased from Townley since the acquisition. The inventory of Rishworth includes goods at a transfer price of $125,000 purchased from Bacup. All transfers were at cost plus 25%.

The receivables of Bacup include an amount owing from Townley of $250,000. This does not agree with the corresponding amount in the books of Townley due to a cash payment of $50,000 made on 29 March 20X7, which had not been received by Bacup at the year-end.

(iv) It is group policy to value the non-controlling interest using the fair value at the date of acquisition. At the date of acquisition the fair value of the non-controlling interest in Townley was $95,000.

Required:

Prepare Bacup's consolidated statement of financial position as at 31 March 20X7.

3 Associates in the consolidated statement of profit or loss

Equity accounting

The equity method of accounting requires that the consolidated statement of profit or loss:

- does not include dividends from the associate
- instead includes the parent's share of the associate's profit after tax less any impairment of the associate in the year, presented below group profit from operations.

Trading with the associate

Generally the associate is considered to be outside the group.

Therefore any sales or purchases between group companies and the associate are not normally eliminated and will remain part of the consolidated figures in the statement of profit or loss.

It is normal practice to adjust for the unrealised profit in inventory. Only P's share of the unrealised profit must be adjusted. Regardless of which company sells to the other, this amount should be deducted from the share of the associate's profit.

e.g

Illustration 2 – Associates in consolidated SPL

Below are the statements of profit or loss for P, S and A for the year ended 30 September 20X8

Statements of profit or loss for the year ended 30 September 20X8

	P	S	A
	$000	$000	$000
Revenue	8,000	4,500	3,000
Operating expenses	(4,750)	(2,700)	(2,050)
Profit from operations	3,250	1,800	950
Finance costs	(750)	(100)	(50)
Profit before tax	2,500	1,700	900
Income tax expense	(700)	(500)	(300)
Profit for the year	1,800	1,200	600

Further information:

- P acquired 80% of S several years ago.
- P acquired 30% of the equity share capital of A on 1 October 20X6.
- During the current year, P sold goods to A for $1 million at a mark-up of 25%. At the year-end, A still held one quarter of these goods in inventory.
- At 30 September 20X8, it was determined that the investment in the associate was impaired by $35,000, of which $20,000 related to the current year.

Required:

Prepare P's consolidated statement of profit or loss for the year ended 30 September 20X8.

Solution

Consolidated statement of profit or loss for the year ended 30 September 20X8

	$000
Revenue (8,000 + 4,500)	12,500
Operating expenses (4,750 + 2,700)	(7,450)
Profit from operations	5,050
Share of associate ((30% × 600) – 20 imp – 15 PUP **(W1)**)	145
Finance costs (750 + 100)	(600)
Profit before tax	4,345
Income tax expense (700 + 500)	(1,200)
Profit for the year	3,145
Attributable to:	
Parent shareholders (Balancing figure)	2,905
NCI (20% × 1,200)	240

(W1) PUP

Inter-company trading between the parent and associate are not eliminated as the associate is outside the group. Therefore, no adjustment in respect of the sale for $1 million needs to be made.

PUP = P's % × profit in inventory

Profit on sale (25/125 × $1,000,000)	$200,000
Profit in inventory (1/4 × $200,000)	$50,000
PUP (30% × $50,000)	$15,000

In the CSPL, the PUP will be deducted from the parent's share of the associate's profit for the year.

Test your understanding 4

Below are the statements of profit or loss of the Barbie group and its related companies as at 31 December 20X8.

	Barbie	Ken	Alice
	$000	$000	$000
Revenue	385	100	60
Cost of sales	(185)	(60)	(20)
Gross profit	200	40	40
Operating expenses	(50)	(15)	(10)
Profit before tax	150	25	30
Income tax expense	(50)	(12)	(10)
Profit for the year	100	13	20

You are also given the following information:

(i) Barbie acquired 45,000 ordinary shares in Ken a number of years ago. Ken has 50,000 $1 ordinary shares.

(ii) Barbie acquired 60,000 ordinary shares in Alice a number of years ago. Alice has 200,000 $1 ordinary shares.

(iii) During the current year Alice sold goods to Barbie for $28,000. Barbie still holds some of these goods in inventory at the year end. The profit element included in these remaining goods is $2,000.

(iv) Non-controlling interests are valued using the fair value method.

(v) Goodwill and the investment in the associate were impaired for the first time during the year as follows:

Alice $2,000

Ken $3,000

Impairment of the subsidiary's goodwill should be charged to operating expenses.

Prepare Barbie's consolidated statement of profit or loss for the year ended 31 December 20X8.

4 Chapter summary

Associate

An entity over which the investor has significant influence.

EQUITY ACCOUNTING

Statement of financial position

Cost of investment	X
Share of post acquisition profits	X
Less impairment losses	(X)
	X

Standard workings

(W5) group retained earnings

(W6) investment in associate.

Fair values

Adjust associate's accounts for consolidation purposes where net assets not recorded at fair value.

Balances with associate

Do not cancel.

Unrealised profit in inventory

Deduct from group reserves and investment in associate

Statement of profit or loss

Group share of the associate's profit after tax less any impairment in the year.

Trading with the associate

Do not eliminate sales or purchases.

Dividends from associates

Exclude from consolidated statement of profit or loss

Unrealised profit in inventory

Deduct from 'Share of profit of associate'

Test your understanding 5

The following are the summarised accounts of H, S, and A for the year ended 30 June 20X9.

Statements of financial position as at 30 June 20X9

	H	S	A
	$	$	$
Non-current assets			
Property, plant and equipment	87,000	98,000	62,000
Investments			
S (100%)	115,000		
A (30%)	15,000		
Current assets	74,000	40,000	9,000
	291,000	128,000	71,000
Share capital ($1 shares)	200,000	75,000	35,000
Retained earnings	89,000	51,000	34,000
Liabilities	2,000	2,000	2,000
	291,000	128,000	71,000

Statements of profit or loss for the year ended 30 June 20X9

	H	S	A
	$	$	$
Revenue	500,000	200,000	100,000
Operating costs	(400,000)	(140,000)	(60,000)
Profit from operations	100,000	60,000	40,000
Income tax expense	(23,000)	(21,000)	(14,000)
Profit for the year	77,000	39,000	26,000

The shares in S and A were acquired on 1 July 20X6 when the retained earnings of S were $15,000 and the retained earnings of A were $10,000.

At the date of acquisition, the fair value of S's non-current assets, which at that time had a remaining useful life of ten years, exceeded the book value by $10,000.

During the year S sold goods to H for $10,000 at a margin of 50%. At the year-end H had sold 80% of the goods.

At 30 June 20X9 the goodwill in respect of S had been impaired by 30% of its original amount, of which the current year loss was $1,200. At 30 June 20X9 the investment in A had been impaired by $450, of which the current year loss was $150.

Required:

Prepare H's consolidated statement of profit or loss for the year ended 30 June 20X9 and consolidated statement of financial position as at 30 June 20X9.

Test your understanding 6

1 **Which of the following are likely to be accounted for as an associate in the consolidated financial statements of TN?**

(i) A 25% shareholding in ZT. TN can appoint a director to the board. There are 4 directors on the board in total, and none have control.

(ii) A 25% shareholding in ZU. ZU is 70% owned by a company called TU.

(iii) A 25% shareholding in ZV. TN have also got an arrangement with other shareholders allowing them access to 55% of the voting rights in TN.

A (i) only

B (i) and (ii)

C (ii) and (iii)

D All three

2 **Which TWO of the following issues would require adjustment in a consolidated statement of financial position?**

A A balance owed from the parent to the associate

B Cash in transit from the associate to the parent

C Unrealised profit relating to goods sold from the associate to the parent

D The value of the associate being impaired at the end of the year

3 On 1 January 20X1, P purchased 30% of the shares in A for $350,000. At this date, A's net assets stood at $700,000.

At 31 December 20X1, A has net assets of $750,000. P sold goods worth $80,000 to A at a margin of 25%. Half of these goods remain in inventory at the year end.

What is the value of the investment in associate as at 31 December 20X1?

$__________

4 On 1 January 20X1, P purchased 30% of the shares in A for $600,000. At this date, A's net assets stood at $400,000.

At 31 December 20X2, A has net assets of $600,000. A made a profit in the current year of $80,000. Since acquisition, P's investment in A has been impaired by $25,000. Of this, $10,000 relates to the current year.

What is the share of profit of associate to be included in the consolidated statement of profit or loss for the year ended 31 December 20X2?

A $14,000

B $21,000

C $35,000

D $50,000

5 On 1 July 20X1, P purchased 90% of the shares in S and 40% of the shares in A. Extracts from the statements of profit or loss for the year ended 31 December 20X1 are shown below.

	P	S	A
	$000	$000	$000
Profit before tax	200	(80)	90
Income tax expense	(80)	20	(20)
Profit for the year	120	(60)	70

During the year, goodwill in S has been impaired by $10,000. The non-controlling interest is valued using the fair value method.

What is the profit attributable to P's shareholders in the consolidated statement of profit or loss for the year ended 31 December 20X1?

A $84,000

B $85,000

C $97,000

D $98,000

Test your understanding answers

Test your understanding 1

Consolidated statement of financial position for P group as at 30 September 20X8

	$000
Non-current assets	
Goodwill **(W3)**	2,600
Property, plant and equipment (14,000 + 7,500)	21,500
Investments	
(10,000 – 5,000 (investment in S) – 750 (investment in A))	4,250
Investment in associate **(W6)**	1,000
	29,350
Current assets (6,000 + 3,000)	9,000
	38,350
Equity	
Share capital	10,000
Group retained earnings **(W5)**	9,625
Non-controlling interest **(W4)**	2,225
	21,850
Non-current liabilities (8,000 + 1,250)	9,250
Current liabilities (4,500 + 2,750)	7,250
	38,350

Workings:

(W1) Group structure

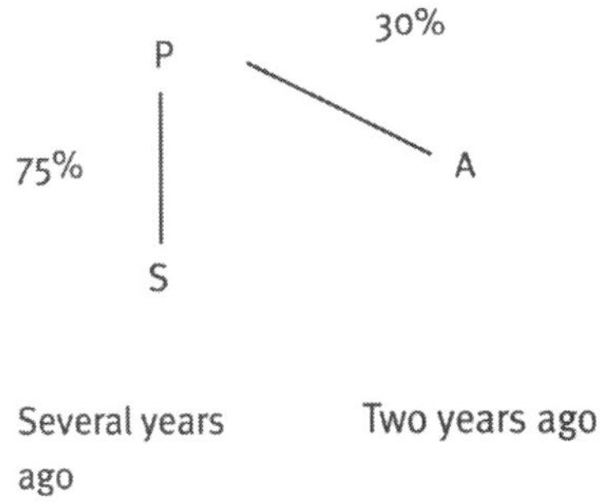

(W2) Net assets

	Acquisition	Reporting date	Post-acquisition
	$000	$000	$000
Share capital	1,000	1,000	
Retained earnings	3,000	5,500	2,500
	4,000	6,500	2,500

(W3) Goodwill

	$000
Parent holding (investment) at fair value:	
Cash	5,000
Fair value of NCI	1,600
	6,600
Less:	
Fair value of net assets at acquisition (W2)	(4,000)
Total goodwill	2,600

(W4) Non-controlling interest

Fair value of NCI at acquisition **(W3)**	1,600
25% × post-acquisition profit (25% × 2,500 **(W2)**)	625
	2,225

(W5) Group retained earnings

100% parent	7,500
Subsidiary (75% × 2,500 (W2))	1,875
Associate (30% × (2,500 – 1,500))	300
PUP **(W7)**	(15)
Impairment of associate	(35)
	9,625

(W6) Investment in associate

Cost of investment	750
Share of post-acquisition profit **(W5)**	300
Impairment **(W5)**	(35)
PUP **(W5)**	(15)
	1,000

(W7) PUP

Profit on sale (25/125 × 1,000)	200
Profit in inventory (1/4 × 200)	50
Group share (30% × 50)	15

Test your understanding 2

Consolidated statement of financial position as at 30 November 20X7

	$000
Non-current assets	
Goodwill **(W3)**	418
Property (1,300 + 850)	2,150
Plant & equipment (450 + 210 + 50 – 30 **(W2)**)	680
Investments (1,825 – 1,700 (subsidiary))	125
Investment in associate **(W6)**	611
Current assets	
Inventory (550 + 230 – 20 **(W7)**)	760
Receivables (300 + 340 – 50 intra-group)	590
Cash (120 + 50)	170
	5,504
Share capital (1,800 + 100 **(W6)**)	1,900
Share premium (250 + 400 **(W6)**)	650
Retained earnings **(W5)**	720
	3,270
Non-controlling interests **(W4)**	234
	3,504

Non-current liabilities	
10% Loan notes (500 + 300)	800
Current liabilities	
Trade payables (520 + 330 – 50 intra-group)	800
Taxation (330 + 70)	400
	5,504

Workings:

(W1) Group structure

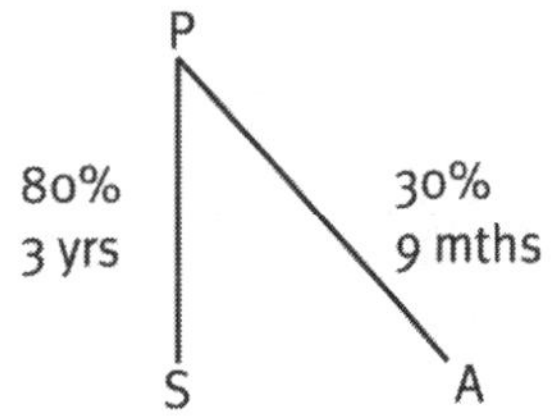

(W2) Net assets

	At the date of acquisition $	At the reporting date $	Post-acquisition $
Share capital	500	500	–
Share premium	80	80	–
Retained earnings	870	400	(470)
FV adjustment plant	50	50	–
Depreciation adjustment (50 × 3/5)	–	(30)	(30)
PURP **(W7)**	–	(20)	(20)
	1,500	980	(520)

(W3) Goodwill

	$000
Parent holding (investment) at fair value:	
Cash	
((80% × 500) × $4.25)	1,700
Fair value of NCI	368
	2,068
Less:	
Fair value of net assets at acquisition	(1,500)
Goodwill at acquisition	568
Impairment	(150)
Carrying goodwill	418

(W4) Non-controlling interest

Fair value of NCI	368
20% post-acquisition loss	
(20% × (520))	(104)
Impairment	
(20% × 150 **(W3)**)	(30)
	234

(W5) Group retained earnings

100% parent	1,145
PURP (W8)	(9)
Sub (80% × (520))	(416)
Assoc (30% × (600 × 9/12))	135
Impairment (150 **(W3)** × 80%)	(120)
Impairment of associate	(15)
	720

(W6) Investment in associate

Cost of investment (30% × 250) × 4/3 × $5)*	500
Share of post-acquisition profit (30% × (600 × 9/12))	135
PUP **(W8)**	(9)
Impairment	(15)
	611

*Share exchange:	
100 shares issued at $5	
Cr Share capital (100 × $1)	100
Cr Share premium (100 × $4)	400

(W7) PUP – Subsidiary

Profit on sale (25/125 × 400)	80
Profit in inventory (1/4 × 80)	**20**

(W8) PUP – Associate

Profit on sale (150 – 100)	50
Profit in inventory (90/150 × 50)	30
Group share (30% × 30)	**9**

Test your understanding 3

Consolidated statement of financial position as at 31 March 20X7

	$000	$000
Non-current assets:		
Property, plant and equipment (3,820 + 4,425)		8,245
Goodwill **(W3)**		370
Investment in associate **(W6)**		420
		9,035
Current assets:		
Inventory (2,740 + 1,280 – 40 **(W7)**)	3,980	
Receivables (1,960 + 980 – 250 intra-group)	2,690	
Bank (1,260 + 50 cash in transit)	1,310	
		7,980
Total assets		17,015
Ordinary shares of 25 cents each		4,000

Reserves:		
Share premium		800
Retained earnings **(W5)**		4,272
		9,072
Non-controlling interest **(W4)**		143
		9,215
Current liabilities:		
Payables (2,120 + 3,070 – 200 intra-group)	4,990	
Bank overdraft	2,260	
Taxation (400 + 150)	550	
		7,800
Total equity and liabilities		17,015

Workings:

(W1) Group structure

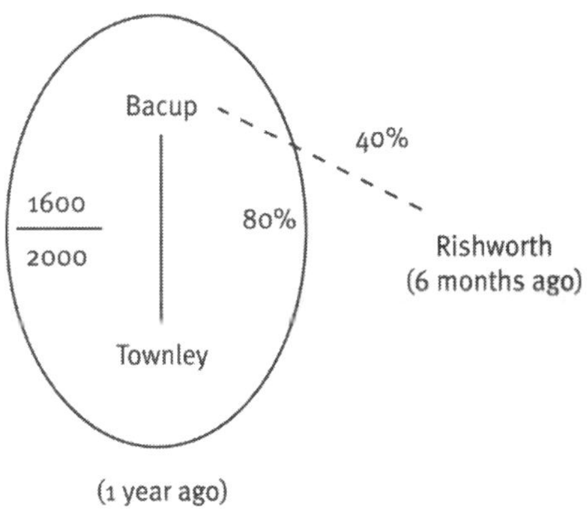

(W2) Net assets in subsidiary

	Acquisition	Reporting date	Post-acquisition
	$	$	$
Share capital	500	500	–
Share premium	125	125	–
Retained earnings	380	780	400
Development w/off	(80)	(200)	(120)
PUP **(W7)**	–	(40)	(40)
	925	1,165	240

(W3) Goodwill

	$000
Parent holding (investment) at fair value (1,600 × $0.75)	1,200
NCI value at acquisition	95
	1,295
Fair value of net assets at acquisition **(W2)**	(925)
Goodwill on acquisition	370

(W4) Non-controlling interest

	$000
NCI value at acquisition **(W3)**	95
NCI share of post-acquisition reserves **(W2)** (20% × 240)	48
	143

(W5) Retained earnings

	$000
Bacup (2,300 + 1,760)	4,060
P (see below)	(10)
Townley (80% × 240)	192
Rishworth (150 profit for year × 6/12) × 40%	30
	4,272

– PUP = Sold by Bacup to Rishworth, group share only as it is an associate, 40% × ($125,000 × 25/125) = $10,000

(W6) Investment in associate

	$000
Cost of investment	400
Share of post-acquisition profits **(W5)**	30
PUP **(W5)**	(10)
	420

(W7) PUP

$200,000 × 25/125 = $40,000

Test your understanding 4

Barbie: Consolidated statement of profit or loss for the year ended 31 December 20X8

	$000
Revenue (385 + 100)	485.0
Cost of sales (185 + 60)	(245.0)
Gross profit	240.0
Operating expenses (50 + 15 + 3 impairment)	(68.0)
Profit from operations	172.0
Share of profits of associate **(W3)**	3.4
Profit before tax	175.4
Income tax expense (50 + 12)	(62.0)
Profit for the year	113.4
Attributable to:	
Equity holders of the parent	112.4
Non-controlling interest **(W2)**	1.0
	113.4

Workings:

(W1) Group structure

Ken 45,000/50,000 = 90%

Alice 60,000/200,000 = 30%

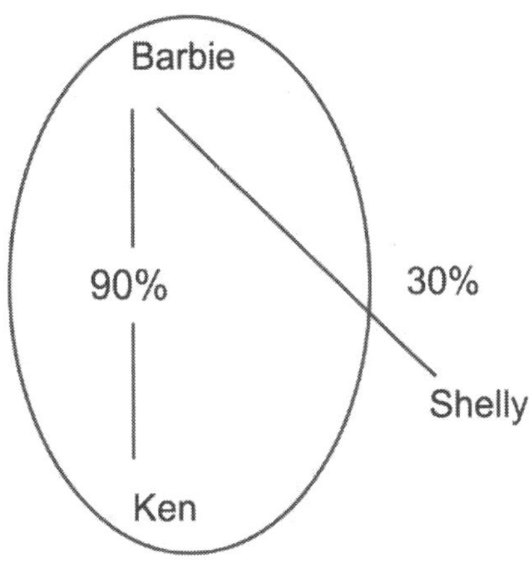

(W2) NCI in Ken

	$000
Subsidiary's profit after tax	13
Less: Impairment	(3)
Adjusted subsidiary profit	10
NCI @ 10%	1

(W3) Share of associate

	$000
30% of associate profit for the year (30% × 20)	6
Less: 30% of PURP (30% × 2)	(0.6)
Impairment	(2)
	3.4

Test your understanding 5

H Group: Statement of profit or loss for the year ended 30 June 20X9

	$
Revenue (500,000 + 200,000 – 10,000 intra-group)	690,000
Operating expenses (400,000 + 140,000 – 10,000 intra-group + 1,200 impairment + 1,000 FV dep'n + 1,000 PUP)	(533,200)
Profit from operations	156,800
Share of profits of associate company (30% × 26,000) – 150 impairment	7,650
Profit before tax	164,450
Income tax expense (23,000 + 21,000)	(44,000)
Profit for the year	120,450
Attributable to:	
Non-controlling interests (N/A)	–
Parent shareholders (balance)	120,450
	120,450

Consolidated statement of financial position as at 30 June 20X9

	$
Non-current assets	
Goodwill **(W3)**	10,500
Investment in associate **(W6)**	21,750
Property, plant and equipment	
(87,000 + 88,000 + 10,000 FV – 3,000 FV dep'n **(W2)**)	182,000
Current assets (74,000 + 40,000 – 1,000 PUP **(W2)**)	113,000
	327,250
Equity	
Share capital	200,000
Retained earnings **(W5)**	123,250
Non-controlling interest **(W4)**	–
Liabilities (2,000 + 2,000)	4,000
	327,250

Workings:

(W1) Group structure

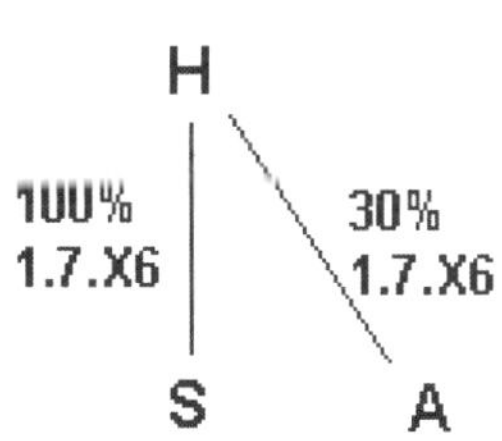

(W2) Net assets

	Acquisition	Reporting date	Post-acquisition
	$	$	$
Share capital	75,000	75,000	
Retained earnings	15,000	51,000	36,000
Fair value adjustment	10,000	10,000	
Depreciation (3/10 × 10,000)	–	(3,000)	(3,000)
PUP (10,000 × 50% × 20%)		(1,000)	(1,000)
	100,000	132,000	32,000

(W3) Goodwill

	$
Cost of investment	115,000
Fair value of net assets at acquisition **(W2)**	(100,000)
	15,000
Less: Impairment loss (30% × 15,000)	(4,500)
	10,500

(W4) Non-controlling interest

N/A, 100% subsidiary

(W5) Retained earnings

	$
Parent	89,000
Less: Impairments (4,500 **(W3)** + 450)	(4,950)
Share of post-acquisition profits	
(S: 100% × 32,000 **(W2)**)	32,000
(A **(W6)**)	7,200
	123,250

(W6) Investment in associate

	$
Cost	15,000
Share of increase in net assets	
(30% × (34,000 – 10,000))	7,200
Less: Impairment **(W5)**	(450)
	21,750

Test your understanding 6

1 **A** – Item (ii) is likely to be regarded as a financial asset, as TN have no significant influence. Item (iii) is likely to be classed as a subsidiary, as TN seem able to exercise control.

2 **C and D** – Balances between the parent and associate are not adjusted, whether there are items in transit or not. Unrealised profits and impairments are items that must be adjusted in the consolidated statement of financial position.

3 **$362,000** – See below.

Investment in associate

	$000
Cost of investment	350
Share of post-acquisition profits (30% × 50)	15
PUP **(W1)**	(3)
	362

(W1) PUP

With an associate PUP, we only adjust P's share of the PUP.

$80k × 25% = $20k × 1/2 left in inventory = $10k × 30% = $3k

4 **A** – See below.

Share of profit of associate

	$000
P's share of profit for the year (30% × 80)	24
Impairment in the year	(10)
	14

In the statement of profit or loss, we are only looking for the current year's profit and impairment, not the cumulative amount.

5 **D** – see below.

	$000
100% × P's profit	120
90% × S's profit (90% × (60) × 6/12)	(27)
40% × A's profit (40% × 70 × 6/12)	14
90% × Impairment (90% × 10)	(9)
	98

Note: Remember to time-apportion the subsidiary and associate, as both were mid-year acquisitions. As the NCI is valued at fair value, the impairment is split between P and the NCI.

Chapter

21

Group disposals

Chapter learning objectives

Upon completion of this chapter you will be able to:

- explain how a disposal is treated in the parent company financial statements
- explain how a disposal is treated in the consolidated financial statements
- account for the disposal of an entire subsidiary.

PER

One of the PER performance objectives (PO6) is to record and process transactions and events. You use the right accounting treatments for transactions and events. These should be both historical and prospective – and include non-routine transactions. Working though this chapter should help you understand how to demonstrate that objective.

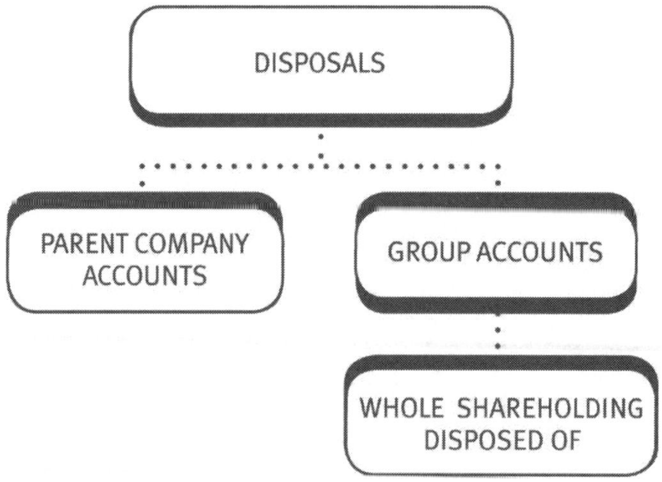

In this chapter we will be considering how to deal with the situation where a parent sells its shareholding in a subsidiary during the year. We will have to calculate a profit or loss on disposal in the statement of profit or loss of both the parent and the group.

In the FR exam, a 20-mark group accounts preparation question will not include disposal of a subsidiary, but aspects of this can be tested elsewhere in the exam, including within interpretations questions, where candidates may be required to analyse the impact of a disposal. This chapter contains an example of a disposal showing the effect on the consolidated financial statements as an illustration, but a candidate will not be required to do this in the exam.

1 Disposals

When a shareholding in a subsidiary is disposed of it must be reflected in:

- the parent company's individual financial statements and
- the group financial statements.

2 Parent company financial statements

Gain to parent company

The gain/loss on disposal in the parent company's accounts is calculated as follows:

	$
Sale proceeds	X
Carrying amount of investment	(X)
Parent gain/loss on disposal	X(X)

The gain is reported as an exceptional item –

- must be disclosed separately on the face of the parent's SPL
- after profit from operations.

Any tax on the gain is calculated by reference to the gain in the parent's individual financial statements.

3 Consolidated financial statements – Full disposal

Disposal of whole subsidiary

The impact of the disposal on the financial statements can be seen below.

- **Statement of profit or loss**
  - 100% of the subsidiary's results consolidated up to date of disposal
  - Gain/(loss) on disposal.
- **Statement of financial position**
  - At the year-end no shares are held by the parent and therefore the disposed subsidiary is not included in the group statement of financial position.
  - Gain/loss on disposal to be included within retained earnings

Gain on disposal

	$	$
Sales proceeds		X
Net assets at date of disposal	X	
Net goodwill at date of disposal	X	
NCI at date of disposal	(X)	
		(X)
Group gain/loss on disposal		X(X)

This gain will be included in the consolidated statement of profit or loss.

Note: Any tax on the gain is calculated using the gain in the parent's individual financial statements.

Carrying amount of goodwill at the date of disposal

	$
Calculated as seen before:	
Consideration transferred	X
NCI at acquisition (fair value or proportional method)	X
	X
100% of the fair value of net assets at acquisition	(X)
Goodwill at acquisition	X
Less: Impairments to date of disposal	(X)
Goodwill at disposal	X

Carrying amount of net assets at date of disposal

Calculated as follows:	
Net asset b/f	X
Profit/(loss) for current period to disposal date	X(X)
Dividends paid prior to disposal	(X)
Net assets at disposal	X

Note: The net assets at disposal may also include any remaining fair value adjustments to the subsidiary's net assets. The amount to include in net assets at disposal is the fair value adjustment made on acquisition, less fair value depreciation to date between acquisition and disposal. It may be helpful to use a standard W2 for the figures at the disposal date.

Non-controlling interest (NCI) at disposal

(i) **Fair value (FV) method**

If using the FV method, you will either be given the FV at the date of disposal, or you will need to calculate as below:

NCI at acquisition	X
NCI % of S's retained profits post-acquisition up to disposal	X
NCI % of impairment	(X)
Non-controlling interest at date of disposal	X

(ii) **Proportion of net assets method**

If non-controlling interest is valued as the proportion of net assets, then the NCI at disposal is NCI % of S's net assets at the date of disposal.

Alternatively, you can use the method below.

NCI at acquisition	X
NCI % of S's retained profits post-acquisition up to disposal	X
Non-controlling interest at date of disposal	X

Test your understanding 1

Rock acquired a 70% investment in Dog for $2,000 two years ago. It is group policy to measure non-controlling interests at fair value at the date of acquisition. The fair value of the non-controlling interest in Dog at the date of acquisition was $800 and the fair value of Dog's net assets was $1,900. The goodwill has not been impaired.

Rock disposed of all of its shares in Dog for sale proceeds of $3,000. The fair value of Dog's net assets at the date of disposal was $2,400.

Required:

Calculate the profit/loss on disposal that would be recorded in:

1 Rock's individual statement of profit or loss.

2 Rock's consolidated statement of profit or loss.

Test your understanding 2 – Kathmandu

The statements of profit or loss for the year ended 31 December 20X9 are as follows:

Statements of profit or loss for the year ended 31 December 20X9

	Kathmandu	Nepal
	$	$
Revenue	553,000	450,000
Operating costs	(450,000)	(400,000)
Operating profits	103,000	50,000
Investment income	8,000	–
Profit before tax	111,000	50,000
Income tax expense	(40,000)	(14,000)
Profit for the period	71,000	36,000

Additional information:

On 1 January 20X5 Kathmandu acquired 70% of the shares of Nepal for $100,000 when the fair value of Nepal's net assets was $110,000. Nepal has equity capital of $50,000. At that date, the fair value of the non-controlling interest was $40,000. It is group policy to measure the NCI at fair value at the date of acquisition.

Nepal paid a $10,000 dividend on 31 March 20X9.

Nepal had retained earnings of $80,000 on 1 January 20X9.

Goodwill has not been impaired.

Required:

Prepare the group statement of profit or loss for the year ended 31 December 20X9 for the Kathmandu group on the basis that Kathmandu sold its holding in Nepal on 1 July 20X9 for $200,000. This disposal is not yet recognised in any way in Kathmandu's statement of profit or loss.

Alternative presentation – if subsidiary represents a discontinued operation

The disposal of a subsidiary may meet the definition of a discontinued operation in accordance with IFRS 5, and would therefore be presented as such.

This would mean that in the statement of profit or loss, the results from the subsidiary would be presented as a single line 'Profit/(loss) from discontinued operations', rather than being consolidated line by line.

4 Chapter summary

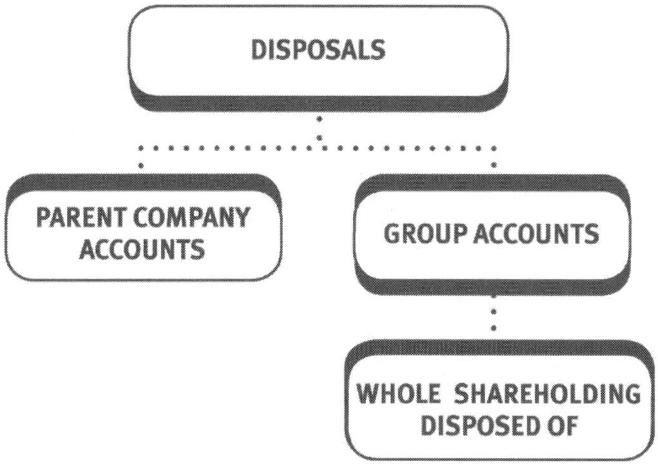

Test your understanding 3

Hague has held a 60% investment in Maude for several years, using the fair value method to value the non-controlling interest. A quarter of the goodwill has been impaired. The group's year end is 31 December 20X5. A disposal of this investment has been made on 31 October 20X5 for sale proceeds of $10,000. Details are:

	$
Cost of investment	6,000
Maude – Fair value of net assets at acquisition	2,000
Maude – Net assets at disposal	3,000
Maude – Fair value of NCI at acquisition	1,000

Required:

Calculate the profit/loss arising:

(i) in Hague's individual financial statements

(ii) in the consolidated financial statements.

Test your understanding 4

1 **Which of the following facts about disposals of a subsidiary are true?**

A The profit or loss on disposal of a subsidiary should be recorded in Other Comprehensive Income

B The disposal of a subsidiary has no impact on the parent's individual financial statements

C The non-controlling interest at the date of disposal must be removed from the statement of financial position

D Only the parent's share of the subsidiary's net assets must be removed from the statement of financial position

Data for Questions 2 and 3

Pulis acquired 70% of Seedorf's 1 million $1 shares on 1 January 20X2 for $2.5 million, but decided to sell the entire holding on 1 July 20X5 for $4 million. Goodwill had not been impaired during this period. The non-controlling interest was valued using the fair value method at $500,000 at the date of acquisition and $700,000 at the date of disposal. Seedorf had retained earnings of $600,000 on 1 January 20X2, and $900,000 on 1 January 20X5. Seedorf made a profit of $200,000 during 20X5. No fair value adjustments were required at acquisition.

2 **What is the goodwill to be removed in the calculation of profit or loss on disposal?**

$__________

3 **What are the net assets of Seedorf at the date of disposal?**

$__________

4 Papa acquired 100% of Son's 1 million $1 share capital on 1 January 20X1, and sold it on 1 January 20X6 for $8 million. All of the goodwill in relation to Son has been impaired prior to the disposal. When Papa acquired Son, Son's retained earnings were $2 million, and the retained earnings at disposal were $3 million. The fair value of Son's net assets were equal to their carrying amount with the exception of Son's property, which had a fair value of $2 million above its carrying amount. The property had a remaining life of 20 years at the date of acquisition.

What is the profit on disposal to be recorded in Papa's consolidated financial statements?

$__________

5 Price acquired 80% of Spoon's share capital on 1 January 20X1 for $15 million when Spoon's net assets were $10 million. Price sold all of its shares in Spoon on 1 January 20X7 for $16 million when Spoon's net assets were $12 million. Spoon uses the proportion of net assets method for valuing the non-controlling interest, and there has been no impairment of goodwill since acquisition.

What is the profit or loss on disposal of Spoon to be recorded in Price's consolidated financial statements?

A $600,000 loss

B $3,000,000 loss

C $600,000 gain

D $3,000,000 gain

Test your understanding answers

Test your understanding 1

1 **Gain in Rock's individual statement of profit or loss**

	$
Sale proceeds	3,000
Carrying amount of investment	(2,000)
Gain on disposal	1,000

2 **Gain in consolidated statement of profit or loss**

	$	$
Sale proceeds		3,000
Less: Carrying value of subsidiary at disposal		
Net assets at disposal	2,400	
Goodwill at disposal **(W1)**	900	
Less: NCI at disposal **(W2)**	(950)	
		(2,350)
		650

Workings:

(W1) Goodwill

	$
Fair value of P's investment	2,000
Fair value of NCI at acquisition	800
Fair value of sub's net assets at acquisition	(1,900)
Goodwill at acquisition/disposal	900

(W2) NCI at disposal date

	$
NCI at acquisition	800
NCI% × post-acquisition reserves (30% × (2,400 – 1,900))	150
	950

Test your understanding 2 – Kathmandu

Consolidated statement of profit or loss

	$
Revenue ($553,000 + (6/12 × $450,000))	778,000
Operating costs ($450,000 + (6/12 × $400,000))	(650,000)
Operating profit	128,000
Investment income ($8,000 – ($10,000 × 70%))	1,000
Profit on disposal **(W4)**	80,040
Profit before tax	209,400
Tax ($40,000 + (6/12 × $14,000))	(47,000)
Profit for the period	162,400
Attributable to:	
Equity holders of Kathmandu (balance)	157,000
Non-controlling interest **(W5)**	5,400
	162,400

Workings:

(W1) Net assets – Nepal

	Net assets at disposal $
Share capital	50,000
Retained earnings b/f	80,000
6/12 × 36,000	18,000
Less: Dividend (paid pre-disposal)	(10,000)
	138,000

(W2) Goodwill

	$
Consideration	100,000
FV of NCI at date of acquisition	40,000
	140,000
FV of net assets at date of acquisition	(110,000)
Goodwill	30,000

(W3) NCI at disposal date

FV of NCI at date of acquisition	40,000
NCI share of post-acquisition net assets (30% × ($138,000 – $110,000)	8,400
	48,400

(W4) Profit on disposal

	$	$
Proceeds		200,000
Less: Carrying amount of subsidiary:		
Net assets at disposal **(W1)**	138,000	
Goodwill at disposal **(W2)**	30,000	
	168,000	
NCI at date of disposal **(W3)**	(48,400)	
		(119,600)
Profit on disposal		80,400

(W5) Profit attributable to NCI

	$	$
Profit of Nepal (6/12 × $36,000)	18,000	
Profit attributable to NCI × 30%		5,400

Test your understanding 3

(i) **Gain in Hague's individual accounts**

	$
Sale proceeds	10,000
Less: Carrying amount of shares sold	(6,000)
Gain to parent	4,000

(ii) **Gain in Hague Group accounts**

	$
Sale proceeds	10,000
Less: Carrying value of subsidiary disposed of:	
Goodwill at disposal date **(W1)**	(3,000)
Gain to parent	(3,750)
Add: NCI at disposal **(W2)**	900
Gain before tax	4,150

Workings:

(W1) Goodwill

	$
Fair value of P's investment	6,000
NCI at fair value	1,000
Fair value of subsidiary net assets at acquisition	(2,000)
Goodwill at acquisition	5,000
Impairment (1/4 × 5,000)	(1,250)
Goodwill at disposal	3,750

(W2) NCI at disposal date

	$
NCI at acquisition **(W1)**	1,000
NCI% × post-acquisition reserves	
(40% × (3,000 – 2,000))	400
NCI% × impairment (40% × 1,250)	(500)
	900

Test your understanding 4

1 **C** – The gain or loss on disposal should be recorded in the statement of profit or loss, not other comprehensive income. The disposal of a subsidiary will still affect the parent's financial statements, as the subsidiary will have been recorded as an investment in the parent's books. All of the net assets of the subsidiary should be removed, as the consolidated financial statements include 100% of the net assets of the subsidiary, regardless of the percentage owned.

2 **1,400,000**

	$000
Fair value of consideration	2,500
NCI value at acquisition	500
	3,000
Less:	
Fair value of net assets at acquisition ($1 million share capital + $600, 000 retained earnings)	(1,600)
Goodwill on acquisition and disposal	**1,400**

3 $2,000,000. The net assets of Seedorf consist of share capital and retained earnings. Seedorf's share capital is $1 million. Seedorf's retained earnings at 1 January 20X5 are $900,000. As Seedorf has made a profit of $200,000 for the year, $100,000 (6/12) would have been made up to the date of disposal.

Net assets = $1 million + $900,000 + $100,000 = **$2,000,000**

4 **$2,500,000**

	$000
Sale proceeds	8,000
Less: Carrying value of subsidiary disposed of:	
Net assets of subsidiary at disposal date **(W1)**	(5,500)
Goodwill at disposal date (fully impaired)	–
Less: NCI at disposal (No NCI as 100% owned)	–
Gain on disposal	**2,500**

(W1) The net assets on disposal consists of the share capital of $1 million, the retained earnings of $3 million and the remaining fair value adjustment of $1.5 million, which is the $2 million fair value adjustment on acquisition less the fair value depreciation since then ($2 million/20 years × 5 years post-acquisition). This can be easier to see using the table seen in the consolidated statement of financial position workings for net assets.

	Acquisition	**Disposal**	**Post**
	$000	$000	$000
Share capital	1,000	1,000	0
Retained earnings	2,000	3,000	1,000
Fair value adjustment	2,000	2,000	0
Fair value depreciation (5/20)	0	(500)	(500)
	5,000	**5,500**	500

5 **A**

	$000
Proceeds	16,000
Interest in subsidiary disposed of:	
Net assets at disposal (given)	(12,000)
Goodwill at disposal **(W1)**	(7,000)
NCI at date of disposal **(W2)**	2,400
Loss on disposal	(600)

(W1) Goodwill

	$000
Consideration	15,000
NCI at date of acquisition	
(20% × 10,000 net assets at acquisition)	2,000
FV of net assets at date of acquisition	(10,000)
Goodwill	7,000

(W2) NCI at disposal date

NCI at date of acquisition	2,000
NCI share of post-acquisition net assets (20% × (12,000 – 10,000)	400
	2,400

An alternative working for the NCI at disposal date would be to take the NCI's share of the net assets at disposal, which would be $12,000 × 20% = $2,400.

Chapter

22

Interpretation of financial statements

Chapter learning objectives

Upon completion of this chapter you will be able to:

- indicate the problems of using historic information to predict future performance and trends
- explain how financial statements may be manipulated to produce a desired effect (creative accounting, window dressing)
- explain why figures in the statement of financial position may not be representative of average values throughout the period
- define and compute relevant financial ratios
- explain what aspects of performance specific ratios are intended to assess
- analyse and interpret ratios to give an assessment of an entity's performance and financial position in comparison with an entity's previous period financial statements
- analyse and interpret ratios to give an assessment of an entity's performance and financial position in comparison with another similar entity for the same period
- analyse and interpret ratios to give an assessment of an entity's performance and financial position in comparison with industry average ratios
- interpret an entity's financial statements to give advice from the perspective of different stakeholders

- explain how the interpretation of current value based financial statements would differ from those using historical cost based accounts
- explain the limitations in the use of ratio analysis for assessing corporate performance
- explain the effect that changes in accounting policies or the use of different accounting policies between entities can have on the ability to interpret performance
- indicate other information, including non-financial information, that may be of relevance to the assessment of an entity's performance
- explain the different approaches that may be required when assessing the performance of specialised not-for-profit and public sector organisations.

PER

One of the PER performance objectives (PO8) is to analyse and interpret financial reports. You analyse financial statements to evaluate and assess the financial performance and position of an entity. Working though this chapter should help you understand how to demonstrate that objective.

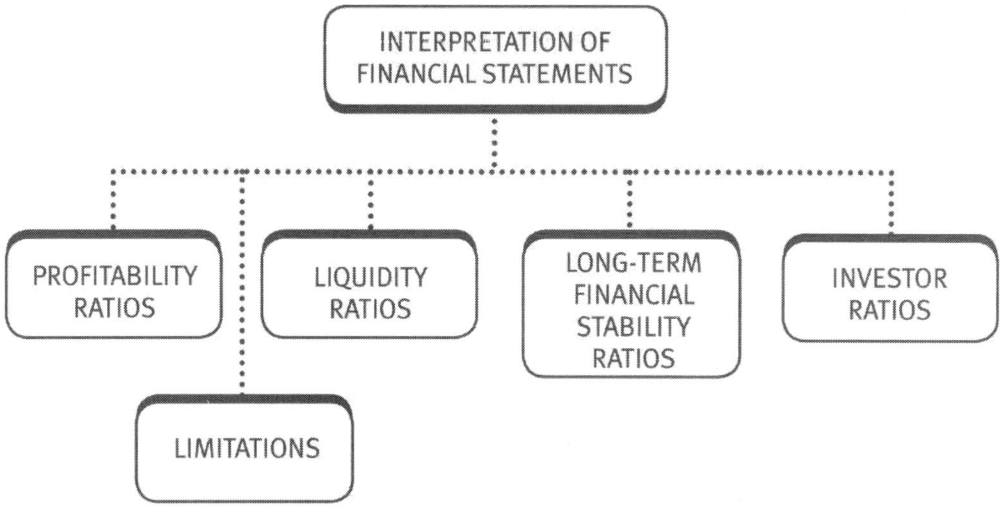

1 Interpreting financial information

Introduction

Financial statements on their own are of limited use. In this chapter we will consider how to interpret them and gain additional useful information from them.

In the FR exam, ratios and interpretation are likely to be examined in two ways:

- Objective Test Question (section A or B) – This is likely to involve the calculation of a ratio, or drawing a conclusion from a small piece of information given
- Constructed Response Question (section C) – This is likely to involve the calculation of a small number of ratios, followed by the analysis of a larger scenario, assessing a business.

In a larger question, it is important to note what is being asked and to tailor the answer accordingly. For example, if the scenario relates to whether a loan should be given to a company, the answer should focus on items such as cash flow, ability to meet interest payments and current levels of debt.

In a 20-mark interpretation question, candidates may be asked to interpret information for a single entity or a set of consolidated financial statements. A set of consolidated financial statements could include an addition or a disposal of a subsidiary.

Users of financial statements

When interpreting financial statements it is important to identify the users of financial statements and the information they need:

- shareholders and potential investors – primarily concerned with receiving an adequate return on their investment, but it must at least provide security and liquidity
- suppliers and lenders – concerned with the security of their debt or loan
- management – concerned with the trend and level of profits, since this is the main measure of their success.

Other potential users include:

- bank managers
- financial institutions
- employees
- professional advisors to investors
- financial journalists and commentators.

Ratio analysis

A number of ratios can be calculated to help interpret the financial statements.

In an examination question you may not have time to calculate all of the ratios presented in this chapter so you must make a choice:

- choose those relevant to the situation
- choose those relevant to the party in the question
- make use of any additional information given in the question to help your choice.

Analysts will, in practice, be limited in the analysis that can be performed by the amount of information available. They are unlikely to have access to all the facts which are available to an entity's management.

In the examination the information which can be provided about a company in any one question will be limited. The first part of such a question may ask you to interpret the available information, while you may also be asked to state what further information you require.

If you are asked to request further information, make the request specific to the scenario given and state the reason you would be looking for that particular piece of information.

Commenting on ratios

Most of the marks in an examination question will be available for sensible, well-explained and accurate comments on the key ratios.

If you doubt that you have anything to say, the following points should serve as a useful checklist:

- What does the ratio literally mean?
- What does a change in the ratio mean?
- From the information given, what is likely to have led to the changes in the ratio?

Your answer to a section C question on analysis should use the information in the scenario to produce the reason for movements in performance and position. Your knowledge of the business will be limited to that provided within the question, so the reasons for the movement in ratios should be linked back to this at all times.

2 Different sections to analyse

In a report, you are often asked to analyse specific sections. The broad categories are:

- Performance – This looks largely at the statement of profit or loss and associated ratios, such as profit margins, return on capital employed and net asset turnover. This section looks at the results that the business has generated in the year.
- Position – This looks at the statement of financial position, and the associated ratios. This could be broken down further into short-term liquidity, looking at working capital, and long-term solvency, looking at levels of debt.
- Investor – This looks at items that would specifically matter to investors. This will cover items such as the share price, dividends and earnings.

3 Performance

The ratios relating to performance are detailed in the next section. However, comments on performance should not simply be limited to talking about ratios.

Revenue

Revenue is key in relation to performance and should always be commented on.

Comments on revenue should not be limited to basic analysis such as 'Revenue has increased, which is good'. Comments should look to explain why revenue has increased in the year, examining items such as new products, new markets, promotional activity or anything relevant to the scenario.

Gross profit margin

Gross profit margin or percentage is:

$$\frac{\text{Gross profit}}{\text{Sales revenue}} \times 100\%$$

This is the margin that the company achieves on its sales, and would be expected to remain reasonably constant.

Since the ratio is affected by only a small number of variables, a change may be traced to a change in:

- selling prices – normally deliberate though sometimes unavoidable, e.g. because of increased competition or entry into a new market
- sales mix – often deliberate (company discontinuing some products)
- purchase cost – including carriage inwards or discounts
- production cost – materials, labour or production overheads

A good way to analyse gross profit margin is to ask yourself:

- Are there any reasons why the selling price has changed?
- Are there any significant changes to the costs in the year?
- Has there been any indication of a change in sales mix?

Gross profit margin

Comparing gross profit margin over time

If gross profit has not increased in line with sales revenue, you need to establish why this is so. Is the discrepancy due to:

- increased 'purchase' costs: if so, are the costs under the company's control (i.e. does the company manufacture the goods sold)?
- inventory write-offs (likely where the company operates in a volatile market-place, such as fashion retail)? or
- other costs being allocated to cost of sales – for example, research and development (R&D) expenditure?

Inter-company comparison of gross profit margin

Inter-company comparison of margins can be very useful but it is especially important to look at businesses within the same sector. For example, food retailing is able to support low margins because of the high volume of sales. A manufacturing industry would usually need higher margins to offset lower sales volumes.

Low margins usually suggest poor performance but may be due to expansion costs (launching a new product) or trying to increase market share. Lower margins than usual suggest scope for improvement.

Above-average margins are usually a sign of good management although unusually high margins may attract competition.

Operating profit margin

The **operating profit margin** is calculated as:

$$\frac{\text{Profit from operations}}{\text{Sales revenue}} \times 100\%$$

An alternative to operating profit margin is to calculate net profit margin, using either profit for the year or profit before tax as the numerator.

Any changes in operating profit margin should be considered further:

- Are the changes in line with changes in gross profit margin?
- Are the changes in line with changes in sales revenue?
- As many costs are fixed they need not necessarily increase/decrease proportionately with a change in revenue.
- Look at individual categories (administration, distribution expenses)

If there are significant changes within operating expenses, it is important to consider:

- Are these due to one-off items, such as redundancies or litigation? If so, these items should be stripped out of the ratio to provide a meaningful comparison.
- Are there likely to be ongoing future consequences? For example, a company opening a website to sell directly to the public is likely to have much higher distribution costs into the future.

Operating profit margin

This is affected by more factors than the gross profit margin but it is equally useful and if the company does not disclose a cost of sales it may be used on its own in lieu of the gross profit percentage.

One of the many factors affecting the trading profit margin is depreciation, which is open to considerable subjective judgement. Inter-company comparisons should be made after suitable adjustments to align accounting policies.

By the time you have reached operating profit, there are many more factors to consider. If you are provided with a breakdown of expenses you can use this for further line-by-line comparisons. Bear in mind that:

- some costs are fixed or semi-fixed (e.g. property costs) and therefore not expected to change in line with revenue
- other costs are variable (e.g. packaging, commission).

Return on capital employed (ROCE)

$$\text{ROCE} = \frac{\text{Profit}}{\text{Capital employed}} \times 100\%$$

This shows the ability of the entity to turn its long-term financing into profit. Profit is measured as:

- operating (trading) profit, or
- the profit before interest and taxation (PBIT), i.e. the profit before taking account of any returns paid to the providers of long-term finance.

Capital employed is measured as:

- equity plus interest-bearing finance, i.e. the long-term finance supporting the business. This usually includes ALL lease liabilities, whether they are shown as current or non-current, or
- total assets less current liabilities

ROCE for the current year should be compared to:

- the previous year ROCE
- the cost of borrowing
- other entities' ROCE in the same industry.

Movements in ROCE should be analysed by looking for the reasons why profit has moved, and reasons for any changes in the long-term funding, such as loans or share issues to fund acquisition of non-current assets.

It is important to note that ROCE can be significantly affected by an entity's accounting policies. A company that revalues their non-current assets will have a revaluation surplus in equity. This will make their ROCE lower than a company that does not revalue their assets, making comparison meaningless.

Similar to ROCE is return on equity (ROE):

$$\textbf{ROE} = \frac{\text{Profit after tax}}{\text{Equity}} \times 100\%$$

This can be used to show the return made for the year on the total equity in the business. Pre-tax ROE can also be calculated using profit before tax rather than profit after tax.

Return on capital employed (ROCE)

Once calculated, ROCE should be compared with:

- previous year figures – provided there have been no changes in accounting policies, or suitable adjustments have been made to facilitate comparison (note, however, that the effect of not replacing non-current assets is that their value will decrease and ROCE will increase)
- the company's target ROCE – where the company's management has determined a target return as part of its budget procedure, consistent failure by a part of the business to meet the target may make it a target for disposal
- the cost of borrowings – if the cost of borrowing is, say, 10% and ROCE 7%, then further borrowings will reduce EPS unless the extra money can be used in areas where the ROCE is higher than the cost of borrowings
- other companies in same industry – care is required in interpretation, because of the possibility, noted above, of different accounting policies, ages of plant, etc.

The ratio also shows how efficiently a business is using its resources. If the return is very low, the business may be better off realising its assets and investing the proceeds in a high interest bank account! (This may sound extreme, but should be considered particularly for a small, unprofitable business with valuable assets such as property.) Furthermore, a low return can easily become a loss if the business suffers a downturn.

Further points

- Treatment of associates and investments: where the profit excludes investment income, the statement of financial position carrying amounts for associates and investments should be excluded from the capital employed to give an accurate measure of trading performance. If associates and investments are not excluded, the overall profit figure should include income from investments and associates.

- Large cash balances are not contributing to profits and some analysts therefore deduct them from capital employed (to compare operating profits with operating assets). However, it is usually acceptable not to make this adjustment as ROCE is a performance measure and management have decided to operate with that large balance.

Net asset turnover

The **net asset turnover** is:

$$\frac{\text{Sales revenue}}{\text{Capital employed}} = \text{times pa}$$

Note: Capital employed can be calculated as equity plus interest-bearing debt. As an alternative, net assets (total assets less total liabilities) could also be used.

It measures management's efficiency in generating revenue from the net assets at its disposal:

- the higher the asset turnover, the greater the efficiency.

Note that this can be further subdivided into:

- non-current asset turnover (by making non-current assets the denominator) and
- working capital turnover (by making net current assets the denominator).

Relationship between ratios

ROCE can be subdivided into profit margin and asset turnover.

Profit margin × Asset turnover = ROCE

$$\frac{\text{PBIT}}{\text{Sales revenue}} \times \frac{\text{Sales revenue}}{\text{Capital employed}} = \frac{\text{PBIT}}{\text{Capital employed}}$$

Profit margin is often seen as an indication of the quality of products or services supplied (top-of-range products usually have higher margins).

Asset turnover is often seen as a measure of how intensively the assets are worked.

A trade-off may exist between margin and asset turnover.

- Low-margin businesses (e.g. food retailers) usually have a high asset turnover.
- Capital-intensive manufacturing industries (e.g. electrical equipment manufacturers) usually have relatively low asset turnover but higher margins.

Two completely different strategies can achieve the same ROCE.

- Sell goods at a high profit margin with sales volume remaining low (e.g. designer dress shop).
- Sell goods at a low profit margin with very high sales volume (e.g. discount clothes store).

4 Position

When analysing position, this can be split down into short-term liquidity (looking at working capital) and long-term solvency (focusing on debt levels).

Working capital ratios

There are two ratios used to measure overall working capital:

- the current ratio
- the quick or acid test ratio.

Current ratio

Current or working capital ratio:

$$\frac{\text{Current assets}}{\text{Current liabilities}} :1$$

The current ratio measures the adequacy of current assets to meet the liabilities as they fall due.

A high or increasing figure may appear safe but should be regarded with suspicion as it may be due to:

- high levels of inventory and receivables (check working capital management ratios)
- high cash levels which could be put to better use (e.g. by investing in non-current assets).

Current ratio

The current ratio measures the adequacy of current assets to meet the company's short-term liabilities. It reflects whether the company is in a position to meet its liabilities as they fall due.

Traditionally, a current ratio of 2:1 or higher was regarded as appropriate for most businesses to maintain creditworthiness. However, more recently a figure of 1.5:1 is regarded as the norm.

The current ratio should be looked at in the light of what is normal for the business. For example, supermarkets tend to have low current ratios because:

- there are few trade receivables
- there is a high level of trade payables
- there is usually very tight cash control, to fund investment in developing new sites and improving existing sites.

It is also worth considering:

- availability of further finance, e.g. is the overdraft at the limit? – very often this information is highly relevant but is not disclosed in the accounts
- seasonal nature of the business – one way of doing this is to compare the interest charges in the statement of profit or loss with the overdraft and other loans in the statement of financial position. If the interest rate appears abnormally high, this is probably because the company has had higher levels of borrowings during the year
- long-term liabilities, when they fall due and how will they be financed
- nature of the inventory – where inventories are slow moving, the quick ratio probably provides a better indicator of short-term liquidity.

Quick ratio

Quick ratio (also known as the liquidity or acid test) ratio:

$$\text{Quick ratio} = \frac{\text{Current assets} - \text{Inventory}}{\text{Current liabilities}} :1$$

The quick ratio is also known as the acid test ratio because by eliminating inventory from current assets it provides the acid test of whether the company has sufficient liquid resources (receivables and cash) to settle its liabilities.

As well as analysing how 'safe' a business is by looking at the current and quick ratio, it is important to look at why the ratios have moved by considering working capital in more depth.

Cash

As well as the working capital ratios below, it is also useful to comment on any movement in cash in the year.

- Identify where any major cash inflows have come from in the year.
- Identify where the cash has been used in the year.

As far as possible, any comments should be made with reference to the scenario. A simple statement of 'cash has gone up, which is good' is unlikely to be worth many marks. A discussion should be based around whether cash has gone up from the company's performance or from other sources, such as taking on more debt.

Quick ratio

Like the current ratio it is relevant to consider the nature of the business when calculating the quick ratio. Again supermarkets have very low quick ratios.

Sometimes the **quick ratio** is calculated on the basis of a six-week time-frame (i.e. the quick assets are those which will turn into cash in six weeks, quick liabilitics are those which fall due for payment within six weeks). This basis would usually include the following in **quick assets:**

- bank, cash and short-term investments
- trade receivables.

thus excluding prepayments and inventory.

Quick liabilities would usually include:

- bank overdraft which is repayable on demand
- trade payables, tax and social security
- dividends.

Income tax liabilities may be excluded.

When interpreting the quick ratio, care should be taken over the status of the **bank overdraft.** A company with a low quick ratio may actually have no problem in paying its amounts due if sufficient overall overdraft facilities are available.

Inventory turnover period

Inventory turnover period is calculated as:

$$\frac{\text{Inventory}}{\text{COS}} \times 365 \text{ days}$$

An alternative is to express the inventory turnover period as a number of times per annum:

$$\frac{\text{Cost of sales}}{\text{Inventory}} = \text{times pa}$$

An increasing number of days (or a diminishing multiple) implies that inventory is turning over less quickly which is regarded as a bad sign as it may indicate:

- lack of demand for the goods
- poor inventory control
- an increase in costs (storage, obsolescence, insurance, damage).

However, it may not necessarily be bad where management are:

- buying inventory in larger quantities to take advantage of trade discounts, or
- increasing inventory levels to avoid stockouts.

Inventory days

Year-end inventory is normally used in the calculation of inventory turnover. An average (based on the average of year-start and year-end inventories) may be used to have a smoothing effect, although this may dampen the effect of a major change in the period.

Inventory turnover ratios vary enormously with the nature of the business. For example, a fishmonger selling fresh fish would have an inventory turnover period of 1-2 days, whereas a building contractor may have an inventory turnover period of 200 days. Manufacturing companies may have an inventory turnover period of 60-100 days. This period is likely to increase as the goods made become larger and more complex.

For large and complex items (e.g. rolling stock or aircraft) there may be sharp fluctuations in inventory turnover according to whether delivery took place just before or just after the year end.

A manufacturer should take into consideration:

- reliability of suppliers: if the supplier is unreliable it is prudent to hold more raw materials
- demand: if demand is erratic it is prudent to hold more finished goods.

Receivables collection period

This is normally expressed as a number of days:

$$\frac{\text{Trade receivables}}{\text{Credit sales}} \times 365 \text{ days}$$

If the figure for credit sales is not available, revenue should be used. The collection period should be compared with:

- the stated credit policy
- previous period figures.

Increasing accounts receivables collection period is usually a bad sign, suggesting lack of proper credit control which may lead to irrecoverable debts.

It may, however, be due to:

- a deliberate policy to attract more trade, or
- a major new customer being allowed different terms.

Falling receivables days is usually a good sign, though it could indicate that the company is suffering a cash shortage.

Receivables days

The trade receivables used may be a year-end figure or the average for the year. Where an average is used to calculate the number of days, the ratio is the average number of days' credit taken by customers.

For many businesses total sales revenue can safely be used, because cash sales will be insignificant. But cash-based businesses like supermarkets make the substantial majority of their sales for cash, so the receivables period should be calculated by reference to credit sales only.

The result should be compared with the stated **credit policy**. A period of 30 days or 'at the end of the month following delivery' are common credit terms.

The receivables days ratio can be distorted by:

- using year-end figures which do not represent average receivables
- factoring of accounts receivables which results in very low trade receivables
- sales on unusually long credit terms to some customers

Payables payment period

This is usually expressed as:

$$\frac{\text{Trade payables}}{\text{Credit purchases}} \times 365 \text{ days}$$

This represents the credit period taken by the company from its suppliers.

The ratio is always compared to previous years:

- A long credit period may be good as it represents a source of free finance.
- A long credit period may indicate that the company is unable to pay more quickly because of liquidity problems.

If the credit period is long:

- the company may develop a poor reputation as a slow payer and may not be able to find new suppliers
- existing suppliers may decide to discontinue supplies
- the company may be losing out on worthwhile prompt payment discounts.

In most sets of financial statements (in practice and in examinations) the figure for purchases will not be available. Therefore cost of sales is normally used as an approximation in the calculation of the accounts payable payment period.

Note: In an exam, you may be asked to calculate the working capital cycle, or asked to work out the receivables/inventory/payables period from the working capital cycle.

Working capital cycle (cash cycle)

Working capital cycle = Inventory turnover period (days) + receivables collection period – payables payment period

The working capital cycle shows the average length of time between paying production costs and receiving cash returns from the inventory.

Example 1 – Interpretation

Statements of financial position and statements of profit or loss for Ocean Motors are set out below.

Ocean Motors statement of financial position

	20X2		20X1	
	$000	$000	$000	$000
Non-current assets:				
Land and buildings				
Cost	1,600		1,450	
Depreciation	(200)		(150)	
		1,400		1,300
Plant and machinery:				
Cost	600		400	
Depreciation	(120)		(100)	
		480		300
		1,880		1,600
Current assets:				
Inventory	300		100	
Receivables	400		100	
		700		200
Total assets		2,580		1,800
Equity:				
Share capital – $1 ordinary shares		1,200		1,200
Retained earnings		310		220
		1,510		1,420
Current liabilities:				
Bank overdraft	590		210	
Payables and accruals	370		70	
Taxation	110		100	
		1,070		300
		2,580		1,800

Ocean Motors statement of profit or loss

	20X2	20X1
	$000	$000
Sales revenue	1,500	1,000
Cost of sales	(700)	(300)
Gross profit	800	700
Administration and distribution expenses	(400)	(360)
Profit before tax	400	340
Income tax expense	(200)	(170)
Profit for the year	200	170

The dividend for 20X1 was $100,000 and for 20X2 was $110,000.

Calculate the following ratios for Ocean Motors and briefly comment upon what they indicate:

Profitability ratios:

- gross profit margin
- operating profit margin
- ROCE
- net asset turnover.

Liquidity and working capital ratios:

- current ratio
- quick ratio
- inventory collection period
- accounts receivable collection period
- accounts payable payment period

Solution

Profitability ratios

	20X2	20X1
ROCE	400/1,510 = 26.5%	340/1,420 = 23.9%
Gross profit margin	800/1,500 = 53.3%	700/1,000 = 70.0%
Operating profit margin	400/1,500 = 26.7%	340/1,000 = 34.0%
Asset turnover	1,500/1,510 = 0.99	1,000/1,420 = 0.70

Comment

Key factors:

- revenue has increased by 50%
- gross profit margin significantly decreased, maybe due to lowering of
  selling prices in order to increase market share and sales revenue
- operating profit margin has decreased in line with gross profit margin
- ROCE has increased, which must be due to the improvement in asset turnover.

Liquidity and working capital ratios

	20X2	20X1
Current ratio	700/1,070 = 0.65 : 1	200/380 = 0.53 : 1
Quick ratio	400/1,070 = 0.37 : 1	100/380 = 0.26 : 1
Inventory holding period	300/700 × 365 156 days	100/300 × 365 122 days
Accounts receivable collection period	400/1,500 × 365 97 days	100/1,000 × 365 36.5 days
Accounts payable payment period	370/700 × 365 193 days	70/300 × 365 85 days

Comment

Overall the liquidity of the company would appear to be in some doubt:

- Both the current ratio and quick ratio appear very low although they have improved since the previous year.
- We do not know anything about the type of business, so it is difficult to comment on these absolute levels of liquidity.
- Inventory holding period indicates that inventory is held for a considerable time and that this period is increasing.
- Accounts receivable collection period has deteriorated rapidly although given the increase in revenue this may be due to a conscious policy of offering extended credit terms in order to attract new custom.
- Accounts payable payment period has also more than doubled and is even longer than the period of credit taken by customers.
- Clearly the business is heavily dependent upon its overdraft finance.

5 Long-term financial stability

Introduction

The main points to consider when assessing the longer-term financial position are:

- gearing
- overtrading.

Gearing

Gearing ratios indicate:

- the degree of risk attached to the company and
- the sensitivity of earnings and dividends to changes in profitability and activity level.

Preference share capital is usually included as part of debt rather than equity since it carries the right to a fixed rate of dividend which is payable before the ordinary shareholders have any right to a dividend.

Gearing will include all interest-bearing debt, and show it as a proportion of equity, or as a proportion of the total long-term financing (being equity plus interest-bearing debt).

High and low gearing

In highly geared businesses:

- a large proportion of fixed-return capital is used
- there is a greater risk of insolvency
- returns to shareholders will grow proportionately more if profits are growing.

Low-geared businesses:

- provide scope to increase borrowings when potentially profitable projects are available
- can usually borrow more easily.

Gearing

Not all entities are suitable for a highly-geared structure. An entity must have two fundamental characteristics if it is to use gearing successfully.

Relatively stable profits

Loan interest must be paid whether or not profits are earned. A entity with erratic profits may have insufficient funds in a bad year with which to pay the interest. This may result in the appointment of a receiver and possibly the liquidation of the entity.

Suitable assets for security

Most issues of loan capital are secured on some or all of the entity's assets which must be suitable for the purpose. An entity with most of its capital invested in fast-depreciating assets or inventory subject to rapid changes in demand and price would not be suitable for high gearing.

The classic examples of entities that are suited to high gearing are those in property investment and the hotel/leisure services industry. These entities generally enjoy relatively stable profits and have assets which are highly suitable for charging. Nonetheless, these are industries that could be described as cyclical.

Entities not suited to high gearing would include those in the extractive, and high-tech, industries where constant changes occur. These entities could experience erratic profits and would generally have inadequate assets to pledge as security.

Measuring gearing

There are two methods commonly used to express gearing as follows.

Debt/equity ratio:

$$\frac{\text{Loans + Preference share capital}}{\text{Ordinary share capital + Reserves + Non-controlling interest}}$$

Percentage of capital employed represented by borrowings:

$$\frac{\text{Loans + Preference share capital}}{\text{Ordinary share capital + Reserves + Non-controlling interest + Loans + Preference share capital}}$$

Interest cover

$$\textbf{Interest cover} = \frac{\text{Profit before interest and tax}}{\text{Interest payable}}$$

Interest cover indicates the ability of a company to pay interest out of profits generated:

- low interest cover indicates to shareholders that their dividends are at risk (because most profits are eaten up by interest payments) and
- the company may have difficulty financing its debts if its profits fall
- interest cover of less than two is usually considered unsatisfactory.

Interest cover

A business must have a sufficient level of long-term capital to finance its long-term investment in non-current assets. Part of the investment in current assets would usually be financed by relatively permanent capital with the balance being provided by credit from suppliers and other short-term borrowings. Any expansion in activity will normally require a broadening of the long-term capital base, without which 'overtrading' may develop (see below).

Suitability of finance is also a key factor. A permanent expansion of an entity's activities should not be financed by temporary, short-term borrowings. On the other hand, a short-term increase in activity such as the 'January sales' in a retail trading company could ideally be financed by overdraft.

A major addition to non-current assets such as the construction of a new factory would not normally be financed on a long-term basis by overdraft. It might be found, however, that the expenditure was temporarily financed by overdraft until construction was completed, when the overdraft would be replaced by a long-term borrowing secured on the completed building.

Overtrading

Overtrading arises where a company expands its sales revenue rapidly without securing adequate long-term capital for its needs. The symptoms of overtrading are:

- inventory increasing, possibly more than proportionately to revenue
- receivables increasing, possibly more than proportionately to revenue
- cash and liquid assets declining
- trade payables increasing rapidly.

Overtrading

The symptoms of overtrading simply imply that the entity has expanded without giving proper thought to the necessity to expand its capital base. It has consequently continued to rely on its trade payables and probably its bank overdraft to provide the additional finance required. There will come a point where suppliers will withhold further supplies and bankers will refuse to honour further cheques until borrowings are reduced. The problem is that borrowings cannot be reduced until sales revenue is earned, which in turn cannot be achieved until production is completed, which in turn is dependent upon materials being available and wages paid. Overall result – deadlock and rapid financial collapse!

This is a particularly difficult stage for small- to medium-sized companies. They have reached a stage in their growth when conventional payables and overdraft facilities are being stretched to the maximum, but they are probably too small to manage a flotation. In many cases, by proper planning, the company can arrange fixed-term loan funding from the bank rather than relying exclusively on overdraft finance.

Test your understanding 1

Interpretation of financial statements

Neville is a company that manufactures and retails office products. Their summarised financial statements for the years ended 30 June 20X4 and 20X5 are given below:

Statements of profit or loss for the year ended 30 June

	20X5	**20X4**
	$000	$000
Revenue	1,391,820	1,159,850
Cost of Sales	(1,050,825)	(753,450)
Gross profit	340,995	406,400
Operating expenses	(161,450)	(170,950)
Profit from operations	179,545	235,450
Finance costs	(10,000)	(14,000)
Profits before tax	169,545	221,450
Tax	(50,800)	(66,300)
Profit for the year	118,745	155,150

Statements of financial position as at 30 June

	20X5	**20X4**
	$000	$000
Non-current assets	509,590	341,400
Current assets		
Inventory	109,400	88,760
Receivables	419,455	206,550
Bank	–	95,400
	1,038,445	732,110
Share capital	100,000	100,000
Share premium	20,000	20,000
Revaluation surplus	50,000	–
Retained earnings	376,165	287,420
	546,165	407,420
Non-current liabilities	61,600	83,100

Current liabilities		
Payables	295,480	179,590
Overdraft	80,200	–
Tax	55,000	62,000
	1,038,445	732,110

The directors concluded that their revenue for the year ended 30 June 20X4 fell below budget and introduced measures in the year end 30 June 20X5 to improve the situation. These included:

- Cutting prices
- Extending credit facilities to customers
- Purchasing additional machinery in order to be able to manufacture more products.

The directors are now reviewing the results for the year ended 30 June 20X5 and have asked for your advice, as an external business consultant, as to whether or not the above strategies have been successful.

Required:

Prepare a report to the directors of Neville assessing the performance and position of the company in the year ended 30 June 20X5 compared to the previous year and advise them on whether or not you believe that their strategies have been successful.

6 Investor ratios

Earnings per share (EPS)

The calculation of EPS was covered in an earlier chapter.

Price / Earnings (P/E) ratio

$$\textbf{P/E ratio} = \frac{\text{Current share price}}{\text{Latest EPS}}$$

- Represents the market's view of the future prospects of the share.
- High P/E suggests that high growth is expected.

P/E ratio

This is the most widely referred to stock market ratio, also commonly described as an earnings multiple. It is calculated as the 'purchase of a number of years' earnings', but it represents the market's consensus of the future prospects of that share. The higher the P/E ratio, the faster the growth the market is expecting in the company's future EPS. Correspondingly, the lower the P/E ratio, the lower the expected future growth.

Another aspect of interpreting it, is that a published EPS exists for a year and therefore the P/E ratio given in a newspaper is generally based on an increasingly out-of-date EPS. To give an extreme but simple example:

Company X

- For the year ended 31 December 20X6, EPS = 10c
- Overall market P/E ratio = 10.
- P/E ratio for X = 20 (because market expects above average growth).
- Market price at 30 April 20X7 (date of publication of previous year's accounts) = $2.
- During the year, X does even better than expected and by 29 April 20X8, the share price is up to $3, therefore giving a P/E ratio of 30 (based on EPS for year ended 31 December 20X6).
- Year ended 31 December 20X7, EPS = 15c, announced on 30 April 20X8. This is in line with expectations so share price is unchanged and P/E ratio drops again to 20 ($3/15c).

The earnings yield is the reciprocal of the P/E ratio, calculated as earnings as a percentage of market price. For Company X at 30 April 20X8 it is 5% (15c as a % of $3).

Dividend yield

$$\textbf{Dividend yield} = \frac{\text{Dividend per share}}{\text{Current share price}}$$

- can be compared to the yields available on other investment possibilities
- the lower the dividend yield, the more the market is expecting future growth in the dividend, and vice versa.

Dividend cover

$$\textbf{Dividend cover} = \frac{\text{Profit after tax}}{\text{Dividends}}$$

- This is the relationship between available profits and the dividends payable out of the profits.
- The higher the dividend cover, the more likely it is that the current dividend level can be sustained in the future.

Example 2 – Interpretation

Given below are the statements of profit or loss for Pacific Motors for the last two years.

Statements of profit or loss

	20X2	**20X1**
	$000	$000
Revenue	1,500	1,000
Cost of sales	(700)	(300)
Gross profit	800	700
Administration and distribution expenses	(400)	(360)
Profit before tax	400	340
Income tax expense	(200)	(170)
Profit for the year	200	170

In 20X1 dividends were $100,000 and in 20X2 they were $110,000.

The company is financed by 1,200,000 $1 ordinary shares and the market price of each share was $1.64 at 31 December 20X2 and $1.53 at 31 December 20X1.

For each year calculate the following ratios and comment on them briefly:

- EPS
- P/E ratio
- dividend yield
- dividend cover.

Solution

	20X2	20X1
EPS	200/1,200	170/1,200
	= 16.7 c	14.2 c
P/E ratio	164/16.7	153/14.2
	= 9.8	= 10.8
Dividend yield	(110/1,200)/164	(100/1,200)/153
	= 5.6%	= 5.4%
Dividend cover	200/110	170/100
	= 1.8 times	1.7 times

Comment

There has not been a significant amount of change in the investor ratios over the two years but the following specific comments could be made:

- both EPS and dividend per share have increased by a small amount over the two years which is a policy often designed to satisfy shareholders
- the P/E ratio has declined which indicates that the market does not think as highly of the shares this year as last year
- dividend cover is slightly higher which means that a slightly higher proportion of the profits for the year have been retained within the business.

7 Limitations of financial statements and ratio analysis

Historical cost accounts

Ratios are a tool to assist analysis.

- They help to focus attention systematically on important areas and summarise information in an understandable form.
- They assist in identifying trends and relationships.

However ratios are not predictive if they are based on historical information.

- They ignore future action by management.
- They can be manipulated by window dressing or creative accounting.
- They may be distorted by differences in accounting policies.

Asset values shown in the statement of financial position at historical cost may bear no resemblance to their current value or what it may cost to replace them. This may result in a low depreciation charge and overstatement of profit in real terms. As a result of historical costs the financial statements do not show the real cost of using the non-current assets.

Creative accounting/window dressing

Creative accounting refers to the accounting practices that are designed to mislead the view that the user of financial statements has on an entity's underlying economic performance. Typically creative accounting is used to increase profits, inflate asset values or understate liabilities.

In the past companies could smooth profits to maintain a steady upward trend by making use of general provisions (no longer allowed per IAS 37, see Chapter 15). An upward profit trend is reassuring to both existing and potential investors or of benefit to bonus-seeking directors. As the restrictions on provisions have tightened, companies have found other ways to manipulate profit, such as unsuitable revenue recognition or inappropriate accruals.

Creative accounting techniques can also be used to manipulate the gearing level of a company. A company that is highly geared has high interest payments that reduce the amount of distributable profit available to shareholders and increases the risk associated with the company, making it more difficult to obtain future lending.

Other reasons for creative accounting could include the desire to influence share price, to keep the company's financial results within agreed limits set by creditors, personal incentives or to pay less tax.

Window dressing

Window dressing is a method of carrying out transactions in order to distort the position shown by the financial statements and generally improve the position shown by them.

Examples of window dressing include:

- a company might chase receivables more quickly at the year end to improve their bank balance;
- a company may change its depreciation estimate i.e. by increasing the expected useful life of an asset, the depreciation charge will be smaller resulting in increased profits; and
- an existing loan may be repaid immediately before the year end and then taken out again in the next financial year.

Choice of accounting policies

It is necessary to be able to assess the impact of accounting policies on the calculation of ratios. Comparison between businesses that follow different policies becomes a major issue if accounting standards give either choice or judgement to companies e.g. IAS 40 or IAS 16.

Transactions with related parties

If an entity trades with related parties, such as other entities within the same group or other entities run by the same directors, then these transactions may not be at market price. This can involve items such as purchase or sale transactions at rates other than market value or loans carrying interest rates not at market value.

The impact of these transactions on the entity must be assessed to give a fair comparison with other entities, and to show the position if the entity was removed from the group and no longer enjoyed the benefit of such transactions.

Seasonal trading

Ratio analysis can be distorted when a company has seasonal trading. For example, a company may position their year-end to be after a particularly busy period so that inventory levels are lower than usual making the inventory count a less time-consuming process. This in turn will generally mean that current asset levels are higher from a bank/receivables point of view and that trade payables are lower (where suppliers have been paid for the supply of the inventory to meet demand for the busy period). The timing of such financial reporting would improve the appearance of the ratios and make the company seem more solvent. In comparison if the financial statements had been drawn up at a different period in time then the results could appear quite different.

Limitations of ratio analysis

- Although there are general guidelines (for example, the quick ratio should not normally be less than 1:1), there is no such thing as an 'ideal' ratio. A quick ratio of less than 1:1 would be acceptable in some businesses, but dangerously low for many others.
- Unless ratios are calculated on a uniform basis, from uniform data, comparisons can be very misleading.
- The statement of financial position shown in the financial statements may not be representative of the financial position at other times in the year. Many businesses set the end of their accounting period to a date on which there is a relatively low amount of trading activity. Retail organisations often have an end of February accounting date (after the peak pre-Christmas trading and the January sales). As a result, the balances on a statement of financial position are not representative of the average position throughout the accounting period.

Consider inventory levels in a retail organisation. They may vary throughout the year with lows at the end of a season and highs at the start of the season.

Adding opening and closing inventory and dividing by two will not produce a fair average.

- Ratios based on historical cost accounts do not give a true picture of trends from year to year. An apparent increase in profit may not be a true increase, and may simply reflect the effects of inflation.
- Financial statements only reflect those activities which can be expressed in money terms. They do not give a complete picture of the activities of a business. For example, the size of the order book is normally ignored in financial statements.
- The application of accounting policies in the preparation of financial statements must be understood when attempting to interpret financial ratios.
- Ratios must not be used as the sole test of efficiency. Concentration on achievement of target ratios by managers may inhibit the incentive to grow and expand, to the detriment of the long-term interests of the company.
- A few simple ratios do not provide an automatic means of running a company. Business problems usually involve complex patterns which cannot be solved solely by the use of ratios.

Inter-firm and sector comparison

It can be useful to compare ratios for an individual entity with those of other firms in the same industry. However, comparing the financial statements of similar businesses can be misleading because:

- the businesses may use different accounting policies
- ratios may not be calculated according to the same formulae. For example, there are several possible definitions of gearing and ROCE.
- large organisations can achieve economies of scale, e.g. by negotiating extended credit periods, or discounts for bulk buying with suppliers, whereas these measures may not be available to smaller businesses, and may distort comparison.
- entities within the same industry can serve completely different markets and there may be differences in sales mix and product range. These can affect profitability and activity ratios such as profit margin and ratios of expenses to sales.

Sector comparisons

It can be useful to compare ratios for an individual company with the sector as a whole. However, it must also be noted that the sector will incorporate companies of different sizes so it may not be a like for like comparison.

Additional information

In practice and in examinations it is likely that the information available in the financial statements may not be enough to make a thorough analysis.

You may require additional financial information such as:

- budgeted figures
- other management information
- industry averages
- figures for a similar business
- figures for the business over a period of time.

You may also require other non-financial information such as:

- market share
- key employee information
- sales mix information
- product range information
- the size of the order book
- the long-term plans of management.

Test your understanding 2

Comparator assembles computer equipment from bought-in components and distributes them to various wholesalers and retailers. It has recently subscribed to an inter-firm comparison service. Members submit accounting ratios as specified by the operator of the service, and in return, members receive the average figures for each of the specified ratios taken from all subscribing entities in the same sector. The specified ratios and the average figures for Comparator's sector are shown below.

Ratios of companies reporting a full year's results for periods ending between 1 July 20X3 and 30 September 20X3:

Return on capital employed	22.1%
Net asset turnover	1.8 times
Gross profit margin	30%
Net profit (before tax) margin	12.5%
Current ratio	1.6:1
Quick ratio	0.9:1
Inventory days	46 days
Receivables days	45 days
Payables days	55 days
Debt to equity	40%
Dividend yield	6%
Dividend cover	3 times

Comparator's financial statements for the year to 30 September 20X3 are set out below:

Statement of profit or loss

	$000
Revenue	2,425
Cost of sales	(1,870)
Gross profit	555
Other operating expenses	(215)
Profit from operations	340
Finance costs	(34)
Exceptional item (note (ii))	(120)
Profit before tax	186
Income tax expense	(90)
Profit for the year	96

Extract from statement of changes in equity

	$000
Retained earnings – 1 October 20X2	179
Profit for the year	96
Dividends paid (interim $60,000, final $30,000)	(90)
Retained earnings – 30 September 20X3	185

Statement of financial position

	$000	$000
Non-current assets		540
Current assets		
Inventory	275	
Receivables	320	
		595
		1,135
Equity		
Ordinary shares (25 cents each)		150
Retained earnings		185
		335

Non-current liabilities		
8% loan notes		300
Current liabilities		
Bank overdraft	65	
Trade payables	350	
Taxation	85	
	———	500
		———
		1,135
		———

Notes:

(i) The details of non-current assets are:

	Cost	Accumulated depreciation	Carrying amount
	$000	$000	$000
At 30 September 20X3	3,600	3,060	540

(ii) The exceptional item relates to losses on the sale of a batch of computers that had become worthless due to improvements in microchip design.

(iii) The market price of Comparator's shares throughout the year averaged $6 each.

Required:

(a) Calculate the ratios for Comparator equivalent to those provided by the inter-firm comparison service.

(b) Write a report analysing the financial performance of Comparator based on a comparison with the sector averages.

Specialised, not-for-profit and public sector organisations

Not-for-profit and public sector organisations cover a range of entities, such as charities, schools, healthcare providers and government departments. Their main focus will to be to achieve certain objectives rather than make a profit. For example, a school's primary aim may relate to exam pass rates. While their aim may not be to make a profit, there are many accounting standards which would still be relevant, such as IAS 16 *Property, Plant and Equipment*, IAS 20 *Government Grants* and IFRS 16 *Leases*.

The International Public Sector Accounting Standards Board (IPSASB) issue International Public Sector Accounting Standards (IPSAS) which are based around IFRS, but tailored towards not-for-profit entities.

The main financial aim of specialised, not-for-profit and public sector organisations is not to achieve a profit or return on capital but to achieve value for money. Value for money is achieved by a combination of the three Es:

- Effectiveness – success in achieving its objectives/providing its service.
- Efficiency – how well its resources are used.
- Economy – keeping cost of inputs low.

As profit and return are not so meaningful, many ratios will have little importance in these organisations, for example:

- ROCE
- gearing
- investor ratios in general.

However such organisations must also keep control of income and costs therefore other ratios will still be important, such as working capital ratios.

As the main aim of these organisations is to achieve value for money, other, non-financial ratios take on added significance:

- measures of effectiveness such as the time scale within which outpatients are treated in a hospital
- measures of efficiency such as the pupil-to-teacher ratio in a school
- measures of economy such as the teaching time of cheaper classroom assistants in a school as opposed to more expensive qualified teachers.

8 Interpretation of consolidated financial statements

Interpreting group financial statements

A 20 mark interpretation question could involve transactions between a parent and a subsidiary, or an acquisition/disposal of a subsidiary. It is therefore essential that you are comfortable with the information contained within Chapters 17-20 in terms of acquiring a subsidiary and any adjustments required for intra-group trading with a subsidiary. In addition to this, the calculation of profit or loss on disposal of a subsidiary from Chapter 21 is also essential.

A question involving group financial statements is likely to require you to make some adjustment to figures, whether through making adjustments to consolidated figures, or looking at goodwill or the gain/loss on disposal.

In this case, your analysis should consider the overall impact to the group as well as the underlying performance of individual companies if information is given about them.

The relationships within the group should be considered, looking at any items which may not be at fair value in order to attempt to manipulate performance of a particular aspect of the group.

In addition to looking at any group adjustments, the overall impact on the financial statements should be considered, taking into account any trend analysis for future periods. Examples of this are shown below.

Subsidiary acquired during the year

Statement of profit or loss:

- Income and expenses should increase due to the new subsidiary being included in the year
- This will not have a full year's results from the subsidiary, as the results will only be consolidated from the date of acquisition
- Acquisition costs may be included, which affect the performance of the group in the current period
- Margins will be affected as the newly acquired subsidiary is likely to have different margins to the rest of the group

Statement of financial position:

- 100% of the assets and liabilities of the subsidiary will be consolidated at the reporting date
- This will mean that there could be significant increases in assets or liabilities depending on the position of the newly-acquired subsidiary
- Working capital ratios, such as receivables collection period, are likely to change due to the new subsidiary having different credit terms to the rest of the group
- Working capital ratios may also be affected adversely as the ratio uses the year-end assets or liabilities, but the income/expenses included may be time-apportioned in the statement of profit or loss. For example, a subsidiary with revenue for the year of $1,000,000 and closing receivables of $90,000 would have a receivables collection period of 33 days in its individual financial statements (90,000/1,000,000 × 365). If this had been acquired exactly halfway through the year, only $500,000 revenue would be included within the consolidated statement of profit or loss, with the full $90,000 of receivables included in the consolidated statement of financial position. This would effectively give a receivables collection period of 66 days (90,000/500,000 × 365), giving a distorted picture.
- Return on capital employed and net asset turnover may decrease as the subsidiary's profit will be time apportioned, but any debt held by the subsidiary will be included in full at the reporting date (see the statement of financial position below).

Future periods:

- Future years' statements of profit or loss will include a full year's results from the subsidiary so will show a more accurate reflection of the performance going forward.
- Any costs associated with the acquisition will not be included, giving a more accurate picture of the underlying performance.

Subsidiary disposed of during the year

Statement of profit or loss:

- The previous year's statement of profit or loss would include a full year's results from the disposed subsidiary
- The results for the current year may have the subsidiary shown as a discontinued operation (shown as one line below the profit for the year from the continuing operations) or have the results consolidated into income and expenses for the period up to the date of disposal
- The consolidated results may also include any gain/loss on disposal, which should be stripped out for comparative purposes
- Any costs associated with the disposal, such as professional fees or redundancies, may be included in the current period which would not be recognised in future periods
- Margins are likely to be incomparable, as the prior year will include the disposed subsidiary but the current year may only include the companies remaining in the group

Statement of financial position:

- The previous year's statement of financial position would contain 100% of the assets and liabilities of the disposed subsidiary
- The current year's statement of financial position would contain none of these as the subsidiary will not be controlled at the reporting date
- Cash may be increased by the sales proceeds of the subsidiary
- Ratios such as working capital ratios, return on capital employed and net asset turnover may be distorted if some of the subsidiary's results are included in the statement of profit or loss, as no assets or liabilities from the subsidiary will be included in this calculation

Future periods:

- There will be no distortion of ratios due to the partial results of the subsidiary being included
- Future analysis could involve an examination of how the group have invested any proceeds raised from the disposal of the subsidiary

Test your understanding 3

Summarised below are the recently issued financial statements of Hoof, a listed company, for the years ended 30 September 20X7 and 20X6.

Statements of profit or loss for the year ended 30 September

	20X7	**20X6**
	$000	$000
Revenue	250,000	180,000
Cost of sales	(200,000)	(150,000)
Gross profit	50,000	30,000
Operating expenses	(26,000)	(22,000)
Finance costs	(8,000)	–
Profit before tax	16,000	8,000
Income tax expense (at 25%)	(4,000)	(2,000)
Profit for the year	12,000	6,000

Statements of financial position as at 30 September

	20X7	**20X6**
	$000	$000
Non-current assets		
Property, plant and equipment	210,000	90,000
Goodwill	10,000	–
Current assets		
Inventory	25,000	15,000
Receivables	13,000	8,000
Bank	Nil	14,000
	258,000	127,000
Equity		
Share capital	100,000	100,000
Retained earnings	14,000	12,000
Non-current liabilities		
8% loan notes	100,000	–
Current liabilities		
Bank overdraft	17,000	–
Trade payables	23,000	13,000
Taxation	4,000	2,000
	258,000	127,000

On 1 October 20X6 Hoof purchased 100% of the net assets of Foot for $100 million. To finance this, Hoof issued $100 million 8% loan notes on 1 October 20X6.

Foot's results for the year ended 30 September 20X7 can be seen below.

Statement of profit or loss

	$000
Revenue	70,000
Cost of sales	(40,000)
Gross profit	30,000
Operating expenses	(8,000)
Profit before tax	22,000
Income tax expense (at 25%)	(5,500)
Profit for the period	16,500

Foot paid no dividend during 20X7, but Hoof paid a dividend of 10 cents per share.

The following ratios have been calculated for Hoof for the year ended 30 September 20X6:

Return on capital employed (Profit before interest and tax/loan notes + equity)	7.1%
Gross profit margin	16.7%
Net profit (before tax) margin	4.4%

Required:

(a) Calculate the equivalent ratios for Hoof for 20X7:

   (i) including the results of Foot

   (ii) Excluding all effects of the purchase of Foot

(b) Analyse the performance of Hoof for the year ended 30 September 20X7.

(c) Analyse the cash position of Hoof.

Test your understanding 4

The Pure group operates in the farming industry and has operated a number of 100% owned subsidiaries for many years. Its financial statements for the last two years are shown below.

Consolidated statements of profit or loss for the year ended 30 September

	20X3	20X2
	$000	$000
Revenue	94,000	68,500
Cost of sales	(46,000)	(28,000)
Gross profit	48,000	40,500
Distribution costs	(21,200)	(19,300)
Administrative expenses	(25,600)	(15,400)
Profit from operations	1,200	5,800
Investment income	–	600
Finance costs	(120)	–
Profit before tax	1,080	6,400
Income tax expense	(300)	(1,920)
Profit for the year	780	4,480
Attributable to:		
Shareholders of Pure	1,580	4,480
Non-controlling interest	(800)	–
	780	4,480

Consolidated statements of financial position (extracts) as at 30 September

	20X3	20X2
	$000	$000
Current Assets		
Inventories	6,500	4,570
Trade receivables	17,000	15,600
Bank	610	6,000
Equity		
Share capital	25,000	6,000
Retained earnings	73,500	72,500
Non-controlling interest	510	–
Non-current liabilities		
Loan	20,000	–

The following information is relevant:

(i) Pure has become increasingly worried about two major areas in its business environment. Firstly, there are concerns that reliance on large supermarkets is putting pressure on cash flow, as the supermarkets demand extended payment terms. Secondly, consistent increases in fuel prices mean that delivering the produce nationally is becoming extremely expensive.

(ii) To manage this, Pure acquired 80% of Howard on 1 October 20X2. This was the first time Pure had acquired a subsidiary without owning 100%. Howard operates two luxury hotels, and Pure acquired Howard with a view to diversification and to provide a long-term solution to the cash flow concerns.

(iii) The Pure group raised finance for the acquisition from a number of sources. Part of this came from the disposal of $11 million held in investments, making a $4.5 million gain on disposal, which is included within administrative expenses.

(iv) Howard opened a third hotel in March 20X3, its largest yet. After poor initial reviews, Howard appointed a new marketing director in May 20X3. Following an extensive marketing campaign, online feedback had improved significantly.

(v) The following ratios have been calculated for the year ended 30 September 20X2:

Gross profit margin	59.1%
Operating margin	8.5%
Return on capital employed	7.4%
Inventory turnover period	60 days
Receivables collection period	83 days

Required:

(a) For the ratios provided above, prepare the equivalent figures for the year ended 30 September 20X3.

(b) Analyse the performance and cash flow of Pure for the year ended 30 September 20X3, making specific reference to any concerns or expectations regarding future periods.

9 Chapter summary

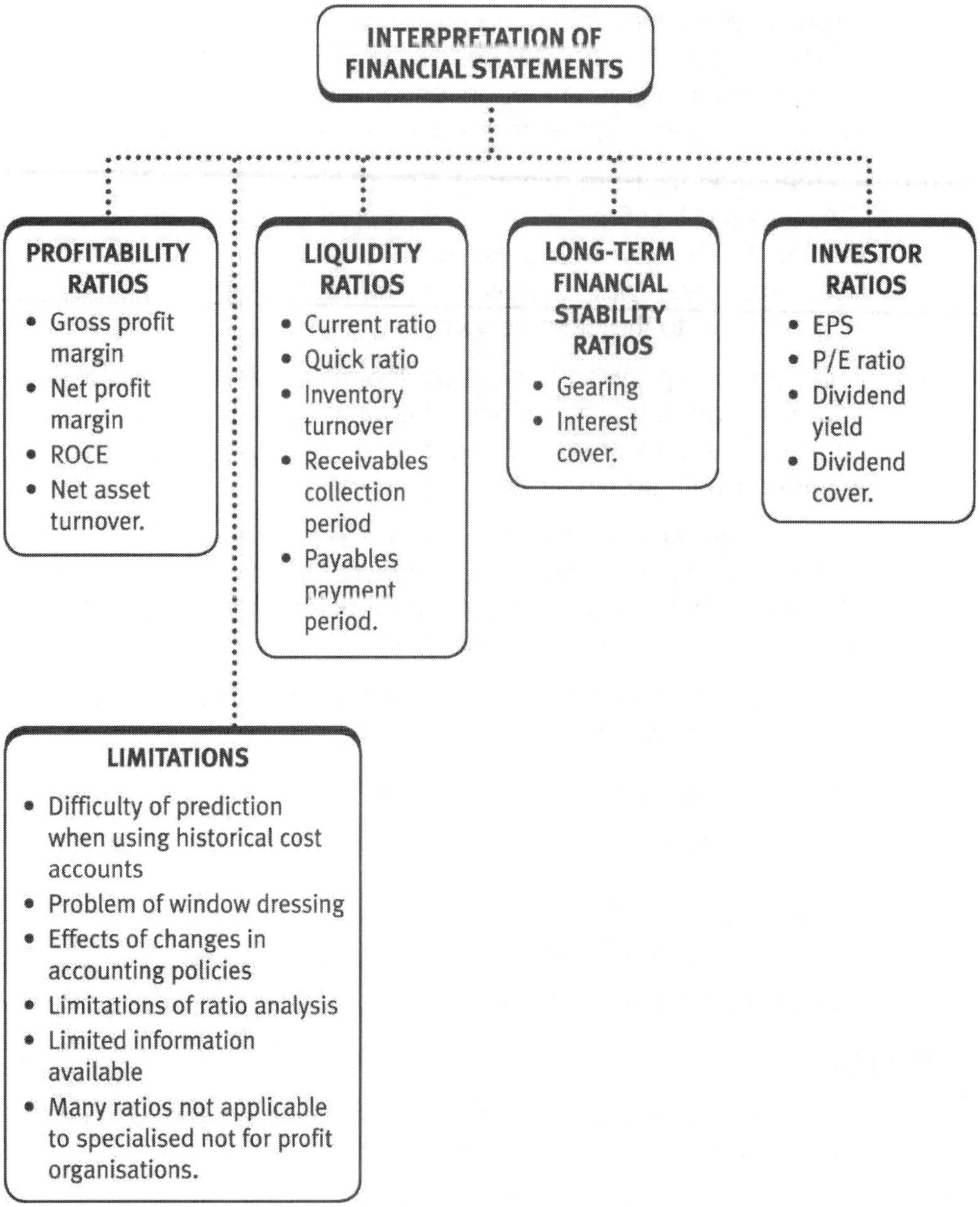

Test your understanding 5

1 The following extracts of Jim's financial statements are available:

	$000
Redeemable preference share capital	50
Ordinary share capital	900
Share premium	400
Retained earnings	400
10% loan notes	150

The gearing (debt to debt plus equity) ratio of Jim will be:

A 8.3%

B 10.5%

C 15.8%

D 22.2%

2 The following extracts from Patel's financial statements are available:

	$000
Profit from operations	400
Finance costs	(50)
Profit before tax	350
Ordinary share capital	900
Retained earnings	300
10% loan notes	500

What are the return on capital employed (ROCE) and pre-tax return on equity (ROE)?

	ROCE	ROE
A	23.5%	23.5%
B	20.6%	29.2%
C	23.5%	29.2%
D	28.6%	23.5%

3 **The acid test or quick ratio should include**

A raw materials

B work in progress

C trade receivables

D non-current liabilities

4 Lytham plc recognised an impairment loss in relation to property, plant and equipment in profit or loss during the year.

What was the effect its recognition on Lytham plc's gearing and non-current asset turnover?

A An increase in gearing and an increase in non-current asset turnover

B No change in gearing and a decrease in non-current asset turnover

C An increase in gearing and a decrease in non-current asset turnover

D No change in gearing and an increase in non-current asset turnover

5 JT operates in a highly seasonal industry. An analyst has sought to assess JT by comparing its ratios to ratios of the business sector average for the year ended 31 December 20X3.

Which of the following is likely to be a limitation of this analysis?

A The average figures have been taken from entities whose year ends occur at different points across the year

B The industry has experienced significant falls in demand over the past two years

C All of the entities in the sector prepare financial statements under IFRS Standards

D An error was discovered relating to JT's 20X2 financial statements. This was corrected in 20X3.

6 The following information has been taken from the accounting records of FX for the year ended 31 December 20X4.

FX's working capital (cash) cycle is 55 days.

FX's trade payable payment period is 40 days

Credit sales amounted to $2 million, and year end receivables were $274,000

All calculations should be made to the nearest full day. The trading year is 365 days.

What is the inventory turnover period as at 31 December 20X4?

A 50 days

B 45 days

C 65 days

D 35 days

7 **Incorrectly treating a lease rental as an operating expense is likely to have what impact on ratios?**

A Non-current asset turnover will be understated

B Interest cover will be understated

C Return on capital employed will be understated

D Gearing will be understated

Data for Questions 8 and 9

The following extracts of Greg's financial statements are available:

Dividend paid	$140,000
Ordinary $1 share capital	$1,000,000
Retained earnings	$2,900,000
Share price	$2.50
Profit for the year	$330,000

8 **What is the dividend yield for Greg?**

A 14%

B 42.4%

C 4.8%

D 5.6%

9 **What is the dividend cover?**

A 2.4 times

B 17.9 times

C 20.7 times

D 7.1 times

10 **Which of the following ratios is likely to be most relevant for a local charity?**

A Earnings per share

B Return on capital employed

C Operating profit margin

D Quick (acid test) ratio

Test your understanding 6

Farrell is a listed company with a number of subsidiaries. On 1 April 20X6, it disposed of its 75% holding in Daly for total cash consideration of $10 million. The net assets of Daly at the date of disposal were $14 million, and the value of the non-controlling interest at this date was $2 million. Farrell acquired its interest in Daly on 1 April 20X0, at which time goodwill of $4 million was recognised. This goodwill had been fully impaired by 30 September 20X3. The loss on disposal has been included within operating expenses for the year to 30 September 20X6.

The consolidated summarised financial statements of Farrell at 30 September 20X5 and 30 September 20X6 are shown below.

Consolidated statements of profit or loss for the years ended 30 September

	20X6	20X5
	$000	$000
Revenue	89,000	93,000
Cost of sales	(71,550)	(74,400)
Gross profit	17,450	18,600
Operating expenses	(9,210)	(7,800)
Profit before tax (operating profit)	8,240	10,800
Income tax expense	(2,400)	(3,000)
Profit for the year	5,840	7,800
Attributable to:		
Equity holders of the parent	4,990	6,900
Non-controlling interest	850	900
	5,840	7,800

Statements of financial position as at 30 September

	20X6	20X5
	$000	$000
Non-current assets		
Property, plant and equipment	41,500	54,600
Goodwill	3,000	3,000
Current assets	54,800	44,000
	99,300	101,600

Equity		
Equity shares of $1 each	40,000	40,000
Retained earnings	22,350	18,700
	62,350	58,700
Non-controlling interest	12,450	13,600
	74,800	72,300
Current liabilities	24,500	29,300
	99,300	101,600

Daley statements of profit or loss for the years ended 30 September

	20X6	**20X5**
	$000	$000
Revenue	11,500	16,000
Cost of sales	(10,570)	(13,100)
Gross profit	930	2,900
Operating expenses	(1,420)	(1,410)
Profit before tax (operating profit)	(490)	1,490
Income tax credit/(expense)	100	(290)
Profit for the year	(390)	1,200

Required:

Using the above financial statements, calculate the following ratios for Farrell for the years ended 30 September 20X6 and 20X5, and comment on the comparative performance, including the impact of the disposal of Daly during the year ended 30 September 20X6:

(i) Return on capital employed (ROCE)

(ii) Net asset turnover

(iii) Gross profit margin

(iv) Operating profit margin

Test your understanding answers

Test your understanding 1

Neville

Report

To: Directors of Neville

From: Business Consultant

Date: XX.XX.XX

Subject: Performance of Neville

Introduction

As requested I have analysed the financial statements of Neville for the year ended 30 June 20X5 compared to the previous year to assess the performance and position of the entity and to determine whether the strategies that you have implemented have been successful. The ratios that I have calculated are shown in an appendix to this report.

Performance

Profitability

The revenue of the entity has increased by 20% on last year. It would therefore appear that the strategy of cutting prices and extending credit facilities has attracted customers and generated an increase in revenue. Whether or not the revenue is now above budget, as was the directors' aim, is unknown.

Despite this increase however, the profitability of the company has worsened, with both gross profit and operating profit being lower than the previous year. Similarly the operating profit margin has declined from 20.3% to 12.9%. There are likely to be several reasons behind this deterioration.

The reduction in sale prices will have contributed to the worsening gross profit. To rectify this, Neville may consider approaching their suppliers for some bulk-buying discounts, as since they are selling more items they will now be purchasing more material from suppliers.

The move of purchasing additional machinery may also have contributed to the lower profitability, with an impact on depreciation expense.

The return on capital employed has dropped significantly from 48% to 29.5%. This is mainly due to the lower operating profit margins and reasons discussed above, as opposed to a decline in the efficient use of assets since the asset utilisation has suffered only a slight fall.

The revaluation of non-current assets will also have contributed to the fall in the return on capital employed and would explain why the asset utilisation has fallen slightly.

The revaluation may have caused additional depreciation charges in the statement of profit or loss if the assets were revalued at the start of the year. This may therefore be another factor in the worsening profits.

The additional machinery purchased during the year may not have been fully operational in the current year, and so would also explain the lower returns. The higher depreciation charges will also have contributed to lower profits.

Position

Liquidity

Again, the company's results are showing a worsening position in this area with the current ratio declining from 1.62 to 1.23.

The cause for this would seem to be the extension of credit facilities to customers.

Receivables days have increased from what seems to be an acceptable level of 65 days to 110 days. Although the benefits of this strategy have been shown by the increase in revenue, it would seem that Neville have now allowed customers too much credit. It would be recommended that receivables days should be reduced to closer to 90 days as a first step.

As a result of the increase in the receivables collection period, Neville have been taking longer to pay their suppliers. Their payables days are now at an unacceptably high level of 102 days. This is likely to be causing dissatisfaction with suppliers and would reduce the ability of Neville being able to negotiate discounts as discussed above.

Inventory holding days have decreased from 43 to 38. Although this increase in efficiency is to be welcomed, it may be caused by supply problems from dissatisfied suppliers.

As a consequence of these factors, by the end of the year Neville are operating a significant overdraft.

Gearing

The gearing ratio has fallen from 16.9% to 10.1% as a result of the reduction in non-current liabilities. Assuming that these are loans, it would appear that Neville have further utilised their cash resources to repay these loans. This does not seem to have been a sensible move given their poor liquidity position.

The revaluation of non-current assets and subsequent increase in equity would also have contributed to the lowering of this ratio.

Further, the gearing ratio last year does not seem particularly high, although comparison with an industry average would confirm this, and the company had a significant level of profits covering their finance costs.

Hence it would have seemed appropriate to have increased the longer term debt of the company to finance the growth rather than increasing their current liabilities.

It was identified above that Neville purchased additional non-current assets. Given the gearing and liquidity positions, it would seem that these have been financed from short-term sources rather than more appropriate long-term sources.

Summary

Although the directors' initial aim of improving revenue has been achieved with the measures taken, the strategies do not appear to have been successful overall. The cutting of prices has caused lowering profit margins and, combined with additional depreciation charges, has resulted in a worsening profit situation overall.

The extension of credit periods has again been successful to the extent that it has helped increase revenue but has caused a poor liquidity position.

It would seem that Neville are showing signs of overtrading.

To rectify the situation it would seem appropriate to increase the long-term debt of the company as a matter of priority.

Appendix

	20X4	20X5	
Revenue	1,159,850	1,391,820	+20%
Gross profit	406,400	340,995	– 16.1%
Operating profit	235,450	179,545	– 23.7%

	20X4		20X5	
Operating profit	$\frac{235,450}{1,159,850}$	20.3%	$\frac{179,545}{1,391,820}$	12.9%
ROCE	$\frac{235,450}{490,520}$	48.0%	$\frac{179,545}{607,765}$	29.5%
Asset turnover	$\frac{1,159,850}{490,520}$	2.36	$\frac{1,391,820}{607,765}$	2.29
Inventory days	$\frac{88,760 \times 365}{753,480}$	43 days	$\frac{109,400 \times 365}{1,050,825}$	38 days
Receivables days	$\frac{206,550 \times 365}{1,159,850}$	65 days	$\frac{419,455 \times 365}{1,391,820}$	110 days
Payables days	$\frac{179,590 \times 365}{753,450}$	87 days	$\frac{295,480 \times 365}{1,050,825}$	102 days
Current ratio	$\frac{390,710}{241,590}$	1.62	$\frac{528,855}{430,680}$	1.23
Gearing	$\frac{83,100}{490,520}$	16.9%	$\frac{61,600}{607,765}$	10.1%

Test your understanding 2

(a) **Calculation of specified ratios**

	Comparator	Sector average
Return on capital employed (186 + 34 loan interest/(335 + 300))	34.6%	22.1%
Net asset turnover (2,425/(335 + 300))	3.8 times	1.8 times
Gross profit margin (555/2,425 × 100)	22.9%	30%
Net profit (before tax) margin (186/2,425 × 100)	7.7%	12.5%
Current ratio (595/500)	1.19 : 1	1.6 : 1
Quick ratio (320/500)	0.64 : 1	0.9 : 1
Inventory days (275/1,870 × 365)	54 days	46 days
Receivables days (320/2,425 × 365)	48 days	45 days
Payables days (350/1,870 × 365) (based on cost of sales)	68 days	55 days
Debt to equity (300/335 ×100)	90%	40%
Dividend yield (see below)	2.5%	6%
Dividend cover (96/90)	1.07 times	3 times

(The workings are in $000 and are for Comparator's ratios.)

The dividend yield is calculated from a dividend per share figure of 15c ($90,000/150,000 × 4) and a share price of $6.00. Thus the yield is 2.5% (15c/$6.00 × 100%).

(b) **REPORT**

Subject: Analysis of Comparator's financial performance compared to sector average for the year to 30 September 20X3

Operating performance

The return on capital employed of Comparator is impressive being more than 50% higher than the sector average. The components of the return on capital employed are the asset turnover and profit margin. In these areas Comparator's asset turnover is more than double the average, but the net profit margin after exceptionals is considerably below the sector average. However, if the exceptionals are treated as one-off costs and excluded, Comparator's margins are very similar to the sector average.

This short analysis seems to imply that Comparator's superior return on capital employed is due entirely to an efficient asset turnover i.e. Comparator is making its assets work twice as efficiently as its competitors. A closer inspection of the underlying figures may explain why its asset turnover is so high. It can be seen from the note to the statement of financial position that Comparator's non-current assets appear to be quite old. Their carrying amount is only 15% of their original cost. This has at least two implications. Firstly these assets will need replacing in the near future and the company is already struggling for funding, and secondly their low carrying amount produces a high figure for asset turnover.

Unless Comparator has underestimated the life of its assets in its depreciation calculations, its non-current assets will need replacing in the near future. When this occurs its asset turnover and return on capital employed figures will be much lower.

This aspect of ratio analysis often causes problems and to counter this anomaly some companies calculate the asset turnover using the cost of non-current assets rather than their carrying amount as this gives a more reliable trend.

A further issue is which of the two calculated margins should be compared to the sector average (i.e. including or excluding the effects of the exceptionals). The gross profit margin of Comparator is much lower than the sector average. If the exceptional losses were taken in at trading account level, which they should be as they relate to obsolete inventory, Comparator's gross margin would be even worse. As Comparator's net margin is similar to the sector average, it would appear that Comparator has better control over its operating costs. This is especially true as the other element of the net profit calculation is finance costs and as Comparator has much higher gearing than the sector average, one would expect Comparator's interest to be higher than the sector average.

Liquidity

Here Comparator shows real cause for concern. Its current and quick ratios are much worse than the sector average, and indeed far below expected norms. Current liquidity problems appear due to high levels of accounts payable and a high bank overdraft. The high levels of inventory contribute to the poor quick ratio and may be indicative of further obsolete inventory, as the exceptional item is due to obsolete inventory.

The accounts receivable collection figure appears reasonable, but at 68 days, Comparator takes longer to pay its accounts payable than do its competitors. Whilst this is a source of 'free' finance, it can damage relationships with suppliers and may lead to a curtailment of further credit.

Gearing

As referred to above, gearing (as measured by debt/equity) is more than twice the level of the sector average. Whilst this may be an uncomfortable level, it is currently beneficial for shareholders. The company is making an overall return of 34.6%, but only paying 8% interest on its loan notes. The gearing level may become a serious issue if Comparator becomes unable to maintain the finance costs. The company already has an overdraft and their ability to make further interest payments could be in doubt.

Investment ratios

Despite reasonable profitability figures, Comparator's dividend yield is poor compared to the sector average. From the extracts of the statement of changes in equity it can be seen that total dividends are $90,000 out of available profit for the year of only $96,000 (hence the very low dividend cover). It is worthy of note that the interim dividend was $60,000 and the final dividend only $30,000. Perhaps this indicates a worsening performance during the year, as normally final dividends are higher than interim dividends. Considering these factors it is surprising the company's share price is holding up so well.

Summary

The company compares favourably with the sector average figures for profitability. However the company's liquidity and gearing position is quite poor and gives cause for concern. If it is to replace its old assets in the near future, it will need to raise further finance. With already high levels of borrowing and poor dividend yields, this may be a serious problem for Comparator.

Test your understanding 3

(a) **Equivalent ratios**

(i) **Including Foot: 20X7**

	20X7
Gross profit margin (50,000/250,000 × 100)	20%
Net profit (before tax) margin (16,000/250,000 × 100)	6.4%
Return on capital employed (24,000/(114,000 + 100,000) × 100)	11.2%

For (ii) it is helpful to re-draft a statement of profit or loss without the effects of Foot.

Statement of profit or loss	$000
Revenue (250,000 – 70,000)	180,000
Cost of sales (200,000 – 40,000)	(160,000)
Gross profit	20,000
Operating expenses (26,000 – 8,000)	(18,000)
Profit before tax	2,000
Tax (at 25%)	(500)
Profit for the period	1,500

Note that there would be no finance costs without the purchase of Foot so these are excluded.

(ii) **Excluding the effects of Foot:**

	20X7
Gross profit margin (20,000/180,000 × 100)	11.1%
Net profit (before tax) margin (2,000/180,000 × 100)	1.1%
Return on capital employed (2,000/(100,000 + 3,500) × 100)	1.9%

Note: Capital employed will be made up of share capital and retained earnings, as no loan notes will exist without the purchase of Foot. Retained earnings without Foot will actually be $3.5 million.

This can be calculated in a number of ways:

- Closing retained earnings of $14 million less $16.5 million from Foot's profit, plus $6 million increase in profit after tax relating to the interest on the loan notes ($8 million interest saved less $2 million tax relief at 25%).
- An alternative calculation of retained earnings would be $12 million in 20X6 plus $1.5 million from Hoofs profit excluding Foot less $10 million dividend (10c per share), which would also give $3.5 million.
- A final alternative calculation of retained earnings would be closing retained earnings of $14 million less the original profit of $12 million plus the $1.5 million profit excluding Foot, to give $3.5 million.

(b) **Performance**

During the year, the revenue of the Hoof group increased by $70 million. However, it can be seen that all of the $70 million increase came from the acquisition of Foot, meaning that the underlying business in Hoof was flat during the year.

Whilst this shows that Foot was a good acquisition in terms of generating revenue, it also highlights a poor performance by Hoof. It appears that Hoof have increased property, plant and equipment in addition to the purchase of Foot as this has increased in the year by $120 million. As Foot was purchased for $100 million, it is unlikely that all of the increase in these assets comes from Foot.

The gross profit margin has increased in the year from 16.7% to 20%. Again, all of this is due to Foot. It can be seen that Foot makes a gross margin of 42.9% ($30 million/$70 million) which is significantly higher than the rest of the group, which has generated 11.2%. This is further indication of both the strength of Foot and the poor underlying performance of Hoof.

Initially, it appears that Hoof would be loss-making without Foot, as Foot's profit before tax is $22 million and the group profit before tax is only $16 million. This suggests that Hoof would make a $6 million loss without Foot. This isn't accurate, as Hoof would not have incurred the $8 million finance costs without the Foot purchase, meaning that Hoof has made a small profit before tax of $2 million.

When looking at both the net profit margin and the return on capital employed, the performance of the Hoof group shows an improvement on the previous year. Investigation shows that without Foot this would again be below the previous year, further highlighting the decline.

The constant improvement in the measures relating to performance shows that Foot has been a successful acquisition and that Hoof's profits without it have significantly declined. It can also be seen that there appears to be some cost savings within operating expenses. These have only increased by $4 million in the year, but Foot's operating expenses are $8 million. This suggests that the group may have benefited from being able to share administrative or head office functions and reduce expenses.

(c) **Cash**

There is a significant decline in the cash position of the Hoof group at 30 September 20X7, going from a cash position of $14 million to being overdrawn by $17 million. While Foot has been acquired for $100 million, this has been funded through the issue of $100 million loan notes, so this cannot be the reason for the decline in cash during the year. There may have been some additional costs linked to the acquisition, but this will not make up a significant part of the cash movement.

There are two major reasons for this decrease. Firstly, Hoof has paid a dividend of $10 million during the year. While this may have kept shareholders happy, the wisdom of this could be questioned, especially in the light of the declining underlying performance in Hoof.

Secondly, there looks to have also been an increase in non-current assets beyond the acquisition of Foot, as these have increased by $120 million after depreciation. More information will be required on where these additions have taken place. If the additions have been made within Foot, this would seem to be a wise move due to the high level of Foot profits. If the assets have been acquired for the Hoof business, it would raise concerns, as it appears that these assets have not been turned into profits during the year.

The interest payment of $8 million will have affected the cash flow, although it must be noted that Foot generates enough profits to cover this payment.

There are no huge concerns over the management of working capital. Without knowing what industry Hoof and Foot are involved in, it is difficult to make judgements on inventory or receivables management, but both balances have increased in line with the increased performance from Foot.

It is possible that Foot may have had an overdraft when acquired, as information on Foot's individual position has not been given.

Conclusion

The acquisition of Foot has clearly been a success for Hoof in terms of profit generation, as this has generated the majority of profits for the year. This has disguised the fact that the underlying Hoof business seems to have struggled with declining profits. Careful attention must be paid to the position, as cash is a significant concern. The wisdom of the dividend could be called into question. It may be that Hoof has finished the expansion in terms of acquiring non-current assets which could relieve some pressure on the future cash flow.

Test your understanding 4

(a) **Ratios for the Pure group:**

	20X3	Working	20X2 (given)
Gross profit margin	51.1%	(48,000/94,000) × 100	59.1%
Operating margin	1.3%	(1,200/94,000) × 100	8.5%
Return on capital employed	1.0%	(1,200/(99,010 + 20,000) × 100	7.4%
Inventory turnover period	52 days	(6,500/46,000) × 365	60 days
Receivables collection period	66 days	(17,000/94,000) × 365	83 days

(b) **Analysis of the performance and cash flow of the Pure group**

Performance

Revenue and expenses have all increased during the year. Some of this will be due to the acquisition of Howard in the year, but without Howard's individual financial statements it is difficult to see how much this has contributed. Howard has been owned since 1 October 20X2 so has contributed a full year's results for the year to September 20X3 which would not have been included in the year to September 20X2.

It is also worth noting that the new hotel was only opened in March, so a full year's revenue has not yet been generated by this.

Whilst revenue has increased significantly, it can be seen that higher expenses have meant that the Pure group has made less profit than in the previous period.

The gross profit margin has fallen in the year. This could be due to the increased pressure on prices from supermarkets or difficult conditions, but could also be due to the addition of Howard into the group.

It may be that the hotel industry generates much lower margins than the farming industry, or it may be that Howard itself generates lower margins. It may also be that the poor reputation associated with the new hotel resulted in the need to offer lower room rates to attract new customers or to bring customers back. Following the improvement in feedback, this will hopefully not need to be repeated in future periods.

The improvement in feedback should lead to increased future bookings, so it may be that the new hotel generates a significantly improved return in future years.

The operating margin has also deteriorated in the year. It is also important to note that there is a significant one-off $4.5 million gain on disposal in relation to the sale of investments. Without this, Pure would have made a worrying loss from operations of $3.3 million.

Analysing this further, the reason for this loss is due to a significant increase in administrative expenses, which would be $30.1 million excluding the $4.5 million profit on disposal.

The Pure group would have incurred costs relating to the acquisition of Howard, which will not be incurred in future periods.

There will have been significant expenses associated with the set-up of the new hotel during the year, which again are unlikely to be repeated in future periods unless Howard plans on opening another hotel. The increased marketing expenses will also have had a significant impact on the profit, though it is unclear whether this is something that may need to be repeated or maintained in the future.

There will be many costs associated with the new hotel which will be recurring, such as the increase in staff numbers, and the running costs of the hotel. The new marketing director is likely to have demanded a significant salary, as they were brought in specifically to address a problem with the hotel's reputation.

Distribution costs have not increased dramatically during the year. This could suggest that there has been a decline in the underlying farming business, as fuel costs have consistently risen. It could also mean that the hotel business has extremely low distribution costs, which is likely.

Whilst the Pure group has managed to reduce its exposure to fuel prices through the acquisition of an entity not dependent on distribution, it is questionable how wise this has been. Howard appears to have lower margins and will still incur significant costs in terms of heat and light, which may rise in a similar manner to fuel costs.

The return on capital employed has deteriorated in the year, which is expected due to the reduced profits. Removing the gain on disposal of the investments would make the Pure group loss-making, meaning that it would make a negative return on capital employed.

It appears that Howard is a loss-making entity, as the non-controlling share of the group's profit is negative. As Howard is the only non-100% owned subsidiary, the non-controlling interest will relate solely to Howard's performance.

It may also be that there is goodwill impairment following the acquisition of Howard. This could have arisen from the poor reputation associated with the new hotel. If the non-controlling interest is valued at fair value, 20% of the impairment would be allocated to the non-controlling interest's share.

In addition to the reduced profits, the capital employed by the Pure group has increased significantly. $19 million of new shares have been issued, probably to fund the acquisition of Howard. There has also been a $20 million loan taken out, although it is possible that Howard already had this loan and this has resulted from the consolidation of Howard's assets and liabilities.

The sale of investments and share issue, and potentially the loan, suggest that the Pure group paid a very high price for Howard. This may not have been wise if Howard has low margins, or is loss-making. If Howard owns the hotel premises, then this may have explained the high price as the land is likely to hold its value, even if Howard performs poorly.

Cash flow

The cash balance has fallen to $0.6 million at 30 September 20X3. It should be noted that the Pure group has raised significant funds during the year through a share issue, sale of investments and the potential receipt of a loan. The vast majority of the cash raised is likely to have been spent on the acquisition of Howard and the new hotel.

The decrease in receivable collection period will have a positive effect on the cash flow of the group. As a hotel will largely be cash- based rather than offering credit, this will aid the cash flow of the group. This means that the acquisition of Howard may help offset the problems caused in the farming sector with the longer terms demanded by the supermarkets.

The inventory turnover period has also reduced. This will be due to the fact that Howard will not carry much inventory, as this is likely to relate to food and drink served in the hotels.

Conclusion

It is difficult to judge the success of the group in the current year, as it has been a transitional year. There are concerns over the performance of Howard, although there are reasons to believe this may improve in future periods. For a more meaningful comparison, individual financial statements of companies within the Pure group would need to be obtained.

Test your understanding 5

1 **B** – Debt is made up of the redeemable preference share capital and the loan notes. The total equity is made up of the ordinary share capital and the retained earnings.

Gearing = debt/(debt + equity) = 200/(200 + 1,700) = 10.5%

2 **C**

ROCE = Profit from operations/Debt + equity = (400/1,700) × 100 = 23.5%

Pre-tax ROE = Profit before tax/equity = (350/1,200) × 100 = 29.2%

3 **C**

4 **A** – An impairment will decrease the profit. This will reduce retained earnings which will in turn increase gearing. The impairment loss will also reduce non-current assets, leading to an increase in non-current asset turnover.

5 **A** – As the industry is highly seasonal, the fact that the financial statements are produced at different points across the year is likely to mean that comparison is distorted. The decline will affect all companies within the sector, so this will not create a difference. The error must be corrected retrospectively, so this would affect 20X2's figures, not 20X3.

6 **B** – Working capital cycle = Inventory turnover period + receivables collection period – payables payment period.

Receivables collection period = $274,000/$2,000,000 × 365 = 50 days.

Therefore inventory collection period + 50 days – 40 days = 45 days.

7 **D** – If a lease rental is incorrectly classed as an operating expense, this will mean that non-current assets, liabilities and finance costs are all understated. This will mean that interest cover is overstated, that gearing is understated, that non-current asset turnover is overstated and that return on capital employed is overstated.

8 **D**

$$\textbf{Dividend yield} = \frac{\text{Dividend per share}}{\text{Current share price}}$$

Dividend per share = $140,000/1,000,000 = $0.14 per share.

Dividend yield = $0.14/$2.50 = 5.6%

9 **A**

$$\textbf{Dividend cover} = \frac{\text{Profit after tax}}{\text{Dividends}}$$

$330,000/$140,000 = 2.4 times.

10 **D** – A local charity is unlikely to be concerned with profit, so A, B and C will be less relevant.

Test your understanding 6

References to 20X5 and 20X6 refer to the years ended 30 September 20X5 and 20X6. Figures in brackets are in $000.

Ratios

			20X6		20X5
(i)	Return on capital employed	(8,240/74,800)	11.0%	(10,800/72,300)	14.9%
(ii)	Net asset turnover	(89,000/74,800)	1.19	(93,000/72,300)	1.29
(iii)	Gross profit margin	(17,450/89,000)	19.6%	(18,600/93,000)	20.0%
(iv)	Operating profit margin	(8,240/89,000)	9.3%	(10,800/93,000)	11.6%

At first glance it appears that 20X6 has not been a good year for Farrell. Revenue and profit have both fallen, and each of the above ratios is worse, in some case significantly worse, than 20X5. However, in order to better understand Farrell's performance and position we need to consider the impact of the disposal of Daly.

The disposal of Daly took place half-way through the year, meaning that six months of Daly's performance will be included within Farrell's 20X6 statement of profit or loss, but none of Daly's assets and liabilities will be included in the 20X6 statement of financial position. It is a straightforward matter to adjust the trading performance to exclude Daly (see Appendix) but the impact on assets is less simple.

Performance

Gross profitability for the group fell slightly but this seems to be due to the poor performance of Daly, whose margin fell drastically from 18.1 % to 8.1 %. From the limited information available it is difficult to know what caused this drop, but the severity of the fall suggests that it may reflect some sort of obsolescence, either through lower sales prices to clear ageing inventory, or reduced inventory valuation at the year-end. Exclusion of Daly's figures shows that the remainder of the group have maintained their gross profitability at 20X5 levels.

The group's operating profit margin will be affected by the inclusion of the loss on disposal of Daly. Figures in the appendix show a loss of $2 million, and the removal of this, together with Daly's expenses, shows the remainder of the group with an improved operating margin, up from 12.1% to 12.6%. This indicates that the remainder of the group have controlled their expenses, reducing them as a proportion of revenue. If we look at Daly's operating expenses we can see that they have increased slightly, despite the fall in revenue, a further sign that things are not as they should be.

Asset turnover has also worsened from 20X5 to 20X6, indicating a fall in efficiency. Again this seems to be due to the impact of Daly, whose revenue fell by 28% in this period. If we eliminate Daly's revenue from the calculation (not entirely valid, but to give some idea of underlying performance) then the asset turnover becomes 1.11 ($83,250/$74,800) in 20X6 and 1.07 ($77,000/$72,300), suggesting that the remainder of the group have maintained their efficiency.

If we combine the asset turnover efficiency and the operating margin efficiency this gives us the return on capital employed measure. We have already seen that Daly has negatively impacted on both efficiency and profitability so it is no surprise that return on capital employed has fallen as a result of this impact. The disposal of Daly should hopefully improve this primary performance measure in years to come.

Daly

The disposal of Daly appears to be a sensible decision, despite the loss on disposal of $2 million. It is clearly a business in decline, with falling revenue and gross profitability and increasing costs. Daly was part of the Farrell group for six years, and although on acquisition it was deemed to have goodwill of $1 million within the business, this has now been completely impaired, another indication of a business in decline. It would seem that Farrell have wisely decided to cut their losses and convert the Daly investment into cash.

The remaining businesses within the group remain fairly robust, with maintained gross profitability, controlled expenses and a healthy 8% ($83,250 v $77,000) increase in revenue. Provided that the cash generated from the sale of Daly is put to good use, results for 20X7 should improve.

Appendix

Daly profitability ratios		**20X6**		**20X5**
Gross profit margin	(930/11,500)	8.1%	(2,900/16,000)	18.1%
Operating profit/(loss) margin	(-490/11,500)	–4.3%	(1,490/16,000)	9.3%

Ratios excluding Daly		**20X6**		**20X5**
Gross profit margin	(16,985/83,250)	20.4%	(15,700/77,000)	20.4%
Operating profit/ (loss) margin	(10,485/83,250)	12.6%	(9,310/77,000)	12.1%

Adjustments to exclude Daly

	Revenue	Gross profit	Operating profit
20X6	$000	$000	$000
Per consolidated statements	89,000	17,450	8,240
Per Daly SPL (× 6/12)	(5,750)	(465)	245
Loss on disposal			2,000
Excluding Daly	83,250	16,985	10,485
20X5			
Per consolidated statements	93,000	18,600	10,800
Per Daly SPL	(16,000)	(2,900)	(1,490)
Excluding Daly	77,000	15,700	9,310

Calculation of loss on disposal

	$000	$000
Proceeds		10,000
Net assets	14,000	
Non-controlling interest	(2,000)	
		(12,000)
		(2,000)

Chapter

23

Appendix 1: Published financial statements

Chapter learning objectives

Upon completion of this chapter you will be able to:

- Published financial statements pro-formas
- Pro-forma workings
- Published financial statements questions

1 Published financial statement pro-formas

Statement of profit or loss and other comprehensive income for the year ended 31 December 20X2

Continuing operations	$
Revenue **(Chapter 11)**	X
Cost of sales **(W1)**	(X)
Gross profit	X
Distribution costs	(X)
Administrative expenses (could include foreign currency gains and losses **(Chapter 10)**)	(X)
Exceptional items	(X)
Profit from operations	X
Finance costs (could include foreign currency gains and losses on loans)	(X)
Investment income (including FV gain on investment properties **(Chapter 2)**, FV gain on FVPL investments **(Chapter 9)**)	X
Profit before tax	X
Income tax expense **(W3)**	(X)
Profit for the year from continuing operations	X
Profit for the year from discontinued operations **(Chapter 5)**	X
Profit for the year from all operations	X
Other comprehensive income	
Gain/loss on revaluation	X
Gain/loss on FVOCI financial assets **(Chapter 9)**	X
Total comprehensive income for the year	X

Statement of financial position as at 31 December 20X2

Assets	$	$
Non-current assets:		
Property, plant and equipment **(W2)**	X	
Right-of-use assets **(Chapter 12)**	X	
Intangible assets **(Chapter 3)**	X	
Investment properties **(Chapter 2)**	X	
Investments (FVPL and FVOCI **(Chapter 9)**)	X	
		X

	$	$
Current assets:		
Inventories	X	
Trade receivables	X	
Cash and cash equivalents	X	
		X
Non-current assets held for sale **(Chapter 5)**		X
Total assets		**X**
Equity and liabilities		
Capital and reserves:		
Share capital	X	
Share premium	X	
Retained earnings	X	
Revaluation surplus	X	
Convertible loan (equity component **(Chapter 10)**)	X	
		X
Total equity		**X**
Non-current liabilities:		
Long-term borrowings	X	
Deferred tax **(Chapter 13)**	X	
Lease **(Chapter 12)**	X	
Government grants **(Chapter 2)**	X	
Provisions **(Chapter 15)**	X	
Convertible loan **(Chapter 9)**	X	
		X
Current liabilities:		
Trade and other payables	X	
Overdraft	X	
Current tax payable **(Chapter 13)**	X	
Short-term provisions **(Chapter 15)**	X	
Lease **(Chapter 12)**	X	
Government grants **(Chapter 2)**	X	
		X
Total equity and liabilities		X

Statement of changes in equity for the year ended 31 December 20X2

	Share Capital	Share Premium	Reval'n surplus	Convertible loan	FVOCI reserve	Retained Earnings	Total equity
	$	$	$	$	$	$	$
Balance b/f	X	X	X	X	X	X	X
Policy change/ error **(Chap 8)**						(X)	(X)
Restated balance	X	X	X	X	X	X	X
Dividends						(X)	(X)
Share issue	X	X					X
Total comprehensive income for the year			X **(Ch.2)**		X **(Ch.10)**	X	X
Reserves transfer			(X) **(Ch.2)**			X **(Ch.2)**	
Convertible issue				X **(Ch.10)**			X
Balance c/f	X	X	X	X	X	X	X

Workings:

(W1) Cost of sales

	$
Opening inventory	X
Purchases	X
Closing inventory	(X)
Depreciation **(W2)**	X
Amortisation of intangibles **(Chapter 3)**	X
Impairment **(Chapter 4)**	X
Research costs **(Chapter 3)**	X
Increase/decrease in provisions **(Chapter 15)**	X(X)
Total	X

(W2) Tangible non-current assets

	Land and buildings	Plant and machinery	Total
Cost b/f	X	X	X
Accumulated depreciation b/f	(X)	(X)	(X)
Carrying amount b/f	X	X	X
Revaluation	X	X	X
Depreciation charge/impairment	(X)	(X)	(X)
Carrying amount c/f	X	X	X

(W3) Tax expense (Chapter 13)

	$
Under/over provision from last year (per TB)	X(X)
Current year estimate	X
Increase/decrease in deferred tax	X(X)
Total	X(X)

Test your understanding 1

The following shows an extract from Archy Ltd's nominal ledger at 30 April 20X1:

	$	$
Administration expenses	950,000	
Distribution costs	531,000	
Purchases	2,875,000	
Finance costs	9,000	
Investment income		5,700
Revenue		5,350,000
Ordinary share capital $1		1,000,000
Receivables	55,700	
Inventory at 1 May 20X0	1,670,000	
Cash and cash equivalents	242,000	
Land and buildings		
Cost at 1 May 20X0	900,000	
Accumulated depreciation at 1 May 20X0		36,000

Plant and equipment		
Cost at 1 May 20X0	102,800	
Accumulated depreciation at 1 May 20X0		36,400
Intangible asset – carrying amount at 1 May 20X0	68,000	
Retained earnings at 1 May 20X0		813,300
Bank loan (repayable on 1 June 20X9)		100,000
Payables		62,100
	7,403,500	7,403,500

The following additional information is available:

1 The tax charge for the year is estimated at $227,000.

2 During the year a piece of plant costing $56,000 with accumulated depreciation of $21,000, met the criteria of IFRS 5 *Non-current Assets Held for Sale and Discontinued Operations*. The plant is available for sale at the price of $32,000 and costs of $1,000 will be incurred in order to complete the sale.

3 Plant and machinery should be depreciated at 20% on cost and charged to cost of sales.

4 The land and buildings were originally acquired on 1 May 20W7 for $900,000 of which $300,000 related to land. Depreciation is calculated on a straight line basis over a 50 year life and charged to administration expenses.

5 At the beginning of the year Archy revalued their land and buildings to $1,400,000 of which $460,000 related to land. The remaining life remains unchanged. This has not been accounted for.

6 Closing inventory was valued at $1,820,000 before any adjustments for damaged items. At the year-end inventory count it was discovered that one line of goods in the warehouse had been damaged. The count shows that 1,250 items were damaged. The inventory was recorded at cost of $150 per item, but following the damage the items have a scrap value of $40 each.

7 The intangible asset is a brand which was acquired for $68,000. The useful life of the brand is considered to be indefinite and therefore Archy carries out an annual impairment review to identify the recoverable amount. An expert has estimated the brand's fair value less costs to sell to be $60,000 and the financial controller has estimated the value in use to be $62,000.

Required:

Prepare a statement of profit or loss and other comprehensive income and statement of financial position for the year ended 30 April 20X1.

Test your understanding 2

The following trial balance relates to Molly at 31 December 20X1:

	Dr	Cr
	$	$
Revenue		50,000
Purchases	20,000	
Distribution costs	10,400	
Administration expenses	15,550	
Loan interest paid	400	
Non-current assets carrying amount	35,000	
Income tax		500
Deferred tax at 1 January 20X1		8,000
Interim dividend paid	1,600	
Trade receivables and payables	10,450	29,000
Inventory as at 1 January 20X1	8,000	
Cash and cash equivalents	8,100	
Ordinary shares $0.50		8,000
Share premium		3,000
10% Loan notes		8,000
Retained earnings at 1 January 20X1		3,000
	109,500	109,500

The following is to be taken into account:

1 Land that cost $5,000 is to be revalued to $11,000.

2 A final ordinary dividend of 10c per share is declared before the year-end.

3 The balance on the income tax account represents an over-provision of tax for the previous year.

4 The income tax for the current year is estimated at $3,000. The deferred tax provision is to be increased to $8,600.

5 Closing inventory is valued at $16,000 at cost for the year. Included in this amount is inventory that cost $8,000 but during the inventory count it was identified that these goods had become damaged and as result the selling price was reduced. The goods are now believed to have a selling price of $4,500 and will incur rectification costs of $500.

Required:

Prepare a statement of profit or loss and other comprehensive income, statement of financial position and statement of changes in equity for the year ended 31 December 20X1.

Test your understanding 3

The following trial balance relates to Marlon at 31 March 20X4:

	Dr	Cr
	$	$
7% loan notes (redeemable 20X9)		18,000
Retained earnings at 1 April 20X3		23,345
Administration expenses	6,020	
Cash and cash equivalents	56,250	
Purchases	84,000	
Distribution costs	5,060	
Dividends paid	1,000	
Dividends received		1,200
Ordinary shares $1		20,000
5% Irredeemable preference shares (dividend at discretion of Marlon)		10,000
Interest paid	630	
Inventory at 1 April 20X3	6,850	
Plant and equipment cost 1 April 20X3	40,315	
Vehicles cost 1 April 20X3	13,720	
Plant accumulated depreciation at 1 April 20X3		7,060
Vehicles accumulated dep'n at 1 April 20X3		2,670
Allowance for trade receivables		600
Redundancy costs	12,000	
Sales revenue		154,900
Irrecoverable debt expense	700	
Share premium		500
Trade payables		18,120
Trade receivables	29,850	
	256,395	256,395

The following is to be taken into account:

1 Non-current assets are depreciated as follows:

- Plant and equipment 20% per annum straight line
- Vehicles 25% per annum reducing balance

Depreciation of plant and equipment is to be considered part of cost of sales, while depreciation of vehicles should be included under distribution costs.

During the year Marlon sold some catering equipment for $2,500. This related to equipment that originally cost $5,000 and had been depreciated by $2,600. No entries have been made at all in the trial balance for this disposal.

2 Current tax due for the year is estimated at $15,000.

3 The closing inventory at 31 March 20X4 was $5,800.

4 The 7% loan notes were issued on 1 April 20X3 and are loans due for repayment by 31 March 20X9. Interest is paid half-yearly on 1 September and 1 April.

5 The redundancy costs represent the initial costs paid as part of a restructuring exercise during the year.

6 On 1 October 20X3, Marlon issued 1,000 equity shares at $1.50 each. All money had been received and correctly accounted for by the year end.

7 The preference dividend for the year has not been paid, and is to be accrued.

Required:

Prepare a statement of profit or loss and other comprehensive income, statement of financial position and statement of changes in equity for the year ended 31 December 20X4.

Test your understanding 4

The following trial balance relates to Arthur at 31 December 20X3

	Dr	Cr
	$	$
Ordinary share capital (50c shares)		200,000
Retained earnings at 1 January 20X3		163,750
7% loan, repayable 31 December 20X5		50,000
Loan interest paid	1,750	
Land and buildings at cost (land element $163,000, note (ii))	403,000	
Plant and equipment at cost (note (ii))	96,000	
Right-of-use asset (note (iii))	28,000	
Accumulated depreciation at 1 January 20X3 (Buildings)		60,000
Accumulated depreciation at 1 January 20X3 (Plant and equipment)		44,000
Trade receivables	48,000	
Inventory at 1 January 20X3	35,500	
Cash and cash equivalents	12,500	
Trade payables		17,000
Lease liability (note (iii))		28,000
Revenue		246,500
Purchases	78,500	
Administrative expenses	34,000	
Distribution costs	51,000	
Interim dividend paid	9,500	
Research and development (note (iv))	24,000	
Deferred tax at 1 January 20X3		15,500
Lease payment (note (iii))	5,000	
Investment income		2,000
	826,750	826,750

The following is to be taken into account:

(i) During the year Arthur made a 1:10 bonus issue. This has NOT been accounted for in the trial balance.

(ii) The buildings had an estimated life of 40 years when built, and are being depreciated on a straight line basis. The directors wish to incorporate a revaluation of the land and buildings as at 31 December 20X3, when the fair value of the land is $250,000 and the fair value of the building is $150,000.

Included in the trial balance is a machine that had cost $8,000 and had accumulated depreciation to date of $6,000. The machine was classed as held for sale from the start of the year. The machine sold in January 20X4 for $1,500, with commission payable of 5% of the sale price.

Plant and equipment is to be depreciated at 30% on a reducing balance basis. All depreciation should be charged to cost of sales.

(iii) Arthur Ltd entered into a seven year lease of plant on 1 January 20X3. The terms of the lease state that Arthur will make annual payments in advance of $5,000. The first of these payments was made on 1 January 20X3. The present value of the lease payments at 1 January 20X3 was $28,000 and the effective interest rate in the lease is 8.16%.

(iv) Research and development comprises research costs of $4,000 and development costs relating to a new product totalling $20,000. Production of this began on 30 September 20X3. Amortisation is to be charged at 4% a year.

(v) Inventory at 31 December 20X3 had a cost of $40,000. This included a damaged item with a cost of $1,500. This item required repairs estimated to cost $500, after which it could be sold for $1,700.

(vi) The directors have estimated the provision for income tax for the year ended 31 December 20X3 at $16,000. Temporary differences at 31 December 20X3 are $32,000 and the tax rate is 30%. All movements in deferred tax should be taken to the statement of profit or loss.

Required:

Prepare a statement of profit or loss and other comprehensive income, statement of financial position and statement of changes in equity for the year ended 31 December 20X3.

Test your understanding 5

Thistle Ltd prepares its accounts annually to 30 June and its trial balance for the year ended 30 June 20X1, before final adjustments, is as follows:

	Dr	Cr
	$	$
Ordinary share capital, 50c shares		500,000
Revaluation surplus at 1 July 20X0		300,000
Share premium		100,000
Retained earnings at 1 July 20X0		540,000
10% Loan, repayable 20X9		80,000
Land and Buildings		
Cost at 1 July 20X0		
(Land element $700,000)	1,400,000	
Accumulated depreciation at 1 July 20X0		58,000
Motor Vehicles		
Cost at 1 July 20X0	67,500	
Accumulated depreciation at 1 July 20X0		30,250
Equity investments at 1 July 20X0	19,800	
Deferred tax liability at 1 July 20X0		8,400
Trade receivables	72,470	
Trade payables		62,180
Inventory as at 30 June 20X1	62,200	
Cash and cash equivalents	217,360	
Profit for year		
(subject to items in the following notes)		160,500
	1,839,330	1,839,330

The following information should also be taken into account:

1 The following transactions have happened during the year in relation to non-current assets, **none** of which have yet been recorded in the books:

- The land and buildings were revalued on 1 July 20X0. The buildings value was unchanged, but the land value increased to $800,000. Ignore deferred tax on the revaluation.
- Motor vehicles which had originally cost $24,000 were sold during the year for $12,000. Accumulated depreciation of $14,000 had been charged on these motor vehicles at 1 July 20X0.
- Depreciation for the year is to be provided using the following policies:

Buildings	2% per annum, straight line
Motor vehicles	20% per annum, reducing balance

2 The directors have estimated that the company's tax liability for the year will be $18,500. The year-end deferred tax balance is estimated at $8,100.

3 Interest on the loan is paid annually in arrears on 1 July. As well as the 10% coupon rate, the loan carries a large premium on redemption, giving it an effective interest rate of 12%.

4 During the year 100,000 ordinary shares were issued at a premium of 40 cents per share. This share issue is reflected in the trial balance.

5 The investment value at 31 July 20X1 was calculated as $20,200.

Required:

Prepare, in a form suitable for publication, the statement of financial position and statement of changes in equity for the year ended 30 June 20X1.

Test your understanding answers

Test your understanding 1

Archy: Statement of profit or loss and other comprehensive income for the year ended 30 April 20X1

	$
Revenue	5,350,000
Cost of sales **(W1)**	(2,881,860)
Gross profit	2,468,140
Distribution costs	(531,000)
Administration expenses **(W1)**	(970,000)
Profit from operations	967,140
Income from investments	5,700
Finance cost	(9,000)
Profit before tax	963,840
Income tax expense	(227,000)
Profit for year	736,840
Other comprehensive income:	
Revaluation gain **(W4)**	536,000
Total comprehensive income	1,272,840

Archy: Statement of financial position as at 30 April 20X1

	$	$
Non-current assets		
Property, plant and equipment **(W4)**		1,402,040
Intangible **(W3)**		62,000
Current assets		
Inventories **(W5)**	1,682,500	
Trade receivables	55,700	
Cash and cash equivalents	242,000	
		1,980,200
Non-current asset held for sale **(W2)**		31,000
Total assets		3,475,240

Equity and liabilities		
Capital and reserves		
Share capital $1	1,000,000	
Revaluation surplus	536,000	
Retained earnings **(W6)**	1,550,140	
		3,086,140
Non-current liabilities		
Bank loan		100,000
Current liabilities		
Trade payables	62,100	
Income tax	227,000	
		289,100
		3,475,240

Workings:

(W1)

Cost of sales	$
Purchases	2,875,000
Opening inventory	1,670,000
Closing inventory **(W5)**	(1,682,500)
Depreciation on plant	9,360
Impairment on asset held for sale	4,000
Impairment on intangible asset	6,000
	2,881,860

Administration expenses	$
As per TB	950,000
Depreciation on building	20,000
	970,000

(W2)

Non-current asset held for sale – valued at the lower of:

Carrying amount ($56,000 – $21,000) = $35,000 or

Net selling price ($32,000 – $1,000) = $31,000

Value at $31,000

Impairment charged to cost of sales ($35,000 – $31,000) = $4,000

The carrying amount of this asset must be removed from the PPE total and shown as an individual line on the SFP

(W3)

Intangible asset

Compare carrying amount with the recoverable amount.

Recoverable amount is the higher of:

Net selling price $60,000

Value in use $62,000

Therefore, recoverable amount is $62,000

The carrying amount is $68,000

Impairment charged to cost of sales ($68,000 – $62,000) = $6,000

(W4)

	Property	**Plant & Equipment**	**Total**
	$	$	$
Cost/Valuation			
At 1 May 20X0	900,000	102,800	1,002,800
Additions	–	–	–
Disposals		–	–
Revaluation	500,000		500,000
Asset held for sale	–	(56,000)	(56,000)
At 30 April 20X1	1,400,000	46,800	1,446,800

Accumulated depreciation:			
At 1 May 20X0	36,000	36,400	72,400
Revaluation	(36,000)	–	(36,000)
Charged during the year *	20,000	9,360	29,360
Asset held for sale	–	(21,000)	(21,000)
At 30 April 20X1	20,000	24,760	44,760
Carrying amount			
At 30 April 20X1	1,380,000	22,040	1,402,040
At 30 April 20X0	864,000	66,400	930,400

* The depreciation on the property on the TB represents 3 years ($900,000 – $300,000)/50 = $12,000 pa. The revaluation happens at the beginning of the year, hence, current year charge should be based on the revalued amount over the remaining life of 47 years =

($1,400,000 – $460,000)/47 = $20,000

The depreciation on the plant and equipment is calculated on the closing cost of $46,800 × 20% = $9,360

We do not depreciate assets held for sale.

(W5)

Inventory	$
Closing inventory at cost	1,820,000
Damaged stock at cost (1,250 × $150)	(187,500)
Damaged stock at NRV (1,250 × $40)	50,000
	1,682,500

Inventory is valued at the lower of cost or NRV

(W6)

Retained earnings	$
Balance at 1 May 20X0	813,300
Profit for the period	736,840
	1,550,140

Test your understanding 2

Molly: Statement of profit or loss and other comprehensive income for the year ended 31 December 20X1

	$
Revenue	50,000
Cost of Sales **(W1)**	(16,000)
Gross profit	34,000
Distribution costs	(10,400)
Administration expenses	(15,550)
Profit from operations	8,050
Finance cost **(W2)**	(800)
Profit before tax	7,250
Income tax expense **(W3)**	(3,100)
Profit for year	4,150
Other comprehensive income:	
Revaluation gain **(W4)**	6,000
Total comprehensive income	10,150

Molly: Statement of financial position as at 31 December 20X1

	$	$
Non-current assets		41,000
Property, plant and equipment **(W4)**		
Current assets		
Inventories **(W5)**	12,000	
Trade receivables	10,450	
Cash and cash equivalents	8,100	
		30,550
Total assets		71,550

Equity and liabilities		
Capital and reserves		
Share capital 50c	8,000	
Share premium	3,000	
Revaluation surplus	6,000	
Retained earnings	5,550	
		22,550
Non-current liabilities		
10% Loan	8,000	
Deferred taxation	8,600	
		16,600
Current liabilities		
Trade payables	29,000	
Loan interest payable **(W2)**	400	
Income tax	3,000	
		31,400
		71,550

Molly: Statement of changes in equity for the year ended 31 December 20X1

	Share capital	Share premium	Reval'n reserve	Retained earnings	Total
	$	$	$	$	$
Balance at 1 January 20X1	8,000	3,000	0	3,000	14,000
Profit for the year (SPL)				4,150	4,150
Dividends paid				(1,600)	(1,600)
Revaluation of land **(W4)**			6,000	–	6,000
Balance at 31 December X1	8,000	3,000	6,000	5,550	22,950

Workings:

(W1)

Cost of sales	$
Purchases	20,000
Opening inventory	8,000
Closing inventory **(W5)**	(12,000)
	16,000

(W2)

Loan interest due (10% × $8,000) = $800 (SPL)

Amount paid (TB) $400, therefore accrual required for $400

(W3)

Income tax	$
TB over-provision	(500)
Current year estimate	3,000
Increase in deferred tax provision (8,600 – 8,000)	600
	3,100

(W4)

PPE	$
TB carrying amount	35,000
Increase in valuation of land ($5,000 to $11,000)	6,000
	41,000

(W5)

Inventory	$
Closing inventory at cost	16,000
Damaged inventory at cost	(8,000)
Damaged inventory at NRV ($4,500 – $500)	4,000
	12,000

Inventory is valued at the lower of cost or NRV

Test your understanding 3

Marlon: Statement of profit or loss for the year ended 31 March 20X4

	$
Revenue	154,900
Cost of Sales **(W1)**	(92,013)
Gross profit	62,887
Distribution costs (5,060 + 2,763 depreciation)	(7,823)
Administration expenses (6,020 + 700 irrecoverable debt expense)	(6,720)
Redundancy costs	(12,000)
Profit from operations	36,344
Income from investments	1,200
Finance cost (630 interest paid + 630 accrual)	(1,260)
Profit before tax	36,284
Income tax expense	(15,000)
Profit for year	21,284

Marlon Ltd: Statement of changes in equity for the year ended 31 March 20X4

	Share capital	Share premium	Retained earnings	Preference shares	Total
	$	$	$	$	$
Balance at 1 April 20X3	19,000	0	23,345	10,000	52,345
Total comprehensive income			21,284		21,284
Share issue	1,000	500			1,500
Dividends (1,000 ord, 500 pref)			(1,500)		(1,500)
Balance at 31 March 20X1	20,000	500	43,129	10,000	73,629

Share issue = 1,000 × $1.50 = $1,500.

Of this, $1,000 goes to share capital with $500 shown in share premium. As the amount has been recorded in the trial balance already, the figures given are the closing balances. The increase in share capital and share premium is included within the SOCIE in order to calculate the opening balances.

Marlon: Statement of financial position as at 31 March 20X4

	$	$
Non-current assets		
Property, plant and equipment **(W2)**		32,079
Current assets		
Inventories	5,800	
Trade receivables		
(29,850 – 600 allowance)	29,250	
Cash and cash equivalents		
(56,250 + 2,500 asset disposal)	58,750	
		93,800
Total assets		125,879
Equity and liabilities		
Capital and reserves		
Share capital $1	20,000	
Preference share capital	10,000	
Share premium	500	
Retained earnings	43,129	
		73,629
Non-current liabilities		
7% loan		18,000
Current liabilities	18,120	
Trade payables	630	
Interest accrual	500	
Preference dividend accrual	15,000	
Income tax		34,250
		125,879

Workings:

(W1)

Cost of sales	$
Purchases	84,000
Opening inventory	6,850
Closing inventory	(5,800)
Depreciation on plant	7,063
Profit on disposal of plant **(W3)**	(100)
	92,013

(W2) Property, Plant and Equipment

	Plant	**Vehicles**	**Total**
	$	$	$
Cost b/f	40,315	13,720	54,035
Disposals	(5,000)	–	(5,000)
At 31 March 20X4	35,315	13,720	49,035
Accumulated depreciation:			
At 1 April 20X3	7,060	2,670	9,730
Disposals	(2,600)	–	(2,600)
Charge for year	7,063	2,763	9,826
At 31 March 20X4	11,523	5,433	16,956
Carrying amount:			
At 31 March 20X4	23,792	8,287	32,079

Depreciation for plant = $35,315 × 20% = $7,063 (taken to cost of sales)

Depreciation for vehicles = (13,720 – 2,670) × 25% = $2,763 (taken to distribution costs)

(W3) Disposal of asset

Asset has been sold for $2,500. This needs to be added to cash, with the carrying value of $2,400 removed from P,P,E (see (W2)) and the gain of $100 taken to cost of sales (W1).

(W4) Accruals

The loan carries 7% interest. 7% × $18,000 = $1,260. As only $630 has been paid, $630 needs to be accrued (Dr Finance costs, Cr accruals).

The preference dividend is 5% × $10,000 = $500. This must also be accrued (Dr Retained earnings, Cr accruals)

Test your understanding 4

Arthur: Statement of profit or loss and other comprehensive income for the year ended 31 December 20X3

	$
Revenue	246,500
Cost of Sales **(W1)**	(104,075)
Gross profit	142,425
Distribution costs	(51,000)
Administration expenses	(34,000)
Profit from operations	57,425
Income from investments	2,000
Finance cost (3,500 **(W4)** + 1,877 **(W8)**)	(5,377)
Profit before tax	54,048
Income tax expense **(W3)**	(10,100)
Profit for year	43,948
Other comprehensive income	
Revaluation gain	63,000
Total comprehensive income	106,948

Arthur Ltd: Statement of changes in equity for the year ended 31 December 20X3

	Share capital	Retained earnings	Revaluation surplus	Total
	$	$	$	$
Balance at 1 April 20X3	200,000	163,750		363,750
Total comprehensive income		43,948	63,000	106,948
Share issue	20,000	(20,000)		0
Dividends		(9,500)		(9,500)
Balance at 31 March 20X1	220,000	178,198	63,000	461,198

The bonus of issue of 1:10 means that 20,000 new shares have been issued for free (10% of 200,000 shares). Usually this would be debited to share premium. However, as no share premium exists, this must be debited to retained earnings instead.

Arthur: Statement of financial position as at 31 December 20X3

	$	$
Non-current assets		
Property, plant and equipment **(W2)**	435,000	
Right-of-use asset **(W8)**)	24,000	
Intangible assets **(W5)**	19,800	
		478,800
Current assets		
Inventories **(W6)**	39,700	
Trade receivables	48,000	
Cash and cash equivalents	12,500	
		100,200
Asset held for sale **(W7)**		1,425
Total assets		580,425
Equity and liabilities		
Capital and reserves		
Share capital $1	220,000	
Revaluation surplus	63,000	
Retained earnings	178,198	
		461,198
Non-current liabilities		
7% loan	50,000	
Lease **(W8)**	19,877	
Deferred tax liability	9,600	
		79,477

Current liabilities		
Trade payables	17,000	
Lease **(W8)**	5,000	
Interest accrual **(W4)**	1,750	
Income tax	16,000	
		39,750
		580,425

Workings:

(W1)

Cost of sales	$
Purchases	78,500
Opening inventory	35,500
Closing inventory	(39,700)
Impairment **(W7)**	575
Depreciation – buildings **(W2)**	6,000
Depreciation – plant **(W2)**	15,000
Depreciation – right-of-use asset **(W8)**	4,000
Amortisation **(W5)**	200
Research	4,000
	104,075

(W2) Property, Plant and Equipment

	Land & buildings	**Plant**	**Total**
	$	$	$
Cost b/f	403,000	96,000	499,000
Held for sale		(8,000)	(8,000)
Revaluation	(3,000)		(3,000)
Cost c/f	400,000	88,000	488,000

Accumulated depreciation:			
Balance b/f	60,000	44,000	104,000
Revaluation	(66,000)	–	(66,000)
Held for sale		(6,000)	(6,000)
Charge for year	6,000	15,000	21,000
At 31 December 20X3	0	53,000	53,000
Carrying amount:			
At 31 December 20X3	400,000	35,000	435,000

Depreciation for buildings = $403,000 – $163,000 land = $240,000/40 years = $6,000

Note: The revaluation takes place at the end of the year and therefore depreciation is calculated on the cost before revaluation.

Depreciation for plant = (88,000 cost c/f – 38,000 acc depreciation (b/f depreciation less held for sale asset depreciation)) × 30% = $15,000

(W3) Income tax expense

	$
Current year estimate	16,000
Decrease in deferred tax provision (9,600 – 15,500)	(5,900)
	10,100

The year end estimate of $16,000 is held in current liabilities

The year end deferred tax liability is $9,600 ($32,000 × 30%). This is held in non-current liabilities, with the decrease in liability from the prior year taken to the tax expense as above.

(W4) Finance costs

The loan carries 7% interest. 7% × $50,000 = $3,500. As only $1,750 has been paid, $1,750 needs to be accrued (Dr Finance costs, Cr accruals).

(W5) Intangibles

Of the $24,000 in the trial balance, the $4,000 research should be taken to the SPL as an expense (taken to COS).

The remaining $20,000 is capitalised as a non-current asset. Amortisation on this begins on 30 September, so there has been 3 months amortisation by the year end. Amortisation is therefore $200 ($20,000 × 4% × 3/12).

The amortisation of $200 is taken to cost of sales, and the carrying amount of intangibles in the SFP is $19,800.

(W6) Inventory

The inventory is in at a total cost of $40,000. Of this amount, some items need to be adjusted. The item costing $1,500 has a NRV of $1,200, and therefore a write-off of $300 is required.

This makes closing inventory $39,700 (Dr Inventory, Cr COS).

(W7) Held for sale

The asset must be removed from Property, Plant & Equipment (see **(W2)**), and then is held under current assets at the lower of carrying amount and fair value less costs to sell.

The asset has a carrying amount of $2,000, but the fair value less costs to sell = $1,500 less 5% commission = $1,425.

The asset should be held at $1,425, with a $575 impairment being shown in cost of sales.

(W8) Lease – right-of-use asset

The right-of-use asset should initially be recognised at $28,000. This should be depreciated over 7 years, giving a depreciation charge of $4,000 (included in cost of sales) and a carrying amount of $24,000.

The liability is then shown as follows:

Year	b/f	Payment	Subtotal	Interest 8.16%	c/f
20X3	28,000	(5,000)	23,000	1,877	24,877
20X4	24,877	(5,000)	19,877		

From this, the interest of 1,877 is taken to finance costs.

The year end liability of $24,877 is split between non-current and current, with $19,877 shown as a non-current liability and $5,000 being held within current liabilities.

Test your understanding 5

Thistle Ltd: Statement of financial position as at 30 June 20X1

	$	$
Non-current assets		
Property, plant and equipment **(W1)**	1,449,800	
Investments **(W6)**	20,200	
		1,470,000
Current assets		
Inventories	62,200	
Trade receivables	72,470	
Cash and cash equivalents **(W9)**	229,360	
		364,030
Total assets		1,834,030
Equity and liabilities		
Capital and reserves		
Share capital	500,000	
Share premium	100,000	
Retained earnings	655,650	
Revaluation surplus	400,000	
		1,655,650
Non-current liabilities		
10% Loan (80,000 + 1,600 (W3))	81,600	
Deferred tax (8,400 – 300 (W7))	8,100	
		89,700
Current liabilities		
Trade payables	62,180	
Loan interest owing (W3)	8,000	
Income tax	18,500	
		88,680
Total equity and liabilities		1,834,030

Thistle Ltd: Statement of changes in equity for the year ended 30 June 20X1

	Share capital	Share premium	Revaluation surplus	Retained earnings	Total
	$	$	$	$	$
Balance at June 20X0	450,000	60,000	300,000	540,000	1,350,000
Total Comprehensive income **(W8)**			100,000	115,650	215,650
Issue of share capital **(W2)**	50,000	40,000		–	90,000
Balance at 30 June 20X1	500,000	100,000	400,000	655,650	1,655,650

Workings:

(W1) Property, plant and equipment

	Land and buildings	Vehicles	Total
	$	$	$
Cost/Valuation			
At 1 July 20X0	1,400,000	67,500	1,487,300
Revaluation	100,000		100,000
Disposals		(24,000)	(24,000)
At 30 June 20X1	1,500,000	43,500	1,543,500
Accumulated depreciation:			
At 1 July 20X0	58,000	30,250	88,250
Charged during the year **(W7)**	14,000	5,450	19,450
Disposals		(14,000)	(14,000)
At 30 June 20X1	72,000	21,700	93,700
Carrying amount:			
At 30 June 20X1	1,428,000	21,800	1,449,800

(W2) Share issue

	No.
Number of issued shares at 30 June 20X1 ($500,000/$0.50)	1,000,000
Number Issued in the year	(100,000)
Number of issued shares at 1 July 20X0 (Balance)	900,000

Total proceeds = 100,000 × $0.90 = $90,000

Nominal value = 100,000 × $0.50 = $50,000 (share capital account)

Premium = 100,000 × $0.40 = $40,000 (share premium account)

(W3) Loan interest

The loan is a financial liability and should be held at amortised cost. The interest charged to the statement of profit or loss is $9,600 ($80,000 × 12%).

Of this, the interest due for the year $8,000 ($80,000 × 10%) is payable 1 July 20X1, so should be held as a current liability.

The remaining $1,600 should be added on to the value of the loan within non-current liabilities to take into account the premium on redemption of the loan.

(W4) Gain on disposal

	No.
Proceeds	12,000
Carrying value (24,000 – 14,000)	10,000
Profit on disposal	2,000

(W5) Depreciation

Building 2% × $700,000 ($1,400,000 – land $700,000) = $14,000

Motor vehicles 20% × (cost $43,500 – depn ($30,250 – $14,000)) = 20% × $27,250 = $5,450

(W6) Investments

The default position for equity investments is fair value through profit or loss (FVPL). As the value has increased by $400 in the year, this will be added to the investment value, with the $400 gain taken to profit for the year.

(W7) Tax

The tax estimate of $18,500 will be taken to profit for the year and held within current liabilities. The deferred tax liability has decreased by $300. This will decrease the liability and reduce the tax expense for the year.

(W8) Profit for year

	$
Per TB	160,500
Gain on disposal **(W4)**	2,000
Depreciation **(W5)**	
– buildings	(14,000)
– motor vehicles	(5,450)
Income tax expense	(18,500)
Reduction in deferred tax **(W7)**	300
Finance cost **(W3)**	(9,600)
Investment gain **(W6)**	400
Profit for the year	115,650

(W9) Cash and cash equivalents

	$
TB	217,360
Proceeds from sale of NCAs	2,000
Cash and cash equivalents	229,360

Chapter

24

Appendix 2: Objective case questions

Chapter learning objectives

This chapter contains a series of objective case questions for question practice. An objective case question involves 5 questions around a scenario, totalling 10 marks.

Test your understanding 1

The following information is to be used for all 5 of the following questions.

Boles has a number of non-current assets in use for its operations, which are detailed below..

Asset	**Date acquired**	**Cost** $000	**Useful life**
Head office	1 January 20X1	20,000	20 years
Factory	1 January 20X3	6,000	15 years
Asset under construction	1 March 20X8	5,000	–
Investment property	1 December 20X8	2,000	20 years

1 Boles decided to revalue its head office and factory for the first time at 31 December 20X8. A surveyor valued the head office at $13.8m and the factory at $3.4m.

What is the total gain to be recorded in the revaluation surplus?

A $1.6m

B $1.8m

C $0.8m

D $0.4m

2 The asset under construction began to be built on 1 March 20X8. This was funded out of general borrowings. Boles had two loans in place during the year, a $2m 6% loan and a $3m 9% loan.

At 31 December 20X8, the asset was still under construction.

How much interest should be capitalised in relation to the asset?

$__________

3 Boles recently bought the investment property to rent to others.

Which of the following are acceptable treatments which could be applied to the property?

(i) Revalue regularly, with the gain or loss being shown in Other Comprehensive Income

(ii) Revalue annually, with the gain or loss being shown in the statement of profit or loss

(iii) Hold at cost, and depreciate the asset over its useful life

A (i) and (iii)

B (ii) only

C (ii) and (iii)

D (i) only

4 Boles is currently undergoing a refurbishment of its head office.

Identify the correct treatment for each of the costs below

	Capitalise	**Expense**
Overhauling the air conditioning units as a result of a safety inspection		
Repainting the entrance to make it more appealing for visitors		
Fixing broken windows on each floor of the office		

5 On 1 July 20X8, Boles received a $2m grant towards new plant which will last 5 years. The grant must be repaid if Boles sells the asset within 4 years.

Boles uses the deferred income method in relation to capital grants.

What amount will be shown in non-current liabilities as at 31 December 20X8?

A $1.8m

B $1.4m

C $1.25m

D $1.75m

Test your understanding 2

The following information is to be used for all 5 of the following questions.

Cook Co operated in the technology industry, involved in developing new games for mobile devices. In the year ending 31 December 20X7, Cook Co had the following assets in the financial statements:

(i) Development costs. The project is still in development at 31 December 20X7. Production is scheduled for 20X8.

(ii) Patent, purchased January 20X6, covering the production process for the next 4 years.

(iii) Brand name, purchased in 20X5 and judged to have an indefinite useful life.

1 **Which of the assets will need an impairment review at 31 December 20X7?**

A (i) and (ii)

B (i) and (iii)

C (ii) and (iii)

D All of the above

2 The patent was purchased on 1 January 20X6 for $10m. On 31 December 20X6, a specialist valued it at $12m due to the benefit that it gives Cook over its competitors.

What is the carrying amount of the patent at 31 December 20X7?

$____________

3 The development project related to a new game for mobile devices and was completed on 30 June 20X8. A total of $16m had been spent up to that point. The game is expected to have a useful life of 5 years. $200,000 was spent on marketing the asset and a further $300,000 has been spent training staff to operate the system to be used to support the production of the game.

What expense should be recorded in the statement of profit or loss for the year ending 31 December 20X8?

A $1.6m

B $1.9m

C $2.1m

D $3.4m

4 The assistant accountant of Cook Co is uncertain about how to deal with intangible assets and has found a website containing a number of statements about them.

Identify whether the statements below are true or false.

	True	False
Intangible assets must be separable		
Intangible assets must never be revalued		
Intangible assets must be identifiable		
Internally generated assets cannot be recognised		

5 In 20X8, Cook Co began developing a new online social gaming platform. The project began on 1 January 20X8 and launched on 31 October 20X8. The directors released the final funds to complete the project following the successful results of testing on 1 June 20X8.

$10 million was incurred on the project evenly from 1 January to 31 October. In addition to this expenditure, an item of plant costing $6 million with a life of 5 years was removed from production and used to develop the project.

What is the total to be capitalised as an intangible asset?

A $5m

B $5.5m

C $10m

D $10.5m

Test your understanding 3

The following information is to be used for all 5 of the following questions.

Cheung Co uses the costs model in relation to property, plant and equipment but has seen a number of issues during the year following a storm on 1 July 20X8 which caused significant damage to a number of items of plant and machinery, as well as Cheung Co's properties. The details of the assets affected are shown below:

Asset	**Remaining life at 1 Jan 20X8**	**Carrying amount at 1 Jan 20X8 $000**
Production machinery	5 years	8,000
Factory	20 years	16,000
Head office	20 years	22,000

Cheung Co produces financial statements to 31 December each year.

1 On the date of the storm, the roof in Cheung Co's factory collapsed, damaging one of the items of production machinery, which had a carrying amount of $5 million at the start of the year. Cheung Co records depreciation monthly and had already accounted for all depreciation correctly up to 30 June 20X8.

Following the damage, the machinery can be used for another 3 years and will generate cash flows with a present value of $4.2 million. The fair value less costs to sell would be $4 million.

What impairment should be recorded in Cheung Co's statement of profit or loss at 1 July 20X8?

$__________

2 On 1 July 20X8, Cheung Co decided to sell the other piece of production machinery and replace it with a new piece of equipment. The production machinery had a carrying amount of $3 million at 1 January 20X8.

At 1 July 20X8, the machinery had a fair value less costs to sell of $2.9 million. Cheung classed the machinery as an asset held for sale from this date. By 31 December 20X8, the asset remained unsold but negotiations with interested parties were ongoing.

What expense should be recorded in the statement of profit or loss for the year ended 31 December 20X8?

A $100,000

B $200,000

C $300,000

D $600,000

3 **In relation to the production machinery to be sold, which of the following is NOT a criterion which Cheung Co must have met in order for the asset to be classified as held for sale?**

A The asset must be actively marketed at a reasonable price

B Negotiations surrounding the sale must be in progress

C The asset is available for immediate sale

D Management must be committed to a plan to sell

4 At 1 July 20X8, an impairment review of Cheung Co's properties was also carried out. The fair value of the head office was assessed at $23 million and the fair value of the factory was assessed at $14 million

Select the correct amount to be recorded for each property at 1 July 20X8.

Head office	Factory
$000	**$000**
23,000	15,600
21,450	14,000

5 Cheung Co's assistant accountant is unsure of some technical details surrounding impairment. A collection of statements she has read are detailed below.

Which of the following statements are true?

(i) Impairments must be taken to the statement of profit or loss

(ii) Impairment reviews are required annually for intangible assets

(iii) Impairment exists when the recoverable amount exceeds the carrying amount

A (i) and (iii)

B (i) only

C (ii) only

D None of them

Test your understanding 4

The following information is to be used for all 5 of the following questions.

Vernon Co holds a number of financial instruments, which are detailed below.

Item	Date acquired/ issued	Value 1 January X4 $000
Equity investments	1 January 20X4	28,700
4% Convertible bonds	1 January 20X4	30,000
4% Loan notes	1 January 20X4	20,000

1 Vernon Co holds the equity investments using the alternative treatment permitted by IFRS 9. During the year, Vernon Co sold shares which had cost $7.8 million for $9.7 million. The fair value of the remaining shares at 31 December 20X4 was $19.8 million.

How much should be taken to the statement of profit or loss for the year ending 31 December 20X4?

$_________'000 gain

2 The $30 million convertible bonds can be converted on 31 December 20X6. Similar loan notes without the conversion option carry an interest rate of 7%. Relevant discount factors are shown below.

Year	Discount factor 4%	Discount factor 7%
1	0.962	0.935
2	0.925	0.873
3	0.889	0.816

How much should be recorded in equity in relation to the convertibles?

A $3,330,000

B $Nil

C $2,100,000

D $2,371,000

3 The $20 million 4% loan notes incurred $500,000 issue costs. The loan notes are repayable at a premium, giving them an effective rate of 8%.

What amount should be recorded in finance costs in relation to the loan notes for the year ending 31 December 20X4?

A $780,000

B $800,000

C $1,560,000

D $1,600,000

4 Vernon Co also factored $2 million of its receivables to a bank during the year. The bank paid $1.8 million to Vernon Co. The bank charged Vernon Co a $100,000 fee for this, and all responsibility for the receivables returns to Vernon Co if the debts are unpaid after 6 months.

Which TWO of the following represent the correct accounting treatment for this arrangement?

A This is a $1.8 million loan and should be held as a current liability

B The $100,000 should be expensed in the statement of profit or loss

C A loss of $200,000 should be recorded in the statement of profit or loss

D The receivables should be derecognised from the statement of financial position

5 During the year, Vernon Co purchased government bonds which are redeemable in 4 years. Vernon Co's business model is to hold bonds until redemption and the cash flows are solely repayments of interest and capital.

If Vernon Co applies the alternative treatment, what is the correct treatment for the bonds?

A Fair value through other comprehensive income

B Split accounting

C Equity accounting

D Amortised cost

Test your understanding 5

The following information is to be used for all 5 of the following questions.

Box produces financial statements to 30 September each year, operating in the farming sector. Box incurs selling costs for animals of 5% whenever they are sold at market.

1 Box's herd of livestock was valued at $3 million at 30 September 20X4 and are generally held for 3 years. The fair value at 30 September 20X5 was $2.5 million.

What expense should be taken to Box's statement of profit or loss for the year ending 30 September 20X5?

A $475,000

B $500,000

C $625,000

D $1,000,000

2 **Which of the following items would be accounted for under IAS 41 *Agriculture*?**

(i) Box's land, used to grow crops and rear animals

(ii) Crops harvested by Box in August 20X5

(iii) Crops planted by Box and still growing

A None

B (i) and (iii)

C (ii) only

D (iii) only

3 When Box calculates the fair value of items, it uses quoted prices in active markets for identical items.

Which level of input is this likely to be?

A Level 1 inputs

B Level 2 inputs

C Level 3 inputs

D None of the above

4 Box has used first-in-first-out to measure its inventory for many years. On 1 October 20X4 Box moved to using average cost. This increased the inventory value at that date by $200,000.

Which of the following is NOT the correct accounting treatment for the financial statements for the year ending 30 September 20X5?

A Increase opening retained earnings in the statement of changes in equity by $200,000

B Increase the prior year comparative statement of financial position inventory by $200,000

C Increase the cost of sales for 20X5 by $200,000

D Reduce the profits in the prior year comparative statement of profit or loss by $200,000

5 Box has uncertainty over two items of inventory at 30 September 20X5.

Item A relates to raw materials purchased for $500,000 for a large profitable contract with a supermarket. Since purchase, the cost of these raw materials had fallen to $400,000.

Item B cost $250,000. It was damaged on 15 September 20X5. After rectification work costing $30,000 it was sold for $260,000 in October 20X5.

What is the value of inventory to be recorded in Box's financial statements as at 30 September 20X5?

$ ________

Test your understanding 6

The following information is to be used for all 5 of the following questions.

Henley Co makes a number of sales that require long payment terms and the new assistant accountant is unsure how to deal with some of these, which are detailed below.

- Sale of equipment with a year's support contract
- Sale of goods with 2 years' interest-free credit
- Construction of an asset for a customer

1 The sale of equipment was made on 31 December 20X4 for $900,000 and included 1 year's free support, which Henley Co usually charges $100,000 for. Henley Co never sells the support as a standalone product.

How much should be recorded in Henley's revenue in relation to this sale for the year ending 31 December 20X4?

$________'000

2 Henley Co offered a customer interest-free credit for 2 years on a sale for $200,000 that was made on 1 January 20X4. Henley Co has a cost of capital of 8% and has recorded $200,000 in revenue.

How much should be reclassified from revenue into finance income for the year ending 31 December 20X4?

A $13,717

B $14,815

C $16,000

D $28,532

3 Henley Co entered into a $10 million contract to build an asset for a customer on 1 April 20X4. The contract is expected to take 2 years and a surveyor has assessed the value of work done as $4 million. The contract will cost $8 million and Henley Co has spent $4 million to date. Henley Co measures progress towards completion using an output method, comparing the work certified to date to the total contract price.

What profit should Henley Co recognise for the year ending 31 December 20X4?

$_________'000

4 On 1 December 20X4, Henley Co began another contract to build an asset for a customer. Henley Co has spent $10,000 so far and believes it may cost $800,000 to complete. The total price of the contract is $1 million. Henley Co uses an output method to measure progress, but as the contract has only just begun, is unable to measure the progress made towards completion at 31 December 20X4.

How much revenue should Henley Co recognise for the year ending 31 December 20X4?

A $Nil

B $10,000

C $12,500

D $16,700

5 Henley Co's assistant has one final question regarding the recognition of revenue. He has read something about the 5 steps for recognising revenue from contracts with customers and is unsure what these are.

Which of the following is NOT a criterion for recognising revenue from contracts with customers?

A Identify the separate performance obligations within the contract

B Identify the price

C Assess recoverability of amounts within the contract

D Identify the contract

Test your understanding 7

The following information is to be used for all 5 of the following questions.

Smith's statement of profit or loss showed a profit of $460,000 for the year ending 31 December 20X1. At 1 January 20X1 Smith had 2 million shares in issue.

1 On 1 August 20X1, Smith made a 1 for 2 rights issue for $2. At this date, the market value of a Smith share was $2.45.

What is Smith's earnings per share for the year ending 31 December 20X1?

A 15.3c

B 17.9c

C 18.4c

D 19c

2 **Identify which types of share issue will require the prior year earnings per share to be restated.**

	Restate prior year EPS	No restatement required
Full price (market) issue		
Bonus issue		
Rights issue		

3 The following year, Smith made $550,000 profit and had 3 million shares in issue for the entire year. Smith also had 1 million options in place giving the holder the right to purchase a share for $2.20. The average share price for the year was $2.50.

What is Smith's diluted earnings per share for the year, to one decimal place?

__________c

4 Smith's assistant accountant is unsure about what diluted earnings per share represents.

Which of the following is true?

A Diluted earnings per share removes any items deemed to be 'one-offs' which could distort comparison

B Diluted earnings per share shows how shares that have been issued post-year end would affect the current year earnings per share

C Diluted earnings per share is widely regarded a more accurate reflection of the current year performance as it takes all items into account

D Diluted earnings per share acts as a warning to shareholders, showing how earnings per share could fall based on items already in existence

5 Smith's assistant accountant is also unsure of what adjustments to make to profit for the year to get to the figure which should be used for profit in the calculation of earnings per share.

Profit for the year will need to be adjusted for which of the following items?

A Redeemable preference share dividends

B Irredeemable preference share dividends

C Reserves transfer for excess depreciation

D Gain/loss on FVOCI investments

Test your understanding 8

Worrell has had a turbulent year, with a number of legal cases arising during the year following problems with a number of components in the products it produces.

Worrell has produced its financial statements to 31 December 20X7. Worrell has a well-documented, strong environmental policy and a record of honouring it.

1 A customer is suing Worrell for burns sustained when using one of its products. Worrell is suing a supplier in response to this, believing that the fault lies with them.

Legal advice suggests that Worrell will probably lose the case with the customer and win the case with the supplier.

Identify the correct treatment for each of the cases below.

Case with the customer	Case with the supplier
Do nothing	Do nothing
Contingent liability	Contingent asset
Provision	Asset

2 Worrell gives a 1 year warranty with one its products. Repair history shows 2% are returned within 1 year for major repairs and 6% for minor repairs. If all goods needed major repairs, it would cost Worrell $800,000. If all goods needed minor repairs, it would cost Worrell $80,000.

What provision is needed at the year end?

$____________

3 Further issues have arisen in Worrell, and Worrell's assistant accountant is unsure how to account for the following:

(i) Worrell operates a number of machines requiring a regular overhaul to pass safety inspections. Many of these are due within the next 12 months.

(ii) Worrell has caused environmental damage during the construction of a new facility. There is no legislation requiring Worrell to repair the ground.

Which of the following should be recorded as provisions?

A (i) and (ii)

B (i) only

C (ii) only

D Neither

4 On 15 January 20X8, the following events were noted by Worrell:

A major customer went into liquidation

Inventory was damaged in a flood. This was sold at a loss on 20 January 20X8.

Which of the items should be treated as an adjusting event according to IAS 10 *Events After the Reporting Period*?

A Liquidation of the major customer

B Damaged inventory

C Neither event

D Both events

5 **Which of the following facts regarding IAS 10 *Events After the Reporting Period* is true?**

A All non-adjusting events must be disclosed in the notes to the financial statements

B IAS 10 covers the period from the reporting date up to the annual general meeting

C Adjusting events provide evidence of conditions in existence at the reporting date

D All adjusting events must be disclosed in the notes to the financial statements

Test your understanding 9

The following information is to be used for all 5 of the following questions.

On 1 June 20X1, Pedro acquired 70% of Sagna. The consideration paid for Sagna consisted of a 2 for 5 share issue and $800,000 payable in 3 years' time.

Pedro's share price at acquisition was $3 and Pedro has a cost of capital of 8%.

The following extracts from the statements of financial position as at 31 December 20X1 are relevant:

	Pedro	Sagna
	$	$
Receivables	31,000	14,000
Cash	14,000	2,000
Ordinary $1 shares	500,000	200,000
Retained earnings	95,000	72,000
Payables	22,000	10,000

1 **To the nearest thousand, what is the amount to be recorded as consideration paid for Sagna?**

A $803,000

B $828,000

C $875,000

D $968,000

2 At the date of acquisition, Sagna's net assets were equal to their carrying amount with the exception of plant, which had a fair value of $12,000 in excess of its carrying amount and a remaining life of 10 years.

Sagna made a profit of $18,000 for the year ended 31 December 20X1.

What are Sagna's net assets at acquisition?

A $272,900

B $273,500

C $274,400

D $275,000

3 During the year, Sagna sold items to Pedro. The year end balances were reconciled, with Sagna showing a receivable of $8,000. This does not agree with the payable recorded by Pedro, with the difference being due to $1,000 cash in transit.

Select the correct options for the consolidated receivables and payables as at 31 December 20X1. Note: One figure should be selected from each column, and the figures selected do not have to be in the same row.

Receivables	Payables
$36,000	$23,000
$37,000	$24,000
$38,000	$25,000

4 The sales from Sagna to Pedro are made at a mark-up of 20%. The total sales in the post-acquisition period are $6,000. Pedro had sold 90% of these on to third parties at the year end.

What is the amount of unrealised profit in inventories at the year end?

$___________

5 **From the adjustments made, which TWO will have an impact on the non-controlling interest?**

A Fair value adjustment

B Intra-group receivable adjustment

C Intra-group payable adjustment

D Cash-in-transit adjustment

E Unrealised profit adjustment

Test your understanding 10

The following information is to be used for all 5 of the following questions.

Given below are extracts from the statements of profit or loss for Pardew and its subsidiary Sherwood for the year ended 31 December 20X5.

	Pardew	Sherwood
	$000	$000
Revenue	411,600	213,120
Cost of sales	(319,200)	(176,400)
Administrative expenses	(50,610)	(33,120)
Finance costs	(2,150)	(600)

The following information is relevant:

(i) Pardew acquired 70% of Sherwood on 1 July 20X5. Since acquisition, Pardew sold goods to Sherwood for $1 million per month, at a margin of 20%. At the year end, Sherwood held 30% of these goods.

(ii) On acquisition, Sherwood's net assets were equal to their carrying amount with the exception of Sherwood's property, which had a fair value of $2 million in excess of its carrying amount and a remaining life at acquisition of 20 years. All depreciation is charged to administrative expenses.

(iii) Goodwill is impaired by $300,000 at the year end. Pardew measures the non-controlling interest at fair value.

(iv) Immediately after acquisition, Pardew loaned Sherwood $10 million, charging interest of 6% per annum.

1 **What is the consolidated revenue for the year?**

A $480,192,000

B $506,160,000

C $512,160,000

D $560,784,000

2 **What is the amount of unrealised profit to be removed from the consolidated financial statements?**

$__________'000

3 How much should be included as consolidated administrative expenses?

A $67,520,000

B $66,820,000

C $67,570,000

D $66,770,000

4 **What amount will be recorded as consolidated finance costs?**

$__________'000

5 **Which TWO of the following adjustments will have an impact on the profit attributable to the non-controlling interest?**

A Intra-group sales between Pardew and Sherwood of $1 million a month

B Unrealised profit on sales from Pardew to Sherwood

C Fair value depreciation

D Goodwill impairment

Test your understanding 11

The following information is to be used for all 5 of the following questions.

Below are extracts from the financial statements of Mariner

Statement of profit or loss for the year ended 31 March 20X1

	$000
Profit from operations	2,250
Income tax expense	(400)
Profit for the period	1,850

Statements of financial position

	31 March 20X1 $000	31 March 20X0 $000
Property, plant and equipment	132,100	136,950
Inventories	90,600	88,400
Trade and other receivables	40,300	45,200
Retained earnings	31,500	36,000
Deferred tax liability	600	400
Trade and other payables	37,050	35,030
Tax liability	1,500	2,000

The following information is relevant:

Mariner disposed of some property, recording a gain on disposal in cost of sales of $3 million. Mariner also purchased new equipment for $1.5 million. Depreciation of $2 million was charged to cost of sales in the year.

1 **Identify whether the following items should be added to or deducted from profit from operations in order to calculate cash generated from operations.**

	Add to profit from operations	Deduct from profit from operations
Depreciation		
Gain on disposal		
Movement in inventories		
Movement in receivables		
Movement in payables		

2 **What amount should be recorded in investing activities regarding the sale of property?**

A $4,350,000

B $5,850,000

C $6,350,000

D $7,350,000

3 **How much tax was paid during the year**

$______________'000

4 **What dividend was paid during the year?**

$______________'000

5 **Match each item to the correct placement in Mariner's statement of cash flows.**

Operating activities	
Investing activities	
Financing activities	

Property disposal proceeds

Tax paid

Dividends paid

Test your understanding answers

Test your understanding 1

1 **B** – The carrying amount of the head office at 31 December 20X8 before the revaluation is $12m ($20m less 8 years depreciation) and the carrying amount of the factory is $3.6m ($6m less 6 years depreciation).

Therefore there is a gain of $1.8m on the head office and a loss of $0.2m on the factory.

The gain should be recorded in the revaluation surplus but the loss should be taken to the statement of profit or loss, as no revaluation surplus exists in relation to the factory.

2 **$325,000** – The interest should be capitalised using the weighted average cost of borrowing, as general borrowings are being used.

The weighted average is calculated as follows:

$$\frac{(\$2m \times 6\%) + (\$3m \times 9\%)}{\$5m}$$

$$= \$390k/\$5m = 7.8\%$$

Therefore the interest should be calculated as 7.8% × $5m × 10/12 = **$325,000**

3 **C** – Boles can either adopt the cost or fair value model for investment properties. The cost model holds the property at cost less accumulated depreciation. The fair value model revalues the asset at each year end, with the gain or loss being shown in the statement of profit or loss.

4

	Capitalise	**Expense**
Overhauling the air conditioning units as a result of a safety inspection	X	
Repainting the entrance to make it more appealing for visitors		X
Fixing broken windows on each floor of the office		X

Boles can capitalise costs relevant to passing a safety inspection, and depreciate these over the time until the next inspection. The repainting and the window repairs are classed as maintenance and cannot be capitalised.

5 **B** – The $2m grant will be released to the statement of profit or loss over 5 years, meaning that $400,000 is released each year. As the grant was received on 1 July 20X8 Boles will have released 6 months of the grant, so $200,000. This leaves a total deferred income at 31 December 20X8 of $1.8m.

Of this deferred income, $400,000 will be released within a year and will therefore be held within current liabilities. This means that **$1.4m** will be held as a non-current liability at 31 December 20X8.

Test your understanding 2

1 **B** – Intangibles with an indefinite useful life will need an annual impairment review, as will development projects which have not been completed. The patent will only require an impairment review if indications of impairment exist.

2 **$5m** – The patent will be held under the cost model, and cannot be revalued as an active market does not exist. At 31 December 20X7, the patent will have been amortised for 2 years, giving a carrying amount of $5m.

3 **C** – As the development project was completed on 30 June 20X8, amortisation should be charged from this point. Therefore by 31 December 20X8 six months amortisation should be charged. In addition to this, the $200,000 marketing and the $300,000 training should both be expensed as they do not meet the criteria for intangible assets.

Therefore the total expense is $16m/5 × 6/12 = $1.6m amortisation + $200,000 marketing + $300,000 training = $2.1 million.

4 See below.

	True	False
Intangible assets must be separable		X
Intangible assets must never be revalued		X
Intangible assets must be identifiable	X	
Internally generated assets cannot be recognised		X

Intangible assets must be identifiable, meaning they can be either separable, or arising from legal rights. They can be revalued if an active market exists. Certain internally generated assets, such as development costs, can be recognised.

5 **B** – The costs on the project can be capitalised from 1 June 20X8, meaning that \$5m can be capitalised (\$10m × 5/10). In addition to this, the depreciation on the plant can also be capitalised as part of the development costs during the capitalisation period, meaning that a further \$500,000 can be capitalised (\$6m/5 years × 5/12).

Test your understanding 3

1 **\$300,000** – At 30 June 20X8, the asset would have had a carrying amount of \$4.5 million, being \$5 million less 6 months depreciation (\$5m/5 × 6/12). The recoverable amount of the asset is the higher of the fair value less costs to sell and the value in use, so is therefore \$4.2 million.

Therefore the impairment loss is \$4.5 million – \$4.2 million = \$300,000.

2 C – Cheung Co should charge depreciation for 6 months to 30 June 20X8 (\$3m/5 × 6/12 = \$300,000). At this point, the asset will have a carrying amount of \$2.7 million. When Cheung Co classes it as held for sale, depreciation will cease and the asset will be moved to current assets at the lower of the carrying amount and the fair value less costs to sell. As Cheung Co will sell the asset for higher than the current carrying amount, the asset will simply be transferred to current assets at \$2.7 million with nothing more taken to the statement of profit or loss.

3 **B** – Negotiations do not need to be in progress.

4 See below.

Head office	Factory
\$000	**\$000**
21,450	14,000

The head office will have a carrying amount of \$21.45 million at 1 July 20X8, being \$22 million less 6 months depreciation (\$22m/20 × 6/12 = \$550,000). Whilst the fair value at 1 July 20X8 is \$23 million, Cheung Co uses the cost model rather than the revaluation model.

The factory will have a carrying amount of \$15.6 million at 1 July 20X8, being \$16 million less 6 months depreciation (\$16m/20 × 6/12 = \$400,000). As the fair value is \$14 million, the factory should be impaired to this value, as it is below the current carrying amount.

5 **D** – Impairments are taken to the statement of profit or loss if no revaluation surplus exists for that asset. Otherwise they are taken to the revaluation surplus first. An annual review is required on intangibles with an indefinite useful life, not on all intangibles. Finally, impairment exists when the carrying amount exceeds the recoverable amount, not the other way round.

Test your understanding 4

1 **$1,900,000 gain** – The gain on disposal of the shares should be taken to the statement of profit or loss. As Vernon Co uses the alternative treatment for equity investments, the fair value loss at the year-end would be taken to Other Comprehensive Income as the alternative treatment for equity investments is to hold them as fair value through other comprehensive income.

2 **D** – When the convertible bonds are issued:

Dr Bank	$30,000,000
Cr Financial Liability	$27,629,000
Cr Equity	**$2,371,000**

Year	Cash flow (4% of $30m)	Discount factor	Present value
1	1,200,000	0.935	1,122,000
2	1,200,000	0.873	1,048,000
3	31,200,000	0.816	25,459,000
		Value of liability	27,629,000

3 **C** – The loan notes should be recorded initially at the net proceeds of $19.5 million, being the $20 million less the $500,000 issue costs. The interest should then be accounted for at the effective rate of 8%.

4 **A and B** – This should be recorded as a loan with a $100,000 expense.

5 **D** – The alternative treatment will be amortised cost as the business model is to hold the bonds until redemption

Test your understanding 5

1 **A** – The livestock should be valued at fair value less costs to sell at each year end. Therefore in 30 September 20X4, the livestock would have been held at $2.85 million ($3m less 5%). At 30 September 20X5 it should be held at $2.375 million ($2.5m less 5%). This means that an expense of $475,000 should be recorded in the statement of profit or loss.

2 **D** – Box's land would be accounted for as property, plant and equipment. The crops that have been harvested would be accounted for initially as agriculture at the point of harvest, but as inventory after that, so will be accounted for as inventories at the year end. The only asset that would be accounted for as agriculture would be the crops that are still growing.

3 **A** – These are likely to be level 1 inputs. Level 2 inputs includes identical assets in non-active markets, or similar items within active markets. Level 3 inputs are likely to involve some element of using valuation techniques or estimates.

4 **D** – The adjustment should be made retrospectively, meaning the prior year financial statements are adjusted, alongside the opening retained earnings. The adjustment will increase the closing inventory of 20X4. This will increase assets in 20X4 and also increase profits, as a higher amount would have been deducted from cost of sales.

5 **$730,000** – Item A should be held at cost, which is $500,000. Replacement cost is irrelevant. As this is for a profitable order, the net realisable value is higher than the cost so no write-down is required. Item B should be held at $230,000, being the net realisable value of $260,000 – $30,000.

Test your understanding 6

1 **$810,000** – As the support contract is worth $100,000, the total value of items sold is $1 million, being the $900,000 equipment and the $100,000 support. As Henley Co are selling the package for $900,000 in total, this represents a 10% discount. This discount should be applied evenly across both elements of the sale, meaning that $810,000 is applied to the equipment at $90,000 to the support contract. As Henley Co made the sale on 31 December, none of the support contract revenue should be recognised as no time has elapsed in relation to this.

2 **A** – The sale should initially be discounted to present value using Henley Co's cost of capital. $200,000 discounted at 8% for 2 years gives an initial present value of $171,468. This should be built up by 8% a year. Therefore the amount to be recorded as finance income in 20X4 is $13,717 ($171,468 × 8%).

3 **$800,000** – Using the output method, the contract progress is assessed at 40% ($4m/$10m). Therefore 40% of the revenue and expenses should be recognised in the statement of profit or loss during the year. This would give revenue of $4 million and cost of sales of $3.2 million (40% of $8m), therefore giving a total profit of $800,000.

4 **B** – As the progress towards completion cannot be reliably measured, Henley Co should recognise revenue to the level of recoverable costs. As Henley Co has spent $10,000 to date, this should be recorded in both revenue and cost of sales.

5 **C** – Whilst recoverability of any amounts is obviously important, it is not one of the criteria for recognising revenue.

Test your understanding 7

1 **18.4c**

Step 1 – Theoretical ex-rights price (TERP)

				$
Prior to rights issue	2	shares	worth $2.45 =	4.90
Taking up rights	1	share	cost $2.00 =	2.00
	3			6.90

TERP = $6.90/3 = $2.30

Step 2 – Rights fraction

Market price before issue/TERP = $2.45/$2.3

Step 3 – Weighted average number of shares

	No.	Bonus fraction	Time	Average
1 January	2,000,000	2.45/2.3	7/12	1,242,754
1 July	3,000,000		5/12	1,250,000
				2,492,754

Step 4 – EPS

$$EPS = \frac{\$460{,}000}{2{,}492{,}754}$$ **= 18.4c per share**

2 See table below.

	Restate prior year EPS	No restatement required
Full price (market) issue		X
Bonus issue	X	
Rights issue	X	

Both a bonus issue and rights issue contain an element of 'free' shares, and therefore the prior year EPS needs to be restated in order to make a meaningful comparison.

3

Earnings	$550,000
Number of shares	
Baslc	3,000,000
Options **(W1)**	120,000
	3,120,000

The DEPS is therefore $\frac{\$550,000}{3,120,000}$ = **17.6c**

(W1) Number of shares at option price

Options = 1,000,000 × $2.20

= $2,200,000

At fair value: = $\frac{\$2,200,000}{\$2.50}$ = 880,000

Number issued free = 1,000,000 – 880,000 = 120,000

(W1) (Alternative)

Alternatively, number of free shares using formula:

1,000,000 × (2.5 – 2.2)/2.5 = 120,000

4 **D** – Diluted earnings per share contains a mix of current and future information, warning shareholders how the current earnings per share could fall in the future, depending on items that are already in existence but may be turned into shares in the future.

5 **B** – The profit to be used is the profit attributable to the owners of the company. Irredeemable preference dividends must be paid before ordinary dividends, but are not included in the statement of profit or loss. Therefore these must be deducted from the profit for the year in order to calculate the profit attributable to ordinary shareholders. Redeemable preference dividends are treated as a finance cost so will have already been deducted in the statement of profit or loss. No adjustment should be made for the FVOCI investments or reserves transfer.

Test your understanding 8

1 See below.

Case with the customer	Case with the supplier
Provision	Contingent asset

As there is a probable outflow, a provision must be made. As there is a probable inflow in relation to the case with the supplier, a contingent asset should be disclosed.

2 **$20,800** – The provision should be recorded at the expected value, as there is a range of outcomes. The expected value is calculated as:

(2% × 800,000) + (6% × 80,000) = **$20,800**

3 **C** The overhaul does not represent a present obligation for Worrell as Worrell has a choice whether to continue using the assets or not.

While there is no legal obligation to repair the environmental damage caused, Worrell has a constructive obligation due to its published environmental policy and record of honouring it.

4 **A** – While the inventory is sold at a loss, this is only because of damage which arose after the year end. The event causing this damage did not exist at the reporting date and this event is therefore a non-adjusting event.

5 **C** – Only material non-adjusting events must be disclosed in the notes to the financial statements. Adjusting events do not need to be disclosed as the financial statements have already been adjusted to reflect their existence. IAS 10 covers the period until the financial statements are authorised for issue, not the annual general meeting.

Test your understanding 9

1 **A** – Pedro have acquired 70% of Sagna's share capital, meaning that Pedro owns 140,000 of Sagna's shares (70% of Sagna's 200,000 share capital). As Pedro have done a 2 for 5 share issue, this means that 56,000 Pedro shares have been issued (2/5 × 140,000). As Pedro's share price is $3, this equates to a value of $168,000.

In addition to this, the future consideration of $800,000 should be discounted to present value. $800,000 × 1/1.08^3 = $635,000.

Therefore the total consideration = $168,000 + $635,000 = **$803,000.**

2 **B** – The retained earnings at acquisition must be calculated by time apportioning the profit for the year. As Pedro has owned Sagna for 7 months, the post-acquisition retained earnings must be $10,500 ($18,000 × 7/12).

Therefore the retained earnings at acquisition = 72,000 – 10,500 = $61,500.

In addition to this, the fair value adjustment of $12,000 must be added to the net assets at acquisition.

The net assets at acquisition is **$273,500** and consists of:

	$
Share capital	200,000
Retained earnings	61,500
Fair value adjustment	12,000

3 See below.

Receivables	Payables
$37,000	$25,000

The $1,000 cash in transit means that Pedro has a payable of $7,000. The $1,000 cash in transit should be treated as received (Dr Cash, Cr Receivables), leaving a $7,000 remaining balance. This is then removed (Dr Payables, Cr Receivables).

Therefore the consolidated receivables =

31,000 + 14,000 – 1,000 – 7,000 = **$37,000**

The consolidated payables = 22,000 + 10,000 – 7,000 = **$25,000**

4 **$100** – The profit made on all sales is $1,000 ($6,000 × 20/120), but the adjustment for unrealised profit only relates to goods remaining in the group at year end. As 10% of the goods remain in the group, this gives an unrealised profit of $100.

5 **A and E** – The fair value adjustment and the unrealised profit adjustment will both have an impact on the subsidiary's net assets and will therefore affect the non-controlling interest.

Test your understanding 10

1 **C** – The income and expenses should be time-apportioned to reflect the fact that Pardew has only owned Sherwood for 6 months. In addition to this, the intra-group sales of $6 million ($1 million a month) should be deducted from the group revenue.

$411,600,000 + $106,560,000 (6 months revenue) – $6,000,000 = **$512,160,000**

2 **$360,000** – The sales are made at a margin of 20%. Pardew has sold $6 million to Sherwood ($1 million a month since acquisition) and therefore the profit on these is $1.2 million ($6 million × 20%). As only 30% of these remain in the group, the unrealised profit is $360,000 (30% × $1.2 million).

3 **$67,520,000** – The administrative expenses of Sherwood should be time-apportioned to reflect the fact that Pardew has only owned Sherwood for 6 months. In addition to this, the fair value depreciation for the property (for the 6 month period) should be included as well as the full goodwill impairment.

50,610 + 16,560 (6/12 × 33,120) + 50 fair value depreciation (2,000/20 × 6/12) + 300 = **67,520**

4 **$2,300,000** – As Pardew have charged Sherwood $300,000 since acquisition ($10m × 6% × 6/12), then Sherwood's finance costs across the whole year must be $300,000 ($600,000 less the intra-group interest). Therefore 6/12 × 300,000 = $150,000.

Consolidated finance costs = 2,150 + 150 = **2,300.**

5 **C and D** – The fair value depreciation always affects the non-controlling interest. The goodwill impairment will also affect it as the non-controlling interest is measured at fair value. The unrealised profit affects Pardew's profits, so has no impact on the non-controlling interest.

Test your understanding 11

1 See below.

	Add to profit from operations	Deduct from profit from operations
Depreciation	X	
Gain on disposal		X
Movement in inventories		X
Movement in receivables	X	
Movement in payables	X	

Depreciation must be added back, as it is a non-cash expense. The gain on disposal is deducted as it is non-cash income. Inventories have increased, which is bad for cash. Receivables have decreased which is good for cash. Finally, payables have increased, which is good for cash.

2 **D**

Property, plant and equipment

	$000		$000
b/f	136,950	Depreciation	2,000
Additions	1,500	**Disposal (balancing figure)**	4,350
		c/f	132,100
	138,450		138,450

Column format:

Balance b/f	136,950
Depreciation	(2,000)
Additions	1,500
Disposal (Balancing figure)	**(4,350)**
Balance c/f	132,100

The carrying amount of the asset disposed is $4,350,000 (see above). As the property has been sold at a $3 million profit, the proceeds must be **$7,350,000**

3 **$700,000**

Tax liabilities

Tax paid (Balancing figure)	**700**	b/f (current + deferred)	2,400
c/f (current + deferred)	2,100	SPL	400
	2,800		2,800

Column format:

b/f (current + deferred)	2,400
Tax charge per SPL	400
Tax paid (Balancing figure)	**(700)**
c/f (current + deferred)	2,100

4 **$6,350,000**

Tax liabilities

Dividends paid (Balancing figure)	**6,350**	b/f	36,000
c/f	31,500	SPL	1,850
	37,850		37,850

Column format:

Balance b/f	36,000
Profit for the year	1,850
Dividends paid (Balancing figure)	**(6,350)**
Balance c/f	31,500

5 See below.

Operating activities	Tax paid
Investing activities	Property disposal proceeds
Financing activities	Dividends paid

Chapter

25

References

The Board (2017) IAS 1 *Presentation of Financial Statements. London*: IFRS Foundation.

The Board (2017) IAS 2 *Inventories*. London: IFRS Foundation.

The Board (2017) IAS 7 *Statement of Cash Flows*. London: IFRS Foundation.

The Board (2017) IAS 8 *Accounting Policies, Changes in Accounting Estimates and Errors.* London: IFRS Foundation.

The Board (2017) IAS 10 *Events after the Reporting Period*. London: IFRS Foundation.

The Board (2017) IAS 12 *Income Taxes*. London: IFRS Foundation.

The Board (2017) IAS 16 *Property, Plant and Equipment*. London: IFRS Foundation.

The Board (2017) IAS 20 *Accounting for Government Grants and Disclosure of Government Assistance*. London: IFRS Foundation.

The Board (2017) IAS 21 *The Effects of Changes in Foreign Exchange Rates*. London: IFRS Foundation.

The Board (2017) IAS 23 *Borrowing Costs*. London: IFRS Foundation.

The Board (2017) IAS 27 *Separate Financial Statements*. London: IFRS Foundation.

The Board (2017) IAS 28 *Investments in Associates and Joint Ventures*. London: IFRS Foundation.

The Board (2017) IAS 32 *Financial Instruments: Presentation*. London: IFRS Foundation.

The Board (2017) IAS 33 *Earnings per Share*. London: IFRS Foundation.

The Board (2017) IAS 36 *Impairment of Assets*. London: IFRS Foundation.

The Board (2017) IAS 37 *Provisions, Contingent Liabilities and Contingent Assets*. London: IFRS Foundation.

The Board (2017) IAS 38 *Intangible Assets*. London: IFRS Foundation.

The Board (2017) IAS 40 *Investment Property*. London: IFRS Foundation.

The Board (2017) IAS 41 *Agriculture*. London: IFRS Foundation.

The Board (2017) IFRS 1 *First-time Adoption of International Financial Reporting Standards.* London: IFRS Foundation.

The Board (2017) IFRS 3 *Business Combinations*. London: IFRS Foundation.

The Board (2017) IFRS 5 *Non-current Assets Held for Sale and Discontinued Operations*. London: IFRS Foundation.

The Board (2017) IFRS 7 *Financial Instruments: Disclosure*. London: IFRS Foundation.

The Board (2017) IFRS 9 *Financial Instruments*. London: IFRS Foundation.

The Board (2017) IFRS 10 *Consolidated Financial Statements*. London: IFRS Foundation.

The Board (2017) IFRS 13 *Fair Value Measurement*. London: IFRS Foundation.

The Board (2017) IFRS 15 *Revenue from Contracts with Customers*. London: IFRS Foundation.

The Board (2017) IFRS 16 *Leases*. London: IFRS Foundation.

A

B

C

D

E

F

G

H

I

U

W